Modern Occult Rhetoric

Modern Occult Rhetoric

Mass Media and the Drama of Secrecy in the Twentieth Century

JOSHUA GUNN

THE UNIVERSITY OF ALABAMA PRESS
Tuscaloosa

Typeface: Sabon

∞
The paper on which this book is printed meets the minimum requirements of American National Standard for Information Sciences-Permanence of Paper for Printed Library Materials, ANSI Z39.48–1984.

ISBN: 978-0-8173-5656-9 (pbk. : alk. paper)
ISBN: 978-0-8173-8541-5 (electronic)
A previous edition of this book has been catalogued by the Library of Congress.

Library of Congress Cataloging-in-Publication Data

Gunn, Joshua, 1973–
Modern occult rhetoric : mass media and the drama of secrecy in the twentieth century / Joshua Gunn.
p. cm. — (Rhetoric, culture, and social critique)
Includes bibliographical references and index.
ISBN 0-8173-1466-0 (hardcover : alk. paper)
1. Occultism—Social aspects. 2. Popular culture—History—20th century. 3. Language and languages—Miscellanea. 4. Mass media. I. Title. II. Series.
BF1439.G86 2005
130′.1′4—dc22
2004029046

Earlier versions or portions of chapters in this study appeared in the following publications: "H. P. Blavatsky and the Magic of Esoteric Language," *Journal of Communication and Religion* 25 (2002): 193–227; "An Occult Poetics, or, the Secret Rhetoric of Religion," *Rhetoric Society Quarterly* 34 (2004): 29–54; and "Prime Time-Satanism: Postmodern Occultism and the Rumorwork of Iconic Topoi," *Visual Communication* 4 (2005): 93–120.

For Robert Icabod Ebenezer Alexander Perry Garcella Philbert Algernon Scott

Contents

List of Illustrations / ix
Acknowledgments / xi
Introduction / xv

Part I: Esoterica

1. What Is the Occult? / 3
Interlude: Erasing the Grooves: On Cold Feet / 27
2. Toward an Occult Poetics / 35
Interlude: Mysteries of the Unknown / 53
3. H. P. Blavatsky and the Magic of Esoteric Language / 56
4. On Textual Occultism / 79

Part II: Exoterica

Interlude: Re-membering Crowley / 109
5. Aleister Crowley and the Hermeneutic of Authority / 116
Interlude: On Stolen Letters and Lettered Secrets / 138
6. The Death of the Modern Magus: "The Masses" and Irony's Other / 143
7. Prime-Time Satanism: Stock Footage and the Death of Modern Occultism / 172
8. The Allegory of *The Ninth Gate* / 204
Epilogue: The Fool's Yapping Cur / 230
Appendix 1: Scholarship on Occultism / 237
Appendix 2: Aleister Crowley's *The Book of the Law* / 249

Notes / 265
Selected Bibliography / 305
Index / 329

Illustrations

1. Eliphas Lévi / 4
2. The Sabbatic Goat / 5
3. Goëtic Circle of Black Evocation and Pacts / 25
4. Helena Petrovna Blavatsky / 55
5. Helena Petrovna Blavatsky / 59
6. Aleister Crowley / 110
7. Aleister Crowley / 146
8. The Baphomet of the Church of Satan / 187

Acknowledgments

This book began as a doctoral dissertation that I wrote during study at the University of Minnesota. I thank the many kind and patient folks at the University of Alabama Press, as well as three important scholarly mentors, for preparing me to do battle with the Demons of the Warmed-Over (if readers notice that these demons have not been completely exorcized, however, then I am entirely to blame). The idea for a book on secrets was hatched in an "Introduction to Rhetorical Criticism" course taught by my adviser, Robert L. Scott, in the very early hours of a cold Minnesota winter day. Despite reading numerous error-filled essays, Professor Scott encouraged further study. He read, reread, and read yet again every chapter, tirelessly recommending changes and suggesting new areas of inquiry. I dedicate this book to Dr. Scott for his kindness, his caring, his parenting, and above all his humanity ("27 April: Old father, old artificer, stand me now and ever in good stead"). Karlyn Kohrs Campbell was also instrumental in the completion of this book. Chapters 2 and 3 began as a project on H. P. Blavatsky in her rhetorical criticism seminar. I learned how to write and teach by working with Dr. Campbell, and her continual encouragement, love, and support has motivated me to do my best. Finally, I owe many thanks to Barry Brummett (otherwise known as "Sheridan, Returned from the Grave"), who has been vetting my scholarship ever since I started sending essays out for review. Barry read the manuscript closely, made numerous, helpful suggestions, and made me my first rum and tonic on Sunday, May 30, 2004.

Other faculty at the University of Minnesota contributed either directly or indirectly to this project. I thank Robin Brown for the many days we have spent in conversation about religion and for going to the exorcisms with me when Bob Larson came to town. Kirt Wilson provided keen insights regarding the magickal texts of Aleister Crowley, which he encouraged me to study in his class on close textual criticism. Edward Schiappa provided invaluable feedback and advice about the theoretical issues of this study, and I thank him, in particular, for helping me to navigate the work of Burke and Rorty (as well as the strange terrain of professorship). Mary Vavrus carefully vetted chapter 7 and spent many afternoons with me in discussion. Ron Greene taught me to be suspicious of the textual magus. In sum, the faculty at the University of Minnesota have been incredibly helpful and supportive during my research.

My friends at Minnesota and elsewhere were also important to the completion of this study. Angela Ray has been like a sister to me, and she continues to teach me what being a scholar is by example. We shared many lengthy discussions about the ideas our work shares in common, and on numerous occasions she provided a shoulder to cry on. David Beard has also been a model friend and scholar, and I thank him for all the conversations we had about the ideas in this book, and those we continue to have as the years fly by. Chani Marchiselli read a number of chapters and offered sharp insights. Aric Putnam and Kristen Brown also provided excellent feedback about key chapters. Mirko Hall and Christopher Swift have listened patiently at the end of a phone as I rambled on endlessly about the occult. Ricca Ducharme also endured an untold number of discussions about this book; her patience and kindness befit the Buddha.

I am blessed to have had such supportive and humane colleagues while a member of the Department of Communication Studies at Louisiana State University. I thank Loretta Pecchinoi, Laura Sells, Tracy Stephenson, and Trish Suchy, in particular, for their encouragement, friendship, and support while I was completing the book, and my colleagues in English, Jim Catano and Michelle Massé, for their cheer and welcome embrace. Dan Grano taught me the virtue of Socratic ignorance, which appears here as its double, humility. I forced Shaun Treat to listen to me read chapters aloud while road-tripping, and I thank him for his feedback, patience, and friendship. Lisa Flannegan, Roger Pippin, Danielle Sears, Stephen Shapiro, Gretchen Stein, David Terry, and the revolving membership of the "Front Porch Action Group" were crucial to my sanity as a scholar, and the periodic evenings with our friend Jim Beam provided ample motivation to write all day.

Many people associated with the occultic objects of study were instrumental to this book's completion. Hymenaeus Beta, Craig Berry, and Marcus Jungkurth of the Ordo Templi Orientis provided good conversation and helped to locate images of Aleister Crowley. Members from the Minneapolis chapter of that organization, the "Leaping

Laughter Oasis," commented on early drafts and invited me to participate in the Gnostic Mass, an unforgettable experience. John Algeo of the Theosophical Society of America helped me to secure images of Blavatsky and provided excellent feedback on chapter 3, correcting a number of errors and misjudgments. Peter Gilmore of the Church of Satan also was very helpful and corrected a number of misperceptions about his organization in good humor, and Michael Aquino of the Temple of Set cheerfully provided access to documents not available to the general public. Joseph Aloysius Becker of Thinkfilm provided me with a copy of his "Mysteries of the Unknown" television commercial, which he produced for Time/Life Books.

Finally, I thank my parents, Dan and Jane Gunn, for their love and support and for being the kind of parents who encouraged me to go to art school when I insisted on going to law school. Without their encouragement and guidance, this book could not have been written.

Quod tacitum velis esse, nemini dixeris.
Si tibi ipsi non imperasti,
quomondo ab aliss silentium speras?
—Seneca (attributed), Proverbs 16

The practice of magic consists in making what is not understood understandable in an incomprehensible manner.
—Carl Jung

Introduction

Many of us have had the experience of picking up a volume in the local bookstore, reading the first few pages, and finding ourselves utterly mystified. Despite the title or the promotional blurbs on the cover, the more one reads this book, the more the words seem to become resistant in their recalcitrant materiality. *Modern Occult Rhetoric: Mass Media and the Drama of Secrecy in the Twentieth Century* is about this experience. It is also about the ways in which individuals use language (and the ways in which language uses individuals) to harbor secrets, creating groups of insiders and outsiders. Consider what some readers may have experienced if, instead of this paragraph, *Modern Occult Rhetoric* began with an epigraph from two celebrated French thinkers and then proceeded to suggest, in tortuous jargon, that these thinkers were secretly students of Freemasonry and the Jewish tradition of mysticism known as the Kabbalah . . .

> Desiring-machines are binary machines, obeying a binary law or set of rules governing associations: one machine is always coupled with another. . . . This is because there is always a flow-producing machine, another machine connected to it that interrupts or draws off part of this flow (the breast—the mouth). . . . Desire causes the current to flow, itself flows in turn, and breaks the flows. . . . Amniotic fluid spilling out of the sac and kidney stones; flowing hair, a flow of spittle, a flow of sperm, shit, or urine that are produced by partial objects . . .
>
> —Gilles Deleuze and Félix Guattari[1]

Speaking in terms of the right-hand path, readers familiar with the work of Gilles Deleuze and Félix Guattari will immediately acknowledge that the un-doing, schizo-phronesis of desiring production and its rippling effects in the worldly, ever-widening, rhizomatic onto-theology of thinking/being was originally mapped by Spinoza. To recognize the flows of desire enabling and disabling a litany of couplings and splits and the many, enercological flows and dams between the conatus and anima—indeed, the fecal gift and the undead eidola—is to celebrate the infinite attributes of "The One." Yet right-handed readers may not immediately realize that the geometrico-mathematical paradox of the syzygy (e.g., the rank-five syzygy expressed as $^{\Sigma}ijk^{\delta}\mathrm{lm} - {}^{\Sigma}jkl^{\delta}im + {}^{\Sigma}kli^{\delta}jm - {}^{\Sigma}l^{\delta}km = 0$)—at base the notion that reality represents itself in the illusion of a dualistic finitude, which is fundamental to most immanent ontologies and which is belied by the unrepresentability of libidinal flows—derives from that ancient art of Jewish mysticism, the Kabbalah.[2]

Speaking in terms of the left-hand path, readers familiar with the goetic arts, the amite arts of Gematria, Notariqon, Temura, and the dogma of the Thrice Great Hermes (Hermeticism)[3] will be familiar with the unfortunate philosophical inversion of the *cogito* ("Something thinks, therefore something exists to think thought"), the macdaddy syzygy of the infinite attribute of thought frequently laid at the unwashed feet of Descartes, which is under attack by Deleuze and Guattari. The liberatory possibilities of the Hebrew Kabbalah or the Greek Qabalah can be understood precisely in terms of their dual-aspect theory of divinity, namely, that the mental and physical are distinct emanations of the Godhead. The monistic foundation of the occult tradition, in this sense, can be located in the Hebrew *Yod* or the Greek *Tau,* both marks of the eternal rendered in the English letter "G": When The One hailed Moses on the mount, He bellowed in terrifying speech, "I am that I am," which is the first axiom of occult philosophy, "being is being."[4] Yet the student of the occult may not immediately recognize that the schizoid-subject-as-desiring-machine is actually cipher for each transitive node on the Tree of Life, each coupling of flows a world or sphere revealed by Plato in the ninth chapter of the *Republic:* Atziluth, Briah, Yetzirah, and Assiah.

Finally, both students of Continental and occult philosophy may not recognize that the binary initially forged by Francis Bacon (principally to keep his head intact), which forever led the scientist and the magician to the independent, institutional pieties reflected in the Doctrine of Twofold Truth (the language of Deity and the language of His Creation),[5] has well served the monis- and monastically minded intellectual since the establishment of the Great Blue Lodge in the eighteenth century. As is well known, the secrets of Freemasonry are transmitted, as Deity to Moses, in the presencing flows of speech, the union of the *conatus* and the *animus,* the threshold of Truth. The cherished letter "G" central to the emblem of Freemasonry (usually centered inside a square and compass) thus yokes the occultist and philosopher of immanence under the noses of the unenlightened masses and betokens a secret shared among only a select few: God is Geometry, and one comes to increasingly deeper understandings of Being only in and by *degrees.*

This book, then, is potentially *earth shattering,* or better, *sphere mapping,* when the reader fully understands my purpose: to reveal the secret that "constitutes the fatal Science of Good and Evil," as Eliphas Lévi once put it, in successive degrees of allegorical correspondence.[6] The secret of all occult traditions is, in fact, that Lucifer is an emanation of Deity, the "light bearer" that makes possible the rhizomatic effluence of desire and knowledge only through worshipful adherence to a false "Master," a revelation perhaps most aptly disclosed by Nietzsche's Zarathustra in terms of the "transvaluation" of all values for the student of philosophy,[7] and by Aleister Crowley in terms of the power of human sacrifice (typically a male baby) for the student of the occult.[8] In short, this book attempts to explain what it means to worship the Devil, particularly in terms of linguistic practice, as well as chronicle the history of our servitude to Satan in the worldwide Order of Freemasonry.

The Secret of the Book

To begin again: if the patient reader has read the last four paragraphs without throwing this book across the room, then he or she may be relieved to learn that the preceding prose was intentionally tortuous, designed to demonstrate formally the primary object of scrutiny in *Modern Occult Rhetoric.* As I hinted, this book is about the object of strange, mysterious, or difficult language, including the reasons or forces behind its invention, the experience of reading, interpreting, and reacting to it, and the ways in which it can get the better of us. It is my hope that by the end of this book the reader can easily take apart the preceding rumination on ontological dualism (the notion that mental stuff, *res cogitans,* and bodily stuff, *res extensa,* are radically distinct), particularly in terms of its rhetorical, or suasive, function: this hodgepodge of esoteric terms and academic jargon is designed to discriminate among those who can read it and those who cannot. When writing the example ruse, I wanted the aesthetic form of the prose to reflect the content or argument: the difficult language of philosophy is akin to the difficult language of the occult tradition; both traditions simultaneously obscure the truths their vocabularies seek to deploy, and both utilize difficult language to create readerships. In short, the content domains of philosophy and the occult share a common logic of discrimination. Their prose, like mine, is designed to delight and to encourage the reader who is "in the know" and to annoy, discourage, or perhaps even intrigue the reader who is not.

Put in more familiar, biblical terms, *Modern Occult Rhetoric* concerns the contemporary equivalent of the shibboleth, a term for the famous speech-password in the book of Judges (12:1–15). Insofar as the King James Bible is the principal source of spiritual secrets in U.S. Freemasonry (a central "Landmark" of the Craft), then the story of warring Semitic tribes certainly can be read as an occult allegory for keeping and telling secrets: the Ephraimites and the Gileadites are warring, and the latter defeats the former. The Gileadites fashion a blockade to catch fleeing Ephraimites and establish a password to let their friends through. Each escapee is asked to pronounce the word "shibboleth," ancient Hebrew for "ear of corn." In the dialect of the Gileadites the word was pronounced with a "sh," while the Ephraimites pronounced it with a "s." Apparently, thousands of folks said the latter and got into some pretty deep "sit" yammering on about corn on the cob.

The concept of the shibboleth underscores the ways in which cipher links human expression to real bodies in space, with real consequences. One literally and figuratively could lose one's head when not paying enough attention to form, the most important, relational meaning of the secret. As a "speech act" or an utterance that does things to and for people,[9] the shibboleth also helps to explain the relationships among the four major concepts or categories of the present study: rhetoric, religion and theological form, the occult, and the occultic.

The Shibboleth of Rhetoric

The performative aspect of the shibboleth underscores why "rhetoric" appears in the title of this book for a number of reasons. The first is that "rhetoric" is itself a difficult term when one recognizes that there is a distinction between "rhetoric" in the popular imaginary and "rhetoric" in the academy. The Ephraimites, today's mass-media spin doctors and politicians, would have us believe that rhetoric is "empty speech" or (dare I say it?) "bulls(h)it," a kind of language use that is purely formal and devoid of content. Yet the Gileadites, or academics who study "rhetoric" and the "rhetorical tradition," wish that the popular media tribes would recognize the term in a very different sense, namely, that rhetoric denotes the serious study of persuasive speaking and writing, which began in ancient Greece in fourth- and fifth-century B.C.E.[10] Among rhetoricians, the way in which rhetoric gets defined has changed dramatically since that time, yet most of us would agree that when a political pundit accuses a public leader of producing "mere rhetoric," he or she does not know the proper password.

The second reason why "rhetoric" appears in the title is because this book is a rhetorical analysis and criticism, meaning that its primary task is to analyze the difficult language of secrecy as a suasive phenomenon. For my purposes I will define "rhetoric" as the study of how representations (linguistic or otherwise) consciously and unconsciously influence people to do or believe things they would not otherwise ordinarily do or believe. This definition means that representation as such is the central, suasive dimension of human drama, the song of the opera of social being.

In light of the example of the shibboleth, the kind of language-doing or rhetoric I am concerned with here is strange or difficult language about secrets. The claims I make in *Modern Occult Rhetoric,* however, go much further than that of providing a history and grammar of the discourse of secrecy. First, I will demonstrate in a number of case studies that difficult language is used to divide and unite readers and that it therefore participates in numerous circuits of power (authorial, authoritative, and otherwise). This element of social discrimination and authority is the core of the discourse of secrecy. Second, I suggest that people cannot help but play the game of secrecy, even in our contemporary age of abject publicity—of webcams, workplace monitoring, and "reality television"[11]—because language and its use easily lend themselves to mystery. Below I discuss each element in terms of "the occultic" and the "rhetoric of religion," respectively.

The Rhetoric of Religion

In the widest sense, the present study can be understood as an examination of the rhetoric of religion, and principally in terms of what I call "theological form." Theological form refers to the recurrent cultural patterns of transcendence that are locatable in human writing and speaking. "Transcendence" is the idea of "moving across or through" and is frequently opposed to "immanence," which means "inside" or "in the here and now." Secular thought and its representation are often described as "immanent," and religious thought and rhetoric are described as "transcendent."

The element that usually types a given discourse as transcendent is the presence (or rather, the impossible absence) of ineffability. The word "ineffability" is a shibboleth of sorts: by definition, the ineffable is that which "cannot be expressed or described in language." It also refers to that which is "too great for words," that which "transcends expression," as well as the "unspeakable, unutterable, and inexpressible."[12] Hence transcendent rhetoric often seeks to communicate something—a spiritual truth, for example—that is beyond representation. For this reason, Kenneth Burke has argued that the rhetoric of religion is inherently paradoxical. In his last major book, *The Rhetoric of Religion,* Burke notes that "the supernatural is by definition the realm of the 'ineffable.' And language by definition is not suited to the expression of the 'ineffable.' So our words for the . . . supernatural or 'ineffable' . . . are necessarily borrowed from our words for the sorts of things we can talk about literally . . . (the world of everyday experience)."[13] Burke's observations about the rhetoric of religion implicate a central, productive ambivalence of theological form: transcendent truths are ineffable, but people invest a lot of time and energy into trying to represent ineffability. In the broadest sense, then, religious rhetoric seems to embody a conflict between representation and ineffability. "Theological form" is my shorthand for this conflict.

I part ways with Burke, however, by arguing that theological form is not limited to supernaturalism. Rather, one of the minor claims I forward in this study (most directly in chapter 2) is that our experience of the world—what we see, hear, touch, smell, taste, and feel—is fundamentally ineffable. This is a fairly noncontroversial claim in philosophical circles, but it is one that rhetoricians sometimes tacitly reject because we tend to be obsessed with rhetoric as an instrument of discovery and social change.[14] I take it as an axiom that our words for things—not only spiritual truths but also simple, everyday encounters with, say, a dirty hairbrush, a pet's accident on the new carpet, or a tasty, buttered ear of corn—always fail to communicate the sensory manifold of human experience.

The key to understanding the link between difficult language and social discrimination is to recognize that, on some level, strange vocabularies are created to better approximate the ineffability of both mundane and spiritual experience. For Burke, the argument for studying rhetoric that is widely recognized as religious—that which typically involves the theological form of transcendence about, toward, or into some *supernatural* ineffability—is that it helps us to see better how rhetoric works in a more general, "natural" sense. Making a similar gambit, I turn to the more general, mundane category of "the occultic" and to the body of supernaturalist discourse from which it is derived, the occult.

The Occultic and the Occult

Modern Occult Rhetoric undertakes an exploration of secret discourse by focusing on what I term "the occultic," a unique version of theological form. The occultic is my "cool, new term" or neologistic substitute for the shibboleth, which too narrowly connotes face-to-face speech. The term "occultic" is derived from the Latin root *occultus,* which means "secret," and which is the past participle of *occulere,* "to conceal." I wish to distinguish the category of the "occultic" from that of the "occult" and "occultism" because the latter no longer exist as terms for a coherent tradition.

The occult should be understood as the study of secrets and the practice of mysticism and magic, comprising a centuries-long dialogue between occultists and their detractors about metaphysical secrets, the role of the imagination in apprehending such secrets, and who has the authority to keep and reveal them. Most of the case studies in this book examine texts that fall clearly within this definition. By the end of the book, however, I argue that the sense of the occult as comprising a "tradition" died at the end of the twentieth century; in postmodernity, the age of surveillance and publicity, there can be no coherent tradition of secrecy.

The decline of occultism as a coherent discourse is immediately discernible when one thinks about its contemporary expression. At the beginning of the twentieth century, occultism was clearly associated with the study of secret knowledge by elites. Today the contexts in which the term "occult" is used are so varied that it is difficult to mention the term in any precise sense without ample qualification. The occult can refer to everything from comic books and horror films to rock music motifs and vague "moods" or states of mind.[15] Although there is an occult tradition—a historical content obsessed with books, spells, and secrets—this has been eclipsed by the form of its rhetoric, which concerns a logic of secrecy, interpretation, and discrimination. Unlike the occult discourse of the early twentieth century, contemporary occult discourse is dominated by image and form. Traditional horror films, for example, are not occult, but they always seem to involve a secret (a hidden monster that suddenly appears, a murderous alter ego, a hidden door or portal to another world, and so on), the ability of the protagonist to uncover the secret or vanquish it, and an array of highly evocative images (of darkness, of blood, perhaps an extreme close-up shot of nice, pointy fangs). A horror film as such is not concerned with the channeling of preternatural power to effect change by means of spells (traditional occultism), but thinking about occultism generically, as the occultic, helps one to understand why, for example, some individuals erroneously claim that all horror movies are "occult." One fundamentalist Christian commentator, for instance, describes the "ghost story" of the 2000 film *What Lies Beneath* in ways that extend the occult to a supersensory experience of dread: "Paramount in this story line [of the film] is Claire's interaction with demonic powers. The occult presence in this story line is what causes the element of terror."[16] The commentator laments that the imagined sense of an "occult presence . . . alas, is the thematic focus of most thrillers."[17] Clearly, as a social form the occult can denote a multitude of objects that have nothing to do, necessarily, with the secret knowledge and practice of magic and mysticism.

Although one of the goals of *Modern Occult Rhetoric* is to characterize the occultic as a distinctive mode of rhetoric, readers expecting a direct or definitive definition of the term are likely to be disappointed. To understand something as "rhetorical" is to understand it as negotiable, as a contingent and protean object that can only be discerned partially and indirectly through case studies. Of course, defining the occult at the turn of the twentieth century is a much easier task than defining the occultic today. In the midst of the now, I'm arguing that what people term the "occult" is best described as the occultic, a form that articulates an inchoate system of beliefs, images, attitudes, and texts together that, nevertheless, reconfigures from individual to group; its meaning is wholly dependent on expert and popular perceptions held in dialectical tension without resolution. Conceptually, we can understand "the occult" as one end of a temporal continuum and "the occultic" as the other. As the category shifts and changes over the course of the twentieth century, so do the number of occultic discourses continue to multiply.

Insofar as the occult has died and been resurrected as something else, then, I'm suggesting that this something else is "the occultic," a brand of contemporary discourse that retains a number of elements of the occult tradition. I have already discussed two of these elements: first, occultic discourse discriminates among groups or kinds of people with strange or difficult language; and second, its strange or difficult language is designed to better apprehend or understand something that is, at base, incommunicable. As the book proceeds, I will continue to build on these two elements.

Although the occultic is a contemporary theological form, it is not necessarily—as I suggested with the rhetoric of religion—supernaturalist. For example, I began this introduction with reference to the philosophical writings of Deleuze and Guattari. As many folks who have tried to read *Anti-Oedipus* or *A Thousand Plateaus* would agree, the authors' principal technique of materialist psychiatry, "schizoanalysis," is anything but straightforward, designed as it is to upset and subvert binary thinking and the philosophical categories of transcendence. My intent here is not to ridicule their language but rather to suggest that their philosophical rhetoric is occultic in terms of, first, its having created a dedicated group of followers who have become absorbed in the argot of "D & G," and second, its explicit claim to a better way of understanding the world—indeed, for understanding the enterprise of philosophy itself. The irony of characterizing a philosophy of immanence as "occultic" is that it shows how its vehicle of expression, its rhetoric, is a transcendent phenomenon. Another axiom I rely on throughout this book is that rhetoric as such is a transcendent thing, regardless of the immanent ends to which it is put.[18]

Understanding the occultic in this general way begins to unravel the tidy distinction between "real science" and the "occult" that was introduced during the Enlightenment. This is not to say that there is no distinction between science and the occult tradition but rather that the rhetoric of each is often experienced by the "outsider" as occultic. One of my favorite examples of the mysterious religiosity of a seemingly atheistic "science" is the rhetoric of psychoanalysis, especially Freud's. Psychoanalysis comprises an academic literature that requires years of study to properly understand its fundamental axioms and analytic techniques. Its "Master," perhaps tired of the accusations of his detractors, revised a number of lectures he originally delivered between 1915 and 1917 to include a discussion of "dreams and occultism," as well as the following apologetic remarks:

> And here, Ladies and Gentlemen, I feel that I must make a pause to take breath—which you too will welcome as a relief—and, before I go on, to apologize to you. My intention is to give you some addenda to the introductory lectures on psycho-analysis which I began fifteen years ago, and I am obliged to behave as though you as well as I had in the interval done nothing but practice psycho-analysis. I know that assumption is out of place; but I am helpless. I cannot do otherwise. This is no doubt related to the fact that it is so hard to give anyone who is not himself a psycho-analyst an insight into psycho-analysis. You can believe me when I tell you that we do not enjoy giving an impression of being members of a secret society and of practicing a mystical science. Yet we have been obliged to recognize and express as our conviction that no one has a right to join a discussion of psycho-analysis who has not had particular experiences which can only be obtained by being analysed oneself.[19]

The occultic logic of discrimination here is as obvious as Freud's self-denial. Clearly someone has the impression that psychoanalysis is occultic, and clearly someone takes pleasure in that impression!

The exemplar of psychoanalysis demonstrates that once we start thinking more broadly about the occult in terms of the occultic, we begin to see a discursive form that involves much more than heavy-metal music, black-clad young adults sacrificing household pets, or Ouija board communiqués from Uncle Earl. Although "dark" cultural myths mark the most conspicuous ways in which people think about the messy term "occult," the form of its discourse is ubiquitous. Nevertheless, to understand the many contemporary manifestations of the occultic, as well as to better flesh out the category, it important and useful to examine the historical roots of the occultic in the occult tradition. Only after examining how the traditional occult text was invented, expressed, and interpreted do we begin to appreciate how widespread the occultic has become as a contemporary rhetorical form.

Focus of Analysis and Outline of Study

One way to understand the occultic is in terms of the variety of ways in which the term "occult" is used. To explain this contemporary variety, *Modern Occult Rhetoric* proceeds historically, beginning in the late nineteenth century, when the term had a more definite meaning and discernible coherence, and ending with the late twentieth century, when that meaning exploded and the coherence was lost. The focus of analysis in each chapter is homologous to this trajectory: I begin by analyzing discrete texts, move to an examination of the relations between multiple texts ("intertextuality"), and end with a kind of genealogy of occult imagery. In short, *Modern Occult Rhetoric* moves from the object of the occult toward the occultic. By approaching a diffuse body of discourse in this way, I hope to provide a historical account of a hitherto ignored body of discourse as well as an argument for its contemporary relevance.

Insofar as I proceed chronologically, what, then, is the story I tell about the occult? Confined to the historical tradition and focused particularly on modernity, I describe occultism as the first drama of religious secrecy in the twentieth century. Before there were alien abductions, crop circles, and secret governmental plots to forge a New World Order,[20] there were newspaper and tabloid articles claiming that charismatic leaders, possibly in league with Satan, were mesmerizing the weak-willed and revealing powerful secrets to an elite cabal. The first part of this book, titled "Esoterica" to refer to the inner, textual, and historical dimensions of occultism, begins this story by detailing the historical origin narrative of the occult tradition, fleshing out its static features in the late nineteenth century. In chapter 1, I answer the difficult question "What is the occult?" by first providing a brief origin narrative of the occult tradition (what students of the occult typically say about its history) and then by examining a number of exemplars to describe the common, generic themes and features of modern occult texts. In chapter 2 the generic features of occultism are embellished with a theory of invention. I argue that modern occultism is a theological form premised on a principled contradiction rooted in the paradoxes of language. Although I term the mode of invention particular to occultism an "occult poetics," I also argue that such a poetics is observable in contemporary occultic discourse that many deem to be atheistic or agnostic, such as the disagreements over theoretical jargon in the academy.

After outlining the generic features of modern occultism and explaining its inventional poetics, I turn in chapter 3 to the first case study, the strange and difficult writings of one of the most popular occultists in the United States, H. P. Blavatsky. By examining the dialectical interplay of Blavatsky's writings and the newspaper texts about them, the relationships among secrecy, authority, and imagination central to occult rhetoric are brought into relief. The analysis of the invention of occult rhetoric is then complemented with an examination of occult modes of interpretation in chapter 4, "On Textual Occultism," which examines Aleister Crowley's *The Book of the Law* to demonstrate how occultists forward a mode of immanent hermeneutics that is mirrored in the criticism of the New Critics and similar schools of close textual reading.

Having detailed occult rhetoric as a conceptual triad of historical tradition, generic form, and modes of invention and interpretation, I undertake in the second part of the book, "Exoterica," a demonstration of the undoing and fragmentation of the occult tradition in the twentieth century. Whereas at the turn of the twentieth century occultism seemed to cohere as a discrete cultural practice with a long and rich historical legacy, at the end of that century the discourse was reduced to an aesthetic form, the occultic. I demonstrate the beginning of this unraveling with the second case study, an examination of Crowley's attempts to establish himself as an occult authority in popular consciousness. Chapter 5 examines the many challenges that religious figures like Crowley face when attempting to establish authority over ineffable secrets in an environment saturated with mass media. Chapter 6 further develops this line of analysis by showing how the cipher and ironic blinds in Crowley's texts, when taken up in the field of mass-media reportage, undermine authority and expose the constructedness of subjectivity. Together, chapters 5 and 6 demonstrate how a central element of the occult tradition, namely the important role of an masterful keeper of secrets, was destroyed by modern paradoxes of publicity, paradoxes that also help to expose the illusion of autonomy.

The fall and eventual ridicule of Crowley in the popular press also betokens a turning point in the history of occult rhetoric in relation to class representation. Whereas occultism was initially the province of a wealthy elite, in the mid-twentieth century the teachings of the occult tradition were democratized in ways that satisfied lower-class curiosity and hatred about the wealthy, so much so that occultism eventually became associated with the lower and middle classes. Chapters 7 and 8 demonstrate how Satanism, which emerged with the reportage about Crowley and eventually crystallized into a coherent belief system in the 1960s, can be read as a measure of the democratizing effects of the mass media. The demystification of occult secrets, however, did not dilute the power of occult form, particularly in terms of the discriminating logic of inclusion and exclusion central to the occultic. The so-called Satanic panic of the late 1980s and early 1990s, for example, is fueled by the excluded disempowered—both those who claim to have supernatural powers (usually young white men) and those who claim to suffer from such powers (usually young and middle-aged white women).

Finally, chapter 7 is the hinge point of the book, capturing a moment when modernity begins to realize itself in the deconstructing movement of floating signifiers or what I term "visual topoi." In addition to providing a glimpse of U.S. class representations in the 1970s and 1980s, this chapter demonstrates how the commodification of occultism loosed traditional occult content from form, enabling its fragmentation into a multitude of objects, from generic horror-film plots to the black-clad fashions of "gothic" youth. Titled "Prime-Time Satanism: Stock Footage and the Death of Modern Occultism," chapter 7 describes the birth of the occultic by mapping a number of visual tropes created by Anton LaVey, the father of the first Satanic church and federally recognized Satanic "religion" in the United States. This cartography provides an explanation for the transformation of occult content from something concerning authority and secrecy to something imaginative and aesthetic. In the concluding chapter, "The Allegory of *The Ninth Gate,*" I observe that the process begun with media portrayals of Satanism is complete. There I argue that Roman Polanski's film concerning Satanists fighting over an important occult book should be read as an allegory for the demise of modern occultism as such—and the persistence of the occultic in alternate social institutions.

In sum, then, *Modern Occult Rhetoric* broadens the more traditional understanding of the centuries-long discourse of secrecy by treating modern occultism as the historical origin of the contemporary occultic, a rhetorical phenomenon or discourse inextricably tied to language and symbol that is no longer confined to a history of magical ritual and practice. *Modern Occult Rhetoric* provides a rhetorical account of the occultic as a ubiquitous theological form, suggesting a way for contending with a popular social phenomenon that is currently difficult to capture and, consequently, rarely discussed in scholarly literature.[21]

Despite my claims about the widespread appearance of the occultic, readers will recognize that most of the texts I analyze are situated within the occult tradition. Because I am interested in introducing this tradition and detailing the reasons for its demise in the twentieth century (particularly as a result of mass-media technologies), I have limited myself to traditional occult texts. Periodically, however, I will remind the reader that I am also writing about what people like me do for a living. Readers seeking a sustained commentary on the academic enterprise will not have trouble finding it here; however, I deliberately withhold most of my explicit judgments about our particular lodge until the very end. In keeping with the occult tradition, I have succumbed to the habit of allegory in order to appeal to, and perhaps to exclude, a number of audiences.

Finally, I should mention that the exigency for broadening how we think about the occult—and by extension its many obsessions, such as cherished books, secret formulas, and authorial power—is, of course, the radical way in which human communication was transformed in the twentieth century. The decentering of speech and text in our society of surveillance and publicity heralds the death of the Great Magus as much as it does the Great Orator. I suggest that these deaths are one and the same, representing a transformation from the age of modern occultism to the postmodern occultic. What great figure, then, have the magus and orator been resurrected into? Read on, and perhaps I will whisper her name.

I
Esoterica

1
What Is the Occult?

> Behind the veil of all the hieratic and mystical allegories of ancient doctrines, behind the darkness and strange ordeals of all initiations, under the seal of all sacred writings, in the ruins of Nineveh or Thebes, on the crumbling stones of old temples and on the blackened visage of the Assyrian or Egyptian sphinx, in the monstrous or marvelous paintings which interpret to the faithful of India the inspired pages of the Vedas, in the cryptic emblems of our old books on alchemy, in the ceremonies practiced at reception by all secret societies, there are found indications of a doctrine which is everywhere the same and everywhere carefully concealed.
>
> —Eliphas Lévi, *Transcendental Magic*[1]

Thus begins Magus Eliphas Lévi's influential 1856 treatise on transcendental magic, which recounts in evocative language the ubiquitous precept of the whole of occultism: the occult concerns secrets. Although the Frenchman claimed to be a devout Catholic (he even studied for the priesthood in his youth under the not-so-secret name Alphonse Louis Constant),[2] his liberal views, his inability to maintain a vow of chastity, and his interest in the secrets of magic eventually led to his expulsion from seminary. After he left the Roman Catholic Church, Lévi supported himself by writing books about secrets and by soliciting a number of well-heeled secret-keepers, anxious to secure his confidence—and livelihood.

In many ways Lévi's writings on magic mark the beginning of "modern occultism," a moment in the occult tradition that is characterized by a popular interest enabled by media technologies of mass production, as well as a general withering of the influence of religious prohibitions against the practice and study of magic. Many scholars of the occult locate the nineteenth-century revival of popular interest in magic and mysticism with the publication of Lévi's occult books, such as *The Dogma and Ritual of High Magic, The History of Magic,* and *The Key of Great Mysteries.*[3] What was significant about these books, and what many a curious reader undoubtedly found attractive, was Lévi's vivid writing style. As Elizabeth Butler notes, Lévi's books "belong more truly to literature than to the science of the occult," for his poetic talents helped him to transform relatively dry books on the

Fig. 1. Eliphas Lévi (1810–1875). Reprinted from *The Secret Tradition in Freemasonry,* by Eliphas Lévi, vol. 1 (London: Rebman Limited, 1911), plate facing p. 300.

subject "into something both radiant and sinister, satanic and sublime," converting descriptions of ritual into something akin to a "sensational novel."[4] Whereas Lévi's lesser-known predecessor Francis Barrett describes the study of the Kabbalah as merely the opening of "many and the chiefest mysteries and secrets of ceremonial magic,"[5] Lévi describes the art of the Kabbalist as that which concerns the most "astonishing formulae" in the service of "The Mother of God," within whom the Kabbalist realizes "all that is divine in the dreams of innocence, all that is adorable in the sacred enthusiasm of every maternal heart."[6] Whereas the father of Renaissance Hermeticism, Henry Cornelius Agrippa of Nettesheim, describes astral travel as a product of "vehement imagination, or speculation altogether abstracted from the body,"[7] Lévi describes the phenomenon as the detachment of the "astral body by which our soul communicates with our organs," which is achieved dramatically by commanding "the material body [to] 'Sleep!' and . . . the sidereal body [to] 'Dream!' Thereupon," continues Lévi, "the aspect of the visible things changes, as in hashish-visions."[8]

Fig. 2. Lévi's illustration of the "Sabbatic Goat." Reprinted from *Transcendental Magic,* trans. A. E. Waite (London: Rider and Company, 1896), 186.

Given Lévi's creative and literary talents, it is not surprising that the imagination plays an important role in his descriptions of the conduct of transcendental magic. The imagination, Lévi says, "is only the soul's inherent faculty of assimilating . . . images and reflections contained in the living light." Yet it is an extremely important capacity for the adept, whose imagination is "diaphanous, whilst that of the crowd is opaque." It is through the imagination that visionary magicians "place themselves in communication with all worlds" or dimensions of reality. The imagination is a place within which "demons and spirits can be beheld really and in truth."[9] Like Barrett, from whom Lévi took many ideas (and, by extension, Agrippa, whom Barrett plagiarized), Lévi emphasizes the importance of imagining magical symbols in the creation and use of talismans and sigils (circles that contain magical formulae), as well as the significant role mental images play in divination and necromancy. Lévi was fond of sprinkling his books with numerous illustrations and magically "charged" symbols. In fact, the imagined deity Lévi created to reside over the magical arts, the Sabbatic Goat, has long eclipsed Lévi's fame as the magus who invented it (see fig. 2).

Lévi's florid style and imaginative embellishments are the bane of many students of occultism, however, for it is commonly argued that his style was a romantic handicap and contributed to distortions of ritual and doctrine. A number of commentators argue that many of the rituals that Lévi "revealed" in his writings contained new elements not to be found in the ancient *grimoires* (spell books) on which he claimed they were based. For example, Lévi's English translator and popularizer, Arthur Edward Waite, says that "as a philosophical survey" Lévi's *The History of Magic* "is admirable" and an example of "literary excellence . . . but it swarms with historical inaccuracies." Although it is an accomplished work, Waite insists, it was in no way an "erudite performance, nor do I think that the writer ever concerned himself with any real reading of the authority whom he cites."[10] Worse, Waite argues that many of Lévi's rituals would offend one of the most celebrated magicians in occult history, the mythic King Solomon, who would "turn in his grave" if he read Lévi's books![11] "Whilst keeping some of the more questionable paraphernalia to witness against the rituals," writes Waite, Lévi "has added much more gruesome ones, and inverted the solemn religious purifications, both spiritual and material, into diabolical parodies."[12] As is the case with any artist, writer, or scholar who elevates cherished subcultural forms to a space of widespread recognition—that is, as is the case with any popularizer—charges of treachery, distortion, disloyalty, inauthenticity, or inaccuracy are inevitable. "Levi's books do not inspire confidence," argues Colin Wilson, a novelist and student of occultism, "for what he is claiming is, unfortunately a lie." His genius consisted of a "highly romantic imagination," continues Wilson, "and little else."[13] Whether or not one agrees with Wilson's assessment of Lévi's genius, his characterization of the writer as a imaginative romantic—and therefore a dubious authority—reflects a common tension in occult works. The legitimacy of an occultist's authority to proclaim supernatural truths or to reveal centuries-old secrets is always questioned by would-be occult-Luthers, staking out their own territory of magical expertise and making their own astral stakes. From this vantage the history of occult discourse is a centuries-long battle of self-proclaimed magi over the best secrets.

The criticisms of Lévi's writings have a lot to do with the suspicion that he was trying to secure fame, perhaps even turn a buck, by sensationalizing occultism and thus distorting the "true" art. During the time Lévi was writing, many of the practices that were considered occult, such as fortune-telling, astrology, spiritualism, and demonology, were sources of entertainment for the literate public. Today this condition is most certainly the case, as scholarly or "learned" versions of occultism are increasingly obscured by the entertaining and imaginary aspects of the tradition. Lévi's Sabbatic Goat, for example, makes frequent appearances on book covers, film posters, record albums, and news programs, while the book from which it is taken is far from a best-seller.[14] In just about every city in the United States one can find an expert in palmistry by looking for that familiar large, outstretched neon hand in a storefront window. While occultism during Lévi's time concerned fetishized books of secrets, today it denotes a large reservoir of cultural imagery and language (often in Latinate form for good effect) that is plumbed for horror movie film plots and television dramas about benevolent soothsayers. Darker variations of contemporary occultism speak to the conjuring of demons at heavy-metal concerts or devil-worshiping youth sacrificing small animals on tombstones. Compared to occultism in the nineteenth century, contemporary occultism seems to reflect a collective imagination unbound: it comprises countless images, texts, films, even sounds, moving about in a swirling mass. What was once Lévi's imaginary and entertaining art of secret knowledge has become a diffuse body of representations that mean different things to different people, depending on the medium and the social or historical context.

So how, then, do we understand occultism as a whole? As I suggested in the introduction, we can split occultism into two separate categories. The larger, overarching category, the occultic, refers to a theological form that underlies a larger reservoir of texts, images, symbols, myths, and so on. The original expression of the occultic was the occult, the smaller category, which is represented by Lévi's work. Briefly, the conceptual hierarchy I set before the reader in the introduction is as follows: the rhetoric of religion concerns the mismatch between language and an ineffable referent. Any discourse that features this mismatch betokens a "theological form." One kind of theological form is the occultic, which manifests itself in any discourse that, first, discriminates among groups of people on the basis of difficult or strange representation, and second, suggests that its representational strategies are better routes to some incommunicable human experience or more primal reality. By understanding the occult as one of many expressions of the more abstract category of the occultic, we can stabilize the occultic as a social form that is composed of the repetition of relatively stable features. To make the task of describing the occultic easier, however, for most of this study I focus on one side of the continuum, the occult side, since it is much easier to discern. Once we are able to contend with the specificity of the historical occult, it will then be easier to see what elements are retained as the category balloons into the occultic at the end of the twentieth century.

Below, I describe the specificity of the traditional occult in two ways. First, we can characterize the occult as a historically contextualized discourse inclusive of a story of its origin. Like the story of Islam, the Wankel rotary engine, or the introduction of corn to the early "American" diet, people have tended to discuss occultism as an object of historical evolution. Whether or not the story is truthful or fanciful is irrelevant, because I am concerned with the way scholars and occultists tend to describe the occult as something that distinguishes it from other discourses—that is, with its rhetoric, not its truth.[15] Second, occult rhetoric can be characterized as a genre, an expression of form, which has a particular pattern that is repeated in multiple occult texts (not the whole, but the bulk). So far I have isolated difficult language as a key "generic" feature of occult content, but I have yet to describe how this content is organized or advanced formally in texts. In order to establish a baseline understanding of the historical occult that can been built on and problematized in succeeding chapters, it is helpful at this point to characterize the specificity of the occult in these two ways.

The Traditional Origin Narrative of the Occult

The "traditional origin narrative" of the occult refers to the common story occult historians and practitioners tend to tell about its origins.[16] I use the term "origin narrative" rather than "history" quite deliberately for two reasons. First, the origin narrative often told by occultists is fanciful and often inaccurate according to even the most relative of documentary standards. Second, although the cursory narrative I provide below is easily documented, the fact remains that any history is shot through with contemporary schemes of coherence. As Ludwig Wittgenstein observed of notions of progressive history, when "we think of the world's future, we always mean the destination it will reach if it keeps going in the direction we can see it going now; it does not occur to us that its path is not a straight line but a curve, constantly changing direction."[17] In other words, history as it is commonly conceived consists of an imposition of pattern only discernible in retrospect, and wed to a common, Hegelian notion of historical progress, the pattern can too easily overwhelm contingency. Acknowledging the contingency of historical narratives with "origin narrative" emphasizes the rhetorically adaptive function of historiography.[18]

However hypocritical the move, Waite's attacks on Lévi's history of occultism testify to the general untrustworthiness of occult origin narratives. In part, the inaccuracies and fictions of the occult tradition are a consequence of the marginalization of occult practice, which has effectively shielded occult scholarship from academic proprieties and standards of accuracy and fidelity. What is important about a general understanding of the history of occultism is not, then, its accuracy or fidelity to past fact. Rather, the origin narrative told by scholars and students of the occult is simply an important part of its specificity as a discourse. This origin narrative of occultism is a crucial part of the meaning of occultism in particular because it provides an explanation for the widespread characterization of the occult as being opposed to science on the one hand and to religion on the other.

In general, the occult as the study of secrets and the practice of magic and mysticism has moved through four periods of history, breaking the surface of popular consciousness in times of general prosperity and retreating from popular notice during times of hardship or widespread misfortune: the medieval era, the Renaissance, the Reformation and Enlightenment, and modernity. As a secret practice, occultism cohered as a distinct discourse during the decline of the Holy Roman Empire, existing largely underground because its practices were illegal. By the arrival of the Renaissance in Europe, however, the occult emerged as natural science and was celebrated by a number of respected humanist intellectuals. It was forced underground again, however, during the Reformation and the ascent of mechanical, physicalist philosophy, which reached its peak in the Enlightenment period. Finally, the occult resurfaced again in the mid- to late nineteenth century, first in France and later in English-speaking countries, as a mysterious and entertaining curiosity for the literate public.[19]

The Medieval Era

Most occult origin narratives begin with a definition of terms, often from an authoritative and fetishized source like the *Oxford English Dictionary,* which defines the occult as that which is "hidden (from sight)" or that which is concealed. Because of the Western tradition of associating knowledge with light (e.g., as evinced in the term "enlightenment"), it makes sense that the older, ocular term was eventually used to describe medieval sciences that were thought to disclose the hidden secrets of nature, namely, alchemy and astrology. But "occultism" can also be said to involve secrets in the sense that many of the practices assembled under its name were forbidden by authorities and had to take place "in secret." The occult as the *secret* study of secrets, then, did not exist until there was a need for secrecy. For this reason many origin narratives found in encyclopedias and similar introductory sources are misleading because they begin with the practice of magic in general, erroneously locating origins in practices like shamanism.

Of course, the idea of magic as the use of supernatural forces to do something secular has been around since antiquity, but magic did not become occult, at least in the Western world, until the Romans adopted

Christianity as the official religion and began persecuting those who held alternative beliefs—including those who studied magic.[20] In light of this important qualification, occultism did not emerge until the medieval period—at the very earliest the fourth century of the common era, when the practice of magic became a capital offense. During the crumbling of the Roman Empire, Augustine's screed against magic and sorcery in his extremely influential tome *City of God* echoed the tenor of popular sentiment:

> Why should I not cite public opinion itself as a witness against those magic arts in which certain most wretched and ungodly men love to glory? For if they are the works of divine beings worthy of worship, why are such arts so gravely punished by the severity of the law? Was it the Christians, perhaps, who enacted the laws by which magic arts are punished? With what other meaning, then, save that these sorceries are beyond doubt pernicious to the human race, did that most illustrious of poets [Virgil] say: "I swear, beloved sister, by the gods, by you, and by your sweet head, that I have recourse to magic arts only against my will?" . . . All the wonders of the sorcerers . . . are accomplished by means of the teaching and works of demons.[21]

Despite what Augustine characterizes as a popular opinion against magic as a demonic art, occultism thrived under the noses of those who would condemn it, especially among priests who understood their practices as that of medicine and what we would now call "natural science."

The Renaissance

Occultism exploded on the popular scene, however, in the Renaissance. During this period, spanning roughly from the late fourteenth to the early seventeenth centuries, magic emerged from the underground and experienced a "revival" among the schooled elite.[22] The primary obsession of occultists during this period was Hermeticism, which refers to the study and practice of alchemy, Kabbalism, and related occult arts under the aegis of a mythic magus known as Hermes Trismegistus. In 1463 the obsession began when a learned physician and priest by the name of Marsilio Ficino published a translation of the *Corpus Hermeticum,* one of the period's most celebrated magical textbooks.[23] The *Corpus* was thought to be the work of an Egyptian priest, rendered in Greek lore as Hermes Trismegistus ("Thrice Great Hermes"), who was mistakenly thought to be a real person.[24] The translation was soon followed by another attributed to Hermes Trismegistus titled the *Asclepius,* and both came to be known collectively as the *Hermetica.*[25] Although the *Hermetica* were probably written in the third century of the common era, humanist magi believed that the Greek texts predated the dialogues of Plato. Because Renaissance humanists fetishized everything from antiquity, the writings were quickly lauded as the fountain spring of all religion, and occultists began to replicate the formulas and rituals described in the texts. The texts became, like the Holy Bible for some Christians, the object used to legitimate any number of occult practices and behaviors. Occultists believed that the texts described an ancient Egyptian religion and contained a number of magical workings in cipher. Thus Hermeticism was born.

Of most interest to the Renaissance magus was the science of alchemy and the mystical art of the Kabbalah,[26] both seemingly supported and thus legitimized by yet another text attributed to Hermes Trismegistus, *The Emerald Table.* Its thirteen verses—said to speak in the "language of the birds" (in allegorical code)—provide a helpful summary of Renaissance magical beliefs and aims:[27]

1. It is true, without falsehood, and most certain.
2. What is below is like that which is above; and what is above is like that which is below: to accomplish the miracle of one thing.
3. As all things were formed from one, by the thought of one, so all things are born from this one thing, by choice.
4. Its father is the Sun, its mother the Moon, the Wind carries it in its belly, its nurse is the Earth.
5. It is the author of all perfection throughout the World.
6. The power is strong when changed into Earth.
7. Separate the Earth from the Fire, the subtle from the gross, gently with care.
8. Ascend from Earth to Heaven, and descend again to Earth, to unite the power of higher and lower things; thus you will obtain the glory of the whole World, and the shadows will leave you.
9. This has more strength than strength itself, for it overcomes all subtle things and penetrates every solid.
10. Thus the world was framed.
11. Hence proceed wonders, which means are here.
12. Therefore I am Hermes Trismegistus, having the three parts of world philosophy.
13. That which I had to say of the operation of the Sun is perfected.[28]

Occultists read this "operation of the Sun" as an alchemic procedure. Moreover, the second verse—perhaps one of the most famous expressions of Kabbalistic method—was thought to validate the priority of the human imagination over other faculties: by working through one's mental, representational, or mimetic capacities (the microcosm), one can comprehend the whole of nature (the macrocosm) and thus know its secrets. The same idea will find favor again in the philosophy, poetry, and literature of the romantic movement of the eighteenth and nineteenth centuries under the more familiar term "reflection."

During the Renaissance a number of prominent occultists became widely known who are deserving of mention. Cornelius Agrippa is the most famous and is celebrated as having written and published the "foundation book of Western occultism," *Three Books of Occult Philosophy.* This work proved invaluable to a number of renowned Renaissance magi, notably Paracelsus and Giordano Bruno, because it brought together into one handy reference a number of occult arts—astrology, herbology and medicine, witchcraft, goety and necromancy, and alchemy. As a sweeping survey of Renaissance occultism, *Occult Philosophy* quickly became a standard against which one measured occult books as well as a mandatory starting point for beginning students of magic. Its influence would stretch well into the Reformation period. John Dee, a gifted mathematician, practicing magician, and royal astrologer for Queen Elizabeth I, was an ardent student of Agrippa's writings and partially responsible for bringing Renaissance occultism into the English-speaking world. A brief description of Dee's occult system helps to illustrate a radical transformation of occultism during the Reformation, which moved back into subcultural obscurity in the sixteenth century at the dawn of the Enlightenment.

Reformation and the Enlightenment

John Dee is most known for having received, by dictation from his magical accomplice Edward Kelley in a trance, a magic vocabulary and a series of verses or "calls" that, when spoken properly, open up different levels of reality—ultimately Heaven itself.[29] The vocabulary, which Dee termed "Enochian language," soon became famous among occultists and has since become the center of what is currently known as Enochian Magic.[30] Although one may agree with Donald C. Lacock's suggestion that "real angels would [probably] speak a more euphonious and more consistent tongue than Enochian,"[31] the language is nevertheless an interesting example of occult cipher. The third Enochian key or "call" for opening a higher level of reality is a good example:

Micma, goho Piad, zir comselh a zien biah os londoh. Norz chis othil gigipah, undl chis ta puim, a q mospleh teloch, auinn toltorg chisi chis ge, m ozien, ds t brgda od torzul. I li eol balzard, od aala thiln os netaab, dluga vomsarg lonsa capmiali vors cla, homil cocasb, fafen izizop od miinoag de g netaab, vaun nanaeel, panpir malpirgi caosg pild. Noan unalah balt od vooan. Dooiap Mad, goholor, gohus, amiran. Micma iehusoz cacacom, od dooain noar micaolz aai om; Casarmg gohia; Zacar, uniglag, od im-vamar pugo plapli ananael qaan.

The English translation is as follows:

> Behold, says your God, I am a circle on whose hands stand twelve kingdoms. Six are the seats of living breath, the rest are as sharp sickles, or the horns of death, wherein the creatures of the earth are and are not, except by my own hands, which also sleep and shall rise. In the first I made you stewards, and placed you in seats twelve of government, giving unto every one of you power successively over 456, the true ages of time, to the intent that, from the highest vessels and the corners of your governments, you might work my power, pouring down the fires of life and increase on earth continually. Thus you are become the skirts of justice and truth. In the name of the same, your God, lift up, I say, yourselves. Behold His mercies flourish, and His Name is become mighty amongst us; in Whom we say: Move, descend, and apply yourselves unto us, as unto the partakers of the secret wisdom of your Creation.[32]

The call cited at length here is significant because of the central place it secures for the Christian God. Augustine's condemnation of magic as being inherently demonic is thus met here with verse that posits a thoroughly Christian magic, one that Dee defended as entirely in keeping with his Protestant faith. The significance of this move—a common one in occult texts during this period—is that it reflects Dee's growing fear of persecution. Although Dee was permitted to practice his magic because of his social status, his royal qualifications, and the company he kept (most especially Queen Elizabeth, who was fascinated by magic), others were not so lucky.[33] During this period the Roman Catholic Church's formal tribunal for crushing heresies, the Inquisition, could no longer control a number of local chapters that were finding "witches" and warlocks in every town and city. Convinced by Augustine's assertion that all occult practices involved demons, the Spanish Inquisition, as is well known, broke from Rome at the end of the fifteenth century in order to continue its unforgiving and ferocious execution of suspected witches. The *Malleus Maleficarum* (*The Witches' Hammer*), a professional manual for witch-hunters written by Heinrich Kramer and James Sprenger sometime in the late 1480s, was being studied and read throughout Europe, undergoing fourteen editions between "1487 and 1520, and at least sixteen editions between 1574 and 1669."[34] Although the Inquisition was never established in England or Scotland, general hardship and unease among the masses fed into fears about magic and the Devil across what would soon become Great Britain under the rule of King James I. Dee's angelic occultism anticipated a widespread, state-sponsored war against all forms of magic and occultism.[35]

Unfortunately for Dee, the last six years of his life were spent in fear, as he was still conscripted by the court in the service of James I (also James VI of Scotland), who apparently mistreated him. Although James I is most known for commissioning the Bible translation that bears his name, he should also be known for his ruthless persecution of suspected witches and occultists. The zealot king wrote and published his own English work on witchcraft, *Daemonlogy,* and often joined in witch-hunts, sometimes directing trials.[36] "Try, by the mediciners' oaths, if Barbara Napier be with bairn [child] or not," writes James about an accused witch and presumed consultant to his political enemy, the Earl of Bothwell. "If ye find she be not, to the fire with her presently and cause bowel [disembowel] her publicly. . . . The rest of the inferior witches, off at the nail with them."[37] James's Augustinian hatred of magic as the work of demons represents yet another turning of the tide for occultism, which became increasingly unfashionable in the Elizabethan and Jacobian eras.

Joining in the religious condemnation were thinkers like Francis Bacon, who vocally denounced the occult sciences as mere superstition and "condemned magic for its secretiveness and its exclusivity," thus forcing a dichotomy between the concepts of science and magic that persists to this day.[38] During this period, insisting on the divide was crucial, for up to a point "the boundaries between 'science,' alchemy and astrology . . . [and] between the theories that underpinned official medical practice and the charms of [occultists] were difficult to draw."[39] Bacon, and later Descartes, Kant, and a host of Enlightenment thinkers, would insist on drawing these boundaries and making the distinctions as sharp as possible. The divide was often based on the Enlightenment precept that understanding nature requires one to think of it in terms of matter in motion, a return to pre-Socratic atomism that secures no role for secret powers.[40] William Eamon argues that occultism had a "profound impact on the scientific revolution," particularly in regard to "a new conception of the scientific enterprise . . . as a hunt for nature's secrets."[41] Be that as it may, Jacobean witch-hunts and religious zealotry on the one hand, and the scientific revolution and Enlightenment philosophy on the other, fashioned both science and religion as the rivals of occultism. Understandably, popular interest in the secret arts during the Enlightenment period dwindled.

The Arrival of Modernity

The traditional origin narrative of occultism comes to an end in the nineteenth century with the arrival of industrial capitalism. The initial seeds were planted by the likes of Francis Barrett, whose largely plagiarized *The Magus, or Celestial Intelligencer; Being a Complete System of Occult Philosophy,* first published in 1801, seemed to satisfy a growing Victorian interest in mysticism and magic. Like Agrippa's system, Barrett's book claims to present the whole of "occult knowledge [which] we have, at a vast labor and expense, both of time and charges, collected whatsoever can be deemed curious and rare, in regard to the subject of our speculations in Natural Magic—the Cabala—Celestial and Ceremonial Magic—Alchemy—and Magnetism. . . . we have impartially examined the probability of the existence of *Magic,* both of the good and bad species, in a vast number of rare experiments in the course of this Treatise."[42] Barrett's description of his system is important for the origin narrative of occultism for three reasons. First, Barrett advances a distinction between "good and bad species" of magic, which reflects a division between "black magic" and "white magic," or the "left hand path" and the "right hand path." Black magic, of course, involves evil spirits and is often engaged to harm people, while white magic is performed to do good. Although this distinction seems to stretch back to the Roman Empire (previous to Christianization, black magic was illegal but white magic was not), Barrett's book devotes a great deal of space to describing black magic, something that, prior to the nineteenth century, would have been very dangerous.

The second reason for the significance of Barrett's system concerns the way in which the black arts are discussed: *The Magus* contains a section on what to do if one "accidentally" conjures an evil or familiar spirit. Moreover, the tome contained four pages of color illustrations of principal "Evil Damons," from "fallen angels" to the "Spirit of Antichrist," so that, in the case of unexpected evocation, the magus could know exactly whom he or she was dealing with! Although past magical books frequently dealt with the problem of evil spirits and demons—most especially hunting and torture handbooks like the *Malleus Maleficarum* and Francesco Guazzo's *Compendium Maleficarum*—Barrett's treatment smacks of sensationalism. His galvanic descriptions of black magic and demonology, in turn, lead to the third reason why Barrett's system of magic is important: *The Magus* had a strong impact on an avid and devoted reader, Eliphas Lévi, who would bring occultism out of the darkness and into the light of mass readership in the middle of the nineteenth century, however ironically, with dramatic descriptions of black magic and striking illustrations of occult paraphernalia, symbol, and ritual.

The distinction between a Renaissance magic with medicinal and quasi-scientific aims and Barrett's colorful pictures of demons thus marks an economic shift in occult discourse, its having moved from a pursuit of knowledge and an investigation of nature to the pursuit of profit through entertainment. It is likely the case that many occultists during the nineteenth century sincerely believed in the arts they wrote about and practiced; however, occult texts began to take on the features of a commodity after they became profitable sources of entertainment. The increasing perfection of the almighty printing press enabled the mass manufacture of books during the Victorian era.[43] A London-based publishing company—Lackington, Allen and Company—mass-produced *The Magus* as "the first readily accessible English translation . . . of rare, long-out-of-print works."[44]

The traditional origin narrative of occultism thus comes to an end with its metamorphosing into a phenomenon of mass culture, a transformation that begins with Barrett but reaches fruition in the "French occult revival" spearheaded by Lévi. Indeed, with Lévi and his contemporaries one can locate the beginning of *modern* occultism as a mass phenomenon, as both an object for serious study and a form of entertainment and, significantly, also something that was no longer burdened by Augustine's famous and long-standing prohibition. The present study will take up the origin narrative where Lévi leaves off, beginning in chapter 3 with the popular literary successes of a boisterous and charismatic Russian immigrant, H. P. Blavatsky, whose massive books *Isis Unveiled* and *The Secret Doctrine* were read by the curious public as much as the private occultist.

The Occult as a Generic Form

The general way in which scholars and students of the occult describe its origin narrative, the first element of the specificity of the occult, sheds light on the rationale behind the logic of discrimination that is at the core of all occultic discourse: to avoid misunderstanding, perversion, or, in some cases, persecution, difficult language was used. Unlike the shibboleth, which marked some for life and others for death, the discriminatory logic of difficult language began as a form of self-protection. In later chapters I will describe how this logic of discrimination was used to create in-groups and out-groups, yet for the remainder of this chapter I would like to address the following question: How was this difficult language used by modern occultists? The answer leads me to the rhetorical features of the occult, or the generic norms that help to make up its specificity. By examining the common features of modern occult texts, we will then be able to determine which among them remain intact in contemporary occultic discourse and which among them have been transformed or simply disappeared.

A Note on "Genre"

I use the term "genre" with some trepidation, because in many disciplines —particularly rhetorical studies, literary studies, and film studies— genre criticism is unpopular and often criticized as being "formulaic."[45] To avoid misunderstanding, a brief discussion of the concept is helpful.[46]

Genres are simply patterns that seem to emerge among texts or social forms in a given cultural discourse. As observed patterns or repetitions, genres are discerned entirely in retrospect by a critic and are generally devoid of predictive value.[47] Although some patterns are restrictive and become loose rules and may be thus said to determine, in limited manner, the formal arrangement of a text (e.g., as is the case with eulogies, romance novels, and "boy band" pop ditties), genres neither predetermine discourse nor are they fixed, as they change and transform continuously over time. Karlyn Kohrs Campbell and Kathleen Hall Jamieson have suggested that genres are akin to dynamic "constellations" of elements that, on the one hand, give an author a sense of what people expect of him or her, but, on the other hand, also detail elements to be violated (such is the case of good poetry or a good speech: "original" or "creative" rhetoric violates expectations).[48] Further, the metaphor of "constellation" is important because it acknowledges that it is the observer of pattern that is responsible for the pattern, not the texts observed. In a manner similar to the historiography of Hayden White, Campbell and Jamieson place the recognition of genre in the mind of the reader or critic, not the text or texts in question. In a "generic" mode of criticism, the "rhetorical critic *chooses a perspective* that will discover and describe one or more patterns that inhere in symbolic action or more sets of rules that human beings in a culture or subculture have created to make symbolic transactions intelligible and meaningful to each other. Inevitably, the critic argues that the patterns of or the rules inherent in a rhetorical act or body of rhetorical action reflect and account for that act or body of action as fully as possible" (my emphasis).[49] Although I would disagree that any text or discourse contains "inherent" features in the sense that such features exist independent of the observer, I agree with Campbell and Jamieson that genres, as much as origin narratives, are offered by the critics as useful organizing schemes.[50] In the discussion of genre below, the patterns that I suggest are common among occult texts are not offered as objective features but rather as items that I have noticed tend to recur in my experience of reading occult texts, items that help us to better contend with the diffuseness of occult discourse in general. Only a complete and exhaustive account of all occult texts could prove that such patterns are inherent to all occult texts—an impossible task.

The Generic Features of Compositional Form: Revelation, Neologism, and Irony

One of the many entertaining aspects of modern occult texts is the title page, which, more often than not, is presented in the language of revelation, the dialectical counterpart to secrecy. In the nineteenth century, title pages often featured long titles and subtitles as an advertisement, a function that extends to jacket covers and dust-flap summaries in regard to contemporary occult texts.[51] Insofar as self-identified occult writers understand the occult as the study of secrets, it is not surprising that title pages tout a given book's content as a whispering: "Herein you will find the mysteries of the world revealed." Barrett's lengthy title page to *The Magus* is a great example:

The Magus,
or
Celestial Intelligencer;
being
A Complete System of
Occult Philosophy.
In Three Books:
Containing the Ancient and Modern Practice of the
Cabalistic Art, Natural and Celestial Magic, &c.;
shewing the wonderful Effects that may be performed by
a Knowledge of the

Celestial Influences, the occult Properties of metals,
Herbs, and Stones,
and the
Application of Active to Passive Principles.
Exhibiting
The Sciences of Natural Magic;
Alcymy, or Hermetic Philosophy;
and
The Nature, Creation, and Fall of Man;
His natural and supernatural Gifts; the magical Power
inherent in the Soul, &c.; with a great Variety of
rare Experiments in Natural Magic;
The Constellatory Practice, or Talismanic Magic;
The nature of the Elements, Stars, Planets, Signs,
&c.; the Construction and Composition of all sorts of
Magic Seals, Images, Rings, Glasses, &c.;
The Virtue and Efficacy of Numbers, Characters,
and Figures, of good and evil spirits.
Magnetism,
And Cabalistical or Ceremonial Magic;
In which the secret Mysteries of the Cabala are
explained; the Operations of good and evil Spirits;
all Kinds of Cabalistic Figures, Tables, Seals, and
Names, with the Use, &c.
The Times, Bonds, Offices, and Conjuration of Spirits
To Which is Added
Biographia Antiqua, or the Lives of the most eminent
Philosophers, Magi, &c.
The Whole Illustrated with a great Variety of
Curious Engravings, Magical and Cabalistical Figures,
&c.
By Francis Barrett, F.R.C.
Professor of Chemistry, natural and occult Philosophy,
the Cabala, &c. &c.

Barrett's title promises all but the moon (or, rather, promises the moon but only in terms of its imaginative, astrological reality)! Later in the nineteenth century the fashionability of long titles would dwindle, but they nevertheless proceed in the same sensationalistic tone. Lévi's prized opus is titled *The History of Magic, Including a Clear and Precise Exposition of Its Procedure, Its Rites and Its Mysteries,* thus promising a clarity and precision of revelation. Blavatsky's *Isis Un-*

veiled: A Master-Key to the Mysteries of Ancient and Modern Science and Theology betokens a disclosure of the true face of occultism as well as the ultimate "key" for decoding all "mysteries." Contemporary texts continue the tradition: the full title of Israel Regardie's classic account of the Hermetic magic of the famous secret society, the Golden Dawn, is *The Golden Dawn: A Complete Course in Practical and Ceremonial Magic, Four Volumes in One; The Original Account of the Teachings, Rites and Ceremonies of the Hermetic Order of the Golden Dawn (Stella Matutina) as Revealed by Israel Regardie;* the title uses revelation as a key term.

More contemporary, commercially successful, characteristically occultic work, such as that of mystics like Gary Zukav and psychics like Sylvia Browne, have more modest titles but preserve the rhetoric of revelation on their dust jackets. The back cover of Browne's *New York Times* best-seller, *Life on the Other Side: A Psychic's Tour of the Afterlife,* reads:

> Praise for Sylvia Browne: "Sylvia Browne is a master at conveying the truth that exists in the fourth dimension," Carolyn Myss, bestselling author of *Anatomy of the Spirit.* "I've personally witnessed Sylvia Browne bring closure to distraught families . . . and open people's hearts to see the good within themselves," Montel Williams [talk-show host]. From *Life on the Other Side*[:] "I happen to be one of the most naturally skeptical people you'll ever meet, and I'm almost addicted to research. My faith in God has always been unshakable, but until and unless I've seen, tasted, smelled, felt and experience the details about how this whole creation of reality works, I take nothing for granted. . . . I would never waste your time with a book of pretty fantasies and illusions about The Other Side. The Other Side is more thrilling, comforting, loving, and empowering than any fairy tale could ever be."

I have cited the jacket copy at length because it highlights an element that has persisted since the nineteenth century. The language of revelation—that the given occultist will be telling secrets—is always couched in terms of "the truth." In addition, the jacket copy features a concern with authority, particularly in terms of testimonials from presumed experts (one, another psychic; the other, a television talk-show host). Any nonfiction book necessarily claims authority; both "author" and "authority" are derived from the Latin *auctor,* which means "creator." In occult books, however, the authority claimed is always in terms of something that previously has been concealed or gravely misunderstood, and this something typically has to do with powers that derive from alternate realities most immediately accessible "within" one's mind.

Browne's book (published in 2000), however, also highlights a rhetorical move found in many historical occult works that bears mention: prefatory piety. "My faith in God has always been unshakable," she suggests. As I noted in the origin narrative, after Augustine's influential condemnation of magic and occultism as having derived its powers from demonic forces, occultism was thought to be evil by many religious authorities. This belief waxed and waned throughout history; the evidence of its strongest application is the thousands of suspected witches who were burned alive and tortured during the heyday of the Spanish Inquisition. The consequence of this belief was the inclusion of prefatory remarks in occult texts that serve as testaments to Christian faith. Agrippa's *Occult Philosophy* begins with an open letter to the Chancellor of Italy that reads, "To the reverend father in Christ, and most illustrious prince, *Hermannus,* . . . Agrippa . . . sendeth greeting," signaling his servitude and religious conviction. Barrett's *The Magus* is careful to describe magic and astrology as God-given and in general "agreement" with the "Holy Scriptures."[52] Lévi introduces his *The History of Magic* by stressing that the "three wise men" of the story of nativity were, in fact, magi, a move he repeats in *Transcendental Magic:* "Science, notwithstanding, is at the basis of Magic, as at the root of Christianity there is love, and in the Gospel symbols we find the Word Incarnate adored in His cradle by Three Magi, led thither by a star—the triad and the sign of the microcosm—and receiving their gifts of gold, frankincense and myrrh, a second mysterious triplicity. . . . Christianity therefore owes no hatred to Magic."[53] Similarly, Waite opens his self-described "canon of criticism," *The Book of Ceremonial Magic,* with a lengthy discussion of "Christian Mystical Theology." As is the case of all white magic, Waite writes, the literature of Christian occultism "is full as to that which it understands in respect to Divine life; it is grace which fills the heart; it is the Holy Spirit of God which makes holy the spirit of man; it is life in God. There is no doubt that in its formulation it was presented to the mind of Christian Mysticism as the life which was hidden with Christ in God."[54] That contemporary occultists continue to introduce their texts as compatible with a "faith in God," even the Christian God, is a compositional regularity in much occult literature.

The device of prefatory piety in occult texts seems to suggest that many occultists thought of themselves as traditionally religious individuals.

Or so it would seem. Unlike contemporary occultic texts that proclaim religious affinities with Christianity and other dominant religions, the prefatory piety in modern occult texts, beginning most notably with Lévi, is a deliberate rhetorical blind. The primary, compositional contrivance of modern occult texts is an irony designed to mislead the less discerning. Indeed, deliberately misleading language and prose has been a common element in occult texts since the medieval era, when magi and occultists were forced to compose their texts in an allegorical code, or "the language of birds." For example, the alchemic word *VITRIOL* found in a number of occult texts was meaningless to non-alchemists. It refers to the Latin phrase *Visita Interiora Terrae Rectificandoque Invenies Occultum Lapidem,* which could be translated as "visit the interior of the earth, and by rectifying, you will discover the hidden stone."[55] The hidden stone here is the famous Philosopher's Stone, a rock or gem that would presumably turn baser metals into gold, provide eternal youth, heal illness—or not. Given the ubiquity of cipher in occult texts, scholars are uncertain as to whether the Philosopher's Stone is the attainment of a state of consciousness, a secret book, or perhaps a procedure itself.

Because occult practice has been, throughout its origin narrative, a punishable offense, allegorical and figurative language was common. Neologisms and otherwise strange terms are rife in occult texts. For example, Charles Walker suggests that members of a secret occult order, the Rosicrucians, "were aware of these different levels of meaning [in the use of strange occult terms] and could speak in their esoteric language on a level which was beyond comprehension to the uninitiated."[56] John Dee's Enochian language could also be read as cipher, a symbolic language with which to communicate with others about occult matters in ways that were unrecognizable to a public increasingly suspicious of magic and the occult. Given this rationale, it is not surprising that many occult texts are deliberately ironic in their use of prefatory piety.

Lévi's ironic turns in many of his books are a good example of textual irony, which seems to be used instead of difficult esoteric language or jargon for the same end. Rather than alienate a curious reading public, Lévi avoids the language of birds and instead uses a self-referential and (if one is "in the know") humorous brand of irony. In *The History of Magic,* Lévi insists "to Christians that the author of this book is Christian like yourselves. His faith is that of a [Catholic] strongly and deeply convinced."[57] While Lévi may have, in fact, believed this, his implication that the Devil is a fictional "personification" of malevolent force is far from the Catholic doctrine of his time.[58] In *Transcendental Magic* there is a glaring rhetorical blind intended to mislead the uninitiated. That something "sneaky" is happening in his text is cued immediately when one contrasts the contents of the introduction of the book with the lengthy descriptions of black magic at its end.

In the introduction to *Transcendental Magic,* Lévi goes to great lengths to locate the roots of occultism in Christianity. Yet nearing the end of the book, Lévi explains in painstaking detail—tongue undoubtedly firmly implanted in his cheek—how to summon the Devil. The following excerpt demonstrates the lengths to which Lévi would go to secure the misunderstanding of the ignorant and the delight of the initiated:

> Evokers of the devil must before all things belong to a religion that admits a creative devil, who is also rival of God. To invoke a power, we must believe in it. Given such firm faith in the religion of the devil, we must proceed as follows to enter into correspondence with this pseudo-Deity:
>
> MAGICAL AXIOM
> Within the circle of its action, every world creates that which it affirms.
>
> DIRECT CONSEQUENCE
> He who affirms the devil creates or makes the devil.
>
> *Conditions of Success in Infernal Evocations*
> (1) Invincible obstinacy; (2) a conscience at once hardened into crime and most prone to remorse and fear; (3) affected or natural ignorance; (4) blind faith in all that is incredible; (5) an utterly false idea of God. We must afterwards (1) profane the ceremonies of the cults in which we believe; (2) offer a bloody sacrifice; (3) procure the magic fork, which is a branch of a single bough of hazel or almond, cut at one blow with the new knife used for the sacrifice. It must terminate in a fork, which must be armoured with iron or steel, made from the blade of the knife before mentioned. A fast of fifteen days must be observed, taking a single unsalted repast after sundown. It should consist of black bread and blood, seasoned with unsalted spices or black beans

> and milky narcotic herbs. We must get drunk every five days after sundown on wine in which five heads of black poppies and five ounces of pounded hemp-seed have been steeped for five hours, the infusion of being strained through a cloth woven by a prostitute: strictly speaking, the first cloth which comes to hand may be used, should it have been woven by a woman. The evocation should be performed on the night between Monday and Tuesday, or that between Friday and Saturday. A solitary and forbidden spot must be chosen, such as a cemetery haunted by evil spirits, a dreaded ruin in the country, the vaults of an abandoned convent, a place where some murder has been committed, a druidic altar or an old temple of idols. A black seamless and sleeveless robe must be provided; a leaden cap emblazoned with the signs of the moon, Venus and Saturn; two candles of human fat set in black wooden candlesticks, carved in the shape of a crescent; two crowns of vervain; a magical sword with a black handle; the magical fork; a copper vase containing the blood of the victim; a censer holding perfumes, namely, incense, camphor, aloes, ambergris and storax, mixed together with the blood of a goat, a mole and a bat; four nails taken from the coffin of an executed criminal; the head of a black cat which has been nourished on human flesh for five days; a bat drowned in blood; the horns of a goat *cum quo puella concuberit;* and the skull of a patricide. All these hideous objects—though scarcely possible to obtain—having been collected, they must be arranged as follows: A perfect circle is traced by the sword, leaving, however, a break, or point of issue, on one side; a triangle is drawn in the circle, and the Pantacle thus formed is coloured with blood.[59]

The instructions continue for a considerable length. Nevertheless, it should be clear at this point that the task Lévi sets for the neophyte devil worshiper is tremendous! As if to dissuade readers of his English translation from trying it out, Waite writes in a footnote that "readers must be dissuaded from supposing that there is any authority in the records for these diabolical evocations." Lévi, he insists, "supplied most of the pictorial effects by his own imaginative genius."[60] Elsewhere Waite is not so charitable, claiming that Lévi has done nothing short of blasphemy, inverting "the solemn religious purifications" and rites and rendering them into "diabolical parodies."[61] Waite's own descriptions of "the rituals of black magic" in his *Book of Ceremonial Magic,* first published in 1911, however, provide some evidence to support the claim that his protests were somewhat disingenuous, if

Fig. 3. Lévi's illustration of the "Goëtic Circle of Black Evocation and Pacts." Reprinted from *Transcendental Magic,* trans. A. E. Waite (London: Rider and Company, 1896), 318.

not a continuation of the magical joke. As most occultists during this period would argue, the forces of good and evil come from the same supernatural force; thus, to distinguish between good and bad magic was to misunderstand the "nature" of magic. Were Lévi's remarks meant to be taken seriously, then? Not by the ardent adept who would recognize Lévi's playfulness and look elsewhere for a more fundamental teaching. With Lévi's finger to his lips and with a wink of his left eye, it is as if he is saying, "Shhhhh. Don't tell, but this is not the real deal. Read deeper."

Concluding Remarks: Characterizing "Modern" Occultism

In the context of its origin narrative, in this chapter I have suggested that the contemporary incoherence of occultism is best managed by dividing the discourse into a larger and smaller category. The larger category, the occultic, concerns the many ways in which "the occult" is used in contemporary discourse. The smaller category, the occult, is both an expression and the origin of the larger category. I then suggested that we could learn more about the larger occultic by examining the historical occult. Finally, I suggested that the specificity of the occult reduces to its origin narrative and its generic features.

In terms of the origin narrative, I argued that *modern* occultism can be identified by its commodification, particularly in terms of the wider dispersal of texts designed for audiences much larger than a small cabal of true believers. To the traditional, expressed motive of the will to knowledge, then, in modern occultism we can add an economic motive. Second, I suggested that modern occultism can be described in terms of the relaxed prohibitions against its practice; although some religious authorities continued to think of all occultism—good or bad, white or black—as demonic, it is clear that practicing occultism no longer risked the consequence of social alienation or death. Widespread public interest among the literate elite is testament enough that the stigma of occultism was not as bad as it had been during the Enlightenment. In the next chapter I will describe further the contextual forces that contributed to an explosion of popular interest.

Finally, I have detailed a number of generic features typical of occult texts: the compositional forms of revelation, allegorical and figurative language, and the frequent use of misleading, ironic blinds. As the occult transforms during the twentieth century, the first two of these features will survive in the form of the occultic, but the ironic blind becomes increasingly difficult to control as society becomes increasingly "public."

To deepen our understanding of the occult in terms of difficult and figurative language, the next two chapters turn to an examination of the processes of "invention," or the ways in which occult rhetoric is created ("occult poetics"). Once the reasons behind the generic element of allegorical and figurative language are explained, I then turn in chapter 4 to the processes of interpretation, or how occult texts were read and asked to be read. An examination of occult interpretation or hermeneutics will, finally, lead us to the generic element of irony, a distinctive part of occult rhetoric and an important reason for its demise. In the wake of irony, the occultic emerges.

Interlude

Erasing the Grooves: On Cold Feet

On a chilly evening in mid-October 1999, my friend Erika and I attended an informational meeting held by the Minneapolis chapter of the Society for Ascension. The meeting was advertised in a pamphlet I picked up one day while browsing in an occult bookstore near the University of Minnesota campus. The pamphlet described the Society for Ascension in vague and evocative terms, which were splashed across the background image of a turbulent and cloudy sky. I suppose the pamphlet caught my eye because it was oddly disturbing. The color scheme is intense: a series of dark red and lighter orange shades on the inner flaps leads one's eye to lightly painted webs of lightning. It is as if the text on the front of the page is bursting out from a cataclysmic sky, heralding the coming of something quite monumental (the fourth horseman of the Apocalypse, I thought, or perhaps the Messiah himself). The text on the cover reads: "The Ishayas' Ascension: Ancient Teachings brought fourth for the third millennium. Woven throughout the tapestry of time . . . practiced and cultivated by the Masters for a millennia . . . preserved since the time of Christ . . . the Teaching of Ascension is again being released into a world ready for the fruits of enlightenment." As someone trained to ruminate on words, I was drawn to "tapestry." For me the term resonates with "fabric" and "woven," two metaphors Erika and I would hear time and time again during our experience with the group. This trinity of terms suggests the exotic and antique, a cherished cloth, an ancient veil. Coupled with the red-and-orange image of a foreboding sky, the pamphlet reminded me of the Western romance of India, the collective appropriation of Indian "exotica" in the pages of coffee-table books and on the screens of televisions: the chalky reds speak of images of poverty, closely associated with a dusty, orange earth; brown bodies bathing in sacred polluted rivers; a meditation and turning inward through the third eye which unites the external with the eternal; Ben Kingsley walking through dusty streets, trailed by children, tanned and Gandhi-ed, demonstrating how class boundaries become porous though self-denial and a highly theatrical version of starvation. In the Western popular imaginary, it seems that the rigid caste system of India is erased in this swirl of evocative, romantic imagery.

In the popular imaginary of the United States, where Horatio Alger's Ragged Dick spits on a shoe, polishes, and sees reflections of inevitable future successes, the sovereign individual is key. The antagonism of class that I see through the edges of these aesthetic imbrications of Indian imagery—the Sanskrit transliterations, the wisdomatic guru, the snake charmer, the hues of red—is elided in favor of an individual ascension into classless spheres of reality: "Whether you are looking for simple stress relief or the key to Full Human Consciousness," the pamphlet continues, like Coca-Cola, "the Ishayas' Ascension is it." The theme of effortlessly produced empowerment is common in the group's literature. For example, an undated newsletter reads: "Any discussion of the Ishayas' historical tradition should begin with a reminder that the Ishayas' teachings are centered around personal experience and empowerment only, and require no belief whatsoever. All religious traditions teach some form of inward contemplation and prayer, and the Ishayas' Ascension—being a very powerful tool to achieve this inward movement—can exist within and even without any system of belief." There is no expenditure of labor. There is no discernible class. Effortless enlightenment, along with that much-needed stress relief, is guaranteed. Reading these materials, I kept thinking about the tension between the individualist, consumerist language of the pamphlet's linguistic economy and the exotic images that its graphic design cued in my own imagination. It all seemed much too American. I had to learn more.

After phoning the society's "center" and getting directions, Erika and I drove toward a destination in north Minneapolis. I was initially uncomfortable after I hung up the phone because I learned that the "center" was actually someone's home. That it was an intimate as opposed to a public space seemed odd. I thought about the phenomenon of "love-bombing," presumably a technique of indoctrination and brainwashing that cult groups use to collect members. This invitation to learn more about the Society for Ascension within an intimate space, I figured, was deliberate.

It was dark outside when we arrived, and the house in which the meeting took place was difficult to find because there were no streetlights. We approached a house that seemed occupied and looked inside a screened porch, where we noticed a large pile of shoes outside the front door. There was no street number, but I thought "this must be it" because of the stereotypes I had about Eastern religious practice, which involved the removal of shoes. We were going to have to remove our shoes. I didn't like the idea because my feet get cold easily, and I was wearing thin nylon socks. Worse, Erika whispered that in the event something horrifying happened, we would not be able to run away.

We entered the porch and knocked on the front door. Immediately the door opened and we were greeted by a white (as opposed to Indian) woman who we later would learn was celebrating her thirty-ninth birthday (a large arrangement of thirty-nine roses was prominently displayed on a coffee table in the living room). She smiled and was eating something. Her mouth still occupied, she said that we were welcome and in the right place. She told us her name and asked us to remove our shoes. As we did Erika and I introduced ourselves. The woman was wearing a white sweater and white cotton pants and had a number of brown, wooden-bead necklaces conspicuously hung around her neck. She continued to block the doorway but not in a threatening manner, stressing that we could not enter the home until our shoes were removed. The seeming routineness of our visit was comforting.

As we entered the home, I noted a white man with long, brown hair in his mid- to late twenties putting food into Tupperware in a kitchenette just beyond the foyer. To our left was a staircase to the upper part of the house, and to our right was a living- and dining-room area crowded with couches. The room was very comforting: the carpet was white and the walls were painted with a soft rose color, also trimmed in white. There was a large painting of wide pink swathes and green splotches hanging on the dining-room wall. Scattered throughout were smaller framed pictures of Chinese calligraphy, which we were told were charming proverbs.

No one asked us to find a seat, so I (bravely, I thought) decided to blaze a path to a couch on the far wall. I chose this seat so that I could observe most of the room, especially the doorway. I knew this was a self-protective move (Wild Bill Hickok never sat with his back to a door). Erika sat beside me. To our right was a young woman; although her legs were crossed, her arms were open in a gesture of friendliness. She welcomed us and thanked us for coming. Like the woman we met at the door, she was also wearing white. She had long, curly hair, and around her neck was a large, conspicuous jeweled cross. She began asking questions of Erika and did not seem interested in talking to me. As they conversed, more people entered the room. The woman we met at the door entered with a man wearing red clothes and sat on a couch facing us. After the man was seated, the woman tucked her feet under him.

While Erika continued talking to the young woman, the man in red stood up and extended his hand for a handshake. He told me his name and identified himself as the person with whom I had spoken on the phone. He was a young man in his mid-twenties with a goatee and a short ponytail. He smiled a lot. The man in the kitchen entered the room and sat in a chair (part of a dining-room set) to our right. Next to the chair was a white "dry-erase" marker board balanced across two dining-room chairs. On the board was written "The Ishayas' Ascension." Below this phrase were a number of Sanskrit words (transliterated), which we later learned were the names of our four hosts. The names were so unusual (to me, at least) that I had difficulty remembering them.

There was a knock on the door, and the woman whom we first met untucked her feet and got up to answer. A white woman in her forties or fifties and a man of similar appearance and age entered the room without their shoes. As they were greeted, the woman speaking to Erika told us that their names were Bob and Karen (here, pseudonyms). We were told that Karen was coming tonight for Bob's benefit. Karen was about to endure a seven-day "intensive" retreat and wanted Bob to know a little more about why she was going and what the group was all about. Karen and Bob entered the living room and introduced themselves. Erika and I stood up and shook their hands. I noticed that they both were dressed casually in ways that were not like that of our hosts.

Once Karen and Bob found seats on the remaining, empty couch (there were three), a formal presentation began. The young man from the kitchen began to speak in a soft tone, as if he were a shy person. As he talked his hands fiddled with his rings and he avoided eye contact. He began by telling us that "the Ascension" was a set of "mechanical techniques," absent a belief system, which one could use to get in touch with "the Infinite." We learned that the Society for Ascension is a group of like-minded adults dedicated to spreading a message of universal brotherhood and peace. They believe this message is best taught by mastering certain meditative techniques, variously termed "attitudes," that enable the individual to access the Infinite. The Infinite is, paradoxically, individuated within each of us at the center of our consciousness. The woman whom we met at the door cut the man off and began explaining further. The young man looked relieved. She picked up a marker and drew a small circle, which she called "the Infinite," and then drew the symbol for infinity in its center.

I decided to tuck my feet underneath me on the couch. They were getting cold. I decided this was a good gesture because it mirrored the behavior of our hosts (all of whom were sitting on their feet in one way or another). I briefly thought of tucking my feet under Erika but quickly decided that might be too much mirroring.

The woman then drew another circle around the smaller circle. She said that this new circle represented a childhood experience of failure, which in their literature they term a "limitation" or "groove." This "groove," she said, made it more difficult to access the Infinite. The woman sitting next to Erika interrupted the demonstration and asked that the concept of "groove" be explained further. The woman at the marker board then told us a story about her childhood. When she was very young, she said, she wanted to wash the hair of one of her baby dolls. When she did, all the hair fell out and she was very upset. She said that this experience of "failure" created a groove in her consciousness. She elaborated the point at some length and then moved to tell another autobiographical anecdote about her teenage years (being told to stay in her bedroom as a punishment), which led to yet another story, drawing more concentric circles as she chronicled her life.

Eventually, Ascending was described as "erasing" a path through the groves to the Infinite, the most divine part of self united with the entire cosmos. The woman used a felt eraser and made a path of white to the middle of the circles. The man in red then began to tell us how much Ascending has helped his life. He said he was "now full of joy." He talked about a "void" that we all feel in our lives, and how this "void" is our "true self" calling us to the Infinite. He explained that he read philosophy and tried a number of religions, that he experimented with sex and heavy drugs, all in an effort to navigate this void. The Ishayas' Ascension, he testified, revealed to him that the void was nothing more than spiritual distance from the Infinite.

During this discussion I kept thinking of Freud and Lacan, and how the discussion we were hearing closely resembled the notion of "lack" that Lacan suggests marks one's entry into self-consciousness. I decided to ask a question. I asked why Ascending was superior to psychoanalysis. The woman whom we met at the door made a unpleasant face and blurted out, "What?" in a startled and inquisitive tone. I was surprised by this and didn't know if she was mocking or simply unsure about what I was asking. The man in red explained to her that psychoanalysis concerns a talking cure, and the woman seemed satisfied. The man then addressed me and said that psychoanalysis was, in fact, a "groove" itself and only addressed the problem of the void on a superficial level. Ascending went beyond "mere psychobabble," he said. In fact, "psychobabble is part of the problem" because it creates a difficult jargon that has to be learned, thus creating a "limitation" and therefore a groove. I was still struck by the similarity between what I was being told and psychoanalytic theory, so I asked a question about the Id, which I phrased in terms of sexual desire. "What is the relationship between Ascending and sex?" I asked. The man answered that sexual desires, which were natural and important, were dirtied by accumulated limitations and groves. Through the grooves sexual pleasure becomes an avenue for self-confidence (or worse, self-hatred) or a means by which notions of masculinity and femininity are reinforced, rather than an expression of the true, unbridled, spiritual purpose of sex. He said that once he began Ascending, he no longer needed sex as much as he had thought, and that sex was also much more enjoyable. He then said: "You know, I still love chocolate though. It's not that this desire for chocolate-eating is going to go away."

Erika then asked a number of questions. "Is ascending meditation, then? Is there a God-figure, or just the Infinite?" Others around the room joined in answering Erika's questions. It was clear to me that they were more interested in Erika and that my questions marked me as a skeptic. Erika asked the hosts their lives were changed as a result of Ascending. The man in red answered first. He said that he was once an architectural student and then a student of homeopathic medicine. He said that his mother was always on an endless quest for the next "New Age thing" and that she always told him about her spiritual discoveries. She stopped moving from New Age group to New Age group when she found the Society for Ascension, and this made him take notice. He said he read the literature written by MSI (an acronym for the name of the founder of the society, Maharishi Sadashiva Isham, formerly a practitioner of transcendental meditation from Seattle, Washington) and had an "epiphany." The other young man (from the kitchen) said that he was also introduced to the group by his mother. The woman at the marker board then related a long, complicated story about being a successful photojournalist, but then one day she had a sudden need to lock herself in a cabin in the mountains for some days, presumably to think through a profound unhappiness. Ascension helped her find a way to happiness and joy. Although she didn't explain how she discovered the society, she said that she was convinced of the authenticity of MSI's teachings because they are "woven into the fabric of reality itself." One recognizes the Truth, she said, when one experiences the Infinite for the first time.

The meeting devolved into a series of questions and answers, as well as a number of inside jabs and jokes between the hosts that Erika and I did not understand. During these questions and answers sometimes Karen would jump in to explain a concept that she believed we needed to have explained to us. The young woman at the marker board announced that Karen had been Ascending as long as they have but that Karen is still "working on herself." What this meant was never explained except in terms of the hosts' having "taken the next step by dedicating their lives to the Society and spreading its message of joy." True enlightenment, said the woman at the marker board, was already "wired" into our bodies and minds and only needed to be "teased out."

We learned that the hosts made their living from donations and the fees charged at weekend workshops, during which the secret techniques were revealed.

Karen described herself as the ever-searching "soccer mom" looking for spiritual truth. She spoke as if the Society for Ascension was the place where her seeking had finally led her. Bob (her second husband, we were told) was not convinced. When one of the hosts asked Bob what he thought, he said that he was the "Doubting Thomas" and that he simply "doesn't get it." He said that he tolerated Karen's spiritualism, however, because it was helping her to cope with an issue that we were not privy to. The most interesting thing that happened during the evening, however, was an outburst from Bob. When it was nearing 9:00 P.M., nearly two hours after we had arrived, I was asking a lot of questions about their claim that "no belief is necessary," which seemed contradictory to me. I also asked why our hosts changed their birth names to Sanskrit names. The woman at the marker board explained that although she harbors no resentment toward her parents, her Sanskrit name resonates with "who I really am." She explained that Sanskrit is a special language because the sound of each word vibrates at the same frequency as its referent. For example, she explained, the spoken sound for tree actually vibrates at the same frequency of the atoms that comprise a tree. She said that this is analogous to speaking a word through a plastic cup in sand (I wondered what the Sanskrit term for "unicorn" was). At this point Bob blurted out a defiant "Hogwash!" His reply was very vehement and turned into a screed. He said that he had taught German for twenty-five years and that Sanskrit was an Indo-European language. He went on for three or four minutes about the "preposterous" claims of our hosts, and the atmosphere of the room became negatively charged. The hosts were visibly uncomfortable. The man in red offered to research the matter and get back to him. Erika began to squirm during this exchange, indicating to me that it was time for us to go.

Once the conflict began to abate somewhat, I asked a few more questions to help reestablish a more comfortable environment. I learned that progress in Ascending is marked by moving through various teaching units or "spheres." The first sphere involves the adoption of "four attitudes," which we could learn about at a center workshop that weekend for $200 a person.

After a number of thank-you's and well wishes, we stood up and headed for the door. I made it a point to shake everyone's hand. Erika went to the porch and put on her shoes. Just as I was about to step outside and join her, the man in red tapped me on the shoulder and gave me an audiotape, which he said would give me a deeper understanding of their teachings. The tape was labeled "Introduction to the Ishayas' Ascension." I never listened to the tape, convinced I knew what I would hear.

As I detail more fully in chapter 2, what I would have heard on the Ishayas' Ascension tape is a contemporary "remix"—to riff in the idiom of hip-hop—of Platonic teachings that are over two thousand years old. Human language, precisely because it is human, is incapable of "cutting through the grooves" to the Source, the One, the Infinite, or for Plato, the sphere of the Eternal Forms, all of which are synonymous in respect to ineffability. Rather, the best once can do is dialectic, the method of using language against itself in order to transcend it. But not just any dialectic—certainly not Plato's—will do for modern occultists. Rather, the secrets that each occult or New Age group reveals (at $200 a workshop, of course) concern their privileged vocabularies, their better allegories, for that which cannot be expressed in human representation. In short, the uniqueness of this or that occult or occultic group can be located in its particular version of "invention," of what I call an "occult poetics."

2
Toward an Occult Poetics

> Yogibogeybox in Dawson chambers. *Isis Unveiled.* Their Pali book we tried to pawn. Crosslegged under an ubrel umbershoot he thrones an Aztec logos, functioning on astral levels, their oversoul, mahamahatma. The faithful hermetists await the light, ripe for chelaship, ringabout him. . . . Lotus ladies tend them i'the eyes, their pineal glands aglow. Filled with his god, he thrones, Buddh under plantain. Gulfer of souls, engulfer. Hesouls, shesouls, shoals of souls. Engulfed with wailing creecries, whirled, whirling, they bewail.
>
> —James Joyce[1]

> Every night before retiring, relax on the bed and watch the going to sleep process. . . . As the body relaxes and the mind settles down, and the change of viewpoint takes place which we call sleep, maintain the attitude of awareness for the upper levels. . . . Then you will come into the state of beingness which is characterized by the clarity of mental vision. . . . [W]hile the body is resting you awaken in the Atma Sarup (soul body) which is when we find ourselves in eternity, the overcoming of death. This is the freedom which is spoken so much about in ECKANKAR.
>
> —Paul Twitchell[2]

In the ninth chapter of Joyce's *Ulysses,* Stephen Dedalus, a witty young aesthete and aspiring poet seeking atonement (and eventually finding it in his intellectual father, Leopold Bloom), enters a room at the National Library and encounters a number of boisterous scholars. The scene is based on the mythic Ulysses' navigation of a tumultuous sea amid the Scylla, a nasty, multiheaded creature, and the Charybdis, a treacherous whirlpool. The dangers for Stephen, however, are the barbed remarks of the scholars, presently engaged in a discussion of Goethe's novel *Wilhelm Meister.* In other words, the danger of this particular navigation is not physical but rhetorical.[3]

Determined to outwit them, Stephen attacks the arguments, observations, and platitudes of the talkative scholars with sharp remarks, often at their personal expense. The mightiest Scylla is "A. E.," or George Russell, an avowed Neoplatonist and romantic who believes that art reveals a hidden, spiritual world behind the world of appearances.[4] On the basis of textual clues, it seems that Russell has embraced an occult cosmology known as Theosophy, a "New Age" system of beliefs revealed by a Russian spiritualist and psychic, H. P. Blavatsky, in the late nineteenth century. Seeing Russell in the library, Stephen is reminded of the difficult, esoteric language of Theosophy. "Yogobogeybox," thinks Stephen in mockery of the Theosophist's vocabulary. "*Isis Unveiled.* Their Pali book we tried to pawn," he continues thinking, signaling his distaste for Blavatsky's famous New Age book, which, incidentally, was popular among the learned elite during Joyce's lifetime. "Aztec logos, functioning on astral levels, their oversoul, the mahamahatma," muses Stephen, likening Theosophical language to a "whirled" and "whirling" Charybdis, drowning true believers in "*quintessential triviality.*" As if suffering from the weight of Stephen's psychic disapproval, Russell retreats, "afraid [that he is] due at the *Homestead.*"[5]

In the fall of 1998 I attended the ECKANKAR "World Wide Seminar" at the Minneapolis Convention Center in Minnesota. ECKANKAR, a religion based on "Soul Travel" and the "Ancient Science of Prophecy" known as the *Eck-Vidya,* was founded by Kentuckian Paul Twitchell in 1965.[6] When I walked into the convention hall I was overwhelmed by number of people there. The size of this contemporary religious movement surprised me because it is premised on what other occultists or "metaphysicians" would term astral projection—the notion that one's conscious soul or ego could leave the body and travel to different geographic regions as well as multiple dimensions or "planes of reality." Given the rise and fall of the transcendental meditation movement in the late 1960s and early 1970s, I had assumed astral projection was unfashionable. I was wrong. There exists a vast, little-seen, and little-known subcultural world of occult and New Age groups who claim to travel mentally, projecting their astral bodies through the imagination and into the many worlds beyond the here and now.

Over the course of three days, in numerous workshops and seminars, the ECKers (as they prefer to call themselves) discussed dreams and soul travel, past-life regression and hypnosis, reincarnation and karma, meditation, and other metaphysical fare. The highlight of the conference was the keynote address, which was delivered by the sole Living Spiritual Master, or Mahanta, appointed by the (presumably superhuman) ECK Masters. In one large convention hall almost thirty-five hundred people from around the world convened to hear Sri Harold Klemp, a mild-mannered, middle-aged man from Wisconsin with a charming smile, wide-framed spectacles, and a suit that seemed just a tad too large for his small frame. He spoke in a monotonous, hypnotic tone, and despite a dry sense of humor and a general lack of dynamism, the audience was transfixed.

What was particularly interesting to me about Klemp's talk was not so much his CEO-style presentation as it was his conspicuous use of specialized terms. Throughout the evening one heard of "karma," the spiritual and material "planes of existence" ("soul," "etheric," "mental," "causal," and "astral"), the "Golden Heart," the "ECK-VIDYA," the "SHARIYAT," and most important, "HU" (pronounced "hue"), the divine name of the "SUGMAD" (God). As with the more familiar "OM," at one point during the keynote address everyone in the audience—excepting myself and my partner at the time—chanted "HU" simultaneously. The effect was jarring, unsettling, and strangely pleasing; the large, domed convention hall rumbled with a continuous, harmonic drone that undoubtedly goose-pimpled many participants. It certainly goose-pimpled me.

I did not think of these strange terms as composing a *quintessential triviality,* as Stephen Dedalus puts it; the sheer number of chanting ECKers was refutation enough of Stephen's thesis.[7] Rather, I think that the specialized vocabulary of ECKers, as much as the "yogibogeyboxes" and "mahamahatmas" of the imagined Theosophy of *Ulysses,* comprises a particularly meaningful poetics for the true believer. Esoteric language allows the occultist to express or perhaps do things that ordinary language does not seem to permit. For the occultist, esoteric language reaches, with hope and promise, toward the ineffable.

I suggested in chapter 1 that the generic features of modern occult texts included the compositional forms of neologism and irony. In this chapter my investigation of occult rhetoric more fully explores the neologism, including not only its discriminatory function but also its revelatory function. Specifically, I focus on the function of what I term "esoteric language" in order to describe modern occult discourse as a creative linguistic practice or poetics (by using the term "poetics" I mean to evoke the dynamic, creative, and imaginative connotations of the term that are based on its rooting in the Greek *poiêtikos,* "inventive," and *poiein,* "to make").[8] Considered sympathetically, I argue that occult discourse can be understood as the end result of a dynamic, generative paradox or antinomy (a stark contradiction between two principles) that structures and in some sense determines the invention of difficult or strange language. The antinomy is composed of a seemingly contradictory stance among occultists and mystics that, on the one hand, regards spiritual truths as ineffable but, on the other, assumes that there is much to say about ineffability. In order to describe this antinomy and how it contributes to a poetics particular to the occultic in general, this chapter is divided into two main sections. First, I describe the relationship between modern occultism and the concept of the ineffable. Contending with the concept of ineffability in occult discourse gives one a better sense of how secrets are understood and discussed by occultists. Then, I show how occult notions of ineffability are, ironically, wed to what I term the Platonic or "fixed" view of language. With this background, I then move to the second main section of the chapter, where I describe how the uneasy fit between ineffability and the fixed view of language creates a productive paradox or contradiction that animates occult texts in ways that are relatively independent of the intention or will of a given author. I conclude the chapter by comparing the esoteric language of modern occultism to the theoretical jargon of academics.

Ineffability and the Occult

Central to the use or creation of strange vocabularies in occult texts is what is sometimes referred to as "the problem of mystical speech."[9] The most famous articulation of the problem comes from Lao Tzu's *Tao Te Ching:* "The name that can be named is not the enduring and unchanging name."[10] To name the Tao is to fail to know the Tao. Expanded to the central problematic of all mystical speech, this notion can be described in the following way: true wisdom and spiritual knowledge cannot be expressed in human language, for it resides beyond or outside human signification. This common belief is premised on the idea that language cannot characterize ultimate reality precisely because language is human, and humans are imperfect. Occultists, as much as the traditionally religious, respond to this problem in one of three ways. First, occultists deny ever having direct access to ultimate reality and often prescribe meditation and silence as a better tack. The silence strategy is often characterized as "mysticism" and is a common route to spiritual enlightenment in Eastern religious traditions. Insofar as silence can be characterized as the dialectical counterpart of rhetoric, however, I will not concern myself with this strategy except to acknowledge that it exists among occultists (as the absence of speech, silence leaves the critic little to analyze). The second and third strategies, however, are important and generate texts. The second strategy concerns the attempt to gain access to ultimate reality by transcending human language in some sort of imaginative dialectic. The strategy here is to use language against itself in order to ascend to higher states of awareness. I call this strategy "Platonic dialectic" for reasons that I will detail shortly. The third strategy concerns an occultist's claim to have discovered or been given a privileged, divine vocabulary for accessing, by means of ritual, chant, and so forth, spiritual realities. I characterize this third strategy as the articulation of a "pure language."

Platonism for the Masses

I opened this chapter with a passage from Joyce's *Ulysses* because it seemed to encapsulate the concerns of this chapter. It is not mere happenstance that Stephen Dedalus engages the Neoplatonist "A. E." as the multiheaded Scylla, for the body of occult discourse is, indeed, that of Plato—its heads but so many variations of a common poetics or logic of invention. Because occult strategies for contending with ineffability are rooted in the Platonic dialogues, a sketch of the Platonic views on language, ineffability, and ultimate reality provides a useful foundation for analyzing occult discourse.

In the *Republic,* Plato has Socrates instruct readers that natural language cannot disclose the Absolute, expressed to the enlightened soul as knowledge of the immutable, abstract, and eternal Forms. Plato's Socrates urges the rigorous study of mathematics, geometry, astronomy, and harmonics in order to condition the mind of the student of Truth to think beyond natural language and free him from the gross and illusory world of appearances to which natural language necessarily refers.[11] Only after one has mastered formal abstraction is he ready to practice dialectics, which for Plato is the use of dialogic speech as a means of mentally ascending toward ultimate reality and harmonizing with the eternal Forms, and eventually apprehending the ultimate Form of the Good.[12] Training the mind to think in terms of form as opposed to content (e.g., the meaning of particular words) enables the philosopher to "intuit" ultimate reality.

Key to Platonic dialectic is the power of speech, which Plato suggests is more immediate and "real" than writing. In the *Phaedrus,* Plato explains that dialectic is necessarily premised on the present-tense or "now" that is part of the spoken word. Once words are spoken, they are lost forever and replaced by new words. Spoken words survive only as "traces" in the memories of those in dialogue. The fleeting quality of speech is important to Plato for two reasons. First, the intangibility of speech better "mirrors" the materiality of ultimate reality (which is abstract, not concrete). Second, speech is a presencing phenomenon that features the quality of immediacy. Thus speech has a power of adaptation that writing does not. The immediacy of speech gives the individual the ability to use words that mean something particular to the individual he is conversing with, often in ways that can better address his inner being. Plato also argues that speech is better than writing because it can attend to the contingencies of one's speaking situation (by clarifying misunderstandings between participants of a dialogue, and so on) and thus can more directly address the "soul of the hearer."[13] Because of its presence or proximity to the moment of utterance, active speech is able to communicate ideas immediately, and further, it promises a window for transcending the horizon of utterance by inspiring a nonlinguistic intuition between participants. Speech is preferred to writing because the latter undermines the possibility of interpersonal inspiration or intuition. For Plato, speech holds out the promise of silence, the moment when Truth is intuited in its translinguistic immanence and glory.

Although the primary medium of occultism is the book, Plato's views on human language and the necessity of dialectic appear frequently in occult texts: many occult texts assume the ability of specialized language to "presence" elements of ultimate reality better than ordinary language. For example, writing about the early ECKANKAR teachings of Paul Twitchell, the current Mahanta, Harold Klemp, suggests that Twitchell struggled with the "petty, awkward words of the human language." Twitchell "did what he could to find the proper words and metaphors that would strike an image in the reader's mind. Sometimes he used a world that wasn't quite right; at other times he would leave an extra word or two that appeared to cause a contradiction. . . . [I]t's foolishness to think that the words come out golden the first time; they don't. The human language, at best, is only a poor reflection of the truth that comes from a higher level. What is known as truth on each plane is but a poor reflection of the truth on the next, higher plane. This is life."[14] Like Plato's Forms, the spiritual truths of ECKANKAR teachings expose the limitations of human language. Klemp stresses, however, that it "is important for [ECKers] to use the ECK language among ourselves. Our terminology—words such as SUGMAD, ECK, ECKANKAR, *Arahata*, and *Shariyat-Ki-Sugmad*—has a special meaning for us; it is one of our bonds."[15] The ECKANKAR vocabulary, stresses Klemp, is a better approximation of the divine and helps to create a sense of community and belonging. "Our terminology" thus signifies the ability of the ECKANKAR vocabulary to address the soul of the reader or hearer better than ordinary language, as well as the linguistic equivalent of a secret handshake.

In a similar, predictable manner, the spiritual truths revealed in *The Urantia Book*, a 2,097-page cosmology presumably revealed by superhuman "Counselors," are described as being impossible to capture in English:

> It is exceedingly difficult to present enlarged concepts and advanced truth, in our endeavor to expand cosmic consciousness and enhance spiritual perception, when we are restricted to the use of a circumscribed language of the realm [Urantia, or earth]. But our mandate admonishes us to make every effort to convey our meanings by using the word symbols of the English tongue. We have been instructed to introduce new terms only when the concept to be portrayed finds no terminology in English which can be employed to convey such a new concept partially or even with more or less distortion of meaning.[16]

An example of one of the hundreds of these "new terms" is "Solitarington," which refers, confusingly, to " 'the bosom of the Father and the Spirit' and . . . the rendezvous of a magnificent host of unrevealed beings of origin in the conjoint acts of the Universal Father and the Infinite Spirit, beings who partake of the traits of the Father in addition to their Spirit inheritance."[17] In the gradual comprehension of a number of neologisms and new concepts, presumably the Urantian (or "Reader," as believers refer to themselves) is better able to intuit the Truth.[18]

Finally, one of the best examples of the Platonism of occult texts is G. I. Gurdjieff's *Beelzebub's Tales to His Grandson*. In this 1,238-page "allegory," Gurdjieff deploys his occult cosmology in a strange and frequently incomprehensible story of extraterrestrial beings witnessing the folly of humanity from on high. A humorous, exemplary passage comes from the chapter titled "The Law of Heptaparaparshinokh":

> In order that you may approximately represent to yourself and understand just how such exceptions may occur among [three-headed beings of our great Megalocosmos], you must first of all know that, in spite of the fact that from the time when all the consequences of the properties of the organ Kundabuffer began to be crystallized in them and it became proper to them to have automatic-Reason during their responsible existence, yet, nevertheless, always and up to the present time, at the arising and the beginning of the formation of each one of them, there is always in their presence the germs of all possibilities for the crystallization, during their completing formation into responsible

> beings, of corresponding being-data, which later during responsible existence could serve for the engendering and function of objective-Reason, which should be the common presences of three-brained beings of all natures and of all external forms, and which, in itself, is nothing else but, so to say, the "representative-of-the-Very-Essence-of-Divinity."[19]

Followers claim that Gurdjieff's neologisms and long, tortuous sentences in *Beelzebub's Tales to His Grandson* are deliberately designed to "dismay automatic thinking" and expand consciousness to higher levels of reality.[20] Unlike the vocabulary of ECKANKAR, which is deployed as a better, pragmatic approximation of Truth, or the neologisms of *The Urantia Book,* which are advanced as being the closest to the divine or pure language of God, Gurdjieff holds out the language of his system as pure fiction. Just as Plato frequently resorted to allegories to give the reader or hearer a catalyst for apprehending something translinguistic, so too Gurdjieff clothes his teachings in deliberate obfuscations and misdirections.

Despite their unique differences, all three occult vocabularies I have touched on here are premised on the idea that spiritual truths are somehow ineffable and that one must cultivate a type of thinking, memory, or cognition that is beyond language in order to access the Truth. Each features a privileged vocabulary that is either built on a pure language or invented from scratch to better approximate the divine. Yet there is a discernible tension in these systems: if ultimate reality is ineffable, then how does one know if one's vocabulary or language is, in fact, a better approximation? Unlike a traditional priest, who would likely invoke the necessity of faith, the occultist would typically answer with the confirmation of occult experience: if a given esoteric vocabulary did, in fact, provide one with glimpses of ultimate reality, if the language seems to work, then it must be true. The problem with this answer, however, is that it is premised on a paradox.

The Bases of Paradox: Presence and the Fixed View of Language

The Platonic views of the function of speech, language, and dialectic are paradoxical because they are based on a fixed understanding of language which maintains that signification presences the signified. In more basic terms, the paradox concerns saying one thing and doing another, aptly illustrated in the dialogues of Plato. While Plato condemns writing as evil, the dialogues are, in fact, written. While Plato describes the Forms as ineffable, dialectical language enables their apprehension. Or in other terms, as William James observed of all mystical and occult belief systems, true believers necessarily believe that an experience of the Truth cannot be expressed in human language.[21] Ironically, testimony about the ineffability of ultimate reality and spiritual truths is expressed with human language. Is this contradiction between belief and action a problem?

One answer to this question is the resounding and complex "yes" located in the linguistic philosophy of Jacques Derrida. Derrida argues that the difficulty Plato highlights in the *Phaedrus* concerns his ironic preference for "speech" over that of "writing," which Plato believes is more immediate and closer to Truth. In his famous "deconstruction" of the conclusion of the *Phaedrus,* Derrida asserts the primacy of writing over speech and uses this experimental inversion to illustrate how Plato's condemnations of writing presuppose a logic common to writing *and* speech: the "play" of absence. Although Derrida's argument is complex, a brief sketch is helpful for highlighting the bases of the paradox or "problem" of mystical and occult discourse.

Derrida argues that Plato's privileging of speech over writing is premised on an erroneous commitment to what he calls the "the metaphysics of presence," a concept that speaks to the central ontological commitment of occult discourse. The metaphysics of presence simply refers to the assumption that something external to language (a presence) guarantees the correctness or correspondence of language to a reality. For Derrida, the metaphysics of presence is a common mistake that everyone makes, but it is a mistake nonetheless and one that we ought to avoid if possible. In reference to Plato's celebration of the immediacy of speech, Derrida argues that speech, like writing, is a representation of something else, and hence is a "sign function" or representational scheme of sounds and words that is premised on a necessary absence of that which is represented, not a presence. Derrida says that representation or signification is based on both a distance from a signified and a difference among terms. He expresses the simultaneity of this kind of distance and difference with the term *différence,* which he describes as "neographism."[22] Notwithstanding Derrida's own brand of neologistic occultism, the term *différence* is useful because its terminological strangeness underscores the idea that meaning is fundamentally referential and intersubjective—that one can only mean, and purportedly understand, in the interior of a language and in the absence of a signified.[23] Thus the notion of absence is related to the concept of *différence* in two important ways. First, words refer to objects that are not present. Second, words can only mean in relation to other words that are, by virtue of the positivity of utterance, unspoken. The signification of "cat" on this page, for example, is distant from an actual cat in a patently material way and is meaningful only to the extent that I am aware of the absent differences implied by the term, such as "not dog," "not parrot," "not goldfish," "not ear of corn," and so on (e.g., the paradigmatic axis). In rhetorical studies a similar notion has been expressed as the "dialectic of rhetoric and silence": "In speaking we remain silent," observes Robert L. Scott, "and in remaining silent, we speak."[24] Silence speaks a positivity in the absence of language as much as speaking must inevitably refer to the unspoken or silent. Hence the possibility of pure presence or immediacy which Plato argues that speech promises—a metaphysics of presence—is a deceptive fantasy; not even silence is "pure" of distance or difference.[25]

With the neographism of *différence,* then, Derrida deconstructs Plato's claims that speech discloses a "presence" or is the proper avenue to Truth by analyzing the practice of writing. Derrida suggests that despite the philosopher's striving toward the apprehension of the materiality of the Forms (which exist in an ideational, non-physical or anti-physical realm), the Forms cannot be meaningfully ineffable because of the absence-logic of language itself: nothing means for human beings outside language, written *or* spoken. There is no outside "guarantee" for language that language "presences" in writing or speech. This implies that the ineffable as a discursive locality can be a "silent" space only in the sense of a negative signification or absence. As H. P. Blavatsky has expressed the idea, there is always a linguistic positivity in any negative expression: it is the voice of *Nada,* "the Voice of Silence," the positivity (voice) of no-thing (silence).[26] Hence Plato is shown to be saying one thing and doing another in a much deeper sense than it initially seems: the contradiction of word and deed is not merely that of writing about the ineffable but is born of an erroneous belief in the presencing power of speech. In other words, Derrida's argument against the metaphysics of presence suggests that the ineffability of the spiritual truths with which occultists are concerned is actually a result of the ineffability that inheres in language: language as such necessarily fails to grasp or capture presences; it fails to disclose *différence* itself.[27] This is tantamount to saying that the paradox of occult discourse speaks the occultist.

It is important to note that Plato's belief that speech evokes the positive presence of the signified is based on the idea that language is "fixed." Indeed, the metaphysics of presence goes hand in hand with a fixed understanding of language. Such an understanding of language holds that meaning is anchored and guaranteed by something external to it (viz., a presence); in Plato this is the Forms, and dialectic helps one to "re-member" the truths once directly apprehended by the soul before it became enfleshed and fell to earth.[28] In Plato's dialogues, as well as traditional religious texts, language is thus an imperfect copy of something translinguistic. For the Christian this external guarantee is God, hence the Gospel of John begins, "In the beginning was the Word, and the Word was with God, and the Word was God."[29] For the occultist the guarantee can be any number of supernatural entities, such as the "astral light" of Eliphas Lévi or the "Divine Principle" of H. P. Blavatsky. The fixed understanding of language thus presumes a meaningful mind-independent reality that language, however inaccurately, represents, a presumption that Derrida has famously dubbed "logocentrism."[30]

In the humanities today the fluid view of language has eclipsed the fixed view, and many scholars would concede that language is contingent and never corresponds to the material world in a direct or transparent way (a presence). After the publication of Wittgenstein's groundbreaking *Philosophical Investigations* (and to a lesser extent, a renewed interest in Nietzsche's theory of language), many philosophers, rhetoricians, and other scholars of linguistic practices have come to understand language in decidedly anti-Platonic terms. Instead of corresponding to some mind-independent reality or divine presence, language is a self-contained, differential system that establishes a horizon for what can be expressed and experienced as meaningful. As social beings, humans are players in a particular "language game" or vocabulary that enables us to do or think some things and prevents us from doing or thinking others (particularly those things that cannot be marked in language).[31] As the pragmatic philosopher Richard Rorty explains, language cannot be a "third thing intervening between self and reality" because language is constitutive of self and reality. Rorty suggests, like Wittgenstein, that language is a tool or a collection of "marks and noises" that enables us to cope with the world. Although there is, undoubtedly, a material world that exists independent of language, Rorty argues that this world is meaningless to humans absent the coping technology of language or representation.

For Rorty, language is also prophetic in the sense that new metaphors can herald new ways of thinking. Vocabularies are a means "for doing [or thinking] something which could not have been envisioned prior to the development of a particular set of descriptions, those which it itself helps to provide."[32] The fluidity of language thus refers to the possibility of expanding the horizons of expressibility through the creation of new metaphors and the destruction of old, "dead" ones. With this perspective, Rorty suggests that "revolutionary achievements in the arts, in the sciences, and in moral and political thought typically occur when somebody realizes that two or more of our vocabularies are interfering with each other, and proceeds to invent a new vocabulary to replace both. [Such new vocabularies] are not discoveries of a reality behind the appearances. . . . To come up with [a new] vocabulary is more like discarding the lever and the chock because one has envisaged the pulley."[33] This characteristically contingent understanding of language denies the occultist (or the supernaturalist of any stripe, for that matter) any ultimate, divine reality that can be signified in language. Instead, the fluid view regards the occultist from an exterior vantage and describes him or her as a poet attempting to expand the limits of expressibility through the creation of new vocabularies. Whether the occultist-poet is conscious of his or her literary expansions is inconsequential.

These strivings to expand vocabulary and the range of expression are premised on feelings that we all have about the inadequacy of language, the ineffability of human experience signified by Derrida's concept of *différence*. As Barry Barnes has eloquently expressed the problem, for "all the complexity and richness of language, experience is immeasurably more complex, and richer in information."[34] Or in other terms, our attempts to expand vocabularies are born of an experience of absence (as opposed to the ineffability of presence presumed by the religious). Despite the limits of language, there remain aspects of experience that elude our attempts at meaning-making. The poet is an individual who can work within a language game to extend and make previously inexpressible and meaningless elements of human experience expressible and meaningful.

The refutation of old vocabularies and the creation of new ones is made possible by experiences that are not immediately expressible in a given vocabulary. The possibility of creating language for new meanings necessarily involves the occultist-poet in a political process insofar as his or her vocabulary is to replace another. That there is something political at stake in a poetics will be familiar to readers of critical theory and Continental philosophy. Because works like Heidegger's *Being and Time* and Horkheimer and Adorno's *Dialectic of Enlightenment* are deliberately difficult, readers are forced to work exceedingly hard to understand them. Adorno and others argue that intense intellectual labor is needed because it helps to denaturalize a comfortable linguistic horizon and in turn point to new ways of thinking about ourselves and the world that make change possible.[35] Commenting on her own, dense writing, for example, Judith Butler argues that "some newness of the world [is] opened up through messing with grammar" and that her playful neologisms and difficult sentence structures help to locate spaces in which people can resist oppressive cultural logics, such as heterosexual gender norms (or "heteronormativity"): "Taking for granted one's own linguistic horizon as the ultimate linguistic horizon leads to an enormous parochialism and keeps us from being open to radical difference and from undergoing the discomfort and the anxiety of realizing that the scheme of intelligibility on which we rely fundamentally is not adequate, is not common [or universal to all humans], and closes us off from the possibility of understanding others and ourselves in a more fundamentally capacious way."[36] Hence the idea that language is fluid refers both to the notion that it is not guaranteed or fixed by something external and to the notion that new forms of expression and meaning are possible despite the obvious limitations of language at any given moment in time.

The Specificity of Occult Poetics: The Rhetorical Antinomy

Read internally and sympathetically, I have suggested that occultists—as well as the traditional religious supernaturalist—understand their creation or use of strange, esoteric vocabularies as a Platonic quest to apprehend translinguistic truths. Read externally, however, I have suggested that esoteric language presumes a number of things. First, esoteric language is based on the assumption that its terms signify something external to human language, a metaphysics of presence. This assumption of presence implies, in turn, the second presumption of esoteric vocabularies, that language in general is "fixed." Finally, I have suggested that esoteric language represents an occult poetics striving toward an expansion of possible meanings within a given language game, precisely because a translinguistic ineffability of presence is impossible. It is to the specificity of this poetics that I now turn.

Placed in front of the historical backdrop of the encroachment of scientific discourse in the modern era, many brands of occultism—from ECKANKAR to Gurdjieff—can be understood as confronting the "rational" and scientistic vocabulary of modernity, a vocabulary that Kenneth Burke warned reduced the ambiguity and fullness of human experience, the "drama" and "action" of life, to mere "motion."[37] Yet as a particular brand of poetics, occult discourse must have a unique "logic" to it that explains its strivings to expand or transcend vocabularies in ways that are different from traditional religious discourse contending with scientism. An occult poetics must be, as Aristotle suggests of the making of tragedy and epic, a "productive science" in the sense that occultism is premised on a set of rules or conditions (a logic) that help to generate a rhetoric distinct from others.[38] An occult poetics qua poetics must contain a logic of rhetorical invention particular or specific to itself.

Given the foregoing discussion of the limits of language, it would seem that the esoteric language of occult discourse functions in ways that are similar to that of traditional, supernaturalist religious rhetoric and discipline or trade-specific jargon. What distinguishes occult discourse from the traditionally religious is the role of secrecy and the continuous impulse to create new vocabularies for some translinguistic reality. Unlike the Word of God, which is as final as it is eternal, any given occult text announces itself as a better approximation of ultimate reality, novelty thus becoming a central characteristic. The novelty of occult vocabularies, however, is always expressed in terms of revelation and is not necessarily neologistic; hence a "new way" can be introduced that heavily employs the ambiguities of older or "ancient" terms, like "karma."[39] Moreover, occult poetics can also be distinguished from traditional religious forms of invention because of the stability of the rhetorical repertoire of the latter: while God is in fact ineffable, there is a traditional way to go about representing God's truth in language that has gone relatively unchanged for centuries: homiletics.

Although occult discourse is similar to the jargon of academic discourse in terms of its mobility or openness to new vocabularies, it differs significantly in terms of its stake in a meaningful, translinguistic reality. The Platonic assumption behind all occult discourse—that there is something "out there" beyond language that esoteric terms attempt to signify—denies the fluidity of language that academics like Butler draw upon to "open up" spaces of cultural resistance. For this reason, I suggest that the central logic of occult poetics is based on what one could term a "rhetorical antinomy," which I define as the illusion of a fundamental, ontological or metaphysical paradox.

When one speaks of a traditional antinomy, the profoundly influential work of Immanuel Kant on various "conflicts of assertions" is often cued. The "Third Antinomy of Freedom and Natural Law," for example, is the conflict between the assertion that there is a type of "causality" called freedom and the assertion that the world operates deterministically in accord with certain laws of nature that exclude freedom as a cause.[40] In philosophy, W. V. Quine has updated Kant's concept of the antinomy by asserting that it is a paradox of reasoning that requires a repudiation of the concepts that allowed one to express the paradox in the first place.[41] Quine's understanding of the concept of antinomy helps to explain why the qualification of "rhetorical" is apt, because antimonies are actually problems with our vocabularies or language, not with the "real world." The traditional "antinomy" of Kant is about real-world conditions "out there"—what I am calling ontological or metaphysical conditions. To understand an antinomy as "rhetorical" is to recognize the contingency of truth and the social construction of reality, and hence to read contradictions about the "nature" of reality as epistemological or linguistic problems, not ontological or metaphysical ones. In other words, the rhetorical antinomy represents a productive mistake.

In light of the examples of occult texts offered above, I submit that occult discourse is the result of a rhetorical antinomy between a belief (A) and an action (B). The belief is this: (A) spiritual knowledge is translinguistic, or "ineffable." The action is this: (B) one can write and speak about spiritual knowledge. Again, here is the ghost of Plato's famous ironic reversals at the end of the *Phaedrus:* Although writing is condemned at the end of the dialogue as being incapable of communicating spiritual truths (A), it is nevertheless the technology with which Plato attempts to impart spiritual truths (B).[42] The rhetorical antinomy is thus aptly summarized by the following statement: "The Truth is ineffable, but let me tell you about it anyway." This basic contradiction is at the heart of the so-called problem of mystic speech.

What is unique about occult and mystical discourse, however, is that the rhetorical antinomy is believed to be an ontological problem—a problem with something "out there"—and that belief, in turn, generates the discourse (again, the antinomy is different from traditional, religious forms of invention because God's truth *is* describable, and the model of describability is God's authentic Word). A rhetorical worldview, of course, stresses the fluid view of language mentioned previously—a sophistic understanding of meaning that Robert L. Scott termed "epistemic" in the late 1960s.[43] Regardless of one's stance on "the real," the rhetorical view implies that nothing *means* outside human modes of representation and that "truth" is merely the product of sentences. The occultist, like Plato, believes in a transcendent truth that cannot be completely understood in human language; hence the problem of mystic or occult speech is erroneously viewed as an ontological problem. In actuality, the moment an occultist ceases to be silent about the matter of spiritual truth, the moment of the audible voice or the contact of pen to paper, calls forth what Paul de Man would term the "rhetoricity" of the antinomy: the notion of ineffability itself necessitates a rhetoric to express the negativity of ineffability. In other words, the fundamental premise, that spiritual truth is ineffable (A), requires the seemingly contradictory act of speaking or writing (B). What we have in occult poetics, then, is basically a generative contradiction. The rhetorical antinomy is invention by means of an illusory contradiction.

Concluding Remarks: The Magic of Esoteric Language

In this chapter I have further developed a generic feature of occult discourse, the compositional form of neologism as it is expressed in esoteric language. I first suggested that occult discourse is premised on a Platonic commitment to a translinguistic, spiritual realm as well as the idea that language is at best an imperfect copy of the truths of this realm. I then moved to characterize these commitments as constituting a "metaphysics of presence," to use Derrida's phrase, which in turn is based on the "fixed" view of language. I argued that the fixed view was a mistake and that this mistake is responsible for a resulting rhetorical antinomy, or a kind of generative mode of invention in which the motivation for the location or creation of esoteric vocabularies is based on the necessary contradictions that result from a belief in the metaphysics of presence. Although the rationale behind the creation of given occult vocabularies will differ from one occult group to the next, all of them can be described, in general, as a consequence of a paradox: "The Truth is ineffable, but let me tell you about it anyway."

From an internal or sympathetic perspective, I mentioned that occultists, as well as the religious, typically employ one of two kinds of strategies: the prescription of silence (the way of the mystic) or the discovery or creation of a vocabulary or mode of expression that gets closer to the ineffable than does ordinary language. In this chapter I drew on examples that were somewhat pragmatic in tone: the Counselors of *The Urantia Book,* Sri Harold Klemp, and G. I. Gurdjieff seemed to admit that human language could never capture, in an absolute or satisfactory way, supernatural truths. There remains another substrategy as well, which consists of the advancement of a language that is in and of itself the language of the divine. For example, Islamic Sufis believe that Arabic is the language of God, as do Jewish mystics with Hebrew. In the next chapter I will suggest that in addition to making a number of pragmatic arguments for strange terms, H. P. Blavatsky offers up Sanskrit as a pure language as well—a privileged, iconic language that has direct access to spiritual presence if properly understood.

Before I bring this chapter to a close, however, I think it is important to reconsider the descriptions of the differences between traditional religious (supernaturalist), occult, and (my personal, indulgent favorite) academic discourse, for whatever their historical, tropological, and logical differences, the effects of esoteric language might be said to remain constant among all three. As I noted, religious discourse differs from the occult because of its attempts to invite exoteric redemption, a movement against secrecy marked most notably in Christian history, for example, by the Protestant Reformation: God keeps no secrets. Religious discourse also differs from the occult in terms of its repertoire of tropes: the Word of God comprises a very old vocabulary, and there is nothing "new" or exotic in the great holy books of Judaism, Islam, and Christianity. Religious discourse, however, can be characterized as occultic when there are pockets of secrecy (the Vatican, Jewish Kabbalah, Sufi orders, and so on) or when a new language is deployed to establish the authority of one or more individuals (which is usually described in terms of the creation of a sect or, in normative terminology, a "cult").

Academic terminology (most especially theoretical vocabulary) is also deployed in a manner that is said to invite esoteric understanding, often for the purposes of demystifying human behavior or social reality. Yet despite the rampant secularism and agnostic party line of the humanities, the view that the world in itself is "ineffable" and that it makes sense to us only in representation is one that we share, with a little modification, with the supernaturalists: the ineffability of "God" or the "Astral" realm is merely replaced with the ineffability of human experience, *différence,* or Lacan's "Real." The key difference orbits the notion that one should understand language as "fluid" and rhetoric as an epistemic, reality-creating phenomenon. Although theorists in the humanities have long dismissed the criterion of correspondence (and therefore the "metaphysics of presence"), theory should be understood as a proposed alternate vocabulary for describing human reality. For example, Rorty has argued that the difficult vocabularies of Heidegger and Derrida represent a poetic or "literary" attempt to "suggest new questions in new terms."[44] Insofar as everything meaningful is within the domain or map of human representation, new vocabularies help to expand meanings and, as Rorty suggests, possibilities for change. The parallels between academic jargon and esoteric language cannot be ignored, however, because as much as the superhuman Counselors of *The Urantia Book,* Sri Harold Klemp, and G. I. Gurdjieff are revered authorities of esoteric knowledge, so too are Heidegger, Derrida, and Butler authorities in an esoteric language game in which many are discouraged, on the basis of its mystifying aura, from participating directly without the long and sometimes sadistic rites of GEI (i.e., Graduate Education Initiation). In short, current academic theory, particularly that which trucks in neologism and allegory, is the contemporary equivalent to the modern occult text, the postmodern exemplar of the occultic par excellence.

In a widely read essay by Martha Nussbaum in the *New Republic,* for example, Judith Butler's writing is castigated as "ponderous and obscure." Butler's allusions to other thinkers are "never described in enough detail to include the uninitiated," who would simply be "baffled by the thick soup of Butler's prose." In fact, Nussbaum says that "mystification and hierarchy are the tools of [Butler's] practice" and that ultimately Butler has fallen prey to the view of the "philosopher as a star who fascinates . . . frequently by obscurity." Nussbaum argues that Butler's use of enigmatic prose is a deliberate strategy designed to create dependency among her readers by becoming the "originating authority" of an esoteric vocabulary.[45] Although I am sympathetic to Butler's project and agree with the reasons for her call for challenging prose, there is no mistaking the recognition of "truth" (in the weak sense) in Nussbaum's arguments: Butler, as much as Foucault, Deleuze, and even Burke, is a modern-day Gurdjieff.

One problem with Nussbaum's account, of course, is that she fails to recognize that mystery and mystification are inevitable consequences of the rhetorical invention spawned by the ubiquitous confrontation with ineffability, consequences that are aptly and humorously caricatured in Kenneth Burke's modern version of the Tower of Babel as the cacophonous and mundane "human barnyard," with each of its critters chattering and goading each other into hierarchies. Some of us critters are even mysteriously beaming into UFOs.[46]

It is not surprising that Burke, the most priestly and patently mystical of the philosophers of rhetoric, was led to the conclusion that theological discourse was the paradigm of the machinations of rhetorical invention and the "dialectic" of suasive action.[47] The dialectical view, built on the inevitable production of alterity and the necessarily differential structure of language, entails predictable consequences. That language is fluid and contingent necessarily poses the threat and joy of worshipfulness insofar as our theoretical vocabularies are revelations and insofar as they create sites of identification for the creation of an inside and outside group. As the rhetorician Richard Weaver would say, all talk about talk, all theory, is necessarily sermonic.[48] Or as I would have it, all theory is occultic.

Interlude

Mysteries of the Unknown

One of my earliest memories of the "occult" concerns a television commercial for a series of coffee-table books by Time-Life titled "Mysteries of the Unknown." The series featured nine heavily illustrated volumes ranging from *Cosmic Connections* and *Mysterious Creatures* to *Psychic Voyages* and *Visions and Prophecies*. I recall wanting to order the books badly. My parents were not cooperative (perhaps writing a book on the occult is a subtle form of payback?).

I can remember fearful sermons about the evil of Ouija boards and role-playing games in church when I was about eight or nine.[1] I also remember that my father and I used to stay up quite late to watch old horror movies on Ted Turner's Superstation TBS, channel 17. In the fifth grade, Vincent Price was my favorite actor. Yet the most vivid occult images in my mind are from the Time-Life commercial, which aired continuously on UHF channels in the mid-1980s. Whether or not my imagistic memories are actually of this commercial I do not know with any certainty, as memory is reconstructive, choosy, and often unfaithful to past experiences. Yet I can still hear the commercial and visualize it in my mind's eye.

I wanted to reacquaint myself with this commercial because it is a good personal example of how the popular imaginary seems to work. I tried to track it down by writing and e-mailing various media outfits and individuals involved in its production. Although I was unable to locate a copy of the commercial that aired in the 1980s, I discovered that Time-Life had new commercials made in the mid-1990s that utilized the same script.[2] As I watched the newer version, stronger memories of the older one began to surface.

Both versions of the commercial are composed of two kinds of shots: dramatizations of mini-narratives, and close-up montages of the books and the pictures inside them. The new commercial, for example, begins with a series of images depicting a man in an airport. The deep, masculine voice intones:

> Chicago: A man is about to get on a routine flight. Suddenly he pauses. He doesn't know why, but he has got to walk away. An hour later, the plane goes down in flames. It's dismissed as chance.
>
> Britain: A woman has a sudden image of a black mountain that's moving with children trapped underneath it. Two hours later a Welsh schoolhouse is buried by an avalanche of coal slag. It's dismissed as coincidence.
>
> Northern Texas: An unidentified flying object is reported by at least a dozen people. Although there were no storms in the area, it's dismissed as lightning.

Each "mysterious" incident is dramatized with actors adept at making quizzical and terrified faces. After the initial dramatizations, the commercial then moves into a series of shots that feature the books' covers, which then fades into a series of "mysterious" images: a picture of the Sphinx of Egypt, a psychic reading tarot cards, a ritual setting replete with a skull and candles, and so on. The voice-over encourages viewers to "explore the most controversial phenomena of our time in 'Mysteries of the Unknown,' a series that goes deeper into the unexplained than ever before." Eventually the commercial concludes with a 1-800 number and bonus gift offers (a jigsaw puzzle of Stonehenge).

The commercial is interesting to me for a number of reasons, but the most significant reason is that watching it was fun. Seeing the commercial again (or rather, seeing its newer rendition) was like becoming reacquainted with an old friend. During this memorial exercise, however, I realized that the commercial was missing something that I remember distinctly. During one of the montage sequences in the original commercial, there was a close-up shot of the face of an old woman that is not in the new version. I remember that in the old version this face was framed by a scarf and that the woman's countenance was broad and jowly; she seemed to be frowning, but not in the sense of sadness or scorn. Rather, her frown seemed like the inverse of the *Mona Lisa*'s, a darker version of stoic mystery. I remember that the eyes were most noticeable, piercing an assumed distance between subject and object. It was almost as if the woman was defying becoming

Fig. 4. Helena Petrovna Blavatsky (1831–1891). The famous "Sphinx photograph." Courtesy of the Theosophical Society in America.

an object of the camera. The image of the face then faded into another depicting a number of dark, purple clouds with a streak of lightning, jagged and tearing to the bottom of the screen. In the transition from the face to the clouds, the lightning was initially seen as a faint, crooked line beginning in the middle of the old woman's forehead and ending at a hand that was used by the woman to prop up her head.

The disappearance of the old woman's face from the Time-Life commercial is telling. When I began work on this book, I soon discovered that the picture was of H. P. Blavatsky, the leader of the Theosophy movement, whose international fame led to numerous newspaper articles and encyclopedia entries by the turn of the nineteenth century (see fig. 4). The picture itself is described by contemporary Theosophists as the "Sphinx photograph." That this image has been excluded in favor of others can be said to parallel the decline of her influence—imagistic and otherwise—inside and outside occult circles. Although she was, in fact, a household name in the late 1800s, today she is only discussed by those familiar with the Western occult tradition. Regardless, her influence on occult discourse was monumental, and it is to a resurrection of her teachings and rhetoric that I now turn.

3
H. P. Blavatsky and the Magic of Esoteric Language

> *Hartford Daily Times:* Glancing at a pile of letters which the servant had just brought, we exclaimed, "What an immense correspondence must be yours, madame! And in so many different languages! Tell us! What language do you *think* in?"
>
> *H.P.B.:* "In a language of my own! which is neither Russian, French, nor any you know."[1]

Although "New Age" is a hotly contested term among occultists, it originated in occult literature (most especially that of Freemasonry in the United States) and in general referred to the time of the arrival of a new level of human consciousness, the so-called Age of Aquarius, in which people are harmoniously united as one. To this day, occultists continue to debate when, how, and if this "age" will occur, often couching their revelations in unique, esoteric vocabularies or secrets.

Whether one calls it "New Age" or "occultism" ("new" and "secret" are two sides of the same proverbial coin), as I suggested in the previous chapter, the study and revelation of secret knowledge attempts to communicate ineffable, cosmic truths in a manner that can be traced to the mystical discourse of the ancient Greeks. In the *Cratylus,* the *Phaedrus,* and the *Republic,* for example, Plato suggests that literal language is inadequate to express universal truths and that the best devices human beings have at their disposal are indirect allegory (*mythoi*) and dialectical speech.[2] The most popular proponents of occultism today, although less secretive about their secrets than medieval alchemists or nineteenth-century Freemasons, continue to deploy spiritual truths with strange and vague terminology in ways that echo Plato's prescription of indirection.

In one of his sixteen appearances on the *Oprah Winfrey Show* in 1999 and 2000, for example, the best-selling author and mystic Gary Zukav stressed the importance of intuiting the meaning of the difficult concept of "karma," which he said is often misunderstood to mean a penalty for sin. In his March 21, 2000, discussion with Winfrey and to a television audience of thousands, he explained that karma is simply "a natural law of balance." Zukav says that what karma means precisely, however, can only be intuited in its many earthly, and thus imperfect, "reflections," such as the "third law of motion."[3] Similarly, Sylvia Browne, coauthor of the *New York Times* best-seller *Life on the Other Side,* complains that "*karma* is a strange word. No matter how many times I go on TV, no matter how many times I talk about this issue, people are still convinced karma is something they're working through with another person. No—you're working through your *own* karma, which means your *own* experience."[4] The struggle over the signification of "karma," however, is an old one in the United States. It was popularized in what is arguably the first New Age tome, Helena Petrovna Blavatsky's massive, two-volume *Isis Unveiled,* first published in 1877. Indeed, because of her status as one of the first people to popularize Eastern occult lore in the West, much contemporary New Age and occult rhetoric can be said to have its roots in the best-selling work of this exotic Ukrainian émigré.[5]

In this chapter I examine the strange and sometimes incomprehensible vocabulary of the first popular New Age guru in the West and, in so doing, attempt to shed more light on the linguistic features of contemporary occult texts as well. This chapter is offered as a case study that builds on the ideas I introduced in the last chapter. In the last chapter I argued that occult discourse, because much of it presumes a metaphysics of presence and a fixed view of language, is motivated by the mistaken belief that language is capable of signifying external presences. The mistake results, I said, in a rhetorical antinomy that is responsible for the invention of occult texts: the assumption that spiritual truths are translinguistic paradoxically requires a language for expressing ineffability. In this chapter I show how these assumptions animate the rhetorical strategies located in the complex occult texts of H. P. Blavatsky. Further, I illustrate the social and epistemological functions of occult discourse.

I also, however, have a secondary, historiographical goal for this chapter. Because occult discourse has been relatively unexplored by rhetorical scholars, I also provide a brief history of the emergence of modern occultism in the United States through the exemplar of Theosophy, renewing the origin narrative that ended with popular occult writings of Lévi, Barrett, and Waite from chapter 1.[6] It is my hope that this historical narrative can help to provide a foundation for future studies of occult rhetoric. In the contextual section of the chapter, then, I suggest that Blavatsky's rhetoric emerged during a period in U.S. cultural history that was, in many ways, ready for it. In a country recovering from the Civil War and just learning about the threat that scientific discourse posed for religion, Blavatsky's synthesis of scientific concepts and mystical beliefs seemed to promise a middle way. A brief description of the historical context reveals that occultism became popular during social crises.

To these ends, I first contextualize Blavatsky's rhetoric in the backdrop of Darwinism and Spiritualism, two discourses that are and continue to remain crucial for understanding modern occultism as a reactive discourse. Second, I move to a discussion of Blavatsky's writings, focusing on those moments when she appears most conscious of the uses and limitations of language. An analysis of Blavatsky's language, I argue, discloses an attempt to preserve ambiguity in spite of the demands of a dominant language game that stresses logic, reason, and accuracy. Then, I suggest that the function of her often bewildering ambiguities was both social and epistemological in scope. Socially, esoteric language helped to establish Blavatsky's authority as well as create a community through a common argot. Epistemologically, however, esoteric language, because of its ambiguity and terminological strangeness, helped to confront the limits of linguistic representation and, in turn, create the possibility of an indubitable, cosmic, and ineffable Truth. I conclude with a brief articulation of occult poetics and contemporary New Age rhetoric, the most popular occultic discourse today.

The Emergence of Theosophy

In the popular imaginary, Blavatsky is known for her psychic displays and for cofounding the Theosophical Society in 1875. She claimed to have fled her Russian home at the age of eighteen because of an unhappy marriage to a man more than twenty years her senior. During her nomadic travels around the world she had little opportunity to absorb the regionally disparate codes of Victorian propriety, and by the time she settled in New York she had developed a voracious smoking habit and a penchant for cursing in three languages that often brought "angry and amazed stares" from the bourgeois circles she attempted to penetrate.[7] As a bold, outspoken woman with a fondness for colorful and exotic clothing, Blavatsky never wanted for attention. Indeed, her charismatic power and flamboyant style helped her to attract a number of people to one of the oldest "New Age" systems in Western culture, Theosophy.

Blavatsky's Theosophy is a spiritual movement that took its name from the Greek *theos,* "god," and *sophia,* "wisdom." The movement has a number of objectives: "to diffuse among men a knowledge of the laws inherent in the universe; to promulgate the knowledge of the

Fig. 5. Helena Petrovna Blavatsky (1831–1891). This image was probably rendered in 1876, around the time she was writing *Isis Unveiled.* Courtesy of the Theosophical Society in America.

essential unity of all that is, and to demonstrate that this unity is fundamental in nature; to form an active brotherhood among men; to study ancient and modern religion, science, and philosophy; [and] to investigate the powers innate in man."[8] In general, Theosophists claim a knowledge of ultimate reality more profound than that gained from empirical or scientific methods, and they believe that the key to this knowledge lies in "an esoteric tradition of which the doctrines of the various historical religions are held to be the only exoteric expression."[9]

Blavatsky cofounded the society with Henry Steel Olcott, a Union colonel who turned to newspaper reporting after the Civil War. The two met at a "spook shop" (Olcott's humorous term for a place where ghosts make regular appearances) during his investigation of a family's supernatural claims at their Vermont home. Olcott was enchanted by

Blavatsky's "scarlet Giribaldian shirt" and her large, light-blue eyes. Their meeting would eventually result in their renting apartments in the same New York building years later.[10]

Blavatsky's apartment, dubbed "The Lamasery," soon became the center of weekly discussions of the occult. Blavatsky claimed to have sat at the feet of "Mahatmas" during her world travels before coming to the United States and, hence, was privy to a secret knowledge of ancient teachings. Word of her mediumistic performances (although she denied being a "medium" herself) and strange powers began to attract a number of the intellectual and artistic elite to the New York apartment (it is rumored that these included such distinguished guests as poet Ella Wheeler Wilcox and inventor Thomas Edison; however, there is little evidence that either visited Blavatsky).[11] What began as a typical salon evolved, little by little, into a school for Blavatsky's teachings. Blavatsky convinced her audience that she was selected by a secret group of supernatural beings—the Secret Masters—to spread a message of universal brotherhood and peace to the West.

When Blavatsky began to channel the Secret Masters' teachings into a book, she (and her publisher) failed to anticipate its appeal to the general public: *Isis Unveiled,* a mammoth, two-volume book of more than 1,500 pages, sold out of its first 1877 printing of one thousand copies in a week and a half.[12] Despite its fame, the book is unwieldy in its use of scientific, anthropological, philosophical, and occult terminology. For these reasons *Isis Unveiled* was dismissed as "discarded rubbish" by the *New York Sun* and condemned as "a large dish of hash" by the *Springfield (Mass.) Republican.* Yet for the same reasons the *New York Herald* hailed the tome as "one of the most remarkable productions of the century."[13] The *New York World* praised it as "an extremely readable and exhaustive essay upon the paramount importance of re-establishing the Hermetic Philosophy." The *New York Evening Post* found *Isis Unveiled* a "mine of curious information," and the *New York Daily Graphic* said it was "a marvelous book both in matter and manner of treatment."[14] As a result of this and similar publicity in northeastern newspapers, the book brought fame to Blavatsky and the Theosophical Society. Exposés of Blavatsky and her books would continue to appear in U.S. newspapers and magazines until well after her death in 1891, although she left the country in 1878 for India.

Perhaps inspired by the popular success of *Isis Unveiled,* Blavatsky would go on to write thousands of pages of "secrets," the most significant of them appearing in two journals that she edited, *The Theosophist* and later *Lucifer,* and in books like *The Secret Doctrine* (1888),

The Voice of Silence (1889), and the *Key to Theosophy* (1889). None of these works was as popular as *Isis,* and their sum was not as widely read as the many "curiosity" pieces written *about* Blavatsky's life and teachings in newspapers and magazines.

Religious Tolerance and the Challenge of Darwin

The success of Blavatsky's *Isis Unveiled* can be explained in reference to a number of broader social transformations in the nineteenth century, the most notable being religious crisis and the growing public interest in the supernatural. Theosophy emerged in the United States after the Civil War in the middle of a larger social conflict between the discourse of science and the discourse of religion.[15] The uniqueness of the U.S. religious response to this conflict is frequently discussed in literature about Evangelicalism, Fundamentalism, Seventh-day Adventism, and the like, which arose in opposition to the encroachment of scientism, and in literature about movements such as Mary Baker Eddy's Christian Science, which strove toward "wedding the spiritual and immaterial dimension of Christianity with scientific empiricism."[16] Broadly conceived, this conflict can be traced to the squabbles between the scholastics and the natural philosophers in the seventeenth century. Descartes's famous compromise helped the parties sparring over the authority of knowledge strike a deal: the natural philosophers would study the natural scene, a passive, and hence safe, panoply of substance in motion; religious scholars would help to animate this scene with divine action and agency.[17]

By the late eighteenth and early nineteenth centuries, the mystical gnosis of orthodox Jewish and Christian doctrine was challenged by the "development hypothesis." At that time the tiny thread holding the natural world of motion and the divine world of action together was the argument from design, eloquently expressed by natural theologians such as William Paley: the world is so intricate in design and movement, so complex in its order, that there must be a God to establish and maintain it.[18] By century's end, however, the public concessions of theologians inside and outside the academy had so significantly weakened their authority that Darwin's *Origin of Species* was unquestionably devastating for popular perceptions of American Protestantism. First, Darwin's popularization of the development hypothesis (as the theory of evolution) countered the literal reading of Genesis, now thoroughly entangled in the Protestant imagination with Milton's lively embellishments in *Paradise Lost.* Second, Darwin's suggestion that even the "most sophisticated organism" could develop without a divine blueprint was a formidable challenge to the argument from design.[19] As Barbara Warnick has noted, Darwin's theory of natural selection—not evolution per se—was most troublesome because it "removed from nature the reassuring element of divine guidance and made God a creator of an organic world that seemed capricious, cruel, and arbitrary."[20]

Aside from this devastating critique, Christianity was also undergoing an "intellectual assault" as new forms of biblical criticism and the comparative study of religion spread across the U.S. academy.[21] In part, an intense interest in biblical history was inspired and revived by the theories of evolution circulating before Darwin, Huxley, and Spencer popularized them.[22] Yet it was mostly the discoveries made by classical archaeologists, particularly in India and Egypt, as well as the growth of a new method of extrinsic biblical exegesis at Oxford, that initiated a succession of biblical interpretations wed to reading the Scriptures in light of "ecclesiastical antiquity." The work of archaeologists, philologists, and linguists also sparked an interest in comparative religion and, for the "literate masses," a new fascination with memoir and travel literature.[23]

The Heyday of Spiritualism

In the United States, response to the growing religious tolerance among the scholarly, hastened by academic innovations in interpretation and archaeological discovery, as well as new communication technologies like the telegraph, helped to ease the growth of Spiritualism. Spiritualism (or "modern Spiritualism") refers to the late-nineteenth- and early-twentieth-century movement which held that spirits of deceased persons could communicate with the presently living.[24] During this period the "occult" became synonymous with supernatural communication in the popular imaginary.

The story of American Spiritualism begins in the scene surrounding the strange performances of two young women, Kate and Margaret Fox. It was amid the Second Great Awakening that the Fox sisters claimed to be able to communicate with the spirit of a man who died in their Hydesville, New York, home. By the spring of 1848, the spirit was producing "knocks" or "rappings" in answer to questions the young women asked of it, and soon the sisters were holding what came to be known as séances, with the curious traveling for miles to witness the spectacle. The Fox sisters eventually traveled the Northeast on a lecture tour, claiming that the spirit they conjured began demanding public performances. Partly as a result of the publicity of these lectures and performances, mediums of all kinds began to surface. By the 1860s, Spiritualism had become a full-blown movement, with mediums and psychics from all over the United States and Europe claiming they could communicate with, and in some cases materialize, the deceased.[25]

Part of the success of Spiritualist discourse can be attributed to the ways in which new technologies of communication catalyzed the long-standing fantasy of communication as the spiritual exchange of thought.[26] The telegraph in particular was a marvel when it arrived, and the possibility of bridging distant locations with cable and, later, broadcasting coincided with the explosion of the popular fascination with spirits and ghosts. Laurence A. Rickels notes that with "the telegraph's instantaneous, or 'live,' transmissions, the origin of new media technologies could be attained or retained. At the same time this kind of 'live' broadcast that the telegraph introduced was the first literalization or realization of telepathy; so it is no coincidence . . . that once the telegraph was introduced, we find societywide preoccupation with the occult."[27] John Durham Peters also points out that Spiritualism "explicitly modeled itself on ability to receive remote messages," right down to the use of Morse code. The ghost communicating with the Fox sisters, after all, did so in knocks and raps. Indeed, spirits would continue speaking in knocks until William Fuld figured out a way to ease the taxing labor of counting: the Ouija board.[28]

The success of Spiritualist discourse also had much to do with the accessibility of its literature, which was written in a simple, pseudoscientific style. Even though the attitude toward white literacy and popular education was highly positive in the United States in the late nineteenth century, most people were not scholarly and were ill-prepared to read the popular philosophical works of the day (from Kant and Darwin to Spencer, Dewey, and James).[29] What could be understood and read with relative ease were the pamphlets and books written in less-academic prose. Spiritualist books, such as Andrew Jackson Davis's five-volume *The Great Harmonia,* published between 1850 and 1859, were easily digestible for a public familiar with the tincture of scientific terminology but unable to articulate its underlying philosophical complexity. Davis's prose was penned in a quasi-religious and scientific tone that his followers found appealing: "Far, far away beyond countless constellations of suns and planets and deep, deep in the fathomless bosom of the immeasurable Univercoelum, throbs the HEART of all life and animation. Its deep harmonious pulsations flow through innumerable vessels to the unimaginable circumference of all planetary existence."[30] Like Davis's writings, many other Spiritualist texts donned the mantle of scientism, which was appealing to readers for two reasons. First, because the concept of "science" had taken on the connotation of truth and authority by the middle of the nineteenth century, it makes sense that those who read about the spiritual life in ways that were compatible with the idea of science would find pseudo-scientific writing appealing (as readers still do today). Such motives help to mark the success of contemporary Protestant sects like Christian Science, which holds tightly to a radical idealism (there is no matter, only mind; healing occurs by means of mental correctness). Second, pseudo-scientific writing was easier and more entertaining to read. Although inspired in part by Kant's ruminations on the immanence of God, the literary movement known as transcendentalism, which orbited works like Emerson's *Nature* and the writings of George Ripley, Bronson Alcott, and Margaret Fuller in *The Dial,* paralleled the scientific romanticism of Spiritualist writings. For a largely white, somewhat literate middle class, Emerson's likening himself to a transparent eyeball beholding the divinity of creation was probably more accessible than Kant's "transcendental" apprehension of "synthetic a posteriori" principles. Likewise, Davis's "inexhaustible source of celestial essences" was probably more appealing than Darwin's dry and plodding outline of the geographical distribution of the species and the nature of horse breeding in the *Origin of Species.*

During the 1850s a number of Spiritualist journals and newspapers were launched that fed the popular desire for more "scientific" yet simple accounts of supernatural phenomena. In the shadow of scientific discourse, which regarded the supernatural with a high degree of skepticism, Spiritualists were determined to amass evidence of the supernatural—a determination that finds modern analogues in the famous British Society for Psychical Research and the contemporary scholarly field known as parapsychology. The first American Spiritualist paper, *Banner of Light,* was published during Blavatsky's time by J. R. M. Squire, and it was soon followed by a more popular journal called the *Spiritual Scientist.*

It was amid the heyday of Spiritualism that Blavatsky's writings emerged. Her rhetoric entered public discourse at a time when many were grappling for some confirmation of divine purpose. Assailed by science and new, more tolerant scholarly investigations of foreign cultures, Christianity finally suffered its most devastating blow from Darwin's theory of natural selection. As the increasingly dominant vocabulary of science made its way into newspapers, pamphlets, and novels, the language of religion—of ambiguity, of magic, of uncertainty—came increasingly under assault. Finally, technologies of telepresence like the telegraph were emerging, fueling the fantasy of spiritual communication and increasing the desire to believe in Spiritualism.

Theosophical Cosmology and Audience

Blavatsky's response to the encroachment of scientism emphasized the comparative study of sacred and occult texts, including the Bible. Whereas Spiritualists tended to champion scientism and hence a clarity of prose more typical of contemporary New Age literature in its search for evidence of the paranormal, Blavatsky continually urged the study of occult texts. The "true" science could not be empirical, as empiricism was concerned with matter, not spirit. For her, it was only though careful reading and the acquisition of a newer vocabulary, cobbled together from various "ancient" texts, that one could "lift aside the curtain, and, in the brightness of that Night made Day, look with undazzled gaze upon the UNVEILED TRUTH."[31]

Theosophical Cosmology

Although a precise account of Blavatsky's Theosophical system is impossible here (literally hundreds of thousands of pages detail every aspect of reality), a summary of her cosmology is helpful.[32] According to Blavatsky, everything in the cosmos (the universe as a whole) has metaphorically spun outward from an unknowable, ineffable, centrifugal center, the "Divine Principle." The manifested existence, or thingness, of this mysterious source unfolded eons ago in undulations of astral light, eventually succumbing to a "knowable" cosmos. This creative act gave rise to our home universe as well as numerous others (called "spheres") that vary in their degree of advancement. Theosophists believe that the cosmos is a conscious entity. The communication of the universe with itself is expressed to individual beings who have fallen from its center as "law."[33] The most important law of the cosmos—karma—is that every universe or sphere constantly strives toward equilibrium (variously, "harmony" or "balance"), which is hampered on earth by the essential polarities of matter and spirit. For Blavatsky, earthly life is merely one step in a long pilgrimage back to unity. She promises that the study of the "Secret Doctrine"—the entire "body of mystical and sacred teachings" of multiple mystics, philosophers, and occultists—will aid the soul on its cosmic journey.[34] Blavatsky seems to present the universe in a way which suggests that it is some grandiose brain and that people are its neurons. Further, she argues that the priestly monopoly on divine knowledge has unfortunately led to the creation of unnatural hierarchies and misguided spiritual teachings.[35] Because of the twin evils of Christianity and "materialism" (basically, what one would call "science" today), Blavatsky believed that Western thinkers are forsaking the opportunity to unite "all races" in the peaceful bonds of "universal brotherhood."

Esoteric Language and the Problem of Audience

The uniqueness of Blavatsky's cosmology is that it is deployed in difficult and obtuse language; for instance, in *The Secret Doctrine* Blavatsky's alternative to Darwin's theory of evolution and natural selection is clothed in strange mix of scientific and Hindu terminology:

> The *Tertiary* Atlantean part-cycle, from the "apex of glory" of that Race in the early Eocene to the greedy mid-Miocene cataclysm, would appear to have lasted some 3½ to four million years. If the duration of the Quaternary is not rather (as seems likely) overestimated, the sinking of the Ruta and Daitya [both are claimed to be submerged continents] would be post-Tertiary.[36]

Further,

> leaving the classification of the geological periods to Western Science, esoteric philosophy divides only the life-periods on the globe. In the present *Manvantra* [a period between two *manus,* or beginning times of manifestation] the actual period is separated into seven Kalpas [a period of roughly four billion years] and seven great human races.[37]

Blavatsky is discussing the evolution of the "seven root races" that evolved independently from other animals. She explains that during her time, people were members of the fifth "Aryan" root race.[38] A supporter of special creationism (in the sense that evolution could not account for the development of the human mind), Blavatsky intended *The Secret Doctrine* as a scientifically verifiable explanation of the way these root races evolved to the present. Yet as these examples illustrate, many of Blavatsky's explanations are more likely to confuse readers. Also characteristic of Blavatsky's rhetoric is a penchant for Greek, Hindu, and Buddhist terminology, which was sprinkled liberally in essays that range from ruminations on the psychic forces of hair to the spiritual significance of hypnotism.[39]

Accounting for the size of the audience of this unfamiliar cosmology is difficult. The initial pressruns of *Isis Unveiled* suggest that her first U.S. audience numbered in the lower thousands.[40] If one expands the audience to those who might have read exposés of Blavatsky or reviews of her books, the audience for Theosophical rhetoric numbered in the hundreds of thousands. By the turn of the century it seems that for the reading public Blavatsky had become a household name, representing the mysteries of occultism; she had enough of a name to merit its inclusion the 1902 edition of *Encyclopaedia Britannica.* That she was a well-known person is further supported by the numerous stories about her that begin by noting her fame. The following excerpt from an 1889 edition of Cincinnati's *Commercial Gazette* is a good example:

> Since the time, many years ago [1875–1880], when the daily papers told us of a mysterious and gifted woman in our midst who was preparing a book of occult lore, such as had never before been given to the readers of our western world, up to the present time, when the author of "Isis Unveiled" is recognized in the literary world as one of its indefatigable workers, in the religious world as an enemy to old beliefs, and in the social world as incomprehensible as a sphinx—Madame Blavatsky is without doubt the most remarkable woman of the age. Shrug your shoulders, my friend, and utter the word infamous if you choose—but you will find it no easy task to prove aught that will derogate from her character or ability, and no one will venture to assert that any other woman is known around the world like her.[41]

Similarly, the *New York Daily Graphic* describes the Lamasery as "widely known," and the *Hartford Daily Times* describes the Theosophical Society in a way that suggests "wide discussion" among the reading public.[42] Blavatsky is also frequently described as famously scandalous, since many—especially religious—authorities accused her of plagiarism and fraud. A reporter from the *Philadelphia Inquirer* observed that since "Blavatsky came to New York in the early seventies . . . scandal and misrepresentation have made free with her name."[43] An editorial in Horace Greeley's *New-York Daily Tribune* laments that "few women in our time have been more persistently misrepresented, slandered and defamed than Madame Blavatsky."[44] Indeed, a story in the *New York Sun* begins by describing a farewell party for "the famous heathen of Eighth avenue, Madame H. P. Blavatsky."[45]

Just who, then, was reading Blavatsky? How does one characterize the "reading public" that deigned to digest her "*Tertiary* Atlantean part-cycles" and dharmic, polysyllabic conceptions? Unfortunately, there is no satisfactory answer.[46] In newspaper stories, on the one hand, we do have lists of people who visited Blavatsky. A reporter from the *New York World* documented a lengthy list of names from that "brilliant crowd of Bohemians" who were wont to gather for "an evening to drink tea from Madame's samovar and indulge in a feast of reason and a flow of soul":

> Prof. Weiss, of the New York University; Thomas A. Edison, A. L. Rawson, the painter; Prof. Wilder, the genial and lamented Sam Ward, poet, philosopher, lobbyist and bon vivant; his *chere ami,* William Henry Huribert, then editor of THE WORLD; the Earl of Dunraven, whose father wrote a monumental book on Spiritualism, and who is now Lord Salisbury's Under-Secretary for the Colonies; David A. Curtis, of the *Herald;* Edward P. Mitchell, then, as now, exploiting his brilliant imagination in the *Sun*'s columns; Albert Bierstadt, the artist; Charles Sotheran, mystic and bibliophile; Linda and Eda Diez, the actresses . . . [47]

The list continues at some length. If these individuals are any measure, then it was the well-educated, white, and wealthy elite who were reading Blavatsky.[48] Only those with the money and, therefore, leisure could afford to spend time with Blavatsky's difficult books. On the other hand, individuals of lesser social standing were reading her work as well. These individuals are of most interest and significance insofar as the popular imagination is concerned—individuals whom historians sometimes referred to as the "English common reader" or "common reader."[49]

Esoteric Language as Authority Appeal

Rhetorically, accounting for the limited popularity of Blavatsky's writings is simply baffling. Her explanations and refinements of Theosophical doctrine span thousands of pages, and many casual readers likely found her books daunting. Worse, the complexity of her language in her most popular works is often overwhelming. Yet if one looks at Blavatsky's esoteric language as a poetics, the common reader begins to look like a patient individual for whom clarity or uncluttered prose was relatively unimportant. In fact, clarity may have worked against Blavatsky's popularity insofar as the novelty of her rhetoric, however difficult, contributed to her mystery. In other words, esoteric language and complex argumentation helped to imbue Blavatsky with authority. Her frequent use of comparative exegesis was a common means by which she introduced strange terms and was one of her favorite ways of transferring the sacred authority of a fetishized text to her textual persona:[50]

> [The] doctrine, that man is trine—spirit, or *Nous,* soul and body—was taught by the Apostle of the Gentiles [Paul] more broadly and clearly than it has been by any of his Christian successors (see *I Thess.,* v, 23). . . . The Buddhists, who separate the three entities in man . . . yet divide the soul into several parts. . . . The old Greeks did likewise, holding that *psyche* was *bios,* or physical vitality, the *epithumia* or concupiscible nature, and the *phren, mens,* or mind.[51]

For a number of her readers, this strategy worked. Elizabeth L. Saxon's letter to New Orleans's *Daily Picayune* in November 1877 suggests how Blavatsky's deployment of esoteric language may have been interpreted by the curious reader:

> Her book [*Isis Unveiled*] reads like the wonders of the "Arabian Nights" in some of its statements, but she assures me the "half was not told," and certainly testimony of this mystic power is not wanting elsewhere. Her book comprises two large volumes of over six hundred pages each. It is issued by Bouton, and is bound to meet with large sales. I read the first volume, and would advise others to read them: whether for or against her opinions. Her long life in the East and her command of sources of information gives her great power. She is a formidable antagonist from the fact that the languages of the East are perfectly familiar to her and their literature has been at her command.[52]

The *Boston Evening Transcript* was just as charitable, for although Blavatsky's "work abounds in quotations from a dozen different languages," it is "not for the purpose of vain display of erudition, but to substantiate her peculiar views."[53] The *New York Tribune* said that *Isis Unveiled* "amply confirms [Blavatsky's] claims to the character of an adept in secret science."[54]

Although her esoteric language seemed to establish Blavatsky as an expert for the true believer, it also provided ammunition for skeptical blasts. For example, one of the most explicit public controversies about Blavatsky's use of language concerns a battle of pamphlets between Blavatsky and the editor of London's *The Freethinker,* George W.

Foote. Apparently, this battle of words was widely known among the U.S. reading public.[55] In 1889 Foote printed a pamphlet titled *Mrs. Besant's Theosophy,* which challenged Theosophical teaching and Blavatsky's intellectual heir, Annie Besant. Blavatsky responded with *The Thersites of Freethought.* In turn, Foote replied to Blavatsky with *The New Cagliostro:* "I am aware that you are extensively read in useless literature. You have a prodigious knowledge of occult authors. You have made a wonderful collection of the maggots of the human brain. There is hardly a superstition which [is] not wholly or partially sanctioned in your four portly volumes. Your heap of rubbish is colossal."[56] As many critics in her time noted, Blavatsky's later Theosophical writings are derived largely from Eastern religious doctrines and employ their terminology indiscriminately. Max Müller, a renowned anthropologist and scholar of ancient Eastern religious texts during Blavatsky's time, remarked that in *The Secret Doctrine* he "could find nothing 'that cannot be traced back to generally accessible Brahmanic [Hindu] or Buddhistic sources, only [that] everything is muddled or misunderstood.' "[57] As my brief remarks on the authority-establishing function of esoteric language might indicate, however, these indelicate uses were deliberate. A quick glance at Blavatsky's explicit discussions of language discloses both an awareness of the limits of language and a desire to develop an ambiguous and novel vocabulary for moving readers toward the ineffable truth—an awareness and a desire that is best characterized as an occult poetics.

The Occult Poetics of Theosophy

Blavatsky's books and essays are rife with contradiction, ambiguity, and tedious etymological explications that obscure, rather than clarify, occult doctrine. Editors of her books were often forced to rewrite them repeatedly, presumably to eliminate obfuscating vocabulary. Indeed, even those within the Theosophical Society sometimes found her writing incomprehensible.[58] If Blavatsky's writings were so difficult to penetrate, why were they read at all? If Blavatsky persuaded people to believe in her cosmology, how do we explain the deliberate use of complex esoteric language? If she was claiming to reveal secrets, why did she slow their uptake in difficult terminology? The answers to these and similar questions are not straightforward. First, lest one commit what is sometimes described as the "intentional fallacy," one must admit that there is no way to posit what Blavatsky intended to do with her difficult language. This does not mean we are prevented from reading the deployment of esoteric language sympathetically, however, which means that we can accept the occultists' argument that esoteric language is an attempt to help the reader or hearer escape the constraints of language by means of language. In this internal sense, esoteric language represents the use of language against itself in a Platonic, dialectical fashion in order to transcend its limits. Because ordinary language cannot capture the essence of transcendent and universal truths, the occultist uses esoteric language as a better—however inaccurate—descriptor of the divine. For the occultist, a better brand of naming enables the true believer to leap intellectually from the imperfect name to the essence of the named more easily.[59]

As I suggested in the previous chapter, however, a fruitful way to answer these kinds of questions is to proceed symptomatically, analyzing Blavatsky's rhetoric from an external or characteristically rhetorical perspective. From this vantage, one does not read Blavatsky's texts as reflecting a world but rather as calling one into being. One can understand the deployment of esoteric language commonsensically as therapeutic rhetoric or as a rhetoric of reassurance: the world called into being is one in which the supernatural persists, which eases doubts of the true believer. An alternate symptomatic reading is one that focuses on the logic or function of esoteric language, one that can account for the creation and motility of the ambiguous term. From this vantage I suggest that one can understand occult texts as a reactive practice that confronts the limitations of language—occult poetics.

As I detailed in the previous chapter, the central logic of occult poetics is based on what one could term a rhetorical antinomy, which I defined as the illusion of a fundamental, ontological paradox or contradiction between two observations about reality. In this respect, occult discourse is the end result or consequence of a rhetorical antinomy between a belief (A) and an action (B). The belief is this: (A) spiritual knowledge is translinguistic, or "ineffable." The act is this: (B) one can write and speak about spiritual knowledge. The rhetorical antinomy is summarized by the statement, "The Truth is ineffable, but let me tell you about it anyway." As I will illustrate below, this statement is an apt characterization of the structure of many of Blavatsky's challenging occult texts.

Blavatsky and the Limits of Natural Language

Because I have argued that the esoteric language of the occult can be understood as the somewhat inevitable result of a rhetorical antinomy, Blavatsky's use of esoteric language was demanded, to some extent, by the assumption that the ineffable (for her the "Divine Principle") is beyond representation and thus commands the use of the peculiar term or unusual phrase to better approximate the divine. That is, regardless of the occultist's intentions, ambiguity is a better approximation of the ineffable than is accuracy or precision. Throughout her own writing, and in particular in her defensive and reflexive essays and pamphlets about her use of esoteric language and flawed English, Blavatsky is clear about the inability of natural language—and especially English—to convey supernatural meaning. She argues:

> In our highly civilized West, . . . in the wake of ideas and thoughts —as happened with every tongue—the more the latter become materialized in the cold atmosphere of Western selfishness and its incessant chase after the goods of this world, the less was there any need felt for the production of new terms to express that which was tacitly regarded as obsolete and exploded "superstition." Such words could answer only to ideas which a cultured man was scarcely supposed to harbor in his mind. "Magic," a synonym for jugglery; "Sorcery," an equivalent for crass ignorance; and "Occultism," the sorry relic of crack-brained, medieval Fire-Philosophers. . . . They are terms of contempt, and used generally only in reference to the dross residues of the Dark Ages. . . . Therefore we have no terms in the English tongue to define and shade the difference between such abnormal powers, or the sciences that lead to the acquisition of them, with the nicety possible in the Eastern languages—pre-eminently the Sanskrit.[60]

In this passage Blavatsky explicitly acknowledges her discomfort with the fixity of language. This fixity or rigidness of signification, she says, is inherently entangled with materialist worldviews insofar as the drive toward pure denotation is akin to the push toward reductive, physicalist explanations of human reality and experience. Further, although she notes a desire to get away from Western terms for magical and mystical experiences because of their negative connotations, she also seems concerned with nuance that she thinks is impossible in the dominant vocabulary. In fact, she is eventually led to admit that all languages, including Sanskrit, will fail to characterize the divine unless the user is divinely inspired. "There are no words to express the lights and shadows," she says, to "draw the demarcation between the sublime and the true, the absurd and the ridiculous."[61] From a rhetorical perspective that would characterize the problem as epistemic, this inability to draw a line is the impossibility of a metalangauge that could help to adjudicate competing significations of the ineffable.

Blavatsky's frustration with the impossibility of a metalangauge, as well as with the constraints of the dominant vocabulary—reasoned English—is echoed in her defense of *Isis Unveiled,* which was attacked as plagiarized gibberish:

> What I am determined to do is to give facts, undeniable and not to be gainsaid, simply by stating the peculiar . . . circumstances under which I wrote my first English work [*Isis Unveiled*]. I give them seriatim.
>
> 1. When I came to America in 1873, I had not spoken English—which I had learned in my childhood colloquially—for over thirty years. I could understand [it] when I read it, but could hardly speak the language.
>
> 2. I had never been at any college, and what I knew I taught myself. . . . I then hardly read any scientific European works, knew little of Western philosophy and sciences. The little which I had studied and learned of these, disgusted me with its materialism, its limitations, its narrow cut-and-dried spirit of dogmatism, and its air of superiority over the philosophies of sciences and antiquity. . . . I had not the least idea of literary rules.[62]

Blavatsky continues at some length. What is important to note in these defensive remarks is an implicit, offensive linking of "Western philosophy and sciences" with English grammar, a linking that implicates a dissatisfaction with the dominant, Western language game. William Covino has characterized attacks on an era's "literary rules" as a challenge to dominant systems of "articulate power," which are composed of the tacit rules of correct communication, inclusive of grammar and social mores.[63] Failure to conform to the dominant system of articulation relegated one to a classed yet competing system of the "inarticulate," but this does not mean one was powerless. Blavatsky appears to counter the dominant vocabulary by challenging its semiotics as materialist and by offering a competing system of terminology that required a new logic of articulation—an understanding of occult poetics.

It makes sense, then, that to deploy her "ancient wisdom" Blavatsky turned to Eastern vocabularies—vocabularies that would undoubtedly be prima facie connotative for the English common reader. First, Sanskrit terms, like most words in an unfamiliar language, are initially ambiguous, and hence the possibility for multiple meanings is open. Such terminological openness prolongs the indeterminacy of meaning, and this is desirable because indeterminacy is closer to ineffability—much, much closer—than accuracy or precision. Second, Sanskrit marks the exotic Other, an Other that would appeal to popular audiences that were reading, in ever increasing numbers, travel literature. Third, Blavatsky could actively forge the rules of a new language game based on unusual terms from another language, and she was thus free to link strange, exotic terms to the philosophical or cosmological precepts that she, magically, decreed. One observes this rule-making time and time again in Blavatsky's writings, usually signaled by a criticism of another's discussion of a concept (like "karma") or in self-conscious attempts to avoid "misapprehensions." For example, in the clearest of her works, *The Key to Theosophy,* Blavatsky endeavors to "remedy" a "confusion of ideas" about the "Principles" (components or aspects) of the human constitution. One is quick to note, however, that Blavatsky's clarifications are still quite vague:

> To avoid henceforth such misapprehensions, I propose to translate literally from the Occult Eastern terms their equivalents in English, and offer these for future use.
>
> THE HIGHER SELF is Atma the inseparable ray of the Universal and ONE SELF. It is the God above, more than within us. Happy the man who succeeds in saturating his inner Ego with it!
>
> THE SPIRITUAL divine EGO is the Spiritual soul or Buddhi, in close union with the Manas, the mind-principle, without which it is no EGO at all, but only the Atmic Vehicle.
>
> THE INNER, or HIGHER "EGO" is Manas, the "Fifth" Principle, so called, independently of Buddhi. The Mind-Principle is only the Spiritual Ego when merged *into one* with Buddhi,—no materialist being supposed to have in him such an Ego, however great his intellectual capacities. It is the permanent Individuality or the "Re-incarnating Ego."[64]

The assignment of meaning here is the counterpart to the Indian mystic's "*neti neti*" method of defining the ineffable negatively (it's not this, but it's not that either): each weird term corresponds to another weird term, neither of which has a clearly denotative meaning. The assignment of meaning becomes purely an analytics of definition in the sense that nothing new about reality is said (e.g., the famous example of analytics, "a bachelor is an unmarried man"), and thus the possibility of what "Buddhi" might mean to the reader is still open despite its being bound by the network of terms set in relation to it. Aside from the authority-establishing function of resisting precise denotation, such an openness of meaning also works to promote the fourth function of esoteric language: the enthymematic function. The reader can tailor the meaning of "Buddhi" or "Atma" to individual experience or an individual need. Further, the terms' deliberate vagueness leaves open the possibility that they do in fact implicate something true beyond a human's capacity to signify it—an epistemological function.[65]

Finally, Sanskrit functions as the original "pure language," a feature common to many occult origin narratives. The pure language is the universal mother tongue, a language whose signs and referents line up in perfect iconicity. Only a few can use the pure language correctly, and it is that language from which all other natural languages have fallen.[66] In *The Secret Doctrine,* Blavatsky muses:

> However incomplete and feeble as an exposition, it [the book thus far] is, at any rate, an approximation—using the word in the mathematical sense—to that which is the oldest basis for all the subsequent Cosmogonies. The attempt to render in a European tongue the grand panorama of the ever periodically recurring Law—impressed on the plastic minds of the first races endowed with Consciousness by those who reflected the same from the Universal Mind—is daring, for no human language, save the Sanskrit—which is that *of the Gods*—can do so with any degree of adequacy. But the failures in this work must be forgiven for the sake of the motive.[67]

This language of the gods is only truly intelligible to a few:

> All the ancient records were written in a language which was universal and known to all nations alike in days of old, but which is now intelligible only to a few. . . . [A]ll the words of that mystery language signified the same thing to each man whatever nationality. . . . It is maintained that INDIA (not in its present limits, but including its ancient boundaries) is the only country in the world which still has among her sons adepts, who have the knowledge of . . . the key to the entire system.[68]

Blavatsky claims that Kabbalists, with their mathematical approach to divine language, and occultists more familiar with the mathematical significance of the Bible and other sacred texts, are the most likely to comprehend the "mystery of Being" by means of their access and understanding of the pure language.

Of course, the concept of a pure language is not peculiar to modern occult discourse, as its pursuit can also be located in the scientific quest for a transparent language in the work of countless thinkers, such as Francis Bacon and the scientists associated with the Royal Society. That occultists seem constantly to strive toward a pure language (each occultist claims to have a better vocabulary), however, highlights the rhetorical antinomy at the center of occult poetics: the striving for the discovery of the pure language is motivated by one's encounter with the limits of language in the face of ineffability. In his or her strivings to speak the astral, the occultist is led to believe that there must have been an Adamite language in which the signified and signifier were one in perfect iconicity. The contradiction of Blavatsky's rhetoric—and the very tension that keeps it moving in a hermeneutic circle—is mapped by the rhetorical antinomy. Although there is no language that can fully communicate astral truth, there is or once was a pure language for which there are better and worse copies. Blavatsky, like every other occultist of her stature, claimed to have assembled one of the best facsimiles of that divine signification.

Concluding Remarks: Same as It Ever Was

> *The Seat of the Soul* is written for the largest, fastest-growing market the world has ever seen or ever will see. That is because the new species is being born inside us.
>
> —jacket copy from Gary Zukav's *The Seat of the Soul*

In this chapter I have examined the work of H. P. Blavatsky, continuing the origin narrative of occult discourse that I began in chapter 1 and illustrating how esoteric language operates by applying the model of occult poetics that I developed in chapter 2. Regarding the latter, I have argued that one can understand Blavatsky's rhetoric internally and sympathetically as an attempt to reassure believers and, presumably, to move them in a Platonic fashion toward glimpses of ultimate reality. Externally, I have suggested that we can understand Blavatsky's rhetoric, particularly her esoteric language, as reflecting a process of invention peculiar to occultism. As the most conspicuous part of this rhetorical process—that is, occult poetics—esoteric language has a number of functions for the occultist or mystic that need to be summarized. First and foremost, esoteric language has an epistemological function for the true believer. Because the terms in question are odd or strange, their ambiguity helps to preserve the notion that what they denote may actually be beyond signification, and thus assertions about it are "true." In this respect, esoteric language reassures readers of their faith on the basis of possibility. Second, the vague or elusive meanings of specialized terms can cater to true believers enthymematically, allowing them to work it into their own experience and perhaps tailor the terms' meaning to personal needs. Third, esoteric language is used to remind aspirants of the limits of language and to thrust them into higher states of awareness beyond language. Fourth, esoteric language is often deployed in order to establish one's authority, a strategy exemplified expertly in the work of Blavatsky. Finally, I argued that from a external, rhetorical perspective, esoteric language is the inevitable outworking of a contradictory confrontation with the limits of language. I have suggested that the kind of confrontation particular to occultism is aptly described as a rhetorical antinomy.

As the most conspicuous result of the rhetorical antinomy central to occultism, however, esoteric language is easiest to notice and overshadows other, less conspicuous strategies, such as the deliberate paradox or contradiction, complex metaphor and analogy, and negative dialectics. These other ways of navigating the rhetorical antinomy are also common, and in recent years they may have come to overshadow the use of esoteric language as a rhetorical strategy. The most popular occult books today—at the time of this writing, works by psychic Sylvia Browne and mystic Gary Zukav—are written in a much plainer, more straightforward style than the works of Blavatsky. Despite their striving for clarity, however, these New Age systems continue to stress, perhaps unwittingly, the inadequacy of language and preserve the function of esotericism by selectively choosing a handful of strange terms and especially by stressing the novelty of their own revelations. For example, Zukav's *The Seat of the Soul,* which rose to the number one slot on the *New York Times* best-seller list in the early 1990s and again more recently because of promotion by Oprah Winfrey, opens with a forward about the need for a "new vocabulary":

> Humanity, the human species, is longing now to touch that force [an emerging transhuman force], to shed that which interferes with clear contact. Much of the difficulty in doing this lies in the fact that the vocabulary with which to address this new force, which is indeed the eternal force, is not yet born.

> In this moment and in this hour of human evolution this proper vocabulary and means of addressing that which longs to transcend religiosity and spirituality and assume the position of authentic power is longing to be born. We need to give that which . . . we are touching consciously for the first time a vocabulary that is not clouded . . . not . . . seen . . . through the veils of mystery or mysticism.[69]

The need for a new vocabulary signals the first element of any occult poetics: the rhetorical antinomy that holds the truth to be ineffable yet describable. The vocabulary Zukav offers is predictable. He speaks of karma, the soul, and of the superior multisensory human and the inferior and limited five-sensory human. He talks of a "Light" that is intuitively known but not easily described: "The Light that flows through your system is Universal energy. It is the Light of the Universe. You give that Light form. What you feel, what you think, how you behave, what you value and how you live your life reflect the way that you are shaping the Light that is flowing through you."[70] The vagueness of "the Light" preserves the basic epistemological and enthymematic functions of esoteric language without terminological strangeness. Or rather, one could argue that esoteric language is still present in form, as Zukav's writing continues to exhibit its ambiguity despite his using the common yet wildly connotative term "light."

Like Zukav, Sylvia Browne stresses the need for a new vocabulary because humanity has reached a "new" stage of evolution (indeed, she even refers to the teachings of the Theosophical Society as an important part of her spiritual education).[71] One can say the same of many other occult and occultic texts, because most of them tend to stress the novelty of their revelations and the necessity of new vocabularies, from ECKANKAR's *Eck-Vidya* to Scientology's *Dianetics*. The most obvious feature of New Age rhetoric, the most recognizable form of the contemporary occultic, is its claim to novelty, its "newness," fresh esoteric terms (often ironically "discovered" in presumably "ancient" texts) being the primary example. Yet as the Blavatsky of modernity might say while channeling the singing spirit of the Talking Head that was David Byrne, "same as it ever was."[72]

4
On Textual Occultism

> All this secrecy is very silly. An indicible Arcanum is an arcanum that *cannot* be revealed. It is simply bad faith to swear a man to the most horrible penalties if he betray . . . , etc., and then take him mysteriously apart and confide the Hebrew Alphabet to his safe keeping. This is perhaps only ridiculous; but it is a wicked imposture to pretend to have received [a magical alphabet] from Rosicrucian manuscripts which are to be found in the British Museum. To obtain money on these grounds, as has been done by certain moderns, is clear (and I trust indictable) fraud.
>
> —Aleister Crowley, from 777[1]

Thus the most infamous occultist of the twentieth century, the "wickedest man in the world," introduces the magical alphabet known as the Qabalah.[2] For Aleister Crowley, the Qabalah is a "system of symbolism . . . [as well as] an instrument for interpreting symbols" not vouchsafed to the average person.[3] His indictment of the secrecy surrounding the Qabalah is a reference to the oaths taken by members of the Order of the Golden Dawn, a secret organization whose leaders bid initiates never to reveal their rituals or their teachings. The Qabalistic alphabet and its many tables of correspondence, published by Crowley in 1907, were, in fact, the biggest "secret" taught by the elite order. Crowley's revelation of the Golden Dawn's secrets would invite many social and civil indictments in the years to come.

More important for the concerns of this chapter, however, is Crowley's critique of modern occultism as an organized, economic enterprise. The occult can be understood as both an institutional arrangement of people into hierarchies (leaders over followers) and as a cultural modality that advances a set of organizing principles for its key activity, that intellectual labor more commonly recognized as the practice of textual interpretation. After years of study, Crowley came to realize, like the critic Kenneth Burke, that the occultist's control of secrets begets mystery, which in turn suggests a kind of readerly obedience for those who wish to know the secrets—especially "insofar as the acceptance of a mystery involves a person in the abnegation of his own personal judgment."[4] For Crowley, the social power inevitably produced by the mystery of occultism should only be used to form helpful arrangements, such as that of teacher and student or author and reader. Hoarding "secrets" for monetary gain is the most egregious abuse of occult power because, fundamentally, occultism is about cosmic truths and the care of the soul. Indeed, at least in this respect Crowley practiced what he preached, for despite the potential of his many published essays and books to bring him a modest income, he stuck to his oath never to "make money out of Magick."[5]

Insofar as money is the paradigmatic condensation symbol of social power, Crowley's complaints speak directly to the central concern of this chapter: the power of interpretation, and the act of interpretation as an exercise of power. If one understands power as the ability to get someone to do what he or she would not otherwise ordinarily do, or to think what he or she would not otherwise ordinarily think—in the most extreme sense as the ability to invite some degree of abnegation of personal judgment in others (e.g., readers or followers)—then all critical interpretation is necessarily a practice of power. This is not to say that every attempt to ferret meaning from a text is born of some barbaric will to dominate others ("might makes right"), although one could certainly say that there are multiple religious histories that would support this observation. Nor is this to say that critical practice results in monetary gain (were that but true!). Rather, understanding critical interpretation as a form of power implies an understanding of power as productive and born of a kind of "will to knowledge." By saying that interpretation is a practice of power, one suggests that the simple activity of reading, of assigning meaning, is always already caught up in a complex social network that helps one to determine, often unconsciously, what a text should mean. This social network consists of a multiplicity of influences, the most basic of which is the use of language itself. By knowing a language, one understands the rules (grammar, syntax, and so on) necessary to assign meaning to utterances, a mundane variety of interpretive power. Michel Foucault also points to more specialized and diffuse domains of interpretive power. In the psychologist's attempt to describe human consciousness, Foucault argues, the human being is defined in ways that come to affect seriously the lives of people in hospitals, clinics, and asylums. For Foucault, power is exercised in the ability to assign meaning in intellectual ways ("knowledge is power"), which may or may not result in a related physical exercise of it ("might makes right").[6]

Because it attempts to fix and isolate meanings, the critical act of textual interpretation is a special exercise of power, particularly because of the fundamental assumptions one makes when producing interpretations. All interpretive claims necessarily begin with the assumption that the meaning or truth of a text under scrutiny is not apparent and that the production of an interpretation is necessary to bring it out. The necessity of interpretation places the interpreter in a position superior to that of the text, and most certainly in a position superior to those consulting the interpretation. As Wlad Godzich has observed of scholarly criticism, interpretation creates an opposition between the "primary" text and the interpretive or "secondary" text that is necessarily caught in the gravitational pull of an authentic meaning or "truth." The act of interpretation "suggests that in the primary text the truth remains somehow burdened by its mode of representation, and it acts upon the belief that the truth can be attained and that indeed it can be given a better representation."[7] Occult texts represent an extreme version of the burden of representation insofar as they are built on the assumption that their truths cannot accurately be represented in human language. This condition inevitably produces hierarchical relationships between those who claim to understand occult texts and those who struggle for understanding.

For Crowley, the burden of occult representation was the inherent arbitrariness of language, for "one of the greatest difficulties experienced by the student [of magick]—a difficulty that increases . . . with his advance in knowledge—is this: he finds it impossible to gain any clear idea of the meanings of the terms he employs."[8] The act of interpreting occult texts, he claimed, was really about managing the ambiguity of language central to the production of occult texts. For Crowley, interpretation was about "establishing a necessary connection between the essence of forms, sounds, simple ideas (such as number) and their spiritual, moral, or intellectual equivalents."[9] In the parlance of literary and rhetorical critics, this kind of interpretation is an attempt to force a congruence between signs and their referents, signifiers and their signifieds, such that true meaning becomes iconic.[10] An understanding of interpretation in this manner presumes what one can fruitfully call a "textual occultism": interpretation is an exercise of power that concerns the revelation of textual secrets and occluded meanings that primary texts fail to disclose in themselves.

In this chapter I complement my previous focus on the composition of occult texts with an examination of the rhetoric of their interpretation and consumption. I have two primary goals. First, I offer a close reading of a difficult occult text, Crowley's *The Book of the Law,* in order to illustrate how occult discourse can be understood as a particular kind of reading or interpretive practice that forces the reader to end a chaining of signifiers at the feet of an occult authority—an end that is assuredly biographical and hence "outside" the text.

Second, I redescribe a central mode of interpretation among many disciplines in the humanities—"intrinsic criticism" or "close textual criticism"—as an occult procedure, using *The Book of the Law* as a point of comparison. I suggest that intrinsic criticism is continuous if not identical with occult modes of interpretation, a practice whose academic and historical trajectory can be traced to methods of the New Critics.

To these ends, the chapter proceeds by offering a description of intrinsic criticism, noting its touted purposes and goals within a interdisciplinary framework. Then I move to an intrinsic analysis of the exemplar text, *The Book of the Law.* In the third part of the chapter I highlight the similarities between Crowley's interpretive practice and that of intrinsic critics, locating their common roots in a hermeneutic of faith. Finally, I conclude with a discussion of the disciplinary effects of textual occultism.

The Textual Erotics of Intrinsic Criticism

In the fields of literary and rhetorical studies, "intrinsic criticism" tends to refer to what Michael Leff has described as the most rigorous and careful kind of "interpretive work."[11] He suggests that one might characterize the practice as "the close reading and rereading of the text, the analysis of the historical and biographical circumstances that generate and frame its composition, the recognition of basic conceptions that establish the co-ordinates of the text, and an appreciation of the way these conceptions interact within the text and help [to] determine its temporal movement."[12] Although Leff is primarily concerned with oratory, he observes that the kinds of texts which best lend themselves to close textual analyses are those that are "well constructed" by "possessing a high degree of artistic integrity and density."[13] The texts best suited for intense, intrinsic analyses or close readings are, hence, great, artistic masterpieces.

The origin narrative of intrinsic criticism can be traced back to the early German romantics, led through the British romanticism movement, and finally seated in the New Criticism stateside. Many histories of romanticism are available elsewhere, so here I will focus on its modern representative, New Criticism.[14] Threatened by the encroachment of scientism and its push for rigorous and thorough "methods" of investigation, and dismayed by the general tendency of literary criticism to generate biography and historical anecdote with little attention to the content of literature itself, the New Critics advanced a series of methods and analytical techniques that obsessed on the formal and structural features of textual content. Although the approaches and goals of New Critics like I. A. Richards, Cleanth Brooks, and René Wellek differed, the general consensus was that criticism should deal with literary art on its own terms, without necessary reference to historical, biographical, or even ideological context.[15] As New Criticism was becoming increasingly unfashionable among literary scholars in the late 1950s, rhetoricians like W. Charles Redding began lamenting the marginalization of the oratorical text in itself, which he claimed was the result of a "heavy reliance upon historical data and historical research techniques."[16] Dilip Gaonkar notes that the origin narrative of "textualism" in rhetorical studies begins as a woeful tale "usually told by stringing together a series of striking but disconcerting phrases from leading authorities that depress the field to supplementary status as hand-maiden to [the discipline of] history."[17] The correction to the proverbial error, to what G. P. Mohrmann ironically described as "puerile biography and vacuous history," was a renewed attention to the text as a valuable interstice, a discrete and self-contained unity that suggested its own means of self-analysis.

The most programmatic statements about intrinsic criticism are few in number, but they do tend to characterize the practice as a whole. Like the New Critics, the approaches and goals of intrinsic criticism differ from critic to critic; however, one can identify a loose consensus about methodology—and I say "methodology" because there is deliberately no formal "method" for interpretation. Indeed, that there is no method is the first guideline for intrinsic criticism, suitably dubbed by Karlyn Kohrs Campbell and Thomas R. Burkenholder as an "organic approach." Such an approach "asks critics to consider a rhetorical act [or text] on its own terms" and "not to approach it with prejudgments and prior assumptions."[18] Elsewhere Campbell describes the intrinsic critic's approach to the text as a paradisiacal encounter with unity, one that "must be unmediated by a predetermined perspective, ideology, or formula, a form of interference that renders the subsequent critical act fraudulent."[19]

This seemingly virginal approach to the text is not the familiar seduction of structural phenomenology, nor is it (necessarily) the detached formalism of the New Criticism. The goal of intrinsic analysis is a perceptual synthesis of text and critic. One must read the warnings against "fraudulent" readings up against scientism, because any contemporary obsession with methodology, just like that of the New Critics, is born of a desire to render interpretive protocols that ensure a respectable verifiability.[20] But for close textual critics, such an insurance seems to take a backseat to romancing the text, for romancing the text is the best way to know it. The intrinsic critical act is characterized as an attempt to forge a "relationship between critic and object" that is "synthetic and holistic" and enables the critic to comprehend, from within, the essence of its "unifying structure."[21] Thus the second guideline of intrinsic criticism opposes the cold and detached tincture of scientism with an erotics: in Leff's terms, the critic should attempt to "merge his or her consciousness into the text." Although this merging will remind the critic that interpretation is "inherently circular" (try as one might, it is impossible to encounter a text absent preconceptions), the cyclical or in-and-out movement from the critic's experience to that contained in the text is precisely what produces critical insight: "The act of interpretation mediates between the experience of the critic and the forms of experience expressed in the text. To perform this act successfully, critics must vibrate what they see in the text against their own expectations and predilections. What critics are trained to look for and what they see interact in creative tension; the two elements blend and separate, progressively changing as altered conceptions of the one reshape the configuration of the other."[22] The power of interpretation is thus a tango, a sympathetic—and ultimately synthetic—penetration or envelopment of textual space. Leff's description of textual erotics is strikingly similar to that of T. S. Eliot, who described the tango as an ecstatic release and recovery: "You have to give yourself up, and then recover yourself, and the third movement is having something to say, before you have wholly forgotten both surrender and recovery. Of course the self recovered is never the same as the self before it was given."[23] Intrinsic criticism is an attempt to explicate the conditions that invited surrender and the subsequent transformation of self in scholarly pillow talk.

The reason that the critic endeavors to vibrate against or merge with the text is because this helps to generate interpretive structures that, in turn, illuminate artistry and demystify a text's "rhetorical power."[24] As Stephen E. Lucas has argued, such illumination deliberately blurs the line between text and context, because intrinsic criticism is built upon the precept that "a text creates its own internal context as it unfolds in time and is processed by a listener or reader."[25] Lucas continues: "Meaning and effect are produced, not by the text as a static entity, but by the progressive interaction of the audience with the temporal flow of ideational, dispositional, stylistic, and syntactical elements in the discourse. . . . The benefit of close textual analysis is that it allows the critic to 'slow down' the action within the text so as to keep its evolving internal context into sharp focus and to allow more precise explication of its rhetorical artistry."[26] This is not to say that intrinsic criticism obviates the need for historical contextualization; most critics would agree that social, political, and historical contextualization are important for understanding any rhetorical act. That the text suggests its own context or interpretive structures, however, does place a high emphasis on the aesthetic and, in turn, recasts "rhetorical power" as the outcome of an art of tropes (incidentally, a perspective first outlined by Nietzsche in his lectures on rhetoric).[27] A focus on style eclipses the traditional focus on invention and argument.[28] Further, the focus on style indicates that intrinsic criticism is a process that actively promotes the collapse of a traditional distinction between form and content.[29] Ultimately, the guideline that emerges from the priority of internal structures and a focus on style is that the critic should interpret texts to help them mean for themselves, to aid them in their own self-construction as a unity.

Finally, the fourth guideline of intrinsic criticism is an extension of the third: one should choose to interpret masterpieces, because the texts best served by intrinsic criticism are artful, discrete, and dense. While this is a very old hat among literary critics (ensconced, as it is, in the debate over the "canon" and "canonizing"), it has only recently emerged as prized grail among scholars of rhetoric and public address in departments of Communication. This concern unquestionably represents an anxiety about the relative lack of sustained analyses of "great texts," analyses that might congeal into something like a disciplinary canon for public-address scholars in particular. Lucas has lamented that rhetorical critics' "persistent neglect of major texts in the history of American oratory is nothing short of astonishing."[30] Similarly, critic Martin J. Medhurst has stated programmatically that rhetorical scholars need to push "close textual analysis to the forefront of agenda" as an "intellectually respectable" practice, and that the best way to do so is to build a canon. "It is time," says Medhurst, "for a nationwide project to produce one or more volumes of criticism of universally recognized oratorical masterpieces."[31] Such aims, however, are also symptomatic of anxiety over "theory" itself, since theorizing about texts can sometimes force their disappearance or occlusion in favor of generalization and abstraction, a phenomenon described by Gaonkar as the "disappearance of the critical object."[32]

Given the ostensive business of this study—an examination of occultism and the occultic as rhetorical phenomena—I would like to read closely a single occult text in order to illustrate how it provides its own interpretive structures. Doing so will help to uncover the important occult textual dynamics, which I will discuss in terms of "internal" and "external" functions, that implicate a negotiation of power among occult authors and their readers. Because the intrinsic approach works best with artistic texts, texts that announce themselves to be "great" in some way, I have selected Aleister Crowley's *The Book of the Law* (included as an appendix in this volume). Although one reason I selected this text is because it is the magnum opus of the most important occultist of the twentieth century, the work also complies with the fourth guideline of intrinsic criticism: it presents itself as a divinely inspired, poetic rebus unparalleled by any other text in human history. As will soon become apparent, intrinsic criticism is precisely the kind of criticism called for by the text for penetrating the depths of its revelations. Yet an intrinsic approach to this text soon reveals that its origins are secular and undeniably "human." Along the way I will try to adhere to the three remaining guidelines of intrinsic criticism as well: first, I attempt to stay within the text and approach it on its own terms; second, I attempt to understand the text sympathetically; and third, I attempt to allow textual structures to emerge and, in turn, to let them suggest ways of interpretation.

A Close Reading of *The Book of the Law*

The Book of the Law is a short work of verse that Aleister Crowley claimed was dictated to him in 1904 by a supernatural ambassador of the Egyptian god Horus. Crowley misplaced the manuscript, but after he relocated it in 1909, nothing received as much attention in his entire corpus than the "law" of this presumably holy book.

The book collects the revelations of three distinct personae, as told by a "praeterhuman intelligence" whom Crowley called "Aiwass" or "Aiwaz." In many writings after the book's dictation, Crowley referred to Aiwass as a supernatural being, as a great white chief or one of the "secret brothers," as his "holy guardian angel," and even as his "subconscious self." Yet for Crowley, "in any case, whatever 'Aiwaz' is, 'Aiwaz' is an Intelligence possessed of power and knowledge absolutely beyond human experience."[33] This intelligence was summoned by means of various invocations that took place in Egypt, beginning on March 16, 1904. The "law" started rolling when, probably trying to impress his new wife, Rose, Crowley successfully invoked Thoth—and unintentionally, Horus—on the next day. All the rituals that the couple performed during the months of March and April are referred to as the "Cairo Working." The uninvited Horus, speaking through Rose on March 17, directed Crowley to a funerary stele in a nearby museum that depicted Horus among two other gods. The stele was given the catalog number 666. Because Crowley associated himself with that ominous number from the biblical Book of Revelation ("the mark of the beast"), he found the stele's two sides rife with magical significance. On the obverse of the stele was a poem. The subject of the poem is the three gods depicted on the front: Nuit (or Nut), Hadit (Behdet, Horus the Behdetite), and Ra-Hoor-Khuit (Re-Horakhty). Nuit is an Egyptian sky goddess. Horus's Heliopolitan origins are various, but he is most commonly recognized as the falcon-god and the son of Isis. Crowley later tells us that Horus's manifestation as Hadit "is a mathematical expression rather than a God."[34] Ra-Hoor-Khuit (or more commonly Re-Horakhty among Egyptologists) is a "Heliopolitan composite of the sun god Re and Horus in his solar aspect, and his compound name means Re-and-Horus-of-the-Two-Horizons (or, in another form, Re-and-Horus-of-the-Horizon)."[35]

In studying the "Stele of Revealing," Crowley claimed to have been searching for new magical formulas for his work in a secret order that he created in the wake of the demise of the Golden Dawn, the A:.A:. (sometimes referred to by others as the *Argentinum Astrum* or "Silver Star," although Crowley eventually denied these significations). His new wife, however, channeling a god (presumably Horus again), shooed him to another task. Hymenaeus Beta, Crowley's intellectual heir and the current head of another organization Crowley headed called the Ordo Templi Orientis (O.T.O.), summarizes that the "culmination of the Cairo Working came on April 8, 9, and 10 of 1904. Following Rose's instructions, Crowley entered the temple [crafted in a hotel room] at noon each day and wrote down what he heard for an hour. He received a direct dictation from an intelligence that described himself as 'the minister of Hoor-paar-kraat' (Harpocrates) named Aiwaz or Aiwass. This is *The Book of the Law*."[36] Crowley claims that he initially hated the book and thought that many of its "ethical" underpinnings were suspect, yet later he found himself mysteriously drawn to it, eventually declaring that his "entire previous life was but a preparation for this event [the reception of *The Book of the Law*], and my entire subsequent life . . . wrapped up in it."[37]

An intrinsic approach to Crowley's texts bids us to poke a bit beyond the wrapping of Crowley's biography to locate what the text announces as its own function. Determining what the text seems to announce it is here to do for humankind can yield a number of insights about it that we might not otherwise ordinarily see if read in the shadow of Crowley's many metacommentaries and interpretations. Then a comparison of the functions Crowley himself afforded the book—external functions—can be fruitfully read against the internal functions.

Internally, *The Book of the Law* invites the reader or hearer to perform orally, and thereby embody, the text. Internally it also invites a comparison of its three chapters—an intrinsic reading that consists of comparative exegesis. These two internal invitations betoken a third mediating function, that of moving readers or hearers to ecstasy, a function that Crowley reinforces externally. Below I suggest that the text itself fails to follow through on its promise to transport readers and hearers to ecstasy, but that it does ingeniously work to establish Crowley's authority and credibility via its very instability.

Humor Me, or, Internally Speaking

In general, *The Book of the Law* is most easily divided into three sections, each of which harbors different speakers and different implied audiences. The three chapters are the messages of three different personae speaking through Aiwass, who is supposedly speaking to Crowley.[38] For simplicity, I will designate the speakers according to their remarks in the opening verses of chapters 1, 2, and 3:

> Had! The manifestation of Nuit.
> Nu! the hiding of Hadit.
> Abrahadabra! the reward of Ra Hoor Khut.

The three personae announced here are, of course, Nuit, Hadit, and Ra-Hoor-Khuit. Because the book was dictated to Crowley by Aiwass on the behalf of Horus via these three entities, the question of primary authorship is ambiguous.[39] Notably, each of the three beginning verses mirrors the others, beginning with an exclamatory (hereafter "ecophonesis," which denotes exclamations of strong emotion) followed by a disclosure. The personae of chapters 1 and 2, of course, link intercourse by removing syllables (acopoce) of their lover's name and rendering the names into commands or calls. This exchange results in a union that is Ra-Hoor-Khuit, whose ecophonectic entrance is not only an exclamation—"Behold! I am here!"—but also, and significantly for Crowley, a gift or formula (ABRAHADABRA, whose Qabalistic number is 418). The various parallelisms of the opening lines of the three chapters announce themselves as interrelated synchronically and paradigmatically on the vertical or associative axis of semiosis: their meanings penetrate in nonlinear ways as well as cumulatively (building upon each other in time). *The Book of the Law* trumpets itself in chapters that are clearly meant to be progressive, not only because of their ordering from front to back but also because each chapter symbolically represents a sexual union and their product in the son of chapter 3, Ra-Hoor-Khuit.

The textual interconnections of these introductory verses indicate that the text need not be read linearly only (beginning to end), however, for it also invites comparative exegesis. Such a request is directly addressed in verse 73 of chapter 3, where Ra-Hoor-Khuit commands a backward reading: "Paste the sheets from right to left and from top to bottom: then behold!" If heeded, such an invitation to comparative readings leads to the recognition of other correspondences among the three chapters, as we find here in chapters 2 (verse 48) and 3 (verse 18):

> 48. Pity not the fallen! I never knew them. I am not for them. I console not: I hate the consoled & the consoler.
>
> 18. Mercy let be off: damn them who pity! Kill and torture; spare not; be upon them!

Similar repetitive movement at the level of the syllable (the mode seems to be five) abides the surface meaning of these ethical commandments, one from Hadit, the other from Ra-Hoor-Khuit (who are, incidentally, different manifestations of Horus). Although it is hard to imagine any sound-puns here, there is a kind of parallelism of sound (paromoiosis) between the two lines.

The invitation to exegetical comparison indicated by the three opening verses of *The Book of the Law,* however, is related to a second internal function indicated by the syllabic repetitions and ecophonetic addresses of "Had!" and "Nu!" and "Abrahadabra!": the text should be performed aloud. The most obvious feature of "Abrahadabra," for instance, is its syllabic repetitions, assonance and consonance, which are particularly divulging of the text's performative function. These exclamatory remarks—perhaps classifiable as apostrophe since they seem to indicate a turning to the different personae of the books as well as to the reader and Crowley—hint at an emotional orality more typical of a poetic impulse and, hence, mark a moment when the text seeks to request admission into the poetic.[40] In general, strongly euphonic and rhythmic texts tend to push silent readers to pronunciation (e.g., Dr. Seuss's occult classic, *Green Eggs and Ham*), perhaps to elide inferior patterns within the visual text, as I think is often the case with *The Book of the Law.*[41]

At the beginning of chapter 1, for example, *The Book of the Law* invites spokenness in a sharp, serrated sequence of cluttered, concatenated consonance:

> 7. Behold! It is revealed by Aiwass the minister of Hoor-paar-krat.
>
> 8. The Khabs is in the Khu, not the Khu in the Khabs.
>
> 9. Worship them the Khabs, and behold my light shed over you!

These verses are typical of the rhythmic aspirations of the text, moving from one "K" sound to the next as the "K" sound helps to denote moments of stress: "The *Khabs* is in the *Khu,* not the *Khu* in the *Khabs.* Worship then the *Khabs* and behold my light shed over you!" announces its most literal or surface meaning as sonorous (Crowley says as much, stressing the "musical simplicity of form" in his commentaries).[42]

The Book of the Law also utilizes rhythm to invite its performance. In chapter 1, for example, when the chief topic of discussion is sex, rhythm is frequently used for an iconic effect:

> 61. I love you! I yearn to you! Pale or purple, veiled or voluptuous, I who am all pleasure and purple, and drunkenness of the innermost sense, desire you. Put on the wings, and arouse the coiled splendor within you: come unto me!
>
> 62. At all my meetings with you shall the priestess say—and her eyes shall burn with the desire as she stands bare and rejoicing in my secret temple—To me! To me! calling forth the flame of the hearts in her love-chant.
>
> 63. Sing the rapturous love-song unto me! Burn to me perfumes! Wear to me jewels! Drink to me, for I love you! I love you!

The orchestration of rhythm here is achieved through a combination of repetitions and sound-imitations.[43] "Me" and "you" come together repeatedly in the author's attempt to resemble sexual union, perhaps with the reader and the text, as some attempt is made toward consonance-as-copulation. Indeed, the sentence length becomes increasingly shorter as it speeds toward a climax, like one's breathing in passionate sexual intercourse. Most significant, however, is the repetition of "to me," which has been read as the Greek "TO MH" ("toe meh") by Crowley and his followers, which means "the not." The claim here is that the construction of "to me" strives toward iconicity insofar as chapter 1 forwards a Taoist principle (to name the Tao is to lose it; to experience the Tao is to know it).[44] "To me" quickens as we reach the end of the chapter, appearing closer and closer to each other in verse until we reach it unclothed in 65: "To me! To me!" Thus, one makes love to the book and embodies it by reading it aloud, a textual erotics remarkably similar to the intrinsic critic's "merging" with and "vibrating" against the text.

Insofar as this passage is doubly seductive—"read me aloud" and "merge with me"—it can also be argued that the book attempts to close the pragmatic divide between form and content. Texts that aspire to the complete collapse of form and content by moving us to speak them and study them—in essence, to embody them—strive toward what Kenneth Burke has called "pure persuasion," a moment of identification so total that one has difficulty distinguishing between self and text.[45] Of course, no text, however great or moving, will ever achieve pure persuasion, because its very existence as text presupposes its discontinuity. Nevertheless, the point here is that texts that request close analysis *and* performance—such as the Bible, the Koran, *Hamlet,* and e.e. cummings's "my specialty is living said"—always work toward the collapse of form and content.

The oral/participatory and interpretative functions of the text, however, do not exhaust the functions revealed with an attention to other elements. Exclamation marks and apostrophe abound throughout, signaling its grandiloquent tone in a kind of bombastic urgency comparable to the ravings of Nietzsche's Zarathustra or the spectacle of wrestling. Further, its choice of archaic words ("thee," "thy," "ye," "availeth," and so on) proclaims the text as sacred document, connoting ancient religiosity and, by extension, divine authority. The text clearly functions as a religious or holy book to be consulted for guidance. Not surprisingly, this external function of *The Book of the Law* mirrors the function and name of the holy book of all Masonic rituals, "The Volume of the Sacred Law," with which Crowley was most certainly familiar.

The Impotence of Ecstasy, or, Externally Speaking

Although Crowley seemed to believe sincerely that *The Book of the Law* was inspired by superhuman intelligences, its clichéd imagery, overwrought style, and overdone ecophonetic displays are too similar to Crowley's other poetic writings to be the product of something supernatural.[46] Crowley claims, however, that "Shakespeare could not have written it [*The Book of the Law*]: still less could Keats, Shelly, Swift, Sterne or even Wordsworth," all of them of inferior skill.[47] Crowley felt that it was the most important thing he ever penned:

> No forger could have prepared so complex a set of numerical and literal puzzles as to leave himself (a) devoted to the solution for years after, (b) baffled by a simplicity which when disclosed leaves one gasping at its profundity, (c) enlightened only by progressive initiation, or by "accidental" events apparently disconnected with the Book, which occurred long after its publication, (d) hostile, bewildered, and careless even in the face of independent testimony as to the power and clarity of the Book, and of the fact that by Its light other men have attained the loftiest summits of initiation in the tithe of the time which history and experience would lead one to expect, and (e) angrily unwilling to proceed with that part of the Work appointed for him which is detailed in Chapter III [the command to bind the book in a certain way, and to write a commentary].[48]

Many of Crowley's writings evince a strong desire to assert the divine nature of *The Book of the Law* in a manner similar to this passage. "I testify, as a Master of English, that I am utterly incapable, even when most inspired, of such English as I find in that Book again and again."[49] Clearly, *The Book of the Law* is Crowley's bible. (Moreover, although Crowley says he is "incapable" of writing *The Book of the Law,* he is nevertheless in the position to judge its divinely inspired perfections—a good indication that the arbitrariness of the authoritative power of interpretation is at issue.)

Crowley argued that *The Book of the Law* is superior to the great literature of the West because of the way in which it operates symbolically. He stressed that work's genius resides not merely at the level of the "vehicle," I. A. Richard's term for a metaphor's signifier or sound-image (e.g., the word or the level of the metaphorical substitution itself), to which literary and rhetorical critics often look for "artistry," but also in a symbolic and melodious phraseology just below the syllabic surface. This is the "tenor," which is not *like* the substitution at all, but rather a surrogate. In this way, for example, Crowley, rescues the metaphorical banality of phrases like "burning desire" from the abyss of pretentious and bad writing by stressing they are poetic and *numerical* substitutions. To understand how the reader is urged to read *The Book of the Law* in this highly symbolic manner (one that cuts against the potentially dismissive reactions to the pretentious surface meaning), then, we have to address the external functions Crowley afforded the text.

In addition to its function as a fetishized, holy book, another external function of *The Book of the Law* is intimately tied to the internal function of embodied performativity: *The Book of the Law* is intended as an opiate, as a transportive device for magicians on their ascent to higher planes of reality. This ascent marks the progress of any magical aspirant in secret magical organizations. Achievement of different levels of reality is called a "degree" or "grade." A more contemporary example is found in the complex hierarchy of the O.T.O., which is premised on a two-tiered degree system (one for the lower grades, one for the higher). The first seven grades concern learning basic magic (currently, reading a good deal of Crowley's writings). Only in the next three grades is one permitted to learn and practice sex magick techniques (reportedly Tantric, although the current author is unfortunately not in the position to know). Admission to the ninth degree means that one can participate in the governance of the O.T.O. It is the second tier of individual or subjective progress, however, that *The Book of the Law* ultimately aims to open for the aspirant. Religious scholar J. Gordon Melton explains that in the O.T.O.,

> while the degree system is related to specific work accomplished and the granting of access to even higher levels of secret teaching material, there is a separate hierarchical system related to one's level of magical occult attainment. While one can be graded and passed upon lessons and exercise which make up degree work, the accomplishments of occult attainment can only be judged by the self as they involve the acceptance of certain tasks, passing through different experiences, and the development of various elements of the self. Especially in the higher grades, the arrival at a new grade is proclaimed not granted, though usually, after a new level is reached, a magician will look to others for confirmation.[50]

Given the text's internal aspirations, it is clear that *The Book of the Law* is intended as catalyst for an experience of the sublime—an aesthetic accomplishment—helping the aspirant toward the attainment higher magical grades.[51] *The Book of the Law*'s internal consonances and invitations toward speech seem intended to motion toward ecstasy externally (as are the text's invitations to get "lost" in its many correspondences through Qabalistic interpretation—a method of reading that assigns numeric value to letters that I discuss in more depth in the next chapter).[52] In relation to the internal dynamic of collapsing form onto content, externally *The Book of the Law* attempts to catch the reader or hearer in the binary of doing and being, the internal and the external thus meeting at the interface of ecstatic experience.

It is not by accident that Crowley often uses the term "sublime" to characterize the way he believes *The Book of the Law* is designed to work. A man schooled in literature at Cambridge, Crowley would have been familiar with the literary discussions and debates that revolved around the "sublime," a concept that first emerged in European literary circles in the sixteenth century after the "rediscovery" of a first-century C.E. manuscript attributed to Longinus titled *On the Sublime*. The treatise, written as a polemical response to a Sicilian rhetorician whom Longinus disliked, details the ways and means by which a writer and speaker can induce feelings of awe and wonder in readers and audiences. By the nineteenth century, the concept of "sublimity" had been expanded by philosophers like Edmund Burke and Immanuel Kant to signify an aesthetic or perceptive experience of awe and speechlessness while in the presence of some indescribably awesome or fantastic object of nature or human design.[53] For Burke such an experience excites the "passions which belong to self-preservation," premised in turn on experiences of pain and danger. This experience, while terrifying, is in some sense delightful but "not pleasure."[54] For Kant the sublime is a "negative pleasure" in that there is no positive boundary or limit to the sublime object that is perceived; the sublime object, signifying "boundlessness" in every way conceivable, does "violence to the imagination" and breaks the hold of reason, in turn profoundly unsettling the "sovereignty" of the experienced and conscious self.[55] In nature these sublime objects were things like the ocean, large mountains or impossibly deep canyons, scenes made famous and inserted into the U.S. popular imaginary by the nineteenth-century paintings of the American landscape and the "American sublime" movement in poetry.[56]

In literary circles, the claim was made by some that truly great poetry—and rarely prose—could also achieve sublime effect on the hearer or reader.[57] It is entirely fitting, then, that Crowley invokes the trope of the "sublime" at numerous places in his commentaries on *The Book of the Law* to signify moments of linguistic transport:

> The style is simple and sublime; the imagery is gorgeous and faultless; the rhythm is subtle and intoxicating; the theme is interpreted in faultless symphony. There are no errors of grammar,

> no infelicities of phrase. Each Book is perfect in its kind. . . . Terse, yet sublime, are these verses of this Book; subtle yet simple; matchless for rhythm, direct as a ray of light. This imagery is gorgeous without decadence. It deals primarily with ideas. It announces revolutions in philosophy, religion, ethics, yea, in the whole nature of Man. For this it needs no more than to roll sea-billows solemnly forth, eight words, as "*Every man and every woman is a star,*" or it burst in a mountain torrent of monosyllables as "*Do what thou wilt shall be the whole of the Law.*"[58]

Further, in an explanation of verses 17–25 in chapter 2, Crowley describes the embodiment of magical language (presumably through chanting in ritual and ceremony) as a kind of sublime perfection: "We therefore empty various magical means to increase the vigor of our bodies and the energy of our minds, to fortify and sublime them."[59] Apparently, *The Book of the Law* is not only a sublime text but also assists in the magician's "subliming" of the body and mind—if there is such a thing—into a perfect unity or magical perfection previously unimaginable in the preceding Aeon of Osiris. In the new Age of Horus, unspeakable perfections are possible. The unification of the body and mind is not merely metaphorical, for it also indicates the authentic movement of magick, which is the unification of one's self on multiple planes of existence, bringing them together, as if the magician is an erect phallus penetrating them all simultaneously (Crowley understands this magickal brand of unification in a patently sexual manner).[60]

As if to present a good role model or to provide a declamatory exercise, sublime experience is modeled for the reader or hearer in chapter 2, where the persona abruptly changes from that of Hadit to Crowley himself, presumably in ecstatic release:

> 61. There is a light before thine eyes, o prophet, a light undesired, most desirable.
>
> 62. I am uplifted in thine heart; and the kisses of the stars rain hard upon thy body.
>
> 63. Thou art exhaust in the voluptuous fullness of the inspiration; the expiration is sweeter than death, more rapid and laughterful than a caress of Hell's own worm.
>
> 64. Oh! thou art overcome: we are upon thee; our delight is all over thee: hail! hail: prophet of Nu! prophet of Had! prophet of Ra-Hoor-Khu! Now rejoice! now come in our splendor & rap-

ture! Come in our passionate peace, & write sweet words for the Kings!

65. I am the Master: thou art the Holy Chosen One.

66. Write, & find ecstasy in writing! Work, & be our bed in working! Thrill with the joy of life & death! Ah! thy death shall be lovely: whoso seeth it shall be glad. Thy death shall be the seal of the promise of our agelong love. Come! lift up thine heart & rejoice! We are one; we are none.

67. Hold! Hold! Bear up in thy rapture; fall not in swoon of the excellent kisses!

68. Harder! Hold up thyself! Lift thine head! breathe not so deep—die!

69. Ah! Ah! What do I feel? Is the word exhausted?

70. There is help & hope in other spells. Wisdom says: be strong! Then canst thou bear more joy. Be not animal; refine thy rapture! If thou drink, drink by the eight and ninety rules of art: if thou love, exceed by delicacy; and if thou do aught joyous, let there be subtlety therein!

The rhythmic exclamations are designed to approximate the experience called forth—sublimity, here as orgasmic release, and as in verses 67 and 68, where we locate the image of a thrusting erection and the exhaustion that ensues, cheekily, in verse 69. Indeed, in 69 Crowley is at a loss for words (or at least announces himself to be, and, of course, in this particular sexual "position" everyone is speechless).[61] Curiously, the torrent of sharp consonant "t" sounds in verse 63 ("Thou art exhaust in the voluptuous fullness of the inspiration; the expiration is sweeter than death") is grating—unmelodious at best—and reminds the reader or hearer that the ecstasy here displayed is solely that of Crowley. Although this passage may be descriptive of an ecstatic experience, the reader or hearer is certainly not going to be moved similarly by reading or hearing about it in this passage.

Strange Bedfellows

Thus far I have argued that an intrinsic reading of *The Book of the Law* uncovers three textual invitations: an invitation to speak it (signified by Nuit), an invitation to study it (signified by Hadit), and an invitation to transcend it (signified by Ra-Hoor-Khuit). As Lucas urges, by parsing the book at "the level of the sentence, phrase, word," and in some cases at the level of the syllable, one is better able to "shed light on both its literary qualities and on its rhetorical power."[62] One discovers, for example, how syllabic repetitions in *The Book of the Law* urge that the text be spoken and thereby embodied; one discovers how the frequent use of exclamation and apostrophe parallels the external functions of sublime transport afforded to the book by Crowley; and one discovers that *The Book of the Law* is not artistically dense enough to keep us comfortably inside it. Despite these insights, when held to the standard of "literary art" that the text and its author invite, *The Book of the Law* fails miserably because of its overwrought metaphor and tired poetic devices. *The Book of the Law* is, in fact, a very ugly text, and its rhetorical power cannot be derived from its attempts at artistry alone.

One is only able to account for the success of the book among Crowley's followers by looking elsewhere, by widening the context of the book beyond its pages to surrounding texts. I suggest that this elsewhere can be described in terms of two kinds of rhetorical power. First, because we cannot locate the rhetorical power of *The Book of the Law* in its internal dynamics, we must locate it externally in the textual persona of Crowley, particularly in his specter as it is embedded within a whole constellation of texts that he left behind (this is my concern in the following chapter). Second, and more pertinent to the textual focus of this chapter, the rhetorical power of *The Book of the Law* is a consequence of its fetishization as an object, the result of the attribution of powers (e.g., artistry, magical transport, and so on) that it does not really possess. The rhetorical power of a fetishized text is an occult power, a suasive force that is not tied to the actual content of a text but rather to its form and appearance. Textual occultism, as the fetishization of a given text as a magical object to be revered, thus entails at least two features by the reading subject: first, faith that the text harbors a secret route to transcendence; and second, a blindness to the fact that the text does not actually possess such a secret.

Crowley understood the power of fetishization and, as his metacommentaries demonstrate, worked hard to make sure his holy book developed an aura. For the remainder of this chapter it is instructive to compare Crowley's occult modes of interpretation to close textual criticism because of the lessons it teaches us about critical power. Both are "occult" procedures obsessed with the disclosure of textual secrets; both work toward an alignment of representation and referent or an iconicity of expression; both invite an erotics—a willed embodiment or penetration of the text, a synthesis of textual and critical experience (Crowley's text quite explicitly: "To me! To me!" it beckons);[63] and both strive toward something extratextual beyond the particular uses of language in a discrete text—a presence, a transcendental signified, an ultimate stop, a trans-rhetorical "truth." Because occult hermeneutics and close textual or intrinsic criticism court fetishization, rhetorical scholars risk the establishment of their own secret societies without continuous and reflexive attempts to mediate text and context, content and form.

Intrinsic criticism's quest for this truth in a text—often in terms of its successful fusion of form and content by means of ingenious artistry—represents a productive, critical blindness to what Hans-Georg Gadamer terms an institutionalized "pre-understanding" or "horizon" of interpretation. This pre-understanding implies that all interpretation is historically and institutionally contingent. That the intrinsic critic attempts to "merge" with the text in circular or cyclical interplays of his or her consciousness with the experiences embedded in the text is symptomatic of a reflexive attempt to overcome this blindness and, in so doing, provide productive insights.[64] In other words, the quest for textual truths or structures with a recognition of institutional constraints, or rather their dialectical interplay, is the motor of critical invention. Gadamer explains that "the horizon of the present is being continually formed, in that we have continually to test our prejudices. An important part of this testing is the encounter with the past and the understanding of the tradition from which we come. Hence the horizon of the present cannot be formed without the past. There is no more an isolated horizon of the present than there are historical horizons. Understanding, rather, is always the fusion of these horizons which we imagine to exist by themselves."[65] The illusion of the autonomy of textual horizons is in fact the source of a given text's seduction, and the failure to recognize the institutionally imposed, historically contingent interpretive frames of our time ("pre-understanding") is a blindness that can quickly fall into, as Godzich puts it, "the isolation of thoughts and ideas and their conversion into autonomous objects of knowledge independent of their productive ground; in other words, their reification."[66] For Gadamer and, by extension, intrinsic criticism, the task of authentic interpretation "involves the experience of the tension between the text and the present. The hermeneutic task consists, not in covering up this tension by attempting a naïve assimilation, but in consciously bringing it out."[67] Consciously bringing out this tension helps to avoid an ironic phenomenon of reification, whereby the text becomes an entity unto itself, fetishized as an object, that may in turn come to govern critical practice.

That the blindness of intrinsic interpretation threatens the fetishization of discrete texts also underscores the religiosity of the critical quest for textual light. Paul Ricoeur would describe intrinsic criticism as a "hermeneutics of faith," one that strives toward the "recollection of meaning" by playing off the horizon-structures that emerge from reading a text against disciplined, interpretive structures in the consciousness of the critic.[68] If one understands religiosity as a strong and faithful reverence for something (be it a fetish or a god, or rather the fetishization of a god), then one might understand the intrinsic critic's quest for artistic structure as a faith in *logos,* the fetishization of the masterpiece being a consequence of this faith. For Ricoeur, the paradigm example of a hermeneutics of faith is Husserlian (transcendental) phenomenology, the key feature of which is the governing principle of the *epochê,* a concept that means "to suspend or step back from our ordinary ways of looking, to set aside our usual assumptions regarding things."[69] It is not coincidental that the *epochê* is almost identical to the intrinsic critic's initial, virginal, and reverent encounter of a text, "unmediated by a predetermined perspective, ideology, or formula." Indeed, in this sense intrinsic criticism and phenomenology must be read in the context of scientific discourse, since for both the critical quest is to discern apodictic structures or "invariant factors." The "faith" of intrinsic criticism is the confidence that language itself will call forth such structures, since "the belief that language, which bears symbols, is not so much spoken by men as spoken to men, that men are born into language, into the light of the logos."[70] The "faith" in a hermeneutics of faith is not, then, a faith in the use of language within a particular text, nor is it necessarily a faith in the text's ability to provide its own context. Rather, the faith cued here is a faith in language writ large, in the capacity of language to signify, in the ability, for example, of the strategic use of consonance to tell us something about "oratorical art" during the reflexive fusion of past and present horizons of understanding in the act of interpretation. The faith is in criticism as a process of recollection, that what is just beneath the surface can be brought out in some authentic way. Ironically, then, the faith of intrinsic criticism is in something external to the particular utterance or text in question: *logos,* language in itself, oratorical art, symbolic interaction, and so on. Like the Qabalist or Hermeticist who seeks intimations of the universe in the particular ("as above, so below"), like Crowley urging us to push beyond what seems to be dead metaphor, the intrinsic critic's microscopic parsing aims for something bound by a text but also something that is well beyond its particular linguistic horizon. Were this not so, there would be no point in a close or deep reading.

What I am suggesting is that in order to avoid fetishizing and thereby occulting texts, the practice of intrinsic criticism should resemble a refitted, Gadamerian hermeneutics that strives toward an authentic interpretation by recognizing and utilizing the pre-understanding (historical contingencies, including modes of interpretation among the scholarly community) to make sense of a text's meaning in the present. More recent explications of Gadamerian approaches to interpretation, such as Steven Mailloux's explication of "rhetorical hermeneutics," do seek to incorporate institutional histories (e.g., the indelible mark of New Criticism on interpretive practice) as a means to articulate the many social forces that contribute to textual meaning, past and present—all in hopes of producing a more "authentic" or true reading. As Mailloux puts it, "rhetorical hermeneutics proposes to set aside the problem of explanation interpretation in terms of the characteristics of readers and the elements of texts and focus instead on the rhetorical dynamics among interpreters within specific cultural settings. In such a hermeneutics, theory soon turns into rhetorical history. . . . Thus rhetorical hermeneutics describes the ebb and flow of the cultural conversation and rejects foundationalist attempts to ground knowledge, interpretation, and reading outside of the rhetorical context of history."[71] By setting aside "the elements of texts" Mailloux does not mean textual structures but rather the articulation of textual structures as absolute and determined by textual limits (at its most basic, the four sides of a page), since pre-understandings always color the interpretation of those structures in a particular, material, historical moment. One should also note, however, that rhetorical hermeneutics locates an authentic reading in institutional histories—controversy over interpretations—not in terms of watershed moments in material history. It is also significant that Mailloux is concerned with the interpretation of fiction.

Within U.S. rhetorical studies, however, intrinsic criticism has elided the important ontological distinction between the "nonfiction" texts of its domain and the fictional status of literary texts. Unlike literary criticism, much rhetorical criticism has staked its disciplinary claim on the notion that rhetorical production, by definition, is a practical art that is embedded within a particular context, that is inclusive of particular individuals, and that addresses some immediate exigency. Literary texts, by contrast, announce their own fictionality in their necessarily symbolic or allegorical formulations, forgoing attempts to represent reality in accord with some logic of coherence, correspondence, or accuracy. For literary theorist Paul de Man, literature is a superior cultural form because it recognizes the impossibility of reconciling the recalcitrance and immutability of the natural world with human desire—in other words, literature rests comfortably within a rhetorical understanding of the contingency of representation, indeed, of "truth." That a synthesis is not possible, says de Man, is premised on a nothingness or lack that literature is tirelessly and "persistent[ly] naming." "In the same manner that the poetic lyric originates in moments of tranquility, in the absence of actual emotions, and then proceeds to invent fictional emotions to create the illusion of recollection, the work of fiction invents fictional subjects to create the illusion of the reality of others. But the fiction is not a myth, for it knows and names itself as fiction."[72] Such a knowing acceptance of the impossibility of unmediated truth is an acceptance of a fundamental negativity of experience (an inability to satiate desire) and an embrace of the figural, which for de Man is an embrace and celebration of the rhetorical.[73] This notion is similar to an occult poetics, one that is premised on the paradoxical notion of the describability of ineffability. One could easily substitute the ineffable for the void that de Man finds literature continually naming in therapeutic gestures. To wit: just as literature ceaselessly continues to name the void, so also do occultists tirelessly attempt to describe truths that are forever beyond human comprehension in language. In its artistic failures, Crowley's *The Book of the Law* demonstrates the frustrations that result from rejecting the contingency of the figural while holding onto a transcendent, translinguistic truth.

Crowley's inability to let go of a translinguistic truth, to succumb to a rhetorical view of language that sees language as constitutive of reality, creates a considerable tension in all his writings. In light of de Man's understanding of "the void," a Lacanian "lack" that literature very consciously attempts to "name" in its many fictions, one might say that Crowley renders this negativity of de Man's description into a positivity, a transcendental signified that guarantees his writings in the astral light. The intrinsic critic makes a very similar move in his or her commingling of the materiality of a text's historical context with the fiction of artistry. The negativity or ineffability that literature continually attempts to name has become a positivity—a historical event, a crisis, a controversy, a "rhetorical situation" that calls forth a response, or on the other side, an artistic genius intentionally and consciously crafting an essay or speech.

Indeed, the significance of the texts studied by intrinsic critics is often established with a stress on the pressing, external recalcitrance of historical moments or the importance of a particular individual (textual pragmatics), but the goal is often an authentic reading of texts in the service of illuminating "great art" (tropological artistry).

Prima facie there does not appear to be a conflict of interest here, and as some have remarked, "the assumption that literary and practical discourse are different in kind . . . is no longer accepted universally and has come under increasingly sharp attack."[74] Yet the problem is not that literary and practical discourse cannot be equally artful (or that, in the end, these modes really are *not* ontologically distinct); rather, the problem is one of internal and external justifications and the way they orient the critic, that the authentic reading of a text must come to terms with historical materiality and artistic forms simultaneously, that one can move among multiple contextual rungs fluidly. Can one even guarantee a coherence among multiple contexts? On the one hand texts are selected because of their extratextual, historical importance, but on the other hand one is urged to let the text suggest its own proper contextualization. The former tends to assume a stability of meaning internal to the text within a continuum of history, while the latter assumes a stability of meaning ironically external to the text—the guarantee of aesthetic form. The critical problematic of intrinsic criticism, then, is precisely that of attempting to preserve the integrity of the discrete text as "art" while uncovering contexts for its interpretation.[75] One observes, simultaneously, an impulse to take up the materiality of discourse as well as an impulse to disclose a general understanding of rhetorical artistry through the analysis of a discrete text.

Outside of historical justification, intrinsic criticism has tended to lean toward an ahistorical investigation of human creativity to resolve the tension between the historical and textual context, between the realist and idealist modes.[76] This is not necessarily because, as some have argued, intrinsic critics fear that extrinsic analysis too easily lends itself to jargon-inspiring "theory," or that intrinsic critics are working toward a reterritorialization of rhetorical studies in the wake of its colonization by the methodological pluralism of communication theorists.[77] To be sure, anxieties over theory do exist and often abide programmatic statements about intrinsic criticism. Still, one would be remiss not to admit that any intense examination of the particular puts the critic "in contact with matters of theoretical interest," primarily because such encounters tend to cue historical and institutional horizons, inclusive of theoretical assumptions.[78] Rather, I think that one can understand the preoccupation with the aesthetic autonomy of the text as a contemporary weigh station on a mystical highway that begins, ultimately, in the desire to know the autonomous self through an interrogation of art. In other words, intrinsic criticism, as much as New Criticism and Crowley's interpretive practice, is an occultic mode of criticism. As de Man might say, it is intrinsic criticism's relative blindness to this important institutional precursor, to the conditions of its own pre-understanding, that is responsible for its most brilliant insights.

Concluding Remarks: Wielding Critical Power without Wands

In this chapter I have done two things. First, I have offered an intrinsic reading of Aleister Crowley's *The Book of the Law* that explains, to some extent, how the text attempts to move readers and hearers. But more important from a theoretical standpoint, I have been using my close reading of a modern occult text, *The Book of the Law,* as a platform for arguing that intrinsic criticism tends toward an occultic mode of interpretation very similar to that prescribed by Crowley. Intrinsic criticism's Qabalistic conflation of method and object in its attempt to render authentic readings of texts creates a number of critical difficulties, the most conspicuous of which is an inability to move among multiple contexts, especially between the historical or practical and the artistic or literary. The consequent tendency has been to neglect the materiality of texts in favor of the art forms disclosed by them—in favor, that is, of fetishization. In closing, I suggest that this tendency risks perpetuating the establishment of secret communities—affinities among scholars regarding fetishized texts, their transcendent truths, and who has the authority to interpret them.

An intrinsic critic's surgical approach to texts belies a general discomfort with the contingency of the rhetorical worldview in its desire to read *through* artful surfaces toward something (falsely) universal. This general anxiety about the rhetoricity of texts, in turn, feeds into a particularly "romantic aesthetic" or "pedagogy" that returns us, once again, to the consideration of interpretation as the exercise of power. Absent an explicit method and denied a context, intrinsic criticism must inevitably rely on the genius model of criticism. Better or worse interpretations of the texts cannot be measured in terms of a scale of widely known values but instead in terms of the virtuoso performance of the critic *without restraint.* Consequently, the intrinsic critic falls under the spell of the fetishized text. As Foucault charged of Derrida's theory of text in one exchange, a romantic pedagogy "teaches the pupil that there is nothing outside the text, but that in it, in its gaps, its blanks, and its silences, there reigns the reserve of the origin; that it is therefore unnecessary to search elsewhere, but that here, not in the words, certainly, but in the words under erasure, in their grid, the 'sense of being' is said. A pedagogy which gives conversely to the master's voice the limitless sovereignty which allow it to restate the text indefinitely."[79] In light of its erotics, the romantic tendencies underlying intrinsic criticism, of course, are obvious. What an analysis of Crowley's *The Book of the Law* and its metacommentaries helps us to see, however, is that intrinsic criticism invites the kind of textual fetishization that produces interpretive authorities. As Foucault observed, for the textual occultist the master hermeneut is the one who is invested with the authority to reveal the transcendent secrets of the text, and only he or she is allowed to "restate the text indefinitely." These tendencies help to explain why the intrinsic criticism of U.S. rhetorical studies often appeals to mysterious criteria for gauging good criticism: the standard of "rigor," for example, is erected by the expert critic, but what this means precisely is never revealed.[80] "Doing good work" is another common criterion of mystification particular to the virtuoso mode of criticism. Hence, for the beginning student or adept, learning criticism is akin to fumbling around in the dark, for its procedures are as mysterious as the intentional processes of the master's critical productions.[81]

Although I am concerned with pointing out the consequences of textual occultism, I do not mean to condemn the practice. I think it is inevitable; intrinsic criticism is a religious mode of study that satisfies, at some level, a human need, and as I argued in chapter 2, this need is catalyzed by the paradoxes of language use in general. In order to resist the undemocratic occult pedagogy that any hermeneutic of faith invites, however, the critic must become suspicious. At some moment in the critical act the critic must pull back from the text and constellate it in and among others in search of a transtextual form, a cultural logic, a social force, a movement of class formations and deformations. In other words, to avoid the perils of fetishization, intrinsic criticism must necessarily merge with extrinsic analyses in order to escape from the occult mode of interpretation that would render itself a variation of blind worship. Jameson characterizes this moving from text to context as movement from content to form, a dialectical mode of criticism. Form is not to be understood as merely a beginning "pattern or mold, as that from which we start, but rather as that with which we end up, as but the final articulation of the deeper logic of the content itself." Ultimately, for Jameson, "form is itself but the working out of content in the realm of the superstructure" or culture. In our pulling back from the text in pursuit of forms, the critic should always regard as "the signs of some deeper corresponding social and historical configuration."[82]

Lest I fall prey to my own critique, then, having meditated on the occult texts of Lévi, Blavatsky, and Crowley, it would now behoove me to articulate occult discourse in relationship to larger social or historical forms. Hence, in the next three chapters analysis moves to articulate occult discourse in relation to prophetic authority and the Hebraic rhetorical tradition, class structure and struggle, and the logics of late capitalism to escape the gravitational pull of the discrete text.

II
Exoterica

Interlude

Re-membering Crowley

I first confronted Aleister Crowley's face in church as a boy during a revivalist's slide show. The revivalist was a traveling Christian Evangelical preacher spreading the word of the Devil's doings in three-day seminars for young Christians. I can remember his coming to town every year since I was about six years old.[1] Before I saw my first "show" I was giddy; I had finally turned nine and was therefore old enough to see the preacher's slides and movies, many of which were "too graphic" and "too scary" for the younger folks.

I cannot remember with any precision what the revivalist did; I recall that he would carefully weave his incendiary sermons with slides of Satanic ritual chambers and movies about Anton LaVey, a Satanic priest (whom I will discuss at some length in chapter 7). He would play creepy music and sometimes would become so impassioned that he would cry. He worked us into a big upset, and then he would have the pianist play "Just as I Am" and make us weep and invite us—young people between the ages of nine to fourteen (maybe sixteen, but once cars were drivable young people tended to stop going to church)—to the altar to kneel and pray for Jesus to come into our hearts. Of course, after the big production, parents were encouraged to donate money to the "ministry."

One night the preacher's talk was about how Lucifer was in control of the rock music industry. He played Led Zeppelin's "Stairway to Heaven" backwards and had us focus on the verse that signaled Robert Plant's "prayer to Satan": in the lyric when Plant sings, "Yes there are two paths you can go by, but in long run, there's still time to change the road you're on," one hears something that sounds like "Satan, my sweet Satan" when the song is played in reverse. Then the preacher obsessed over the "Satanic" aesthetic of one of Ozzy Osborne's records, which Osborne deliberately courted to sell records. He played an "Ozzy" song for us that he characterized as a "hymn"

Fig. 6. Aleister Crowley (1875–1947). This photograph was taken in the 1920s. Courtesy of the Ordo Templi Orientis.

to Aleister Crowley, and pointed out that the "white horse" reference in the lyrics symbolized a penis, thus suggestive of Ozzy's sinful homosexuality.[2] As he showed us Crowley's mug on the cover of the Beatles' *Sgt. Pepper's Lonely Hearts Club Band* album (he is next to Mae West in the top left-hand row of faces), he told us Crowley was a famous Satanist who advocated the killing of babies and saying the Lord's Prayer backwards. The preacher followed this revelation with—I think, although I admit my memory here is dim—a story of a young Satanist whom he interviewed. He claimed that the young man confessed to sacrificing a baby at Satan's urging.

I find this all quite unbelievable today, although I do not dismiss its grave reality for a large number of people. This reality certainly is not the one that a self-labeled Satanist or occultist would claim, although there is something to be said about modern occultism's anti-Christian bent. Nevertheless, the revivalist's presentations scared me a great deal at that time, enough to help me remember them in some detail, at least. I remember I was afraid of Ozzy Osborne's music for years.

My personal introduction to Crowley (see fig. 6) reflects how most people are introduced to the occult today. We come to it through urban legends told around campfires or at church, we learn about it through the stories people tell during card games, we get into its meanings pondering the dark ambiguities of album covers or lyrics, and we make meaning of it watching movies and television. In this everyday respect the occult represents the "unknown," an arena of discourse to which we are necessarily "outsiders." Everyday tales that claim to illuminate the darkness of its inner circle invite a kind of pleasure—a pleasure akin to that of hearing a fictional horror story or watching a scary movie. The caveat, of course, is that these tales announce themselves to be true.

I also wrote about my personal encounter with Crowley because the stories I was told about him, most of which are the gleanings of a rich, collective imagination, persist to this day. Although it is impossible to verify because of the massive number of private and small publishing houses that are involved in evangelizing a Christian hardline, I would argue that most Christian "occult" guidebooks incorrectly characterize Crowley as a "Satanist" who advocated ritual sacrifice. Among the spate of these fear-inspired publications that appeared during the so-called "Satanic panic" of the late 1980s and early 1990s, the evangelical American Family Foundation's *Satanism and Occult-Related Violence: What You Should Know* provides a representative example of Crowley's reputation in fundamentalist discourse:

> A well-educated mountaineer, poet, and author (including works of pornography and sado-masochism), Crowley found his real home in the study of occultism. . . . While living in Cairo in 1904, allegedly under the guidance of his "Holy Guardian Angel," [he] produced a short, ecstatic occultist tirade entitled *The Book of the Law,* which includes such admonitions as "stamp down the wretched and the weak," "the slaves shall serve," "reason is a lie," "these vices are my service; ye do well, and I will reward you," "kill and torture; spare not." . . . In 1916 he assumed the grade of Magus (a high-level title in occultism) during a ceremony in which he crucified a frog and declared his triumph over Jesus Christ. After World War I, Crowley established the "abbey" of Thelema in Sicily, where he indulged in two of his favorite pastimes: ritual sex magic and drug abuse. There were rumors of child sacrifice at the abbey, from which Crowley and his followers were expelled in 1922. . . . [H]is influence on practitioners of "black magic" and Satanism has been enormous.[3]

Although this 1990 guide to "occult-related" violence is rife with innuendo, nothing claimed as factual is, strictly speaking, undocumented. Bob and Gretchen Passantino's less sensational *When the Devil Dares Your Kids* characterizes Crowley similarly and is careful to underscore that possession of Crowley's books is a sign of "your child's" occultist aspirations (the last chapter of the book has a step-by-step guide on how to "rescue your child from Satan").[4]

These charismatic Christian sources are not the best indicators of the wider status of Crowley in the popular imaginary, but they do much to illustrate how cultural logics of representation work through exaggeration. Although more subdued, the innuendo of contemporary mainstream newspaper representations parrots a similar logic, from Crowley's mention in the "Arts and Leisure" section of newspapers as a subcultural touchstone of darkness ("Aleister Crowley, the Satanist, is plotting to overthrow God," says Don Shirley in a *Los Angeles Times* review of a Jeffrey Dorchen play),[5] to his association with the dark rock of Jimmy Page and Ozzy Osborne ("Oh, Crowley would have delighted at Osborne's devilish antics over the years," snickers Howard Cohen of the *Buffalo News*),[6] to his books' mention as important tokens of evil. In the "Zodiac gunman" murder case in the early 1990s, the *New York Times* reported that "detectives seeking the so-called Zodiac gunman have obtained a subpoena for library records and are interviewing people who have recently requested books by an early 20th century Scottish poet who practiced black magic. . . . Investigators sought the subpoena because, they said, . . . the gunman may be inspired by the mystic, Aleister Crowley, a drug addict who practiced black magic and wrote books on the occult."[7] The same kinds of associations persist in Europe as well. A *Sunday Times* (U.K.) article bemoans the growing German interest in Satanism, which is "believed to be particularly strong in the northwestern Ruhr region, the country's industrial powerhouse." The reporter suggests that the interest in Satanism is born of socioeconomic depression, the "lack of work" thus causing them to turn to "devil worshiping." The exhumed corpses and dead chickens discovered lying around area cemeteries are indicative of a cult, and, the police say, such cults "claim Aleister Crowley, an Englishman, as their master. Crowley called himself 'The Beast.' His books are readily available in Germany displayed in specialized shops alongside daggers, chalices and coffins. A self-confessed German disciple of The Beast, charged with spreading Crowley's message, is serving six years for rape."[8] In a highly publicized murder trial, "a mother fascinated by the occult and black magic," the twenty-eight-year-old Ruth Neave, "strangled her six-year-old son and then left him laid out like a sacrificial victim" in Peterborough, Cambridgeshire. Glasgow's *The Herald* reported that "Police found *Magick,* the book written by warlock Mr. Aleister

Crowley, in Mrs. Neave's home."[9] *The Telegraph* gave a more detailed account of the significance of Crowley's book. James Hunt, the prosecuting attorney, speculated in the courtroom that

> "There must have been a reason for the killer to leave the body in that particular way. It must have meant something to the killer. Is it far-fetched to suggest that, from the positioning which it is laid out, it may seem at first almost as though that body was being offered up as a sacrifice?" He said that Neave had a fascination with the occult and black magic, and performed tarot card readings for neighbors. She owned a book entitled *Magic* [*sic*] by the mystic Aleister Crowley, which gave details of sacrifice. The book states that "for the highest spiritual working, one must choose a victim such as a male child of perfect innocence and high intelligence. That is the most satisfactory victim."[10]

Regardless of the truth or falsity of Crowley's being a "black magician," the fact remains that in the Western popular imagination Crowley is legendary, and his figure is an apt condensation symbol for "evil" occultism. Although we expect this kind of mythologizing by newspaper reporters today, the most alarmist outworking of Crowley's mythic status in the popular imaginary comes from presumably more careful scholars in the academy. Valerie Sinason, a respected psychotherapist who compromised her career by claiming that Satanic ritual abuse is widespread and real, characterizes Crowley as the source of much abuse and torture:

> After eight months in which the patient described events that we found unbearable to hear, a picture was painted for us of one aspect of contemporary Satanism. Men and women, dedicated to Aleister Crowley's guiding principle, "Do what thou wilt shall be the whole of the Law," worship Satan as their god in private houses or in churchyards and forests. In so doing they literally turn upside down any moral concept that comes with Christianity. They practice every sexual perversion that exists with animals, children and both sexes. They drink blood and urine and eat faeces and insects. They are involved in pornographic films and drug-dealing as a means of raising money. They are highly organized, successful in their secrecy and have a belief that through this pain and abuse they are getting closer to their god.[11]

Sinason is, in point of fact, wrong about Crowley's followers (Thelemites), and her description of Thelema (Crowley's magickal system) reveals that she has never read anything that the magus wrote. Her observation that Crowley's teachings are an inversion of Christian doctrine, however, is apt.

These contemporary characterizations of Crowley are important for two reasons. First, they help to summarize the relative autonomy of modern occult rhetoric from its author. As I will argue in the chapters that follow, a little bit of mischievous irony on Crowley's part has gone quite a long way—far beyond his ability to control it. Although Crowley's biographies and autobiographies are suggestive of many loathsome activities, what Sinason does not realize is that her rhetoric is structured by a much larger discourse of metaphor and symbol that Crowley understood and went out of his way to exploit. In fact, most Americans and Europeans could probably articulate a similar horrible story of Satanic goings-on, precisely because the narrative elements are so ubiquitous in popular memory. With the figure of Crowley we witness a transformation of the occult to the occultic: what was once the study of secret knowledge increasingly is a reservoir for mythmaking, a source for entertainment, and a general means for establishing inside and outside groups. Further, after the rise of what is known as the "Deliverance" movement in the Christian community, a movement characterized by the exorcism of demons and the laying on of hands, the occult becomes an instrumental, political rhetoric as well.[12]

Second, these contemporary uses of Crowley as a symbol represent a marked shift in the history of occult discourse in the popular imaginary: the mystery and lure of occultism for the reading public, as it was for the illiterate masses during the days of the Spanish Inquisition, has become metonymic for evil yet again. One of the reasons for the association of evil and occultism today is unquestioningly economic: sensationalist stories sell tabloids and newspapers now as much as they did in the 1920s. The religious historian Bradford Verter notes that Crowley

> became prominent at a time when a populist critique of occultism as a sign of the moral degeneration of the cultural elite was rapidly emerging. Crowley's penchant for *blague* [public pranks] made him one of the most prominent symbols of this critique. Esoteric mysticism, once regarded by the media as safe and genteel, now appeared dangerous and immoral. Religious groups once portrayed as eccentric at worst were now redefined as "sex cults." And spiritual leaders such as Aleister Crowley who might

> in an earlier age have been labeled an obscurantist and a charlatan was now labeled, as one headline had it, "the wickedest man in the world."[13]

What the figure of Crowley represents, then, is neither his actual person nor his occult practices and teachings but rather a popular construction or fiction, a new signifier for reviving old stories and ancient myths.

How did these narrative elements—the bloody ritual sacrifices, the urine-drinking, the baby-eating, and the black masses—come to be so ubiquitous in popular accounts of modern occultism? Is the neophyte occultist drawn to magick because these elements seem exciting? How does the occultist negotiate these dark narratives? How does the "public" or the popular audience respond to these narratives? Coming to terms with Crowley's occult rhetoric as the dialectical interplay among his own writings and writings about him enables us to understand the history of occultism in the modern era as a discourse (a whole constellation of texts) enabled and constrained by the mass media. By analyzing texts about Crowley and, later, LaVey, one notices a remarkable shift in popular perceptions about occultism since Blavatsky's time, one that I will suggest maps the democratizing effects of the mass media as well as its ability to amplify class anxieties. Crowley's attempts, as a figure of the ruling class, to establish himself as an occult authority by hoarding secrets only fueled the desire of the middle- and lower-class reading public to know his secrets. In the final analysis, what a study of the rhetoric of and about Crowley, and later the avowed Satanist LaVey, reveals is the autonomy of the occult as a social form once it is released into the multiple, productive, and consumptive circuits of the contemporary mass media. Contending with this autonomy allows us to comprehend the working of larger, extrinsic social forms as a rhetorical process.

5
Aleister Crowley and the Hermeneutic of Authority

The most famous magus of the early twentieth century enjoyed publishing the cherished occult secrets of rival magi. Concerning one controversial revelation, Aleister Crowley carped that "all this secrecy is very silly" and "it is a wicked imposture to pretend to have received [a secret alphabet] from Rosicrucian manuscripts which are to be found in the British Museum."[1] These remarks probably refer to Crowley's former teacher and magical mentor, Samuel Liddell Macgregor Mathers, a striking, charismatic man with long, flowing gray locks, renowned among students of the occult for his masterful translations of two legendary manuals of ritual magic, *The Key of Solomon the King (Clavicula Salomonis)* and *The Book of the Sacred Magic of Abramelin the Mage.* At the height of his power, Mathers claimed to have been in the possession of a secret, magical alphabet (the Hebrew Qabalah), which he confided to members of his secret society, the Order of the Golden Dawn. Crowley was a member of the order and was favored by Mathers as his eventual successor. In the end, however, Crowley was expelled by fellow members who found his ethical conduct and public reputation troublesome.[2]

Because of infighting and various skirmishes over Crowley's legitimate authority within the Golden Dawn, the order eventually disbanded. After a resulting break with Mathers, Crowley decided that the secret rituals and teachings of the Golden Dawn should be made public in his occult journal, *The Equinox.*[3] In response to this bold move, Mathers sued Crowley in 1910 for having violated a "supernatural copyright."[4] The elder magus initially won a temporary injunction preventing Crowley from publishing more issues of *The Equinox* until both men could settle the matter in the courtroom.

The transcript of the court proceedings is an interesting study of occult authority and authorship. A popular belief in the illegitimacy of occult authority, for example, is reflected in the remarks of the British justices who decided the case:

> Lord Justice Moulton: Anyone who knows anything about these [secret] societies knows that the ritual of most of them has been published.

Vaughan Williams: I have not observed any indication that you are, either of you [Mathers and Crowley], Masons. (Laughter)
Frederick Lawrence [for the plaintiff]: I don't propose to give your Lordship any, either. The society is in no way a Masonic society . . . the defendant is publishing the article as an act of revenge for having been expelled.
Vaughan Williams: I see the plaintiff [Mathers] says he is the "earthly chief" of the order, and subject to the guidance of the "Spiritual Order"?
Lawrence: I cannot go into it, my lord. It is clear that [the] spiritual head would not be answerable for costs. (Laughter)[5]

The courtroom melee between Mathers and Crowley is demonstrative of the agonism of the modern occult tradition and illustrates the way in which authority within that tradition is typically achieved: through verbal disagreement and struggle. The courtroom proceedings, which were reported in number of newspapers in the United Kingdom, also help to highlight how the emergence of the "mass public" and the attendant explosion of publicity transformed modern occultism into a star system. Insofar as occult texts became fetishized commodities, so did their authorities become cultural personalities in the early twentieth century. The fetishism of the text was merely "transferred" to mystify the occultist.[6] At least in the popular imaginary, knowing the (spiritual) truth may not be as important as tapping into the mass-mediated cult of personality.

The levity with which the justices discussed the issue of Mathers's supernatural copyright certainly involves the recognition of how the star system works. Yet when considered in contemporary academic terms, the dynamic of authority represented in the battles of magi may not be so funny. On one level, the struggle over authority highlights a general religious problem that occultism helps us to apprehend: If supernatural truths are, in fact, supernatural, then how does one become a legitimate authority of such truths? What are the criteria for legitimate authority? Who or what determines legitimacy? The answers to these kinds of questions are not just important for the supernaturalist, for on another level the modern magi's struggle for authority and recognition reflects the current star system of the academy. We academics in the humanities are currently mired in a genius-virtuoso, superstar model of intellectual authority that has emerged in the wake of "Truth" and the abandonment of absolutes.[7] Understanding the relevance of the authority of the modern magus only requires one to replace the role of supernatural truth with this or that notion of post-truth ineffability that is so central to the project of the posts (e.g., poststructuralism, postmodernism, and so on).

In this chapter I examine the establishment of occult authority in respect to the ways in which a magus instructs followers to interpret occult texts. My argument is that the charismatic, rhetorical strategies used by occultists to establish authority disclose a dialectic of control, or a movement between the autonomy and dependency of a believer, that always threatens to undermine the legitimacy of authority because the status or certainty of spiritual truths is not guaranteed.[8] To these ends the chapter is divided into two main sections. The first section, "The Rhetoric of Religious Authority," more fully explains the rhetorical construction of religious authority in general and locates occultism within a prophetic mode of charismatic authority-creation in particular. In the second section, "Occultism and the Hermeneutic of Authority," I describe the ways in which occult modes of interpretation work to justify the authority of occult leaders, using the example of Crowley's Qabalistic brand of interpretation. Finally, I conclude the chapter by arguing that an analysis of occult rhetoric suggests that all occultic rhetorics of authority, such as that of Jacques Lacan, are fundamentally charismatic and highly precarious.

The Rhetoric of Religious Authority

> Christianity teaches that everything essentially Christian depends solely upon faith; therefore it wants to be precisely a Socratic, God-fearing ignorance, which by means of ignorance guards faith against speculation.
>
> —Søren Kierkegaard as Anti-Climacus[9]

Writing under the deliberately ironic pseudonym of Anti-Climacus in *The Sickness unto Death,* Kierkegaard argues that the basic human condition is one of despair, a psychological illness of fragmentation and self-division. The most unfortunate kind of despair is not knowing that one is despairing, not knowing that one is essentially divided against oneself. The cure for this sickness unto death, he suggests, is faith in God. Yet for Kierkegaard faith is not merely belief but a willed synthesis of the "psychical" and "physical" in spirit, which can only be achieved through a total surrender of one's will to the requests and demands of God or God's messengers.[10]

Kierkegaard's description of faith is an ingenious attempt to resolve the central problematic of religious authority. Unlike the authority of elected public officials, schoolteachers, parents, or professors, religious authority is ultimately rooted in something manifestly absent—a transcendental signified, an astral light, or most commonly, God. Consequently, the most common type of evidence offered by religious authorities is simple tautology, a strategy that scholars of rhetoric term "self-evidence." "It is impossible to adduce evidence for God's law," says James Darsey, "for it contains its own evidence; it is self-evidence, clear upon viewing."[11] Hence the key challenge faced by pastors and preachers, psychics and shamans, is overcoming the feeling, harbored by believers and potential converts, that the self-evidence of divine knowledge or law is not enough. In terms of the challenge that ancient religious prophets faced, James Crenshaw locates doubt and suspicion as the Achilles' heel of radical religious discourse. "The prophet was particularly vulnerable" to attack, suggests Crenshaw, "since he claimed to speak what another had communicated to him, yet when challenged as to the source of his word, he could only affirm that God had indeed summoned him, sent the vision, spoken the word."[12] In addition to self-evidence, Kierkegaard highlights the strategy of convincing believers that their suspicion and doubt are symptoms of a much deeper, spiritual illness, that suspicion and doubt are in fact tokens of a profound despair that will abide with them to the grave. This self-sealing argument is perhaps one of the oldest rhetorical moves in the Hebraic and Christian religious traditions, whether one describes this illness—or better lack—as "sin," "despair," "anxiety," or even "depression."

Thus a religious brand of authority urges subjects to surrender to the mystery or ambiguity of the divine, offering up self-evidence and self-sealing arguments when necessary in order to secure a capitulation that we commonly term "faith." The faith of the true believer is never solely in the existence of God or the supernatural, however, but also in the notion that representatives of God or the supernatural are in a better position to know what we need (a philosopher, a priest, a psychic, and so on). As Theodor W. Adorno observed of astrology, a spiritual authority "attempts to satisfy the longings of people who are thoroughly convinced that others (or some unknown agency) ought to know more about themselves and what they should do than they can decide for themselves."[13] Similarly, in his last major work, *The Rhetoric of Religion: Studies in Logology,* Kenneth Burke argues that religious surrender should be understood as the basis of social hierarchy and order in general: "Once a believer is brought to accept mysteries, he will be better minded to take orders without question from those persons whom he considers authoritative. In brief, mysteries are a good grounding for obedience, insofar as the acceptance of a mystery involves a person in the abnegation of his own personal judgment. . . . So, if a man, in accepting a 'mystery,' accepts someone else's judgment in place of his own, by that same token he becomes subject willingly. That is, subjection is implicit in his act of belief."[14] Faith necessarily entails subjection, and subjection begets hierarchy. As a hierarchical dynamic, religious authority entails the possession of legitimacy (as the ability to have others recognize one's power) and power over others (as the ability of someone to induce others to do or think something). In Burke's broader scheme, even going to a medical doctor can be described as a religious surrender insofar as one faithfully believes in the doctor's ability to correctly diagnose illness. Yet unlike a medical doctor, whose authority is justified legally (via examination and licensing) and institutionally (via schooling and a framed sheep skin hanging on an office wall), the achievement of legitimate religious authority is more thorny. The apparent success of self-evidence and the self-sealing argument is not enough, in and of itself, to secure the subjection of individuals, especially given the inscrutability of the spiritual source or divine essence that secures truth.[15] How, then, does religious authority effectively engender subjection? How does religious authority become legitimate to believers? The most obvious answer to these and related questions is simple: force. The more rhetorical answer, however, is that one can secure authority in reference to traditions and institutions (and by extension, ideology) or legitimize authority by means of individual character and personality.

Although definitions of "authority" are numerous, for this chapter I will refer to the concept as it is often discussed in ordinary terms: authority refers to the ability or power of an individual to do something, or the power of an individual to request or demand something of others.[16] Since the early nineteenth century, discussions about this basic, ordinary understanding of authority have been influenced by the work of Max Weber. In *The Theory of Social and Economic Organization,* Weber argues that in any system of order one will typically find three types of authority (which are not mutually exclusive): rational-legal, traditional, and charismatic. Rational-legal authority is established only on the basis of an "impersonal order" to which relevant parities willingly subject themselves. Rational-legal authorities are thus legitimate only because of a widely held "belief in the legality of patterns of normative rules."[17] The most obvious of rational-legal authorities are, of course, our elected officials, the police, and so on. Rational-legal authority, however, can also include the kinds of authority created in philosophical discussions in which all parties agree to the rules of symbolic logic, linear exposition, and so on. Agreement in this sense, either tacit or explicit, is the paradigm logic of the social contract. Second, Weber suggests that authority can be termed "traditional . . . if legitimacy is claimed for it and believed in on the basis of the sanctity of the order and the attendant powers of control as they have been handed down from the past."[18] A typical example of this kind of authority is the court judge, whose power is legitimized by a judicial institution and who resolves disputes on the basis of precedent. Finally, for Weber the third kind of authority is that which is created on charismatic grounds. Charisma refers to "a certain quality of an individual personality by virtue of which he is set apart from ordinary men and treated as endowed with supernatural, superhuman, or at least specifically exceptional powers or qualities."[19] Authorities who achieve their legitimacy on the basis of personal charm, perceived trustworthiness, goodwill, and wisdom or expertise are charismatic authorities.

In Weber's scheme, the legitimacy of religious authority is typically established with appeals to tradition and to the stability of social institutions.[20] Weber argues that the Catholic priest, for example, "lays claim to authority by virtue of his service in a sacred tradition."[21] Although religious authority is usually and initially (i.e., historically) conferred on the basis of the individual magnetism of a prophet (e.g., Buddha, Muhammad, Jesus Christ, even David Koresh), organized religion tends to justify authority in terms of a preexisting order or institutional tradition, encouraging subjection or loyalty on the basis of its continued persistence. For this reason, Martin Luther's challenge to the legitimacy of the authority of the Catholic Church concerned its patrimony.[22] Luther famously attacked that from which the church derived its authority: sacred custom and tradition, the persistence of the church as an institution that has "always been" such and such a way (presumably because of God's keep). Instead, Luther argued for the legitimate authority of every Christian believer to interpret the Scriptures without the aid of an institutionally authorized intercessor. Absent an institutional justification, Luther's religious authority can be characterized as charismatic because it is rooted in others' perceptions of his character and personality, or rather his ethos. It was Luther's exceptional skills as a persuasive writer and speaker, his ability to convince others that his proclamations were divinely inspired, that are the rhetorical foundation of Protestantism, not a rejection of Catholic doctrine or the content of his proclamations per se.[23]

From a supernaturalist vantage, such a personality-centered approach to authority partakes in the prophetic tradition. The prophetic tradition refers to the legacy of prophets who claimed to have had a direct experience of the divine, from Socrates' guardian angel or *daimon,* to Moses' encounter with the burning bush, to Deborah's divinely inspired war strategies against the Canaanites, to Muhammad's reception of the Koran, to Mary Eddy Baker's "discovery" of Christian Science.[24] In his thoughtful study *The Prophetic Tradition and Radical Rhetoric in America,* James Darsey argues that unlike the secular, Hellenic rhetorical tradition that is rooted in the deliberative practice of the ancient Greeks, the prophetic tradition is molded in a Hebraic ethic that makes no room for reason or argumentative appeal (even those such as Pascal's wager or Kierkegaard's self-sealing argument). Rather, the Hebraic origins of prophetic rhetoric require any aspiring authority to present God's will dogmatically, without room for discussion or negotiation, for God's demands are to be regarded as indubitable, sacred truths.[25] Because prophets or religious leaders are presented as mere vessels of divine truths, the manner of their telling and the exemplar of their person are the most important means of establishing authority. Put simply, to achieve religious authority in a prophetic mode, those who claim to speak divine truths have to look and sound like they are speaking divine truths. Charisma is all one has to work with.

I suggest that modern occult authority is an accelerated or hyperbolic instance of prophetic authority. Indeed, as I have suggested since chapter 1, the history of occultism can be characterized as the chronicle of magi battling over secrets and the best way to communicate them—a discourse of reformation built upon continual protest.[26] Just as Luther protested Catholic tradition, so each occultist announces his or her insights as unique and unprecedented. Just as Luther claimed that each believer is a legitimate authority of biblical truth, so too each occultist announces his or her system as uniquely empowering to the individual aspirant. And just as Luther's authority was grounded in ethos, so does the success of occultists depend on their personality, character, and charm.

Because occultism, like new or emerging Protestant faiths, is a marginal or countercultural discourse, modern occult authority is necessarily limited to charismatic strategies. Whereas any number of mainstream Protestant authorities may appeal to an established tradition (e.g., Lutherans, Baptists, and Mormons all have an institutional basis of legitimizing religious authority), the "secrecy" and mystery that is characteristic of occult knowledge resigns authorial claims to character. Even if a given occultist attempts to claim authority in reference to some occult tradition or institution, such as a "secret" order like the Rosicrucians, for example, such an order tends to remain mysterious, abstract, and out of reach. This is because acceptance of the mystery of the order necessarily entails a hierarchy which reveals that institutional claims are merely the ruse of charismatic authority: An aspirant asks, "How do you know the Great White Brotherhood truly exists?" The occultist responds, "Because I have visited their lodge." The aspirant replies, "Why should I believe you?" and the occultist retorts, "Because I would not lie to you." Successful occult authorities rarely justify their power in relation to traditions or institutions, because the secrets they harbor could be revealed to an unwanted public or, worse, because the traditions or institutions could be exposed as fictions. As Mathers's case against Crowley demonstrates, occult secrets are always at risk of being told. Once the secret teachings, rituals, or languages are exposed to a larger public, mystery evaporates and the occult leader is challenged to prove his or her authority in ways that do not hinge on the stability of institutions.

The two main rhetorical traditions—the Hellenistic, represented by the ancient Greeks, and the Hebraic, represented by the Old Testament prophets—differ most significantly in terms of how each contends with the uncertainty, mystery, and ambiguity in a given rhetorical encounter. In the Hellenistic tradition, doubt is ideally addressed with rational argument, deliberation, and consensus building. Aristotle, for example, suggests that the doubt a given audience has about a rhetor can be remedied within a speech by demonstrating practical wisdom, virtuous character, expertise in his or her field, and goodwill toward others.[27] Creating an impression of these three traits of character presumes an audience will respond to character in relatively predictable ways and thus suggests that charisma is not so much inherent as it is cultivated.

In the Hebraic tradition, however, different epistemological assumptions are at play, for there is a willed "Socratic ignorance," as Kierkegaard says, which holds that the divine word and prophetic *logos* is self-evident and beyond discussion.[28] For Aristotle, one carefully constructed a persuasive speech by inventing its many elements, arranging them in logical order and making sure that the reasoning was sound, and selecting language that was stylistically in keeping with the topic and goals of the speech. Yet for the religious prophet, the divine message comes fully formed and cannot be altered "without violating [God's] sacred trust."[29] In rhetoric that has its roots in the Hebraic tradition, there is no room for Aristotle's call for a demonstration of "practical wisdom" (*phronesis*) because there is no argument; prophetic rhetoric "has no power of invention," claims Darsey, because "it can only reveal that which was already there, the sempiternal; it is always the rhetoric of the messenger."[30]

Because of its stress on charismatic authority and its concern with an absent guarantee, at its most fundamental basis the rhetoric of occult authority has one foot within the Hebraic rhetorical tradition. Like all religious authority, occultists issue a call for subjection and suspension of doubt. Like the supernaturalist, they proclaim to have better routes to the divine or better understandings of occult truths. Like the prophet, their claims to authority are built solely on charismatic strategies. Yet, unlike these religious authorities, the modern occultist is distinctive in regard to the ways he or she creates charismatic authority in a patently Hellenic or argumentative manner. With the other foot in the Hellenic rhetorical tradition, unlike a traditional prophet who has been burdened by God and who is merely a mouthpiece,[31] the occultist has no difficulty extolling his or her own skills or genius as a model. The modern occultist, in other words, participates in the Hellenic rhetorical tradition because of his or her explicit desire to make arguments about the supernatural. Some modern occultists, like Blavatsky and Crowley, for example, even claim that the occult is a "science." For them, self-evidence is not enough to convince the aspirant.

In light of the differences between traditional prophetic and occult authority, the latter is distinctive in its attempt to utilize a Hellenistic means to a Hebraic end. In the pages that follow, I provide a few examples of how occultists go about establishing their authority in modes that are more typically Hellenic or argumentative than Hebraic, particularly in relation to how they ask others to interpret spiritual truths. I will conclude by suggesting that contemporary occultic discourse in general, and the high theory of the academy in particular, similarly features a Hellenistic means to the Hebraic end of securing faith in an authority.

Occultism and the Hermeneutic of Authority

Although occultists resort to the self-evidence and self-sealing arguments of traditional prophecy, their creation of authority is less dogmatic and admits of a number of strategies.[32] The first and most recognized strategy is the demonstration of magical powers or the performance of miracles. This strategy is squarely within the prophetic tradition but is not popular among occultists because it risks the possible exposure of a given occultist as a fraud. Many of those who have pursued public demonstrations of occult power in the past have, in fact, been exposed as frauds (e.g., Uri Geller's amazing spoon-bending powers).[33] Although the psychics and Spiritualists of the mid-nineteenth century were greeted with enthusiasm and interest by a general public anxious to believe in the supernatural, modern and contemporary displays of magical powers were and are met with a high degree of suspicion.

Because of the risks of performance, the more common and safe charismatic strategy, at least in modern occult discourse, has been the writing of occult books. In light of the present discussion of authority, one can redescribe the first section of the present study ("Esoterica") as an analysis of the creation of authority through novel vocabularies and a stress on allegorical and figurative language. In the absence of a stable institution or tradition for grounding, for example, Blavatsky was able to justify her authority by advancing a complex esoteric vocabulary for which only she had a complete understanding. Like the Pentecostal preacher who interprets a follower's speaking in tongues as a revelation of divine truth, the occultist invents charismatic authority by claiming to be the first to understand a strange language or secret scripture.

For the remainder of this chapter, I address the third way occultists often establish authority, which I term the "hermeneutic of authority." Insofar as occultists are concerned with creating secret texts and texts about secrets, then they also must have theories concerning how to read and understand occult texts, or a hermeneutics. Because the exigency for the creation of an occult book is typically a claim to have found a better route to the divine or spiritual, one way in which an occultist can establish authority is by urging followers or potential followers to use an interpretive scheme, especially a scheme that reinforces the authority of the occultist.

In a broader religious context, the most famous hermeneutic of authority is that of scholasticism, a mode of scriptural interpretation that was popular during the Middle Ages and advanced by religious thinkers such as John Duns Scotus, William Ockham, Aquinas, and Augustine. As Augustine described it, scholastic hermeneutics comprised three interpretive principles: first, the scholar must always attempt to understand Scripture in relationship to the time during which it was written; second, the reader must always account for a given passage in relationship to the Scriptures in their entirety; and finally, when a literal reading of a passage is patently absurd, the reader should contend with it as figurative or allegorical. Armed with these three principles and the conviction that God is not a deceiver,

Augustine suggested that the spiritual truths of Scripture could be known.[34] The caveat here, of course, is that only priests had the authority to interpret the Scriptures. For centuries the Bible was cloaked in the secret languages of Greek and Latin (secret at least to the common person who could not read), thus effectively rendering the Bible an occult document.

Augustine's description of scholastic hermeneutics is similar to occult and Platonic modes of interpretation insofar as both are primarily concerned with the restoration or recollection of divine meaning, which could be described as a hermeneutic of faith insofar as an ultimate, metaphysical truth is assumed to exist and is recovered or restored through proper (and inspired) interpretation. In the Platonic dialogues, the flux and turmoil of the manifold world of appearances is stilled in the recollection of a spiritual life and the eternal Forms that the individual has since forgotten.[35] In the Hebraic tradition, scriptural study works toward a recovery of the state of sinlessness before the fall of Adam. Kierkegaard suggested that these hermeneutic modes of remembrance have "the great advantage that begins with loss; the reason it is safe and secure is that it has nothing to lose"—and eternal life to gain.[36] A hermeneutic of recollection and faith is therefore appealing because of its simplicity: the reader or interpreter only has to work toward re-gaining and re-collecting some indubitable thing that is merely lost or forgotten. Thus, the recovery of metaphysical truth or a transcendental signified typical of the hermeneutic of faith could be described as a mode of nostalgia.[37]

An analysis of Crowley's nostalgic, recollective hermeneutic helps illustrate how charismatic authority is established in the absence of institutional or legal sanction. In particular, Crowley's discourse shows that a primary feature of modern occult rhetoric is an invitation to consult a whole system of works, each single text urging the consultation of another. It is the creation of an insular system of texts that works to establish authority on the basis of their common creator. The significance of self-reference is that it functions as a rhetorical surrogate for the tradition and/or institution that is absent, marking the formative stages of an emerging dogma that can later become a tradition or institution. Because the occult hermeneutic of authority is self-referential, it is a higher-order form of self-evidence that mirrors the primary tautology of all religious rhetoric.

Crowley's Nostalgia: Qabalistic Hermeneutics

Although Crowley did a number of things to secure his authority (not the least being the presumably automatic dictation of *The Book of the*

Law), one of the most obvious and interesting elements of his rhetoric of authority is the way in which he urged others to read occult texts, especially his own. Over the course of his long occult career, Crowley specified, often in monotonous detail, how occultists should read occult texts and understand occult symbolism.

Key to Crowley's brand of hermeneutics is a continual, self-referencing invitation to readers to consult a whole system of books and essays that he ceaselessly continued to correct and embellish throughout his life. In a letter to a neophyte occultist, for example, Crowley stresses that his understanding of esoteric language—the Qabalah—is needed to grasp magickal truths. The utility of the Qabalah is

> justified by experience, by the empirical success in communicating thought which has attended, and continues to attend, our endeavors. [A brief lesson in basic semiotics ensues, then] . . . as so often pointed out, all we do is "record the behavior of our instruments." . . . Except in the case of onomatopoeic words and a few others, there is no logical connection between a thing and the sound of our name for it. . . . And then folk wonder how it is that there should be error and misunderstanding in the transmission of thought from one person to another! Rather regard it as a miraculous intervention of Providence when even one of the even simplest ideas "gets across." Now then, even this being so, it is evidently good sense to construct one's own alphabet, with one's own very precise definitions, in order to handle an abstruse and technical subject like Magick. The "ordinary" words such as God, self, soul, spirit and the rest have been used so many thousand times in so many thousand ways, usually by writers who knew not for the necessity of definition that to use them to-day in any scientific essay is almost ludicrous. That is all, just now, sister; no more of your cavilling, please; sit down quietly with your 777, and get it by heart![38]

Here Crowley urges the aspirant to study *Liber 777,* his manual of Qabalistic "correspondences," which he first published in 1909.[39] This kind of self-promotion is ubiquitous in Crowley's work.

So what, then, is the Qabalah? The answer to this question is not easy to provide, for it differs among occultists—even those within the Ordo Templi Orientis, the secret order that currently teaches Crowley's version of the practice. Nevertheless, in general one can characterize the Qabalah is a kind of symbolic, mathematical vocabulary and technique of reading which is employed for reasons that vary from one occultist to another (while derived from the Hebraic Kabbalistic tradition, the Qabalah is significantly different in its use of English and Greek characters, among other reasons). For some the Qabalah can provide a direct route to ultimate reality. For others it is a helpful method of magickal exegesis.

Crowley used the Qabalah principally as a hermeneutics. In various essays and books he describes the Qabalah as comprising a number of techniques that can be imaginatively projected onto the "Tree of Life," a geometric diagram that represents the "planes" or "spheres" of ultimate reality. Crowley urged all magicians to memorize this diagram and what it represents—which is, incidentally, a great number of things—"by heart; you must know it backwards, forwards, sideways, and upside down."[40] Crowley insisted that only with repeated practice do the multifarious connections of everything with everything become apparent. This brand of mental training is exceedingly complex and, properly described, would entail a chapter of its own. Nevertheless, given its prominence in Crowley's writings, and given the ways in which Crowley used it to legitimize his authority as an occult leader, a brief examination of Crowley's rhetoric of interpretation is useful.

Crowley initially learned the Qabalah from Mathers and others as a member of the Golden Dawn. During the demise of that secret order, he began to amend the Golden Dawn's articulation of the practice into something many occultists describe as distinctly original and creative. He published his version in the manual titled *777*. In this book, Crowley describes his Qabalistic project in quasi-scientific terms:

> The book *777* has for its primary object the construction of a magical alphabet. One of the greatest difficulties experienced by the student—a difficulty which increases rather than diminishes with his advance in knowledge—is this: he finds it impossible to gain any clear idea of the meanings of the terms which he employs. . . . In view of this . . . misunderstanding it is clearly necessary to establish a fundamental language. . . . We can easily discard the dogmatic interpretation of the Rabbins. We can refer everything in the Universe to the system of pure number whose symbols will be intelligible to all rational minds in an identical sense. And the relations between these symbols are fixed by nature.[41]

Galileo's insistence that mathematics is the language of the universe is echoed in Crowley's attempts to stabilize Qabalistic correspondences on the intendments of the "rational mind."[42] Given the role of reason (or rather, symbolic logic) that Crowley suggests is crucial to the practice, one could characterize his Qabalah as a kind of "mental yoga" or numerical exercise, whereby "the Work is to reduce all other Conceptions to these of Number, because this thus will lay bare the very Structure of thy Mind, whose rule is Necessity rather than Prejudice."[43]

This more scientistically and pragmatically directed Qabalah attempts to reveal "mental structures" by utilizing "a number of techniques, including the employment of a divine numerology, known as *Gematria,* a shorthand system known as *Notariqon,* and the cryptographic exercises of *Temura.*"[44] *Gematria* refers to the numerical relationships between Hebrew letters, whose addition, subtraction, multiplication, and division by the Qabalist discloses "an endless chain of self-referential correspondences." For example, an English-speaking westerner might find the word "Adam" significant, and convert the word into Hebrew (adm) or ADM (Aleph-Daleth-Mem), which has the numerical value of 1 + 4 + 40, or 45. The number 45 is intriguing for the Qabalist because it is the source of all numbers (45 = 0 + 1 + 2 + 3 + 4 + 5 + 6 + 7 + 8 + 9). *Notariqon* refers to a kind of Gematrian dabbling with an emphasis on the acronymic reduction of sentences. *Temura* refers to a process of substituting some words and letters for others.[45] For followers of Crowley's teachings, Qabalistic mental training is extremely significant, as Crowley insisted on its importance for decoding the cosmic puzzle that is *The Book of the Law.*

The Serious Foolishness of the Qabalah

Crowley uses the Qabalah as a hermeneutic of authority in two ways. First, the Qabalah is used to excuse the poetic shortcomings of *The Book of the Law,* as I demonstrated in the previous chapter. Second, Crowley exploits the arbitrary and interminable logic of the Qabalah to assign himself the role of the ultimate signifying authority. An examination of the term "fool" as it appears in *The Book of the Law* will quickly illustrate both uses.

Crowley argues that key among *The Book of the Law*'s features are "double entendre" and, more interestingly, "paranomasia [*sic*]."[46] *Paronomasia* is a literary term that refers to punning on the basis of sound, and it is consistent with Crowley's emphasis that *The Book of the Law* was orally dictated to him by a supernatural being. Crowley argued that many of these double meanings and "numerical-literal" puzzles can be understood only with Qabalistic modes of interpretation. Because Crowley sometimes described himself as a "serious fool," an analysis of the word and symbolism of "fool" is a good illustration of how he prescribed Qabalistic interpretation.

In *The Book of the Law,* the word "fool" appears nine times. A traditional reading of the word in the context of the sentence or chapter would have difficulty interpreting the term "fool" in a way that does not suggest its common, literal usage: one who is deficient in judgment, sense, or understanding. The examples are from chapters 1 (verses 11, 31, 48, 57), 2 (verses 7, 15, 59), and 3 (verses 57, 63):

> 11. These are fools that men adore; both their Gods & their men are fools.
>
> 31. For these fools of men and their woes care not thou at all! They feel little; what is, is balanced by weak joys; but ye are my chosen ones.
>
> 48. My prophet is a fool with his one, one, one; are not they the Ox, and none by the Book?
>
> 57. Invoke me under my stars! Love is the law, love under will. Nor let the fools mistake love; for there are love and love. There is the dove, and there is the serpent.
>
> 7. I am the Magician and the Exorcist. I am the axle of the wheel, and the cube in the circle. "Come unto me" is a foolish word: for it is I that go.
>
> 15. For I am perfect, being Not; and my number is nine by the fools; but with the just I am eight, and one in eight: Which is vital, for I am none indeed. The Empress and the King are not of me; for there is a further secret.
>
> 59. Beware therefore! Love all, lest perchance is a King concealed! Say you so? Fool! If he be a King, thou canst not hurt him.
>
> 57. Despise also all cowards; professional soldiers who dare not fight, but play; all fools despise!
>
> 63. The fool readeth this Book of the Law, and its comment; & he understandeth it not.

In each case but one, "fool" seems to be used in a straightforward sense, as denoting a misguided or ill-judging person (the sole exception is when "foolish" is used to describe a word or phrase). The immediate context of the term's use—the sentence "frame"—seems to invite a common reading on the basis of the codes they invoke, not the least of which is the basic subject-verb logic. Yet operating Qabalistically, there is potentially no end to the symbolic significance of "fool." Crowley tells us:

> "The fool readeth this Book—and he understandeth it not." This has a secret reverse-sense, meaning: The fool (Parzival = Fra.O.I.V.V.I.O.) understandeth it (being a Magister Templi, the Grade attributed to Understanding) not (i.e. to be 'not').

Here the reader must realize that "Fra." is an abbreviation for Frater, or brother; this is a grade in Crowley's secret order, the "Silver Star." Also, in medieval European mythology, Parzifal is a wise fool. When "Parzifal" is phonetically translated into Hebrew (O.I.V.V.I.O.) and is numerically added up, one gets 418—which for Crowley is rife with significance. Crowley continues:

> This Parzival, adding to 418, is (in the legend of the Graal) the son of Kamuret, adding to 666, being the son of me The Beast [Crowley calls himself "The Beast," and his number is 666, which he took from the Book of Revelation] by the Scarlet Woman Hilarion [Crowley's wife, Rose Edith Crowley, or "Ouarda"]. This was a Name chosen by her when half drunk, as a theft from Theosophical legend, but containing many of our letter-number Keys to the Mysteries; the number of the petals in the most sacred lotus. It adds to 1001, which also is Seven times Eleven times Thirteen, a series of factors which may be read as The Scarlet Woman's Love by Magick producing Unity, in Hebrew Achad. For 7 is the number of Venus, and the sweet seven-lettered Name of my concubine B A B A L O N is written with Seven Sevens, thus:
>
> $$77 + \frac{7 + 7}{7} + 77 = 156, \text{ the number of BABALON.}$$
>
> 418 is the number of the Word of the Magical Formula of this Aeon [elsewhere and in many places, including in *Liber AL,* we are told that this formula is ABRAHADABRA].[47]

The only link between "fool" and Parzival is their Hebrew Qabalistic number, 418, yet Crowley finds "fool" here rife with significance. Intertextual meanings are afforded the concept, which, unfortunately, is easily missed by the neophyte occultist unfamiliar with the myth of Parzival.[48]

Importantly, readers with some background in Crowley's other writings would know that Crowley has also associated himself with "The Fool" in the tarot, a series of cards used for divination. In his own *The Book of Thoth* (Egyptian tarot), written toward the end of his magical career, Crowley explains the card of "The Fool" in more depth: "This card is attributed to the letter Aleph [a], which means an Ox, but by its shape the Hebrew letter (so it is said) represents a ploughshare; thus the significance is primarily Phallic. It is the first of the three Mother letters, Aleph, Mem, and Shin, which correspond in various interwoven fashions with all the triads that occur in those cards, notably, Fire, Water, Air; Father . . . [and on and on]."[49] The Ox reference explains its mention in verse 48 of the first chapter of *The Book of the Law,* although in both old and new commentaries Crowley neglects to explain this Hebrew reference. Nevertheless, Crowley's many, many ruminations on the "fool" in his commentary on *The Book of the Law* and elsewhere are indicative of an inability to stop with the chaining of symbolic reference, which can, of course, continue endlessly.

Of course, Crowley suggests that when *The Book of the Law* reads like bad poetry, there must be a secret meaning that is only apprehended with numerical techniques. In prescribing the Qabalah, however, Crowley opens interpretation to a multitude of possible meanings. Such an opening leads to two interpretive possibilities for Crowley and his readers. First, in liberating words from a mundane fixed signification, Crowley is able re-signify them as he wishes, laying claim to critical power and thus giving him a way to assert his authority (if not to rescue his ugly text from the waste bin of "bad art"). This first possibility, incidentally, is yet another version of occult poetics, ironically, through the use of mundane terms. The second possibility, however, urges others to read *The Book of the Law* Qabalistically as well, which potentially empowers them to re-signify words in ways that Crowley cannot control. As a hermeneutic, the Qabalah is both a way to secure authority and a way to undermine it; it harbors a dialectic of control. For example, whereas Blavatsky used weird terms and hence had the sole power to signify, Crowley's hermeneutic is more democratic in that Qabalistic techniques can be learned by anyone who so chooses (*777* was eventually available to the public). Hence Crowley had to do something, rhetorically, to forestall the polysemic re-significations of followers.

Crowley was aware of the problem of intertextuality and the challenge to his authority that urging figurative readings posed. Presuming that *The Book of the Law* is a secular text created by Crowley, I suggest that he embedded within it a rhetorical inoculation, which he later used to close down polysemic readings (many Thelemites will strongly disagree with this suggestion, however). Speaking directly to Crowley, the supernatural persona that Crowley claims to have dictated *The Book of the Law* says in chapter 2:

> 54. Nor shall they who cry aloud their folly that thou meanest nought avail; thou shall reveal it: thou availest: they are the slaves of because: They are not of me. The stops as thou wilt; the letters? change them not in style or value!
> 55. Thou shalt obtain the order & value of the English Alphabet; thou shalt find new symbols to attribute them unto.

Crowley is commanded to disregard and ignore the "slaves of because," those who would impose linear analytics on the text and focus on meanings Crowley does not like, especially those who would insist on demonstration and evidence. "Because" could mean a number of things here: causality, legitimacy, justification, rationale, communication, or perhaps even "argument" itself. Instead of any of these more rational possibilities, the supernatural author urges a more symbolic reading, not only of *The Book of the Law* but of the English language as well, by claiming to relate new "symbols" to the given order and value (grammar, syntax, and so on) of English. Significantly—and here is the inoculating device—the supernatural being suggests that "the stops as thou wilt." In the context of the hermeneutic of authority, these "stops" refer to symbolic limits, the point at which symbols cease to chain out into relevant texts in a field of occult discourse, the intertextual realm of the imaginary, and thus the end of Qabalistic calculations. In light of his characteristically prophetic insistence that he is "the sole authority competent to decide disputed points with regard to the Book of the Law,"[50] Crowley is thus imbued with the power of magical decree by the text: "All meaning stops with me." Further, since the symbolism of *The Book of the Law* can (theoretically) reach out in infinite directions without any "stop" (especially if we render it numerically with Qabalistic formulae), the "slaves of because" can be read as those who actively look for a justification for "stopping" at one meaning as opposed to another. Read in light of Ra-Hoor-Khuit's bravado, what "the stops as thou wilt" means becomes even clearer in chapter 3:

> 42. The ordeals thou [Crowley] shalt oversee thyself, save only the blind ones. Refuse none, but thou shalt know & destroy the traitors. I am Ra-Hoor-Khuit; and I am powerful to protect my servant. Success is thy proof: argue not; convert not; talk not overmuch!

The "slaves of because" are those who would persuade audiences with good arguments. Here, Crowley is told that the book's authenticity is found in its linguistic and Qabalistic perfections as well as in its predictive truths, in effect undermining one of the most important dimensions of argumentation: the provision of "good reasons."[51]

Although Crowley's hermeneutic of authority concerns a particular kind of occultism (viz., ceremonial magick), the formal ways in which it operates, inclusive of the navigation of the dialectic of control, are common to many of the arts (or "sciences") that are commonly termed "occult." The art of divination, for example, operates similarly: an adept reader of tarot cards spends months, perhaps even years, learning the symbolic correspondences of the major and minor arcana. In the contingent moments of divination, the tarot card reader must decide which particular meanings are appropriate to assign to the cards as they are dealt, for the possible meaningful correspondences are too numerous to be helpful. Likewise, astrologers have similar "wiggle room" in deciding which meanings to assign to zodiac signs, primarily by means of numerical calculation and psychic intuition (otherwise known as "cold reading").[52] From sorcery and witchcraft to alchemy and demonology, occult practices harbor a hermeneutic scheme that Crowley's Qabalism typifies: symbolism is characteristically ambiguous, and such ambiguity is the resource occultists consult to fashion charismatic authority; yet it is also a resource that can just as easily undermine authority—a reservoir or space in which language gets the better of us. In a sense, this occult hermeneutic unwittingly happened upon the significance of the meaningful regress of open semiotic theory, long before Derrida could introduce *différence* or Lacan could deploy the concept of the *chaîne signifiante* ("signifying chain"). "The stops as thou wilt," suggests Crowley's Holy Guardian Angel; the occult hermeneutic is metonymic for the production of linguistic meaning in general, a continuous movement from one signifier to the next until one authority or another—a magus or a priest or a police officer or a rhetorician—prophetically exclaims: "STOP!"

Concluding Remarks: Authority and the Split Subject

In this chapter I have argued that modern occult discourse is best described as being rooted in a Hebraic rhetorical tradition because of its fundamental reliance on appeals to character and because of its calls for faith in the supernatural. Before modernity, occult authority was established by the demonstration of supernatural powers or by advancing complex, esoteric vocabularies. Paradoxically, I have also suggested that modern occult rhetoric has tended to pursue the Hebraic end of prophecy with argumentative appeals that are more in keeping with the Hellenic deliberative tradition. By arguing for a particular method of interpretation that is self-referential, the hermeneutic of authority, I suggested that occultists have utilized a Hellenic strategy. Modern occultism pursues Hebraic ends by Hellenic means. Focusing on this third strategy, I have suggested that the hermeneutic of authority typical of occultism is a nostalgic one that requires the willing subjection of followers to an occult leader whose authority, in turn, is maintained tautologically.

The possibility of an endless chaining of the meaning of occult symbol and metaphor underscores how authority—indeed, autonomous subjectivity itself—is potentially undermined by the logics of language and symbol. Crowley's Qabalistic hermeneutic amplifies problems of figuration in the most exaggerated terms: one can, indeed, go crazy with symbolic reference within a Qabalistic system. Crowley's rhetoric of interpretation illustrates how symbolism can move readers far beyond the text to places where a religious authority would forbid them to go. Thus the mystery and ambiguity of religious discourse in general is reflected in the relationship between tenor and vehicle in particular—in, as Burke aptly states, language itself:

> When we hold that there is a hierarchic incentive (with its "mystery") embedded in the very nature of language, when we insist that one would deceive himself who derived "mystery" purely from institutional sources, we are not arguing for or against any particular set of institutions. . . . [T]o say that hierarchy is inevitable is not to argue categorically against a new order. . . . It is to merely say that, in any order, there will be the mysteries of hierarchy, since such a principle is grounded in the very nature of language and [reinforced] by the resultant diversity of occupational classes. That claim is an important thing, as regards the ultimate reaches of rhetoric. The intensities, morbidities, or particularities of mystery come from institutional sources, but the *aptitude* comes from the nature of man, generically, as a *symbol using animal.*[53]

The claim that the mysteries in hierarchy are ultimately rooted in the ambiguity of symbol use is also important, in respect to the ultimate reaches of rhetoric, because it implies that authority is never the project of an autonomous subject but rather the effect of a relation among individuals. The mystery of order and the ambiguity of symbol use force order and hierarchy on us, as a coping mechanism. Although some authority is achieved by force and violence, in the end no legitimate authority can exist without the consent of the community.

Rhetorical theory, of course, has long recognized the problem of autonomy and ultimately the internal contradictions of the concept of authority. On the one hand, authority implies an egoistic connotation of control and autonomy; charismatic authority in particular is the ultimate expression of an independent, sovereign subjectivity. On the other hand, authority is basically relational (as is any hierarchic subject position) and unavoidably other-focused. Authority thus encapsulates a struggle of divided subjectivity, or the logic of what Hegel termed the "master and slave" dialectic,[54] and underscores the reason why Plato condemned the rhetorical construction of democratic authority. In *Gorgias,* for example, Plato has Socrates condemn rhetoric because it strives to establish a favorable ethos on the basis of direct appeals to the audience:

> What I call oratory is a part of some business that isn't admirable at all. . . . I think there's a practice that's not craftlike, but one that a mind given to making hunches takes to, a mind that's bold and naturally clever at dealing with people. I call it flattery, basically. I think that this practice has many other parts as well, and pastry baking, too, is one of them. . . . [Flattery] takes no thought at all of whatever is best [for the audience]; with the lure of what's most pleasant at the moment, it sniffs out folly and hoodwinks it, so that it gives the impression of being most deserving.[55]

Distrustful of divided subjectivity and most desiring of a transcendent order, Plato called for the ultimate authority and dictatorship of the philosopher-king (a "Master"), whose legitimacy was guaranteed by a knowledge of the true Forms and who, like the Hebraic prophet, adopted the "inflexible posture of righteousness."[56] The "true art of persuasion" consisted of an elite authority who knows how to better address the soul of the hearer than the hearer him- or herself.

In contrast, defenders of the rhetorical worldview understood what Plato termed the "flattery" of audience appeals as a necessary check or limit on authority. For the tradition rooted in Aristotle, Isocrates, and Cicero, the only legitimate way for a rhetor to secure the subjection of the audience was reasoned argument, common emotion or sympathy, and character. For Cicero, in fact, good rhetoric was that which was in some way beholden to the audience as a condition of a free citizenship. In *On Oratory,* through the character of Crassus,

Cicero argued that there is no "more noble [thing] than to be able to fix the attention of assemblies of men by speaking, to fascinate their minds, to direct their passions to whatever object the orator pleases, and to dissuade them from whatsoever he desires. This particular art has constantly flourished above all others in every free state, and especially in those which have enjoyed peace and tranquility."[57] Doing "whatsoever" the rhetor decides or wishes is not, however, entirely arbitrary or self-serving, precisely because of the need to secure the goodwill of the audience. Speeches, in fact, were in part determined by the common beliefs, attitudes, and values of a given community, and to fail to appeal to these commonplaces was to fail at persuading. That the art of rhetoric, traditionally understood, flourished in free and democratic states means that the legitimacy of authority was established primarily in charismatic ways. The priority of charisma in a democratic tradition, however, does not insist on self-evidence and faith but rather on demonstration and appeal. Cicero recognized the rhetor's duty was always to the Other.

What distinguishes a rhetorical view of authority from other views is its emphasis on its construction in contingent moments. In light of its embrace of the necessary appeals to the audience, the need to find "common ground" or the striving toward sites of identification, one might also argue that a rhetorical perspective on authority is unique in its consequent embrace, however implicit, of the fiction of subjectivity that is implied (though not meant) by Aristotle's suggestion that ethos is constructed. Of course, the ancient Greek and Roman rhetorical theorists did not think about subjectivity in these terms, for the concept of the subject itself is a relatively recent invention. Even so, it is significant to note that the Aristotelian and Ciceronian notions of ethos form an important parallel to Lacanian notions of subjectivity, and that the ultimate reaches of rhetoric concern the ways in which symbol use forges and negotiates identity. As Lacan's theory of subjectivity suggests, at base each individual is a fictional unity that is necessarily divided, as the idealized self or *imago* is a representation molded by the Other.[58] The rhetorical construction of authority in discourse is merely a replication of this process, the *imago* thus becoming the *doxa* of the community. Authority is the rhetorical process of establishing an unstable relation between self and Other, and particularly one that elides or obscures the way in which the signifier has more control over us than we would like to admit.

Interlude

On Stolen Letters and Lettered Secrets

> You can't help the play of symbols, and that is why you must be very careful what you say. But the letter, for its part, that goes away. It wanders all by itself.
>
> —Jacques Lacan, "The Purloined Letter"[1]

Edgar Allen Poe's intriguing short story "The Purloined Letter" is built around the circulation of a royal secret. The reader is never privy to what the secret is. All we are told by the narrator is that a letter sent to the queen contains something nasty about the king, which incriminates the queen and which can lead to her death, and the queen knows it. The intrigue begins when the queen spies a royal minister stealing the letter and replacing it with a harmless surrogate, but she is powerless to stop him because the king is in the room. The queen is blackmailed by the minister for months until a witty detective plays the switcheroo game on the original thief, purloining the letter yet again, and thereby reaping a hefty reward from the police. The story closes with the detective fantasizing about the minister continuing to blackmail the queen, not knowing that he is no longer in possession of the now doubly purloined letter, and thus unwittingly bringing about his own punishment.

Poe's story is particularly intriguing to Jacques Lacan, who argues that it helps to explain the role of the signifier in repetition compulsion. The letter is the main character of the story, suggests Lacan, and represents the authority of the signifier over the subject: "The tale of *The Purloined Letter* signifies that there's nothing in destiny, or causality, which can be defined as a function of existence. One can say that, when the characters get a hold of this letter, something gets a hold of them and carries them along and this something clearly has dominion over their individual idiosyncrasies."[2] Indeed, the letter represents the unrepresentable (the unconscious) and the interference the signifier runs between the subject and that which makes the subject singularly singular: his or her inevitable death, the only thing that cannot be gifted.[3] Insofar as Lacan maintains that the signifier is an absence (it "stands in," like the harmless surrogate letters in Poe's story), then it always can get the better of us. The minister believed his authority was vouchsafed by the purloined letter, but in the end he was holding a meaningless surrogate. The letter is its own agent, and the meaning of each character is determined on the basis of his or her relation to the letter.

One of the many ironies of contemporary academese is that the project of the posts, including Lacan's complex understanding of how authority is established (e.g., in terms of the "subject supposed to know"), can be described as both the antithesis of Crowley's hermeneutic of authority as well as its contemporary, occultic manifestation. For example, Lacan's rhetoric, like that of a number of other twentieth-century French intellectuals, has been routinely attacked for its difficulty, and his many followers are quick to acknowledge that reading Lacan's prose is anything but easy. One might say Lacan's letters seem to take on a life of their own, as if they held an authority over the reader.

In what is perhaps his most celebrated essay, "The Subversion of the Subject and the Dialectic of Desire in the Freudian Unconscious," Lacan deploys the notoriously complex "graph of desire" and a number of special, algebraic equations that have invited the frustration of many scholars.[4] As Jason Glynos and Yannis Stavrakakis note, "No one likes to feel stupid. A very rare person indeed is she who, having struggled to make sense of Lacan's *Écrits,* has not entertained such thoughts of vulnerability. This vulnerability is only exacerbated if a Lacanian seminar or essay has been recommended as reading material by a friend or professor whom we respect. It is a vulnerability that can very quickly turn to frustration, intimidation, or even anger."[5] Or in respect to the judges of the Mathers and Crowley trial, the occultic can even be subject to ridicule and laughter. Indeed, laughter and ridicule are often a product of misunderstanding, a frequent recourse of those who are not "in the know" or who do not understand. The detective in Poe's short story, for example, is not interested in the contents of the purloined letter, and even seems amused by the whole affair. But he is not exempt from its authority, insofar as his life participates in its circulation.

Ridicule is precisely what Alan Sokal and Jean Bricmont deploy in their book-length demystification project *Fashionable Nonsense: Postmodern Intellectuals' Abuse of Science* (1998). In their book, which, in general, lambastes the scientistic jargon of academic scholarship in the humanities, Sokal and Bricmont claim to defend the progress and truth-seeking enterprise of "science" against the centerless relativism of the project of the posts. In other words, the authors seek to reestablish the Enlightenment distinction between science and the occult.

Just like the courtroom battle between Mathers and Crowley, we should understand the melee between Sokal, Bricmont, and the postmodernists as a struggle over authority and "secret" meaning. Sokal and Bricmont seem particularly interested in Lacan and psychoanalytic prose, but for reasons of which they are not consciously aware: like the translinguistic truths of Crowley and Mathers, the bedrock of psychoanalysis is that its truth is beyond representation—it is (the) *unconscious.* Psychoanalysis is a contemporary occultic discourse precisely because of the pride of place it secures for the ineffable, yet unlike the occult tradition, this ineffable is impossible to know and, consequently, commands a certain degree of humility. In his discussion of "The Purloined Letter," Lacan questions the very notion that one can distinguish "the understanding of the idiot from that of the intelligent man." Insofar as the detective is able to locate the letter, when the police cannot, by *not* looking too hard, "the intelligent thing to do, in this case, is to play the idiot."[6] Although in Sokal and Bricmont's scientific idiom there is a direct route to the real, in psychoanalysis, letters always already get in the way.

Because Sokal and Bricmont lack any understanding of rhetoric, their failure to acknowledge the psychoanalytic processes of invention and interpretation in respect to ineffability (occult poetics) makes them the unwitting victims of their own lettered thefts. For example, the authors poke fun at Lacan's definition of the phallus as the signifier, understood in terms of the square root of negative one. They find it "distressing to see our erectile organ equated" to the square root of negative one, they say, which reminds them "of Woody Allen, who, in *Sleeper,* objects to the reprogramming of his brain: 'You can't touch my second-favorite organ!'"[7] As Bruce Fink points out, the problem here is that for Lacan the phallus is not the biological penis,[8] just as the Wand, the Sacred Lance, and even the biological penis are symbolic for the "Spiritual Phallus" in Crowley's rituals.[9] Sokal and Bricmont's dick joke, however, "exemplifies the way in which one always says more than one intends to say . . . an aspect of language that Sokal and Bricmont would rather not have to take into account when it comes to understanding 'serious writing.'"[10] Mindful of the unconscious, Fink jokes that perhaps Sokal and Bricmont find their academic "performance lacking."

More seriously, contrary to the outsider who would condemn Lacan's difficult prose as intentionally designed to establish an academic or clinical hierarchy with himself at the top, those who study his work recognize that Lacan's difficult style was designed to achieve the opposite effect. During an explanation of the necessity of the presence of a bar in one of his many algebraic equations, Lacan remarked that "the bar, like everything involving what is written, is based only on the following—what is written is not to be understood. That is why you are not obliged to understand my writings. If you don't understand them, so much the better—that will give you an opportunity to explain them." Fink explains that Lacan's writing is deliberately designed to "jolt" readers out of "conceptual ruts."[11] One of those ruts is the tendency to put faith in an authoritative expert—Lacan as a magus—instead of in our own ability to think though ideas or pursue "the truth." In other words, unlike Crowley's, Lacan's hermeneutic is one of anti- or un-authority to prevent the subjection and hierarchy of an occultic star system.

By characterizing psychoanalysis as the contemporary antithesis of Crowley's Qabalah, however, I do not mean to devalue the theory, nor do I exempt it from the occultic enterprise. Sokal and Bricmont fail to recognize that Lacan's language, considered as a contemporary *occultic* discourse, is designed to combat the very problems they diagnose; they have succumbed to the fetish of esoteric language, which Lacan, like a good occultist, employs to exclude people just like Sokal and Bricmont (if not to invite similar reactions to help demonstrate the point). Nevertheless, insofar as Lacan always urged a close reading of his texts "to the letter," and insofar as he is recognized as the "Absolute Master" or the great "Gongora" or "Grand Dragon" of psychoanalysis,[12] that is, insofar as Lacan is a magus in his own right despite protests, we are led to confront the difficulty of academic authority in postmodernity: as a consequence of media technologies, one is always potentially speaking to audiences that he or she has never considered, audiences who will inevitably misunderstand, who may fetishize you or your discourse, or who may use your letters against you. In our contemporary age of publicity, the contexts into which our rhetoric can be taken "out of context" seem infinite.

Lacan's many difficult seminars were intended for clinicians, and thus his current status as a theoretical rock star in the humanities implicates an occultic system more in control of academic discourse than academics. It is consequently too easy to dismiss in laughter a given academic disagreement over theory as mere "dick-wagging" in pursuit of stature or authoritative power. By paying attention to the rhetorical function of language in the context of authority, we soon discover that every academic debate, at some level, concerns accessibility, concerns who is included and who is not, concerns who gets to speak and who is silenced. Academic debates are certainly about content, about ideas, but they are also about relations and relationships.

Those who refuse to acknowledge the relational and discriminating functions of discourse risk much more than misunderstanding or the loss of a good idea or fruitful insight. As I show in the next chapter, in the age of postmodern publicity, overestimating one's intellectual prowess and mastery of language or *the* fetishized signifier (the phallus) is a mistake. For example, the arrogance of making intellectual jokes at the expense of the Other can lead to castration. You never quite know who is reading your mail.

6
The Death of the Modern Magus
"The Masses" and Irony's Other

In the courtroom battle regarding Crowley's publication of Mathers's secret rituals, the justices had some difficulty finding for Mathers. Not only had the elder magus waited too long to sue (Crowley had published all but a few of the rituals so cherished by Mathers),[1] but the published rituals seemed remarkably similar to those of other secret groups. "Anyone who knows anything about these societies," said Lord Justice Moulton, "knows that the ritual of most of them has been published."[2] By the turn of the twentieth century, for example, the rituals of the largest secret fraternity, the Freemasons, were widely available.[3]

That the secrets of many secret societies were available in print by 1910 marked the beginning of the end of modern occultism. Their availability is a direct consequence of the declining cost of publication and innovations in the forces of mass production and reproduction—most especially the improvements of the printing press that gave rise to the inexpensive daily newspaper and tabloid magazine. For this reason many of the books penned by wealthy, aristocratic occultists like Crowley and Mathers were deliberately costly and hence not widely available to the general public. Crowley's carefully crafted and elaborately illustrated editions of *The Book of the Law,* for example, were simply priced too high to be available to the English common reader; one United States edition of *The Book of the Law* published in the late 1920s was a whopping $418.[4] Yet by the late nineteenth century the general reading public was consuming a healthy diet of occult literature, from nonfiction articles in the *Atlantic Monthly* and the *Nation* to gothic novels, esoteric poetry, and "dime" publications on the topics of black magic, dreams, and fortune-telling.[5] The latter were typically of the how-to variety, which reduced the complexity of occult practice to simple steps. Bradford Verter notes that "although one publisher of cheap paperbacks—'book-a-day' John W. Lovell[—]did inaugurate an Occult Series that issued Theosophical fiction and esoteric works in both paper (50 cents) and cloth ($1.00)[,] most of these booklets emphasized the practical rather than the mystical aspects of esoteric lore. As popular guides to ostensibly secret knowledge, they promised to demonstrate the techniques that would enable the reader to divine the future or penetrate the truth of someone's character; some offered spells culled from Agrippa and Albertus Magnus."[6] The pragmatic and expositive style of popular occult literature contrasts starkly with the texts of occultists like Lévi, Blavatsky, and Crowley. In early chapters I suggested that the challenging style of occult prose was used not only to discriminate but also as a dialectical means to transcend human expression to apprehend the truth. In the previous chapter I argued that another reason for stylistic difficulty is that strange language helps to establish an occultist's authority over others; if occult texts are too easy to comprehend, then there is no need to consult the expert. In this chapter I revisit the discriminating function of the rhetorical blind and show how such stylistic habits began to backfire and undermine the authority they were believed to help establish.

In light of the occult exposés that were becoming increasingly common in the popular press, then, there was not only a battle among occultists as to who had the right to tell secrets but also a battle over the rhetorical style and language of occult literature (in the end, the more simple, direct prose of the popular press would win).[7] This struggle over rhetorical style reflects a concern about the emergence of something new at the turn of the century: the mass audience. The concept of the mass audience speaks to both an emerging "public" constituted or brought into being by various mediated networks of circulation as well as a catch-all category that referred to the great unwashed. In other words, the mass audience is both an empirical and a rhetorical notion.

Empirically, the mass audience denotes the rather large number of people brought into common consciousness by a given media object, such as a newspaper. The wider the circulation of a newspaper, the larger its public or audience became. With the late-nineteenth-century emergence of the popular novel, the dime booklet, the tabloid magazine, and the newspaper a new reading public emerged, and this public seemed very curious about and interested in the occult. Hence Crowley lived during a time of rapid technological transformation, and his writings reflect the challenge of the mass audience that those of the occult aristocracy faced: the secrets of the occult tradition must be protected from the ignorant, misunderstanding rabble. As the secret rituals of the occult elite became increasingly public, so did a number of occult texts become increasingly playful and ironic, designed to appeal to two audiences: the first was the "mass" audience seeking entertainment, and the second was those individuals presumably seeking spiritual enlightenment. Crowley's work provides a number of excellent examples of a conspicuously ironic brand of occultism designed to mislead an inexpert public. The intertextual relationships between Crowley's work and reactions to it, however, also help to articulate why the occult begins to unravel as a coherent tradition: in an age of ever-increasing publicity, keeping secrets is tough! Moreover, when the potential audience of one's work expands exponentially, the likelihood of misinterpretation increases, as does the likelihood that one's rhetoric will take on a life of its own.

Below I examine Crowley's use of irony in order to advance three related claims. The first and most important claim is that, despite the resistance of Crowley and other occultists, the coherence of the tradition began to unravel in the late nineteenth and early twentieth century as the result of a popular press and the publics it brought into being. Second, by analyzing one of Crowley's most famous rhetorical blinds, I illustrate how a rhetoric of religious authority that employs irony as a legitimating strategy is likely to fail in a media-saturated environment. Finally, building on my remarks at the end of the previous chapter, I suggest that the precariousness of occult modes of authority at the end of modernity is demonstrative of the autonomy of social forms. Since the mass audience and the popular imaginary emerged as a result of the explosion and dominance of media technologies, the power of social forms and textual fragments to circulate and generate meaning in spite of the intentions of a concrete individual is tremendous.

To these ends this chapter is divided into three parts. First, because the remaining chapters assume an understanding of the split subject, I begin with a discussion of intentionality and agency that the emergence of the mass audience helps to bring into focus. Then, with an understanding of the intending yet nevertheless socially constructed subject, I move to examine Crowley's misleading call for the sacrifice of children in his magnum opus, *Magick: Book IV,* showing how its intended function as an ironic misdirection is compromised by the logic of publicity. Finally, in the concluding section I examine a number of writings about Crowley that seem to mirror his disdain for the masses: whereas for Crowley the "mass audience" functioned rhetorically as a category for the ignorant rabble, for the press, Crowley came to represent the evils of the wealthy and cultural elite.

The Mass Audience, Irony, and the Arrival of the Occultic

The emergence of a new kind of mediated public or "imagined community" as the result of mass-media technologies is empirically veri-

Fig. 7. Aleister Crowley (ca. 1910) in the headdress of Horus. His hands are making the sign of Pan, which signifies creative energy. Courtesy of the Ordo Templi Orientis.

fiable.[8] Yet as this new kind of "media" public arose, so too did its name become a rhetorical object. In academic circles, the "mass public" or "mass audience" often functioned as a category of derision and as an entity that was to be resisted. Indeed, in 1867 and 1868, Matthew Arnold published a series of articles in which he argued that "culture," understood as the best of a given society, needed to be protected from the homogenizing effects of mass communication and the debased culture it created. Arnold argued for the cultivation of an elite culture that pursues "sweetness" (beauty) and "light" (wisdom) to prevent the anarchy of the masses. This anarchy was an inevitable consequence of "our bondage to machinery" and our "proneness to value machinery as an end in itself."[9] Such views were further promoted (and ironically popularized) in the United Kingdom in the 1930s and 1940s by F. R. Leavis and Q. D. Leavis, who argued that along with the appearance of the mass audience, a tasteless, homogeneous "mass culture" was also appearing. Mass audiences, argued the Leavises, were manipulated into participating in mass culture because commercial interests were appealing to base, primitive impulses.[10] The entertainment industry was particularly naughty, and the Leavises worried about the ability of media producers to engender a kind of "hypnotic receptivity."[11] Stateside, similar fears fueled research on propaganda and the effect of media violence on children.[12]

The thinkers associated with the Frankfurt School of Social Research, originally located in Germany but later centered in the United States after its members fled the Nazis, helped to focus and frame the terms of what is often referred to as the "mass culture debate": Are the "masses" stupid and subject to ideological determination, or is it possible for individuals to resist oppression and escape the increasingly homogeneous "mass culture" that was developing?[13] More often than not, scholars engaged in research on "mass audiences" and "mass culture" in the early to mid-twentieth century were not optimistic about their subjects' capacity for independent thought.

Today our understanding of audiences is much more complex, and for the most part, scholars agree that media consumers are much more savvy, complicated, and resistant than earlier researchers supposed.[14] I have mentioned the mass culture debate, however, because of the rhetorical function of the term "mass audience": as Raymond Williams has pointed out, "the masses" is simply a term for the new, mass-media "mob." "I do not think of my relatives, friends, neighbors, colleagues, acquaintances, as masses; we [*sic*] none of us can or do. The masses are always the others, whom we don't know, and can't know. Yet now, in our kind of society, we see these others regularly, in their myriad variations; stand, physically, beside them. They are here, and we are here with them. And that we are with them is of course the whole point. To other people, we are also the masses. Masses are other people."[15] For the cultured elite in the early twentieth century, the masses were always those "other people" who are prone to misunderstanding or "not getting it right"; the masses, in this respect, function as the Other who threatens to undermine agency and control.

I think we can also read the rhetorical function of "the masses" as an important double of individual anxiety. Fear, hatred, or anxiety about the ability of the masses to misunderstand and destroy one's work is also a tacit suspicion that one may not be in control of one's rhetoric. As I mentioned in the previous interlude, in a media-saturated environment it is easy to have one's rhetoric decontextualized and recast as something that one did not intend (e.g., Crowley's or Lacan's "phallus" is mistakenly read as a penis). What I am suggesting, then, is that the empirically verifiable existence of new, mass-media publics led to the notion of "the masses," which in turn became a surrogate for the Other who threatens individual autonomy.

Insofar as the arrival of the mass audience in both the empirical and rhetorical senses poses a challenge to notions of individual autonomy and intention, at this juncture it is important to take a brief detour to discuss an underlying assumption of this book: there is no such thing as the autonomous, fully conscious, absolutely intending individual.

Some Remarks on Agency and Intention

Some readers may have noticed a tension between my remarks concerning the autonomy of social forms and my focus on the rhetorical acts of discrete individuals such as H. P. Blavatsky and Aleister Crowley. The former view implies a notion of subjectivity that yields "no anteriority or priority over its discourse," what is sometimes described as a "posthumanist" position,[16] while my focus on the acts of certain concrete individuals affords at least some meaningful priority in respect to intent. If it is the case that Crowley's hermeneutic of authority establishes his legitimacy, then it is implied that Crowley intended it to do so. If, however, I maintain that subjectivity is the project of ideology or discourse, then I must also admit that intentionality is born of false consciousness. After all, as Foucault argues, the autonomy of social forms—including language itself—urges the abandonment of "any attempt . . . to see discourse as a phenomenon of expression." In a posthumanist paradigm, Foucault continues, "discourse is not the majestically unfolding manifestation of a thinking, knowing, speaking subject, but, on the contrary, a totality . . . in which the dispersion of the subject and his discontinuity with himself may be determined."[17]

The dichotomy between intentional and non-intentional expression is, of course, false, and the tension I have just outlined is deliberately misleading. I have constructed this argument of straw to draw attention to the fact that dissimulation implies an intent to dissimulate. As Linda Hutcheon has noted, barring the most ironic of theoretical positions (e.g., that of Jean Baudrillard),[18] few theories that assume the critique of humanism and the constructedness of subjectivity "deny that intentions exist" or that "each of us at some time or another has intended," for example, "to be ironic."[19] That I have painted a false dichotomy is proof enough that intentionality is an inevitable and necessary concept for understanding the rhetorical act as such.

In the field of rhetorical criticism, intentionality has been or could be addressed in one of three ways. The first has been to regard the intention of a given speaker or author as irrelevant or even impossible to determine, a position that originated in a 1946 article titled "The Intentional Fallacy" by the New Critics W. K. Wimsatt and Monroe Beardsley. As René Wellek and Austin Warren explain, the "whole idea that the 'intention' of the author is the proper subject of literary history seems . . . quite mistaken. The meaning of a work of art is not exhausted by, or even equivalent to, its intention."[20] Originally the intentional fallacy concerned grounding the aesthetic value of a text in authorial intent and the textual result, although today it also refers to the impossibility of locating intention within a text. Some critics understand avoiding the intentional fallacy to mean that one should not make psychological claims, a characteristically "black box," behaviorist tendency in some of the criticism of U.S. rhetorical studies.[21] From a practical standpoint, however, the weakness of this position is the fact that it is difficult to avoid making assumptions about authorial intent, however fragmented or "dead" one assumes the author to be. Further, most texts contain traces of extrinsic social and historical contexts that inevitably become part of textual interpretation.

A second way to address intentionality is deterministic.[22] Despite the variety of deterministic viewpoints, all are characterized by the idea that intentionality is, at least in part, an illusion, for individual action is the effect of a larger, extrinsic, determining cause such as biology or ideology. This response is rarely advanced in any strong sense, although it is sometimes cast as an ominous foe in rhetorical theory scholarship. Among rhetoricians and literary critics, weaker deterministic responses can be located in scholarship that draws on orthodox Marxism, psychoanalysis, and the early theory of Foucault. For example, in his landmark essay on "critical rhetoric," Raymie McKerrow draws on Foucauldian theory to argue for a reversal of "public address" to "discourse which addresses publics," which he argues can better demystify the discursive sources of oppression and domination. Such a reversal would focus on how symbolism and discourse "address" or constitute individuals and publics. Without such a reversal, McKerrow argues, there is "the danger that a 'public address' vision of popular culture would be constrained to think in terms of 'agent,' rather than symbol as the focus of attention. There also is the danger that such extension of traditional forms of analysis would simply perpetuate the modernist clichés in constructing, through the myopic lenses of a predefined vision of the media as a 'cultural wasteland,' elitist standards of excellence."[23] Although McKerrow does not argue that intention is irrelevant or that individuals are not agents,[24] he has been received as a strong determinist by some for promoting an overly idealist conception of the domination of the symbolic that overlooks the materiality of "real people engaged in struggle."[25]

Finally, a third approach to intentionality, and the one that I advance here, is the proverbial middle road. Although it is difficult to discern the mental states of a given rhetor or author on the basis of a given text, intention and agency nevertheless exist. The distinction that needs to be made is that while individuals intend to do things (and intention is always implied by action, rhetorical or otherwise),[26] the motives structuring intent may be unknown to the individual. In other words, intent may be scripted by ideological forces or unconscious motives and desires. That I tried my hand at dissimulation at the beginning of this book does not mean I did not intend to do so but rather that my intention may be born of a quest for intellectual superiority inspired by an unconscious inferiority (a psychoanalytic rationale), or a desire to move from a lower to a higher social class in writing through the mastery of verbal play, an arrogance which is in turn determined by the economic arrangement of society (a materialist rationale). In short, this third position involves the mindful separation of the concept of intention from the concept of the autonomous and unified subject, even though scholars have habitually assumed their interrelationship. Just as a school of fish can move and act as one in water, so does the divided subject make choices and intend action in the totality of discourse.

It is important to note, however, that divided or split subjectivity is the condition for determination and ideological structuring. When Foucault describes subjectivity as "discontinuous" in *The Archaeology of Knowledge,* it is because of the condition of discontinuity that the subject "may be determined." Even at the most deterministic theoretical stage of his intellectual career, Foucault says that the subject "may" be determined, not that the subject "is" determined. This is because maintaining a strong deterministic position denies that concrete individuals' intentional acts—most especially their rhetoric—do things in the social world that change or alter it, despite the constraints of ideology. To take a strong deterministic position is to deny the empirically observable progress of freedom fighters in the United States civil rights movement in the 1960s, or the strides for legal and social equality that women have made since the nineteenth century. That individuals are merely "bundles" of selves, divided subjectivities, or discontinuous selves is a precondition for determinism, not its absolute guarantee.

The questions a posthumanist understanding of subjectivity raises about agency, intention, and action are vexing, particularly for the rhetorician who stresses that the contingency of language, self, and community is the condition for the possibility of social change. That I can intend to mean or act opens up a world of possibility in which social change may occur. Yet that my intentional acts are ideologically determined (in the weaker sense of constraint) seems to commit me to at least a loose version of fate. As Wittgenstein observed, when we think about the possibility of human progress within the embrace of a progressive history, we tend to think in terms of a straight line. From a rhetorical standpoint, especially a historically mindful perspective that seeks to recapture moments of contingency (and thus moments at which the intentional, rhetorical acts of someone made a difference), the trajectory of human progress must be "a curve, constantly changing direction."[27] As Walter Benjamin observed in his philosophy of criticism, the distinction to be made here is one of retrospection: in the sweep of past social history, we see straight lines and patterns because this is how the determinism of ideology appears—a representation of the success of the constraints ideology places on human action.[28] But the successful observation of these constraints is neither condemning nor guaranteed: from the perspective of the present, one should say harmful and oppressive, ideologically structured consequences will occur unless this or that impedes them.

If the third way of intentionality concerns holding both of these views in dialectical tension, then one comes to the inevitable question: Where does one locate the point at or space in which the intentional acts of individuals are futile and the determination of social forces dominates? I think it is an impossible and ultimately unhelpful task to embark on cartographic quest for an answer. One simply must assume that both deterministic forces and intentional agency exist within the totality of discourse and then work from either end toward some critical goal. The rationale for seeking out moments of historical contingency, as much as for locating instances of structural determination, is a political one, not a metaphysical or ontological one.

The conceptual shift from understanding individual agency as autonomous to understanding it as a dialectical relation between conscious intent and unconscious determinants is a product of social transformation, of the social totality. Only after mass-media technologies led to the expansion of circulatory networks did it become possible to reflect on the many ways in which technology influences and undermines human expression. This realization is reflected in the occult's transition, as a discourse, from a coherent tradition to the repertoire of fragments that are held together by the form of the occultic. The emergence of the "mass audience" as a zombified and mindless rhetorical entity is a reflection of an unconscious or preconscious awareness that we are not as in control of our rhetoric as we like to believe. The term "occultic," consequently, is meant to reflect the autonomy of social forms (e.g., theological form) from occultists, the decentering or death of the Great Magus that is so central to the modern occult tradition. In this sense, modern occult discourse is the discourse of absolute, individual autonomy par excellence, and the occultic is consequently post-occultism.

Below I argue that an analysis of Crowley's attempts to distinguish between the true believers and "the masses" reveals an inability to recognize the limits of agency that were becoming increasingly prominent in the twentieth century. Crowley's inability to control how his work was read reflects the death of the Great Magus in the twentieth century. I suggest that the best way to witness this death is by examining the use of irony, because the principal function of the trope is to distinguish among those who "get it" and those who do not.

Irony, Dialectic, Anxiety

Irony is a figure of speech or trope that demonstrates, with considerable clarity, the logic of intertextuality and the power of language to undermine agency and intent. This is because the rhetorical power of irony concerns its ability to provoke a sense of belonging or exclusion. Because the social logic of inclusion/exclusion—and by extension, self and Other—is most appropriate to irony, its analysis reveals the fissures and cracks of subjectivity. Irony has the power to bring us together as groups and to undo us as subjects.

The concept of irony is rooted in the Greek *eirōn*, which means "dissembler," or one who disguises and conceals. Since Plato's attack on rhetoric as the art of flattery and deception, there has been a longstanding association of rhetoric with irony.[29] Defenders of the tradition, however, have tended to describe irony as one of a number of rhetorical devices that can be used to good effect. Cicero, who discussed irony in terms of the Latin equivalent, *dissimulare,* or "to dissimulate," defines irony as "the humor of saying one thing and signifying another." He notes that using irony is especially pleasing if one manages it well but that it can also have disastrous consequences.[30]

In her exemplary study of the trope, Linda Hutcheon locates the "unbearable slipperiness of irony" in the fact that some audiences fail to recognize when a rhetor or author intends to be ironic, and further, that the "pleasing effect" lauded by Cicero is derived precisely from that risk—"irony's edge." Using irony as a verbal strategy is only successful if it is "stable," which Wayne Booth defines as an ability to be "reconstructed" by readers or an audience in a way that does not invite them to impute unintended meanings.[31] The ironist's challenge is to make sure one supplies enough reconstructive cues to the desired audience such that they will not be encouraged to fabricate a meaning that is not intended. Given the risk, obviously there are also unstable and unintended ironies, situations when someone attributes humor or dissimulation when it is not intended, thereby undermining the control of the ironist. Chaïm Perelman and L. Olbrechts-Tyteca describe this "unbearable slipperiness" as a formal paradox: "Irony always presupposes supplementary information on facts, or norms. . . . Thus irony cannot be used if there is uncertainty about the speaker's opinions. This gives irony a paradoxical character: using it implies that argumentation is necessary; but in order to be able to use it, a minimum agreement is required. . . . Irony is all the more effective when it is directed to a well-defined group. Only by having some idea of the beliefs held within certain social environments can we guess whether or not a given text is ironical."[32] Uncertainty or simply a lack of knowledge about the rhetor or author will likely guarantee the failure of an ironic strategy.

One can understand why those occultists concerned with keeping their secrets secret might find irony an appealing rhetorical strategy: irony can be used to discriminate audiences and to speak in a double voice. In the Middle Ages, occultists spoke to each other in code or the "the language of birds" to avoid religious persecution, an irony in the most basic sense of "saying one thing but meaning another."[33] In modern occult discourse, however, there is no longer a fear of institutional or state-sponsored persecution. Thus irony is resigned to its discriminating function, the creation of in-groups and out-groups. Kierkegaard suggests that verbal irony contains an implicit hierarchical arrangement that mirrors social order. He says that an "ironic figure of speech has [a] property that characterizes all irony, a certain superiority deriving from its not wanting to be understood immediately, even though it wants to be understood, with the result that this figure looks down, as it were, on plain and simple talk that everyone can promptly understand; it travels around, so to speak, in an exclusive incognito and looks down pityingly from this high position on ordinary, prosaic talk."[34] At issue in the deployment of irony is power, especially that which would maintain or create social order. Just "as kings and princes speak French, the higher circles . . . speak ironically so that lay people will not be able to understand them."[35] Hutcheon refers to this classed dynamic as the "politics of irony," the social, structuring work of irony. This politics is particularly dangerous because, unlike "metaphor or allegory, which demand similar supplementing of meaning, irony has an evaluative edge and manages to provoke emotional response in those who 'get it' and those who don't, as well as in its targets and in what some people call its 'victims.'"[36]

The psychic pleasure of "getting it" is inversely proportional to the displeasure of exclusion. For these reasons, Kenneth Burke associates irony with "drama" and observes that from a retrospective, historical gaze, irony can be used as a prophetic formula among the "characters" in any given social order. "There is a level of generalization at which predictions about 'inevitable' developments in history are quite justified," says Burke.

> We may state with confidence, for instance, that what arose in time must fall in time (hence, that any given structure in society must "inevitably" perish). We may make such prophecy more precise, with the help of irony, in saying that the developments that led to the rise will, by the further course of their development, "inevitably" lead to the fall (true irony always, we hold, thus involving an "internal fatality," a principle operating from with, though its logic may also be grounded in the nature of the extrinsic scene, whose properties contribute to the same development).[37]

Irony derives its power from its risks—potential misfires and unintended victims—and thus entails a degree self-destructive potential. Coupled with the highly emotional response individuals have toward irony, it makes sense that the anxiety of individuals who do not "get it" would be more noticeable in reactive texts than with other figures of speech. Because a cartography of discourse is most successful when it successfully locates points of conspicuousness, an analysis of the reactions to verbal irony seems a likely place for traces of anxiety between different publics (e.g., class anxiety).

Given its "prophetic" element, it is not surprising that for Burke another god-term for irony is "dialectic." The significance of the association of dialectic with irony cannot be overemphasized. The relationship between irony and dialectic is twofold. First, although communication itself is a dialogic phenomenon, verbal irony is an exaggerated dialogic trope in the sense that its discriminating function not only excludes others but also needs "the fool," as Burke puts it. Insofar as irony is used to establish charismatic authority among an elite group, for example, ironic authority needs disbelievers and the misunderstanding rabble. In this respect, the irony of modern occultism implies that the occult as such needs its detractors and enemies as much as it needs acolytes and converts. The occult, as such, requires a number of individuals who are not in the know.

Second, "only through an internal and external experiencing of folly could we possess," argues Burke, "sufficient 'characters' for some measure of development beyond folly"—namely, "getting it."[38] Hence the association of dialectic with irony also refers to the power of its symbolic thrust, the ability of irony to push the reconstructing audience to other places, other sites of meaning, other texts, particularly past experiences of not getting it or being played the fool, all of which are other realities or texts not in the here and now. We can term the symbolic thrust of irony its intertextual invitation or quality.

In an important parallel sense, the intertextual invitation of irony can be used to describe the dialectical element of textual criticism, the Gademerian "merging" of the pre-understanding and contextual horizon of the interpreter and the contextual horizons of discourse that was discussed in chapter 4: in the interrogation of texts and "the Other," one ends up interrogating the self. "What goes forth as A," Burke professes, "returns as non-A." Characterizing "dialectical thought," Jameson argues similarly that "the essential movement of all dialectical criticism . . . is to reconcile the inner and the outer, the intrinsic and the extrinsic, the existential and the historical," which allows "us to feel our way with a single determinate form or moment of history at the same time that we stand outside of it."[39]

Thus my methodological concern with moving into the intertextual order and textual strategy are wed at the site of an ironic knot; the relationship between the content of texts and their collective meaning in discourse is formal. As Jameson puts it, "Form is itself but the working out of content in the realm of the superstructure."[40] Irony is not merely a trope but a formal, social dynamic of discrimination. That the ironic content of a discrete text reflects the formal structure of social discrimination will become increasingly apparent with an analysis of Crowley's texts. Crowley's use of irony not only betokens an enormous ego absolutely convinced of his supreme autonomy and individuality but also underscores an association of the "masses" with the "lower classes" that would come to haunt him.

The Problem with Rhetorical Blinds

> *The Book of the Law:* Worship me with fire & blood; worship me with swords & with spears. Let the woman be girt with a sword before me; let blood flow in my name. Trample down the Heathen; be upon them, o warrior, I will give you of their flesh to eat! Sacrifice cattle, little and big: after a child.[41]

> *Crowley:* Those Magicians who object to the use of blood have endeavored to replace it with incense. For such a purpose the in-

> cense of Abramelin may be burnt in large quantities. . . . But the bloody sacrifice, though more dangerous, is more efficacious; and for nearly all purposes human sacrifice is the best. The truly great Magician will be able to use his own blood, or possibly that of a disciple, and without sacrificing the physical life irrevocably.[42]

As was noted in the discussion of the generic features of occult texts in chapter 1, occultists frequently utilize figurative language to speak directly to the initiated and to confuse or discourage the outsider. Like the strategy of self-reference, deceptive rhetorical gestures serve to further justify the authority of a given occultist, since only he or she can claim to know the "true" meaning behind a rhetorical blind. Crowley's scandalous call for the sacrifice of children in occult rituals is one such blind.

One of the most famous of Crowley's writings is chapter 12 of his *Magick in Theory and Practice,* one of the four books of the massive tome *Magick*. Titled "Of the Bloody Sacrifice, and of Matters Cognate," the chapter details how all living beings are but "storehouses of energy, varying in quantity according to the size and health of the animal."[43] Killing the animal to release its energy during rituals, Crowley explains, is perhaps the most important act for the most powerful kinds of magick: "For the highest spiritual working one must accordingly choose that victim which contains the greatest and purest force."[44] Naturally, this is a "male child of perfect innocence and high intelligence."[45] Crowley's explanation of the role of sacrifice in ritual magic here, first published privately by the Ordo Templi Orientis in 1913, sheds some light on Hadit's command from *The Book of the Law* to worship him in fire and blood (see epigraph). The hierarchy established by the life forces of animals is mirrored in verse: incense may represent ritual sacrifice in fire, but in the end it is the shedding of blood that is required; livestock will do, but nothing is more potent than a male child.

Crowley's suggestion to sacrifice children was a rhetorical blind designed to mislead a curious public and to encourage the true adept to read more deeply. The reconstructive clue is located in a footnote: "There is a traditional saying that whenever an Adept seems to have made a straightforward, comprehensible statement, then is it most certain that He means something entirely different. The Truth is nevertheless clearly set forth in His Words; it is His simplicity that baffles the unworthy. I have chosen the expressions in this chapter in such a way that it is likely to mislead those Magicians who allow selfish interests to cloud their intelligence, but to give useful hints to such as are bound by the proper oaths to devote their powers to legitimate ends."[46] The command to sacrifice children contained in *The Book of the Law,* as well as Crowley's elaboration of the blood sacrifice in *Magick,* constitute a deliberate misdirection that is not only verbal but also in some sense "magickal," a technique designed to liberate the magician from language in a unique version of what is known as existential or philosophical irony.

The First Function of Occult Irony: Magickal Irony

Pretending to advocate the sacrifice of children is fun, and this pleasure implicates a state of being in the world—an existentialism—that is "ironic." Throughout his life, Crowley's fondness for staging public spectacles, from pranks (like that of publicly declaring the independence of the Irish Republic in New York Harbor, ripping up his British passport, and declaring war on Britain)[47] to public rituals, never left him. These pranks and public spectacles can be read as Crowley's attempt to become a public ironist through and through. Although it is certainly a means to authority, there is some indication in Crowley's writings that his willed dissimulations were in some sense magically motivated in his attempts to completely depart from the material, human world. In a letter to a follower concerning the "apparent frivolity of some of my remarks," Crowley writes:

> ("How can you expect people to take your Magick seriously!" I hear from every quarter, "when you write so gleefully about it, with your tongue always in your cheek?") The curate's twang, the solemnity of self-importance, all manners that do not disclose the real man, are abominations. . . . I know that I too am at times obscure; I lament the fact. The reason is twofold: (a) my ineradicable belief that readers know [more] about the subject matter better than I do myself . . . (b) I am carried away by the exultant exaltation of my theme; I boil over with rapture—not the crystal-clear, the cool solution that I aimed at. On the Path of the Wise there is probably no danger more deadly, no poison more pernicious, no seduction more subtle than Spiritual Pride . . . so that its victim runs the peril of straying into a Black Lodge.[48]

The irony of existential irony could be described as the paradoxical achievement of humility via an attitude of superiority: by being above the world in leaving it, one is humbled without pride. As it is the goal of the practicing Buddhist to still the mind and leave behind material existence in the quiet transcendence of meditation, a charitable understanding of Crowley's ironies might figure them as part of an existential praxis. Socrates' god-fearing ignorance and his continual, ironic reversals in Plato's dialogues or Nietzsche's tortuous ironies in *Thus Spake Zarathustra* are more familiar examples of the philosophical ironist. Kierkegaard paints the existential ironist as an individual who seeks liberation from the responsibility inevitably entailed by the use of language: "When I am aware as I speak that what I am saying is what I mean and that what I have said adequately expresses my meaning, and I assume that the person to whom I am talking grasps my meaning completely, then I am bound by what has been said. . . . I am also bound with respect to myself and cannot free myself any time I wish. If, however, what I said is not my meaning or the opposite of my meaning, then I am free in relation to others and to myself."[49] That public pranks and ironic spectacles work for this kind of liberation is consistent with the point of magickal ritual and Crowley's own beliefs about magical attainment. For instance, the attainment of the grade of Ipsissimus, the highest grade of spiritual progress, is imagined as the extremely difficult crossing of the "Abyss" on the Qabalist's "tree of life." Crossing the abyss requires a destruction of the ego and all that maintains it, which is what, Crowley claimed, he was invited to do during magickal working in Algiers: "I understood that every disturbance [movement of body or thought alike] (which makes manifestation possible) implies deviation from perfection. It is for this reason that my individuality (which distinguishes me from all other beings) involves the idea of injustice. Therefore, to penetrate beyond the Abyss, where iniquity cannot exist, my personal self-hood must be annihilated."[50] Crowley did not achieve the grade during the working, but it was his pursuit for years to come. He noted the difficulty of attaining the grade in his diary on December 26, 1919: "Attainment is Insanity. The whole point is to make it perfect in balance. Then it radiates light in every direction, while the Ipsissimus is utterly indifferent to it."[51] Kierkegaard characterizes this "insanity" of indifference as an ironist's "radical disassociation from one's society and one's social self,"[52] a break with the "immediacy" of one's physical existence in the "real world."

Kierkegaard's ideal ironist, Socrates, exemplified this break by heeding the Delphic oracle's command "know thyself" through a radical implosion of subjectivity: "Now it is certainly true that the phrase [know thyself] can designate subjectivity in its fullness, inwardness in its utterly infinite wealth, but for Socrates self-knowledge was not so copious; it actually contained nothing more than the separating, the singling out, of what later become the object of knowledge. The phrase 'know yourself' means: separate yourself from the other."[53] This separation is ironic insofar as the ironist achieves a state of indifference toward the Other and toward his or her social self. While such a disassociation never really seemed to happen with Crowley because, clearly, he took much pleasure in his notoriety, one can understand how his pranks and ironic misdirections could be thought to have some magickal or religious purpose. In short, Crowley's ironies and pranks were not merely "fun and games," nor were they completely motivated by a desire to keep esoteric secrets. At the very basic level of language, one can argue that the occultist must be an ironist insofar as he or she must believe that human language is inadequate for expressing and communicating the transcendent truth. The notion that language gets in the way of truth could necessitate the embrace of existential irony as a route to divine knowledge.

The Second Function of Occult Irony: Social Discrimination

Despite the possibility that Crowley could have intended his irony to serve this first, magickal function, an analysis of his texts reveals that his ironies were also meant to discriminate. The ironic command to sacrifice innocent children creates a "secret space" of acknowledgment and, in the words of Cicero, a "pleasing effect" among the initiated who are keen enough to understand the joke. As Crowley says, his rhetorical blind is deliberately advanced to beguile the outsider and "mislead those Magicians who allow selfish interests to cloud their intelligence." Andrew Cross suggests that being a party to the inner circle becomes something akin to "the pleasure lovers sometimes have when speaking to each other in their private code, even when they are by themselves."[54] The deployment of verbal irony does not always require the initiated for it to function as a technology of social discrimination, however. Cross suggests that even in an instance when no hearer catches a ironist's ironic displays, the hearer's relative inability to understand only increases the ironist's "sense of sophistication."[55] In fact, "the more superior [the ironist feels him- or herself] to be, the less need [he or she has] of other's recognition" of his or her authority.[56]

In light of the conceptual discussion of the dialectic of irony, one can begin to sense a socially scripted motive behind Crowley's ironies. We locate extrinsic traces in places that do not announce themselves as ironic—places in which Crowley is either addressing true believers attempting to make sense of the verbal puzzles in *The Book of the Law,* or in places like personal letters, where he addresses the dedicated adept. It is in the texts addressed solely to the initiate that one locates a concern about social position or "class" as motivating the verbal ironies of those texts more likely to be read by a general public.

When we examine Crowley's entire published corpus, his Darwinian and classist views are easy to find. In his second commentary on *The Book of the Law,* Crowley remarks that the "nature of magickal power is quite incomprehensible to the vulgar."[57] Invoking Nietzsche as an important "prophet," Crowley was consistent and unyielding in his stressing the naturalness of social hierarchy: "Nature's way is to weed out the weak. This is the most merciful way, too. At present all the strong are being damaged, and their progress hindered by the dead weight of the weak limbs and the missing limbs, the diseased limbs and the atrophied limbs. The Christians to the Lions! Our humanitarianism, which is the syphilis of the mind, acts on the basis of the lie that the King must die."[58] The masses are a "canting, whining, servile breed of whipped dogs which refuses to admit of its deity" or inner sense of the divine.[59] Classed order is natural and necessary, yet Crowley says (disingenuously) that this order need not be based on material wealth; it is spiritual wealth that naturally pits "the slave mob against us," the "aristocrats of Freedom."[60] Armed with the spiritual message of *The Book of the Law,* he calls for a new spiritual hierarchy:

> We should give every opportunity to the ambitious, and thereby establish a class of morally and intellectually superior men and women. . . . We do not insist on trying to train sheep to hunt foxes or lecture on history; we look after their physical well being, and enjoy their wool and mutton. In this way we shall have a contented class of slave who will accept the conditions of existence as they really are, and enjoy life with the quiet wisdom of cattle. It is our duty to see to it that this class of people lack for nothing. The patriarchal system is better for all classes than for any other; the objections to it come from the abuses of it.[61]

The commentary on the necessity of class (and the reasons why Crowley and his followers are on top) does not end here, however: "Reason is rubbish; race-instinct is the true guide."[62] Crowley's "race-instinct" does not refer to the all-inclusive "human" race of Blavatsky's rhetoric of racial cataclysm in *The Secret Doctrine.* Rather, "race" here very clearly refers to that of the white European. The United States, perceived by Crowley as a heathen "melting pot" of imperialist humanitarianism, is rotten with people who "are desperately anxious to make the Singhalese wear furs, and the Tibetans vote, and the whole world chew gum, utterly dense to the fact that most other nations, especially the French and British, regard 'American Institutions' as the lowest savagery."[63] Echoing the sentiments of a follower in a letter, Crowley speaks of the "'inferior' races, like the Veddah, Hottentot and the Australian Blackfellow."[64] Further, the rotten democratic experiment of the United States threatens "the submergence of the individual in his class," which for Crowley "means the end of all true human relations between men." Crowley argues that "socialism means war," for when "class moves as a class, there can be no exceptions."[65] Class consciousness among the proletariat—and even among the bourgeoisie!—is to be avoided at all costs. Only the true aristocrat of freedom, the enlightened, Thelemic soul, understands class: "How right the politicians are to look upon their constituents as cattle! Anyone who has any experience of dealing with any class as such knows the futility of appealing to intelligence, indeed to any other qualities than those of brutes."[66]

In light of these remarks, the ideal, magickally revealed social order is one that looks remarkably similar to that which Crowley experienced every day: women and people of color were thought of as inferior, less-intelligent beings who were naturally beneath him. In the British Victorian world into which Crowley was born, class distinctions were stark, even for white individuals of the middle class. One finds evidence of the profoundness of this rigidity in flesh and bone: one historian observes that "in the 1870s eleven- to twelve-year-old boys from the upper-class schools were on average five inches taller than boys from industrial schools, and at all teen-agers three inches taller than the sons of artisans."[67] Those with the intelligence and standing enough to be "at the top"—aside from Christians, of course—should be at the top, as it is nature's way. That Crowley himself barely worked a day in his life, spending a life of leisure living in many exotic locations and traveling the world, is not inconsequential. Crowley's father left him an inheritance of forty thousand pounds to draw upon, when he was not living off the wealth of his many spouses.[68] In respect to the social order that Crowley's private discussions seemed to suggest, the irony of the discriminating function of his many verbal ironies is that the secret order of magick is no different from the rigid class structure of Victorian England. As we shall see, the anxieties that emerge in response this particular secret are the source of Crowley's undoing.

The Instability of Occult Irony

The undoing of Crowley's legitimacy as an occult authority has everything to do with how he was portrayed in the popular press, which came as a direct result of his verbal ironies. An understanding of the instability of Crowley's ironies is an apt illustration of Burke's rendition of irony as prophetic formula: what goes forth as A returns as non-A. He who came forth as the prophet of a "new Aeon" returned, by the end of his life, a sad and lonely man, language itself having played him a fool. Because of the uncertainty of audiences both inside and outside the occult subculture, Crowley's rhetoric took on a life of its own that not only undermined his legitimacy as an occult authority but also forever cast him as a bloodthirsty Satanist in the collective memory of the West.

From the vantage of the initiated, blood sacrifice is for the selfish magician (e.g., the one who would not recognize Crowley as the One True Voice of the New Aeon) and the wide-eyed layperson. Its true meaning is only for the most intelligent and devoted of Thelemites. The question arises: So what is an authentic reading of Crowley's seeming advocacy of ritual sacrifice? How are those who "get it" getting it? The answer is more complex than it would seem, even knowing the rules of ironic play and having a healthy dose of reconstructive clues. In a footnote to the chapter on blood sacrifices, we are told that these relatively straightforward accounts of the sacrifice of children signify ejaculate. Lon Milo DuQuette explains that "the preposterous statement written in the above mentioned chapter, in which it appears he confesses to the sacrifice of over 120 male children in one year, was nothing more than an outrageous literary blind. It is obvious to anyone who carefully reads the chapter and its footnotes that the only thing he was confessing to was his practice of a simple technique of sexual magick whereby he ejaculated 120 times that year without making his partner pregnant."[69] DuQuette is at best generous with this reading, for even if we know that Crowley intends irony, no clues are provided to help unravel this intended meaning. In other words, while there is some sense of pleasure in knowing that Crowley is not really advocating murder, the text lacks the clues that might help the reader determine how to signify. Its ironical effect is not "stable" to either the outsider or the initiate if one confines oneself to the context provided by the book. Certainly the same can be said of *The Book of the Law,* which seems to specify human sacrifice twice in chapter 3 without the helpful winks and nods of footnotes.

Irony, then, can pose problems for the knowing initiate if he or she has not been provided the rules for decoding. Presumably, stable irony is discernible on the basis of "four marks": first, the ironical effect is intended by the author; second, the irony is covert (which distinguishes irony from mere metaphor); third, the ironical effect does not initiate a chain reaction of textual deconstruction; and fourth, the irony is "finite." Wayne Booth urges that all ironic constructions "depend on an appeal to assumptions, often unstated, that ironists share," which implies that stable irony is a reconstructive transaction. Hence, for Booth "the act of reconstruction and all that it entails about the author and his picture of the reader become an inseparable part of what is said, and thus that act cannot really be said, it must be performed."[70] The performativity of irony on part of the ironist and the reader is precisely that which is pleasurable, an interplay of power that promises the reward of knowledge for the initiate and an air of superiority for the ironist.

Crowley's apparent ironical blood sacrifice, however, is a dance only those who personally knew him could join, for only they could understand that the ironical mappings here are not stable in the sense that a whole system of correspondences chains out symmetrically. Shared knowledge in the symbolic reference of "blood" and "child" are necessary; DuQuette suggests that they signify "male ejaculate," insofar as spilling one's seed on the floor instead of in one's ritual partner "sacrifices" what could have been a child. Contrary to DuQuette's suggestion, however, there is yet another meaning for blood beyond ejaculate that implicates a movement away from verbal irony into its existential form. DuQuette, a respected Thelemite, purposefully elides the fact that Crowley also prescribed the use of menstrual blood in the creation of "Cakes of Light," honey-soaked delicacies that are used as wafers in his original ritual Mass of Phoenix.[71] The recipe is found in chapter 3 of *The Book of the Law,* per the directions of Ra-Hoor-Khuit:

> 23. For perfume mix meal & honey and thick leavings of red wine: then oil of Abramelin and olive oil, and afterward soften & smooth down with rich fresh blood.
>
> 24. The best blood is of the moon, monthly: then the fresh blood of a child, or dropping from the host of heaven: then of enemies; then of the priest or of the worshipers: last of some beast, no matter what.
>
> 25. This burn: of this make cakes & eat unto me.

Crowley's commentary on these verses is conspicuously brief, and DuQuette and other Thelemites warn that "uninitiated interpretation of *Liber Legis* [*The Book of the Law*] III: 24 involves grave magical danger. He is deliberately vague as to the meaning of the passage, but it should be stressed that a literal interpretation involving the taking of human life is not Crowley's intended meaning."[72]

Even so, the literal and figurative ground here is uneven because there is no intertextual indication of where the realignments of signification are to stop: If blood is not real blood, then does honey signify something else as well? What of the Abramelin oil, an oil only known to Golden Dawn initiates as particularly magical? There is uncertainty about Crowley's irony that cannot be resolved, even in recourse to his whole universe of texts.[73] That "blood" appears in ways that simultaneously mean in literal and figurative senses indicates a different kind of irony is at work that is asymmetrical. This unstable textual irony, on the one hand, cues readers to unravel the text and recode its meaning, but one is uncertain as to where covert meaning ends and the overt begins. This uncertainly, in turn, moves the close reader to a more abstract, meaningful intertextual space that beckons infinite regress. In other words, unstable irony at the level of text forces readers into a chain of questioning about how far to extend ironic meaning, such that uncertainty becomes the product of an endless chain of questioning. In the end, through thousands upon thousands of pages of writing by Crowley, we find Crowley at the terminus of the inferential and figurative chaining.

The uncertainty as to the regress of Crowley's ironies and ambiguous symbolism is as much a part of the success of the occult hermeneutic of authority as it is its greatest weakness. Occult texts typically announce themselves as approximations, since any signification of the truth about ultimate reality is beyond the faculty of language. This implies, then, that occult texts are deliberately, at base, unstable ironies in themselves, texts written to capitalize on the uneasy fit between signs and their (presumably) supernatural, transhuman referents, with the goal of an infinite regress of interpretation (such as that urged by Quabalistic readings), a notion first made popular by early German romantics in terms of the "infinity of reflection." As much as Crowley would construct his persona as the ultimate stop, the fact remains that it is also the enthymematic function of textual ambiguities that invites initiates as well, and the invitation to signify for oneself works to erase Crowley's persona as much as celebrate it. Irony, as much as jargon, leads readers and hearers to contextualize meaning in reference to their lives, most especially so when the instability of the irony is signaled by the relative absence of what Booth refers to as reconstructive cues.

Given the double-edged sword of irony and the reversals it threatens, it would seem that maintaining authority among a group of initiates commits the ironic occultist to perpetual re-significations and ironies in his or her attempts continuously to circumscribe the symbolic maps that are constitutive of the life experiences of initiates. In other words, precisely because of the commitment to extratextual, transcendent truths that form the primary philosophical basis of occult belief systems, any attempt to establish authority and maintain an inner circle by means of a rhetorical blind sets in motion a chaining of signification. In part, this logic of figurative regress helps to explain why Crowley was so prolific, for he had to keep moving the target of the signified to maintain control, so to speak, a continuous widening of the textual circle to manage figurative instability.[74] Language, in this respect, is beyond control.

Occultism Is to Class . . .

The problematic dynamic of intertextual reference that challenges Crowley can be redescribed in terms of "the paradox of authority." According to a number of analytical philosophers and argumentation scholars, the paradox of authority is found in any belief system that encourages and reifies the sovereignty of the individual, such as the democratic state: "Authority is the defining mark of the state in that it is the state which has the right to rule. Autonomy is the primary obligation of man insofar as he may regard himself as the author of his own decisions and hence morally responsible. But if man has a continuing obligation to achieve the highest degree of autonomy there seems to be no way to establish the moral force of the legitimacy of submission to the commands of the state."[75] Magickal systems are very good examples of this paradox. On the one hand, occult authorities urge the absolute autonomy of followers (Crowley insists, e.g., that his "reader knows all about the subject better than I do myself, and may like to hear it tackled from a novel angle").[76] Yet on the other hand, occult authorities are adamant about their authority in prophetic terms ("the Secret Masters chose me!"). The continual creation of text after text rife with ironic blinds and terminological ambiguity could be described as an attempt, unconscious or not, to navigate this paradox.

The textual occurrence of the paradox of authority is connected to the social realm of discourse formally in terms of the relationships that are implied between the author or rhetor and his or her audiences. This connection, the ironic knot between textual content and social form, is the place where Burke's dialectic of irony helps to extract us from the fetishistic pull of a discrete text. One way to characterize an understanding of this formal movement is in terms of the movement between the "text" and "context." Whereas the instability of occult irony threatens the legitimate authority of the occult rhetor or author among the seekers of esoteric wisdom (text), the discriminating functions of occult authority risk resentment from those excluded in the larger community (context). Crowley's exclusions led to a radical re-signification of his persona in the popular imaginary in ways that formally mirror the instability of his textual ironies. The reason one is able to observe this interesting relationship is, as I have suggested, the mass media. Mass-media portrayals of Crowley accelerated, in a hyperbolic manner, the politics of irony on a larger, social scale, so much so that Crowley has become the "wickedest man in the word," the patron saint of all that is evil, and the appointed messenger of Satan on earth—hence the ironic sacrifice of babies metamorphosed into a reality of "unspeakable" evils in the projected "life" of Crowley. A brief description of his portrayal in tabloid magazines and newspapers highlights Crowley's inability to maintain control of his intended meaning.

Crowley's penchant for dissimulation, coupled with his observable public behavior, gradually intensified his sensational portrayal in papers like *American Weekly, John Bull* (England), and the *San Francisco Call.* The European papers, for example, were particularly unkind. After having performed a ritual in London to which many reporters were invited, Crowley's cadre of followers was described as a "blasphemous sect whose proceedings conceivably led themselves to immorality of the most revolting character."[77] Years later, after Crowley had taken refuge in an abandoned abbey in Cefalu, Sicily, rumors exploded about evil goings-on. As the "organiser for pagan orgies," Crowley undoubtedly advocated "free sexual intercourse."[78] His "sexual debauches and drug orgies" at the abbey comprised a "maelstrom of filth and obscenity" inside its walls. Indeed, "the facts are too unutterably filthy to be detailed in a newspaper, for they have to do with sexual orgies that touch the lowest depths of depravity." In fact, "children under ten, whom the Beast keeps in his 'Abbey,' are made to witness horribly sexual debauches unbelievably revolting."[79] This "devil incarnate" seduced young men and women for his black magic, often bewitching them so that they are "powerless to resist his invitation to visit him."[80] In this "cesspool of vice" Crowley made three "unhappy children" observe the "violation of a naked woman in front of the 'altar,' and her subsequent slaying and sacrifice of a goat, which is made to play a principal part in [the] disgusting . . . rites" that take place there.[81]

Popular books such as Dion Fortune's *Winged Bull* and Nina Hamnett's memoir *Laughing Torso* furthered Crowley's evil reputation in the popular imaginary. Although Crowley seems to have enjoyed the initial "evil" portrayals, he undoubtedly became increasingly troubled by them.[82] Angry about his unfavorable portrayal in *Laughing Torso,* Crowley sued Hamnett for libel on two counts: that she wrote he practiced black magic and that she suggested that a baby had disappeared from the abbey (presumably, it is implied, for ritual sacrifice).[83]

Ravenous for sensational stories, *John Bull* painted Crowley as a cannibal: "Possessed at one time with ample private means, he penetrated into the recesses of Egypt, Algiers, Morocco, India . . . even into the 'Forbidden Country' of Thibet. Concerning these travels and his various hunting expeditions some amazing stories are told. . . . One solitary mountain-climbing expedition it is actually affirmed that running short of provisions, he killed two of his native carriers and cut them up for food! This incredible piece of cannibalism is cynically authenticated by 'The Beast' himself."[84] The stories eventually caught up with Crowley and hindered his life. Because of the *John Bull* and *Sunday Express* stories, Mussolini kicked Crowley out of Italy, and his subsequent arrival in Paris, and later London, was widely reported in the United States and abroad.[85]

Crowley made a name for himself in the United States in the early 1910s, mostly as a result of his various public pranks and rituals. Yet by the 1920s, long after his departure for more hospitable environments, his public persona had changed dramatically, undoubtedly as a result of the sensationalist write-ups in the British press. The *American Weekly,* a supplement to the *New York American*, printed a full-page exposé on Crowley that detailed the "trail of wrecked homes, scandals and troubles which have naturally followed from the preaching of that evil doctrine" that is the Law of the New Aeon, "Do What Thou Wilt."[86] The *New York American* reported that in rituals Crowley sacrificed cats.[87] More important for the popular imaginary, however, is that the U.S. stories frequently provided illustrations or photographs. The *New York American* story about the sacrifice of cats depicted a large illustration, with an grotesquely obese Crowley sitting on a throne amid incense, commanding a young man in ceremonial garb holding up cat in his right hand and a "Sacred Sword of

Sacrifice" in his left. An awestruck "Young English Woman" stands off in the distance nearer the reader, horrified at what is taking place.[88]

Thus the figurative instability and discriminating logic of Crowley's rhetorical blinds explain his legendary fame: irony catapulted his persona into the popular imaginary. Although the generation of self-referential texts helps to curtail the tendency of the insider to signify for him- or herself, Crowley is powerless to control the significations of the excluded outsider who is free to signify the sacrifice of babies as he or she damn well pleases. Thus we find ourselves confronting irony as the mechanism through which the occult is springboarded into the popular imaginary and undone thereby: Crowley is "a thoroughly bad man, a Satanist or devil-worshipper steeped in black magic, the high priest of Beelzebub,"[89] an orgy conductor, a drug dispenser, a cannibal, a debauch, and a killer of cats and babies. Occultism, especially of the sort that orbits secret societies, depends on the mystery these kinds of popular myths help to sustain, mystery that is attractive to the curious aspirant who suspects they are not true. But these myths, the fixing of occult's many ambiguities onto social evils—murder, sexual debauchery, bestiality—also effectively undermine the authority of occult leaders who are no longer able to provide the symbolic maps for proper contextualization. Insofar as he or she courts irony and ambiguity, the occultist is necessarily doomed to misunderstanding in a media-rich environment.

In the popular imaginary, the ironic form of the occult is most immediately recognized in terms of who is and is not included as a member of an occult group, who is party to secret knowledge and who is not. In a story about a public performance of Crowley's "Rites of Eleusis," the reporter was careful to note the incomprehensibility of its language, which reveals to some extent an incredulousness: "a person in a red cloak . . . commenced to read some gibberish, to which the attendants made responses at intervals."[90] Worse, when one could catch glimpses of the audience in the darkness, there were "ladies and gentlemen in evening dress, sitting most uncomfortably on very low bamboo stools."[91] The undertone of these reports is one of insult, that one would be subject to the verbal ironies of an inner circle, forced to sit uncomfortably close to a defiling floor. This discussion of the polluting effects of Crowley's ritual betrays class consciousness: "evening dress" is code for class, as is sitting on "low bamboo stools" a violation of Victorian decorum (one does not sit on the floor, especially in evening dress!).

Occult rhetoric cues sensitivities to social rankings and class because it reminds outsiders that they are not insiders. The consequence of this sensitivity is twofold: first, occultists are read as social climbers or as social elitists (not terribly far from the popular image of the college professor, in a way); and second, occultists threaten to erode the social status of the curious. One reporter was aghast that "young girls and married women should be allowed to attend such performances under the guise of a cult of a new religion."[92] Reporters often described the practice of magick as degrading, and one finds numerous stories detailing a otherwise respectable, high-class person falling from grace: "This woman, until her departure from America to join Crowley, enjoyed a high social as well as professional reputation in Los Angeles, and seems an absolutely sincere but devoted dupe of this man, under whose hypnotic influence she has, however, become addicted to heroin and other noxious drugs."[93] Crowley's "devilries" included "luring" a number of unsuspecting students from the socially respectable, high-class schools of Oxford and Cambridge.[94] In story after story one locates a peculiar obsession with the social rank of Crowley as an aristocrat, and the subsequent declassing of his many hapless victims. In the end, the classist basis of Crowley's rhetoric is dialectically mirrored in the rhetoric about Crowley.

Concluding Remarks: . . . as the Occultic Is to Mass

In this chapter I have suggested that the coherence of occultism as the study of secrets began to unravel in modernity, largely for three, interrelated reasons. First, the emergence of large networks of circulation that innovations in mass-media technology helped to create subjected the secrets of the occult tradition to popularization. The centuries-old textual strategies of dissimulation used by occultists, precisely because they fed a popular curiosity about the mysteries of occultism, eventually backfired. By analyzing Crowley's misleading rhetoric I showed how the logic behind the ironic instability of his rhetoric, which was intended to maintain his authority among insiders, eventually led to his own demonization by outsiders. Like the "death of the subject," the Great Magus suffered death by publicity.

Given the anxiety that "secrets" inspire in those who do not know them, it is not surprising that contemporary stories about Crowley reflect an anxiety about the mindless "masses," and usually terms of "class." Yet what distinguishes the exposés of Crowley's time from those of our own is that there has been a shift or inversion of the social hierarchy. Whereas Crowley was cast as an exemplar of the wickedness of the elite and the wealthy, contemporary occultic discourse characterizes the occult as the province of the masses, the rabble, the unwashed lower class. To wit, occultism is the category of the Great Magus, whereas the occultic is the category of the classed Other, "whom we don't know, and can't know."

A *Sunday Times* article on Satanism, for instance, attributes a rise in occult-related crime in Germany to a general "lack of work" among the lower and middle classes—a fall from a previously prosperous social status, indicating implicitly that Satanism is somehow a means of recapturing socioeconomic power.[95] This logic echoes the social sentiment that those drawn to occultism are social climbers seeking a magickal means to prosperity. Newspaper stories in the United States often describe interest in the occult as a middle- to lower-middle-class pursuit as well. A *New York Times* story on witches, for example, begins by describing a ritual: "An hour before sundown, 40 adults have formed a circle in a small backyard, the limbs of a barren tree overhead. Most are dressed in black, many in capes. But the occasion, a gathering of local witches' covens, is expectant, not somber." The location of the ritual is conspicuously mentioned a number of times. The caption to the photographs framing the story reads: "Len Laframboise, during a Wiccan ceremony in Rehoboth, Mass. . . . a gathering of local covens held a sundown ceremony . . . in a backyard." Later, the reporter explains that "season rituals like the backyard gathering . . . connect [witches] with the cycles of nature." Clearly, the backyard is symbolic of a lower socioeconomic status. The implicit logic here is that the more space one has, the higher up on the socioeconomic ladder one is. Further, it is implied that legitimate activities occur in bigger spaces. As descriptions of space become smaller and more cluttered, one can track a rhetoric of classed discrimination. As the article continues, there is a description of a potluck dinner in a witch's apartment, which is "stacked with volumes on witchcraft and other pagan paths." That these spatial descriptions are designed to class participants is corroborated by the biographical detail the reporter provides about interviewees: the witches are normalized as "computer programmers, graphic artists, store managers and others." The author continues that one witch, "Audry Jackson, 23, credit analyst, began studying witchcraft on her own in high school." "Ms. Sulmya-Mass" is 39 and a veterinary technician, and "Josh White, 31," is a firefighter.[96]

The mass-media logic of othering the occultist as a social climber is further emphasized in exposés of occult practices in other countries—especially lesser-developed ones. One glaring example is a story from the *Los Angeles Times* about the rise of exorcism in Mexico: "Mexico is full of people who believe they are possessed. Although it is an overwhelmingly Roman Catholic nation, Christianity here is interwoven with centuries of pre-Hispanic rites of witchcraft, black magic, and faith healing. 'Fortunetelling, consulting the dead, the spirits, astrology—all of these are the terrain of evil,' Juarez said. 'Magic is a breeding ground for the work of Satan.' "[97] The enthymematic message here, of course, is that Mexico is an emblem of socioeconomic depression and that socioeconomic status is inevitably tied to belief in the occult. Hence one finds that Marcel Mauss's key conjecture in *A General Theory of Magic,* that a "disproportionate number of magical practitioners come from the ranks of those occupying a marginal social status," is reflected in the reportage of the occult.[98]

Significantly, however, in Crowley's time marginality consisted of wealth and education. The elite were those drawn to occultism, and as I have implied, this attraction may have been unconsciously motivated by a need to maintain one's elite status or, as is perhaps the case with Crowley, by a fear that one would lose one's social standing. That individuals of lower economic status could become involved in occultism suggests that the secrets of the tradition were becoming increasingly known—and this was because occult discourse was becoming increasingly common in the popular press. This democratization of occult knowledge, enabled by the mass media, has led to an inversion of the social standing of the typical occultist. Whereas the typical occultist in modernity was a figure like Crowley or Blavatsky, today he or she is more likely to be of a lower socioeconomic status. It is not surprising, for example, that those who are most attracted to "the occult" in the United States are those who are most socially and economically disempowered: youth.

7
Prime-Time Satanism
Stock Footage and the Death of Modern Occultism

> This conspiracy must be radically rooted out and execrated. They recognize each other by secret marks and signs [on their bodies] and fall in love before they scarcely know each other . . . they consecrate and worship the head of an ass. . . . Others tell that they reverence even the genital organs of their bishop and priest. . . . And, now, the stories told about the initiation of their novices: they are as detestable as they are notorious. An infant covered with dough crust to deceive the unsuspecting is placed beside the person to be initiated into their secret rites. This infant is killed at the hands of the novice. . . . The infant's blood—oh horrible—they sip up eagerly; its limbs they tear to pieces, trying to outdo each other; by this victim they are leagued together. . . . These sacred rites are more shocking than any sacrilege.
>
> —Minucius Felix summarizes rumors about early Christianity, in *Octavius*[1]

In 1977 a troubled Michelle Smith told her psychiatrist, Lawrence Pazder, some troubling stories. She said that at the age of five she was given to the Devil by her mother. Systematically abused and tortured, she was made to witness the sacrifice of countless animals and babies. To terrify her into silence, she said, she was put into a dark pit with snakes, spiders, aborted fetuses, and rotting corpses. After a car accident, she was given over to a cadre of Satanic nurses who pulled out her teeth. Toward the end of her two-year ordeal, near the age of seven, she claimed, she saw Satan himself.[2]

Despite the outrageousness of Smith's stories, Pazder believed them and was moved to publish them.[3] The result of his zeal was the 1980 international best-seller *Michelle Remembers,* which soon became the most notable survival story of a growing body of popular literature devoted to exposing a vast, conspiratorial underground of devil worship, ritual abuse, and child pornography.[4] Another successful mass paperback, Lauren Stratford's *Satan's Underground,* describes rituals and details instances of childhood torture that are almost interchangeable with those offered by Smith; for example, Stratford also claimed that she was locked away in a small space with four dead babies until she agreed to participate in a ritual sacrifice.[5] By the late 1980s, Pazder, Stratford, and numerous others were frequently appearing as "experts" on television programs that claimed to "expose" a clandestine Satanic underground. These high-profile shows, from the *Oprah Winfrey Show* to *20/20* news specials, helped to propel these conspiratorial claims into the popular imagination.

After the media panic abated in the mid-1990s, however, Smith and Stratford were exposed as frauds, and many of the hypnotic regression techniques used to elicit horrible childhood memories were roundly criticized by scholars within the psychological community.[6] The present consensus of scholars, law enforcement officials, and journalists is that these sensational media events were just that—sensational media events—largely the product of imaginations run wild, fueled by a popular sense of crisis and anomie.[7] Indeed, in the academy these media events have been described as constituting a "rumor panic," a phenomenon in which various folk legends build momentum and metamorphose into realities in the popular media, often because of larger, political struggles (e.g., the rise of the Christian Right) or in response to social crisis and anomie (e.g., economic downturns, a perception of national "moral decline," and so on).[8]

What is particularly interesting from an argumentative perspective is the primary, albeit fallacious, claim offered in support of the victims' stories: those who allegedly have been forced to eat feces and sacrifice babies tell the same story. As a number of self-proclaimed experts on Satanic crime have argued, because the stories are so similar in detail, there must be something horrifically Satanic taking place. Valerie Sinason, a renowned psychologist and champion of "survivors" of Satanic ritual abuse, even argues that the "issue of belief and disbelief . . . is, in the end, 'unhelpful.'"[9] Padzer agrees. Years after the widespread criticism of hypnotic regression, the coauthor of *Michelle Remembers* remarked that "we are all eager to prove or disprove what happened, but *in the end it doesn't matter*" (my emphasis).[10]

The primary reason why the truth or falsity of the survivors' claims about Satanism does not matter to these experts is that many of these survivors were, in fact, abused.[11] My concern in this chapter, however, is that these experts ignore the possibility that Satanism is invoked by abuse survivors because it is the best narrative approximation, the best vocabulary, for describing the abject terror of traumatic experience. Such a perspective implies that Satanism comprises a familiar repertoire of imagery and, hence, suggests the possibility that many Satanic ritual abuse survivors are victims of their own imaginations, drawing on symbols and myths that reside in collective memory and internalizing them as if they were constitutive of a lived past. The relative absence of documented cases of Satanic ritual abuse prior to 1980, and their subsequent appearance after the publication of *Michelle Remembers* and related television programs, marks the Satanic aspect of ritual abuse as a recent embellishment.

In hindsight, the most glaring sin of those who believe in a Satanic underground is their facile dismissal of the fictions of cinema and television as possible source material for "recovered memories" of Satanic crime. For example, in regard to the well-covered McMartin preschool case, in which the preschool owners were falsely accused of running a Satanic child-prostitution ring, police "expert" Sandi Gallant argued categorically that the children's' stories were too consistent and horrific to be fantasies inspired by the cinema.[12] Further, Sinason argues that her "child and adult patients do not find horror films horrifying," because they "are a pale shadow of the reality of their experience." Satanic ritual abuse survivors, she argues, could not possibly "develop ideas or fantasies as a result of watching films."[13]

What is striking about these dismissals is that they are a blatant repudiation of the power of the imagination and, hence, the power of the rhetorical: the ability of discourse to frame and mediate our relationship to the past and render our experience of reality as something meaningful. Indeed, with an eye toward the persistence of Western legends of the past, one discovers that the sacrifice and eating of babies is not a new narrative. These kinds of stories can be traced back to the second century of the common era, when Minucius Felix reported that many pagans believed that Christians were promiscuous, baby-eating mule worshipers (see epigraph).[14]

The uniqueness of depictions of Satanism in the popular media is located in the imagery that is used to abbreviate these long-standing myths: figures chanting in dark robes or hooded garments, altars surrounded by inverted pentagrams, inverted crosses, and blatant images of death (such as skulls) are ubiquitous in Satanic ritual abuse survivor stories as well as televisual and filmic portrayals of Satanism. The imagery is also relatively recent, only appearing with significant frequency in the popular media after the infamous Satanic priest, Anton Szandor LaVey, opened his Church of Satan in San Francisco in 1966.[15] LaVey's imagistic representations of Satanism were and remain profoundly influential in the popular media.

In this chapter I make two arguments about Satanism that help to characterize the rhetoric of occultism at the end of the modern era. First, I suggest that as a discourse, Satanism is largely an imagistic phenomenon devoid of any "secrets" or substantive content. This is because Satanism represents the "fetishization" of the occult into a commodity, or the rendering of occultism into a transactable form. That Satanism transforms the occult into an imagistic, social form marks its rhetoric as the last or final expression of a logic that began with the popular representations of occultism of the mid-nineteenth century: as the occult became increasingly visible in the mass media, its meaning as the elite study of secrets receded behind the aesthetic value of its imagery. Thus the occultic was born.

Second, I argue that the ironic publicity stunts of LaVey and his church are to a large measure responsible for providing the imagery of Satanism to the mass media and, in turn, helped to fashion the visual abbreviations of Satanism that are now ubiquitous in the popular media. By tracing the imagery created by LaVey in the mass media, I provide a map of the dissemination of Satanic, imagistic topoi that helps to explain how Satanism becomes available to people as a collection of visual signs that can be used as touchstones or starting points for the invention of personalized occult narratives. Once available, regardless of their original, ironic context, these visual signs can be re-signified as abbreviations of long-standing cultural myths in a more concrete and memorable way.

To these ends, I redescribe occultism in relation to the commodity form and explain how adopting a political-economic perspective requires one to think about occult discourse as a collection of symbols and images that circulate in patterns typical of the media logics of late capitalism. Then, with the example of LaVey's brand of Satanism, I illustrate how the rhetoric of Satanism comprises the exchange of visual tropes or iconic abbreviations in a number of high-profile television programs. I conclude by suggesting that understanding occultism as a commodity helps one to survey the rhetorical machinations of rumor panics, which is the extreme consequence or result of any occultic discourse today.

Commodity Occultism

In order to understand how the transactability of occult form gives rise to predictable patterns in rumor panic discourse, it is necessary to explain the relationship of the discourse to commodity form. By coming to terms with the logic of the commodity in relationship to "text" in a general sense, one can also better understand how Satanism became so ubiquitous in the popular news media during this time period. As I will explain, the apparently spontaneous mobility of Satanism as a collection of visual abbreviations in the popular imagination is intimately related to its commodification.

The Commodity Form and Late Capitalism

In the first volume of his widely read and profoundly influential study of economics, *Capital,* Karl Marx begins with a discussion of the "elementary form" or fundamental unit of any monied society: the commodity. Simply put, a commodity is something that (a) satisfies a human need of any kind and (b) can be exchanged. Marx held that every society must produce its own material conditions of existence, and that when a society organizes this production in terms of a system of exchange (from bartering to buying and selling), the product is called a commodity.[16] The ways in which these commodities are exchanged and used by individuals determine a society's fundamental "mode of production." In the feudal mode of production, for example, the commodity of food was produced by farmers for their own sustenance, and any surplus went toward the rent of the land they tilled, which was usually run by a feudal lord. Analogously, in the capitalistic mode of production, commodities are produced in ways that generate a "surplus value" by extracting more labor from a worker than is compensated for, a value that typically is liquidated into profit by those who own the means of production.[17]

As I noted previously, the primary mode of production in the United States is often referred to as "late capitalism," a reference both to a moment in the historical trajectory of Western economic development and to an economic system whose quest for surplus value has radically transformed the material features of the commodity and the ways in which it is exchanged.[18] These newer transformations in the logic of capital are discernible in the many synonyms that are used for late capitalism, such as "multinational capitalism," "spectacle or image society," "media capitalism," and "postmodernism." Central to all of these labels is the notion of a global market of exchange and, more important for this chapter, the incorporation of media images and symbolic codes as commodities themselves. The French sociologist Jean Baudrillard has insisted that in late capitalism or postmodernism the primary commodity is the image, a sign that, unlike concrete objects of exchange, has the capacity to "murder" the referent or the reality that it purportedly re-presents.[19] That the West has entered an "economy of information" signals our entrance into an economy of the image: internet web pages, television, movies, and other image-based media have come to dominate the world of commodity exchange. Baudrillard is wary of the economy of image because it extends the commodity form into the popular imaginary and, by extension, the human imagination.

The proximity of the image to cultural forms troubles a number of scholars, since many believe that our cultural world is defined and maintained by the images, or representations, that we exchange among ourselves. Film, for example, is a representation of Western culture that both generates and reflects our ideological landscape. Television programs, especially news programs, help to provide and delimit what is meaningful to a given community with their ideological work. In short, the form of the image, in all its manifestations, is a vehicle of culture and has come to take on an economic value that it did not have previously. Fredric Jameson suggests that the commodification of image is symptomatic of a moment in U.S. economic history when the global economic system collapsed onto cultural systems—a moment when culture itself, inclusive of artifacts, institutions, and ideologies, became commodified and pushed into the circuit of capital.[20] Consequently, because cultural forms like televisual or filmic images have become part of an economic system of exchange, their analysis will necessarily evince the underlying logics of capitalism.

In the United States, the exchange of commodities, now inclusive of cultural forms and the image, is fruitfully characterized as an uneasy conflation of two kinds of systems of exchange, or economies: economies of prestige and economies of sustenance. In the latter system, commodities are created to meet basic human needs (e.g., food); in the former system, commodities take on a symbolic dimension. In economies of prestige, commodities are used to "fix" social meaning, often in relation to social hierarchies or class (Baudrillard has described the capacity of a commodity or good to establish prestige and foreground hierarchy as its "sign-value").[21] In more primitive societies, these economies are often distinct. The economy of sustenance concerns goods that are readily available (e.g., common foods), while the goods in the economy of prestige are scarce. The possession of scarce goods is used to achieve social power and to generate groups of insiders and outsiders. These scarce goods, while potentially useful, are valuable because of their cultural meaning and hence function in ways that are similar to the anthropological concept of the totem: the value of an object of prestige is not its potential utility but rather that it is obtainable by only a few. As a result, the scarce object takes on a mystical quality. In less-developed societies the totem is an animistic object—a plant, a carved image, and so forth. In industrial societies the totem is something like a diamond or a luxury car, both of which are used to signify social status and power. The diamond and the luxury car represent a sign-value that has exceeded notions of utility.

According to the Marxist critic Sut Jhally, modern capitalistic societies have " 'collapsed' the separate spheres of [these two] traditional economies into one of general consumption."[22] For Jhally, this one general economy in the contemporary United States—late capitalism—has advanced advertising as the principal means by which a diffuse yet predictable "culture industry" frames or circumscribes social meaning, primarily if not exclusively by confusing needs and wants, sustenance and prestige. Baudrillard suggests that this collapse, or "implosion," has led to an focus on controlling the communicative or symbolic function of goods over controlling the means of their production. In other words, "control over demand and symbolism"—manufacturing a *social* need for consumption—"becomes the vital focus of advanced capitalism," a modal transformation or evolution that Marx did not foresee.[23] The focus on manipulating the symbolic meanings of goods is the force behind confusing human want and need in the attempt to determine or construct a given commodity's use-value. For Baudrillard, late capitalism confuses want and need with a kind of sleight of (the invisible) hand whereby a commodity's sign-value masquerades as use-value. Hence in late capitalism there is a tendency toward the exchange of an object's image or representation instead of the materiality or concreteness of the object itself.

This tendency to conflate the sign-values and transaction-values of objects of exchange works toward the eclipse of use-value altogether. In Marxian political economy, use-value refers to the material, practical utility of a commodity (inclusive of the labor that was expended to produce it)—what one does with it. As the primary value of a commodity, use-value is opposed to transaction-value or exchange-value, which is the value assigned to an object as something that can be exchanged.[24] The meaning of a commodity or cultural object is always caught in a tension between its material, concrete use and its being an object of exchange, a basic ontological tension. In late capitalism, objects of culture and commodities proper tend to become more valuable by virtue of their reproducibility and transactability as objects. For example, the political economist Jacques Attali has argued that music, a material and ritualistic phenomenon created by human beings, underwent a profound transformation as it moved into the circuit of capital. Once it become commodified as a tangible object that could be "owned" (first with the advent of musical notation, then with the wax cylinder recording device of Edison, then with the advent of the phonograph, and today as a compact disc), the use-value of music, the enjoyment of listing to and creating song, threatens to be overwhelmed by exchange-value. The music or book collector, someone (such as the present author!) who owns more music albums or books than he or she can possibly use or enjoy, is an apt illustration of the transaction-value of music or books overwhelming their use-value. Insofar as the ownership of a high quantity of objects also confers prestige, one can argue that exchange-value and sign-value have become intertwined.

The phenomenon of collecting also illustrates a key concept that is necessary for understanding the logic of the commodity in late capitalism: fetishism. In anthropological literature at the end of the nineteenth century, a fetish was an object that was afforded "secret powers." In non-industrial societies a typical fetish is described as animism. In contemporary society, a traditional fetish would be akin to a colored rabbit's foot as token of the powers of "good luck." Freud appropriated the term from anthropological literature and recast the meaning of a fetish in a way that seems to be more common today: the affording of patently non-human, non-sexual objects with sexual power. Largely defined as a male phenomenon in psychoanalytic literature, the proverbial and ubiquitous fetish in the popular imagination is the woman's shoe.

In Marxian political economy, however, fetishism is used in a related but different sense: it is the phenomenon of attributing to commodities social, non-human power that they do not actually possess absent humans (e.g., the mystique of diamonds, the magical personification of cars). Human beings give commodities their meaning and, hence, their power, but the commodity form works to erase or obscure the role of humans in assigning that meaning and power. As Sut Jhally puts it, "Fetishism consists in seeing the meaning of things as an inherent part of their physical existence when in fact that meaning is created by their integration into a *system* of meaning," a system that is created and maintained by human beings. So, for example, in the object of the musical compact disc, what is obscured or hidden is the labor that went into that disc—the work of musicians, producers, and executives—their late-night disagreements and their studio triumphs; the designing and packaging of the music; the underpaid workers who fashioned the jewel case in stifling factories; and so on. Instead of knowing these things, which are a part of the compact disc's meaning, they are obscured by the value of the compact disc as a transactable good and are replaced with symbolic or imaginary meanings that do not exist in the disc itself.

Form and the Occult Commodity

The logic of late capitalism relates directly to occult discourse insofar as the occult comprises a number of objects, especially books, films, and television programs, that are sold to make money. If it is the case that any one cultural form will reflect, however indirectly, its conditions of production as well as the ideological forces that framed it, then one should be able to explain the proliferation of occult discourse in the 1980s and 1990s in terms of the logic of late capitalism. The challenge is to decide how a political-economic perspective on occult discourse locates suasive dimensions that are otherwise obscured.

The concepts of political economy and occult discourse converge under the phenomenon of mystification, which is the basic effect of commodity fetishism as well as the primary rhetorical feature of occult rhetoric. As I argued in part 1, a key element of occult discourse is the continual revelation and creation of secrets. With Blavatsky I showed how esoteric language was deployed for both contending with the limits of language and for creating a community of insiders. With Crowley I showed how occult modes of interpretation often work to create and, paradoxically, undermine authority. In the work of both figures the promise of occult knowledge and transcendent truths is created by means of a complex interplay of mystification and demystification, often for ends that have little to do with occult knowledge and transcendent truths.

The most straightforward political-economic reading of occultism would be to focus on the mystifications of the occult book, particularly as a fetishized commodity. One could discuss how the scarcity of certain books of secret knowledge, or, in the case of Blavatsky and Crowley, the scarcity of individuals who could properly interpret such books, replicates class structures in local subcultures (or merely recapitulates bourgeois ideology). From a sociological vantage, one could also describe the pursuit of occult knowledge and its mastery among peers as a narrative born of a desire for social mobility and class ascendancy that is actualized within an economy of effortlessly produced value.[25] In this sense the occult becomes a brand of theological gambling, a variation of what is known as a pyramid scheme, whereby an individual circumvents the expenditure of physical labor in an attempt to gain the kind of social power usually conferred by the accumulation of wealth. Thus one creates the fantasy of possessing this social power by becoming involved in an occult group, by possessing the appropriate talisman, or by telephoning the appropriate psychic hot line.

Because I am concerned with the suasive or rhetorical movement of occultism in the televisual age, in this chapter I focus more on the relationship between the content of occultism as "secret knowledge" and the sign-value and exchange-value of its representation or form in order to explain the invention of rumor panics. In other words, I want to focus on a very old and widely discussed concern of textualists: the relationship between form and content. Most rhetoricians and literary critics would agree that, at base, the distinction between form and content is quite arbitrary and is merely a distinction of utility. This consensus, however, reflects a much narrower view of texts than I have advanced in this study. For me, a discourse is a collection of texts, and texts are distinctions between kinds of repetitions. Texts are recognizable kinds of movements, often tangible objects (e.g., Blavatsky's *Isis Unveiled*), but not always (e.g., a melody). In a general sense, however, one can also define a text as a recognizable form, meaning that one distinguishes texts from each other in terms of their formal repetitions. The most familiar understanding of text-as-form is the genre, the notion that features in one kind of text bear similarity to those of another, such that collectively they form a kind.[26]

From a Marxian vantage, however, form implies a materiality, such that the repetition of the text in question is necessarily tangible or concrete or related to something tangible or concrete, such as a medium. Hence a political-economic perspective on texts is concerned with how the medium or materiality of the text relates to its content—if at all. From this vantage, the distinction between form and content concerns how a particular material content determines form (e.g., Lukács's conviction that the formal features of literature bear the impress of its historical and social character), or how a particular ideational form determines content (e.g., how the previous knowledge of a genre determines how some readers understand a romance novel).

In order to wed the traditional textualism of rhetorical criticism with the critiques of objects of material culture more typical of materialist modes, the commodification of "text" must be understood in relation to use-value, sign-value, and exchange-value. As I suggested above, the tendency of commodities in late capitalism is toward an overvaluing of exchange-value (and by extension, sign-value) and the eclipse of use-value. Fused to a textual notion of form and content, then, the tendency of objects of exchange is toward an overemphasis of form at the expense of content. Theodor Adorno's famous critique of popular music, for example, reduces to the parallel between material reproducibility on one level and to textual form and content on another: the mass-produced swing record foregrounds the "banality" of the repetition of sonata form (ABA); thus the pleasures of consumption have more to do with the enjoyment of the music's return to the tonic (home key) than with innovation, artistry, or musical composition.[27] In this way the materiality of mass reproducibility, a formal feature of the musical commodity, is reflected in the "content" of the music itself, a content that capitulates to formal repetitions. Similarly, the pleasures of mass paperback romance novels are products of the recognizable "formula" used to produce them, a formula that is an alternate repetition of the reproduction value of the paperback form.

If the logic of the commodity form holds true for occult discourse, then one would expect that as occultism goes "mass" or goes "pop," the formal features of its exchange as an object of value will come to dominate its use-value. Presumably, the use-value of an occult book concerns the secrets it reveals. Of course, I have argued that in the modern history of occultism, its rhetoric or suasive dimension has as much to do with questions of authority and power as it does with secrets. Nevertheless, the content of occultism, the use-value of secret knowledge, is posed against its sign-value and exchange-value. If late capitalism heralds a stark transition from modernism in terms of the foregrounding of exchange and form and the eclipse of use and content, then commodified occultism should herald its own demise as its content—its secrets—recedes behind its packaging. In other words, commodity occultism is form that inspires mystery without mysterious content. As I argue below, this is precisely what an analysis of Satanic discourse reveals.

Satanomics: Anton LaVey and *The Satanic Bible*

On the night of May 30, 1966, Anton LaVey ceremoniously shaved his head with a straight razor to "leave the world of the descendants of Adam," guilt-ridden and sullied by original sin.[28] This gesture was part of a rite of passage that was assembled from various texts that ostensibly chronicled the rituals of the Yezidi, an Islamic sect of "devil worshippers" who searched for a series of secret, subterranean caverns and rivers that flowed into Hell. LaVey, convinced that "man needs ritual and dogma,"[29] chose the Yezidi rite to mark what he called "year one, *Anno Satanis*," the first year of the reign of Satan and the opening of the United States' first Satanic church. The opening coincided with Walpurgisnacht, the eve of May Day that has "been memorialized as the night that all demons, specters . . . and banshees would come forth and hold their wild revels."[30]

The opening of the Church of Satan was, according to LaVey, the logical outcome of the weekly meetings of his "Magic Circle," a group of friends that met in LaVey's black Victorian home (the "Black House") in San Francisco to dabble in the occult. An adept of Crowley's brand of "magick" and other occult traditions, LaVey claimed that it was time to use magick to "break apart the ignorance and hypocrisy fostered by the Christian churches" by establishing his own.[31] Although the opening was not heavily reported in the press, LaVey and his followers made a concerted effort to publicize the church, an effort that would prove, in the end, extremely successful. In the tradition of Crowley's public pranks and rituals, LaVey staged a "Satanic wedding" that was reported worldwide, followed by a "Satanic baptism" of his six-year-old daughter, Zeena.[32] Because of these widely reported events, as well as the wildly successful film about a young woman bearing the Devil's son, *Rosemary's Baby,* LaVey and his followers proved to be good copy for the press. LaVey and his church were featured in local newspapers across the country as well as in a number of high-profile magazines such as *Time, Newsweek, Cosmopolitan, Seventeen,* and *Look*.[33]

Today the activities of the Church of Satan have fallen far from public view. Despite LaVey's immense popularity in the 1970s, his death in October 1997 received little more than an extended news service obituary circulated in a number of regional newspapers.[34] Having claimed to have once been a lion tamer and circus performer, a carnival hypnotist and magician, a police photographer, an accomplished organist, and an on-call ghost-buster, LaVey had made no secret of his love of spectacle and notoriety, and the irony of his inconspicuous death goes without saying.[35] What has survived LaVey, however, is the iconic existence of his international best-seller, *The Satanic Bible,* and, as I will argue shortly, a widely recognized representation of occultism as a visual idiom—a kitschy, garish, sixties go-go brand of occultism—that, in terms of popular memory, outrivals the rhetorical contributions of all other twentieth-century occultists combined.

LaVey's status in the popular imaginary is secured by *The Satanic Bible,* an average-size paperback that helped to set a new system of occult imagery into motion. Although there were a number of popular occult books in the 1970s (especially those that concerned astrology), none received as much attention or gained as much notoriety as *The Satanic Bible.* The origin of the book is an excellent study of the logics of fetishism, as the dialectic of mystification and demystification is carefully deployed in its marketing. Although the title and packaging of the book betoken an alignment with the supernatural powers of darkness, the philosophy contained within its pages is a secular individualism that dismisses any belief in the existence of deity—good, evil, or indifferent. The book is prima facie ironic insofar as what it contains has little to do with demons or forbidden knowledge. As I argued in the previous chapter, this ironic kind of duplicity is a large source of pleasure for the magickal aspirant.

Two years after establishing the Church of Satan, LaVey had written a number of polemical essays and screeds that he assembled into a mimeographed packet of colored paper, dubbed "the rainbow sheets" by church members. These sheets proved useful at the end of 1968 when Peter Mayer, an editor at the mass paperback publisher Avon Books, contacted LaVey about a book project. Mayer had heard of LaVey's church in the popular press, and in the wake of the success of occult fiction and film in the mid- to late 1960s (not to mention the success of Polanski's Satanic thriller, *Rosemary's Baby*), Mayer concluded that a Satanic bible penned by the already-notable LaVey would sell very well. Mayer was right.[36]

A former friend of LaVey's and fellow Satanist Michael Aquino (currently leader of his own Satanic church, the Temple of Set) recalled that the problem LaVey confronted with Mayer's offer was that he did not have enough written content "to produce a sufficiently-fat paperback."[37] Aquino claims that as the deadline approached, LaVey resorted to plagiarizing a section from a little-known racist tract titled *Might Is Right,* penned by Arthur Desmond under the name Ragbar Redbeard in 1896.[38] Aquino further claimed that LaVey hurriedly appended a number of occult rituals to the end, and the collection went to press in December 1969. In January 1970, *The Satanic Bible* was published. Since then the paperback version has been through multiple reprintings and the book has sold an estimated 700,000 copies.[39]

Although LaVey is most known for writing *The Satanic Bible,* the book's contents are anything but original. By examining the contents of the book, one quickly comes to the conclusion that LaVey's genius resides in his ability to package and market Satanism, not necessarily in his articulation of Satanic philosophy.

In general, *The Satanic Bible* can be divided into two parts. In a how-to manner, one part presents a number of rituals to be performed by the Satanist and details the sorts of materials he or she should acquire, a simple rehash of the directives of ritual magicians found in books like Crowley's *Magick*.[40] The other, more substantive part of the book advances a strident libertarianism reminiscent of Ayn Rand's Objectivist philosophy, which touted the "virtues of selfishness" in books like *The Fountainhead* and *Atlas Shrugged* (in fact, in an interview with the *Los Angels Times,* LaVey remarked that his "religion" was "just Ayn Rand's philosophy, with ceremony and ritual added").[41] The "Nine Satanic Statements" that appear at the head of the book reflect the rational self-interest of Objectivism and are an apt summary of the book's philosophical contents:

1. Satan represents indulgence, instead of abstinence!
2. Satan represents vital existence, instead of spiritual pipe dreams.
3. Satan represents undefiled wisdom, instead of hypocritical self deceit!
4. Satan represents kindness to those who deserve it, instead of love wasted on ingrates!
5. Satan represents vengeance, instead of turning the other cheek!
6. Satan represents responsibility for the responsible, instead of concern for psychic vampires!
7. Satan represents man as just another animal, sometimes better, more often worse than those that walk on all-fours, who, because of his "divine spiritual and intellectual development," has become the most vicious animal of all!
8. Satan represents all of the so-called sins, as they all lead to physical, mental, and emotional gratification!
9. Satan has been the best friend the church has ever had, as he has kept it in business all these years![42]

The idea of Satan has been re-signified by LaVey to represent the essence of human nature, and Satanism is offered as a philosophy of playful individualism that is better equipped than Christianity to cope with this essence.[43]

In light of the nine statements' similarity to Objectivism, the philosophy espoused in *The Satanic Bible* is neither offensive nor surprising, as it is an obvious distillation of ideas common among members of the U.S. counterculture in the 1960s. As Aquino aptly observes, "[*The*] *Satanic Bible,* while exposing [the] scam [of justifying political prescriptions with divine authority], nonetheless drinks at the same well by clothing itself in the supernatural authority of the Prince of Darkness and his daemons. Less this element, *The Satanic Bible* would be merely a social tract by Anton LaVey—not High Priest of Satan, but just one more 1960s-counterculture-cynic atop a soap-box."[44] Aquino implies that formal characteristics of the book and the mystifications of its packaging as "Satanic" have more to do with its commercial success than its actual content. It is not surprising, then, that LaVey himself divests *The Satanic Bible* of possessing the "secret" content typical of books in the occult tradition. True to the generic features of occult and New Age books, LaVey opens *The Satanic Bible* announcing that his is a demystifying intention. However, the demystification is one that goes against the typical proposal of a new vocabulary or the discovery of new, transcendent truths:

> This book was written because, with very few exceptions, every tract and paper, every "secret" grimoire, all the "great works" on the subject of magic, are nothing more than sanctimonious fraud—guilt-ridden ramblings and esoteric gibberish by chroniclers of magical lore unable or unwilling to present an objective view of the subject. Writer after writer, in efforts to state the principles of "white and black magic," has succeeded instead in clouding the entire issue so badly that the would-be student of sorcery winds up stupidly pushing a planchette over a Ouija board, standing inside a pentagram waiting for a demon to present itself . . . in general making a blithering fool of himself in the eyes of those who *know!*[45]

Apparently, those who really know occultism know that the secret is that there *are* no secrets. This brand of demystification denies any content to the occult tradition, refiguring centuries of revealed knowledge as an aesthetic contrivance, a form of human mythmaking and fantasy that appeases a human need for ritual. "Herein you will find truth and fantasy," avers LaVey. "Each is necessary for the other to exist; but each must be recognized for what it is."[46] For LaVey, truth, as much as fantasy, is entertainment.

Unlike its content, the packaging and formal characteristics of *The Satanic Bible* are distinctive, and the book's importance as an element of occult discourse has much more to do with its status as totem or a fetishized object in popular culture than with its 272 pages of directives. With LaVey's remarks about the fantasy function of his bible in mind, one is drawn to the style of the book, which is written in an obvious tongue-in-cheek manner, and more significantly to its noteworthy cover. The front of the popular paperback edition features a

Fig. 8. The Sigil of Baphomet. Courtesy of and copyright © the Church of Satan.

minimalist design, the title and author in a simple white font on a completely black background. Underneath the text, in purple, appears the Sigil of Baphomet, which is the representation of a goat head contained by an inverted pentagram or encircled star. Each point of the pentagram accommodates the goat's horns, ears, and chin. Around the pentagram and goat are two circles, in which appear the ubiquitous occult symbols—Hebrew characters—spelling "Leviathan" (see fig. 8). The back of the paperback is equally striking. Over a black background appears a photograph of LaVey, his glaring eyes, bald head, and meticulously groomed goatee encircled by a large Sigil of Baphomet, such that he appears horned.

In most contemporary depictions of Satanism in books and television programs, the cover of *The Satanic Bible* is often presented as a visual surrogate for the practice of Satanism and sometimes for the whole of occultism. This focus on the cover marks a formal mystification that models the logic of commodity exchange in late capitalism: such a focus is an erasure of the book's content, an eclipse of its use-value by its sign-value and transaction-value. An excellent example of this kind of commodity occultism is found in a video program popular among Evangelical and charismatic Christian groups titled *Devil Worship: The Rise of Satanism*. In the opening segments of the video, LaVey and the Church of Satan are introduced through a series of shots in which *The Satanic Bible* frequently appears. A woman with a British accent narrates the imagery over a characteristically "creepy," synthesized sound track:

SHOT	AUDIO
1. Black-and-white head shot of Anton LaVey.	In 1966, Anton LaVey founded the . . .
2. Medium shot of black Victorian home that houses the Church of Satan.	. . . first Church of Satan in San Francisco, which . . .
3. Medium shot of LaVey in "devil" costume, slow zoom toward his face.	. . . at one point, claimed 10,000 members.
4. Close-up of the cover of *The Satanic Bible.* The Sigil of Baphomet is the focal point.	LaVey authored *The Satanic Bible* and . . .
5. Close-up of the title page of *The Satanic Rituals.* The Sigil of Baphomet is the focal point.	. . . *The Satanic Rituals,* two of Satanism's most important books.
6. Close-up of the back of *The Satanic Bible.* Depiction of Anton LaVey in front of a Sigil of Baphomet.	Astonishingly, when *The Satanic Bible* was first published . . .
7. Close-up of the spine of the Christian Bible.	. . . it outsold the holy bible two to one in many parts of America . . .
8. Long shot of college campus. Students with backpacks walk away from the camera.	. . . and ten to one on some college campuses.[47]
9. Close-up of page 149 of *The Satanic Bible.* It reads, "Invocation Employed Towards the Conjuration of Destruction."	It teaches tenets that are totally opposed to goodness, purity, and selfless behavior.

The final comment in this series of shots illustrates how *The Satanic Bible* is rendered into a visual fetish, its contents ignored and deliberately mystified in order to promote a Christian message of redemption: although *The Satanic Bible* attacks the notion of purity as an impossible ideal, it does not categorically oppose "goodness" and "selfless behavior," nor does it forward a belief in the supernatural. The video presentation focuses on the book's formal aspects at the expense of its actual content.

This fetishization of the image of *The Satanic Bible* is found in all kinds of programs about Satanism, from countless Evangelical video programs that circulate among charismatics to secular "tabloid" news programs like *20/20*. In the next section I illustrate how this strategy was used to re-signify the playful and ironic images of Satanism created by LaVey in an obscure cult film. In the popular imaginary, the intentionally humorous and wildly entertaining rituals created by LaVey for this film have been re-signified to serve as factual and incontrovertible evidence for the existence of blood sacrifice.

Televisual Occultism and Rumor Panic: The Case of *Satanis*

In the previous section I argued that *The Satanic Bible* is a good illustration of commodity occultism, which I have described as the creation of a totem (or fetishized occult object) though the mystification of content or original use-value. I suggested that the book illustrates the triumph of form over content in two ways. First, the content of *The Satanic Bible* is almost depthless, as it forwards a reactive brand of individualism and hedonism that was common in the 1960s counterculture while denying the occult tradition its centuries of secrets. More notable than the content, and what LaVey seemed to emphasize, were the book's formal, aesthetic features: the ominous black cover, the humorous and tongue-in-cheek writing style, the "game" of Satanic ritual and ceremony, and the seeming "forbiddenness" of this philosophy of "common sense" all seem to privilege appearance, surface, and play over depth, profundity, and erudite study. Placed alongside the influential work of figures like Blavatsky and Crowley, *The Satanic Bible* lacks a sophisticated rhetoric of secrecy and depth typical of traditional occult writings.

Second, that portrayals of Satanism often feature the cover of *The Satanic Bible* or the symbol of the Sigil of Baphomet is symptomatic of the emphasis on form typical of commodity fetishism. That media representations often use the image of the book itself without a discussion of its contents heralds the triumph of transaction and sign-value, of form, over original use-value. It is not surprising that media representations often erroneously summarize the content of the book, as well as its companion, *The Satanic Rituals,* as "evil Satanic rites,"[48] despite their presentation as a psychodramatic form of play. "Fantasy plays an important part in any religious curriculum," writes LaVey, and Satanism makes great use of fantasy.

> What constitutes the difference between a Satanic ceremony and a play presented by a theatre group? Often very little: mainly it hinges on the degree of acceptance on the part of the audience. It is of little consequence whether an outside audience does or does not accept the substance of a Satanic ceremony: the strange and grotesque always has a large and enthusiastic audience. . . . [T]he purpose of most Satanic ceremonies is to *elevate* the self rather than *demean it.* [Thus] A ceremonial chamber essentially provides a stage for a performer who wishes complete acceptance from his audience.[49]

Ritual and ceremonial magic are described as forms of therapy, not the manipulation of supernatural forces. In a telephone interview, the current High Priest of the Church of Satan, Peter Gilmore, explained to me that rituals are designed to appeal to the human need for psychodrama. If there are "unexplained magical effects" as a result of ritual, Gilmore said, "that's great," but the primary function is psychological.[50]

The erroneous accounts of *The Satanic Bible* as harboring rituals designed to summon evil, supernatural forces underscore the mystifying effects of commodity fetishism—effects that LaVey knew very well and actively courted to bring his Church of Satan to the public's attention. In many ways, *The Satanic Bible* represents the death of occultism as the study of secrets and its rebirth as an aesthetic form, its function now primarily one of entertainment in the service of capital.

Through the lens of Satanism, an observation of the movement of occult discourse toward form helps to explain how the rather limited repertoire of occult imagery could come to signify the ritual abuse of children. In media depictions of the cover of *The Satanic Bible,* the contents of the book are mystified in the active constructing of a visual repertoire that helped to revive long-standing cultural myths about human sacrifice and blood ritual; the book becomes a thinned-out object, a glossy surface that is divorced from its primary referent system—its actual content—and re-signified into a different referent system as the visual abbreviation of evil. This process of emptying occult texts of their content and resituating their formal elements into alternate referent systems foregrounds the rhetorical dimension of rumor panics in the televisual age: the rather limited iconic repertoire of the occult is at base a site of invention, a locus of highly connotative imagistic forms that are used and reused, signified and re-signified, for extrinsic purposes. The relative paucity of Western representations of evil placed LaVey's intentionally ironic brand of occultism at risk of re-signification, although there is nothing patently "evil," at least in terms of the existence of supernatural forces, about his philosophy.[51] LaVey's Satanic philosophy *is* dangerous insofar as it courts fascistic beliefs, something that LaVey acknowledges,[52] but it is far from any belief in the supernatural. From its inception, the Church of Satan has "made no grandiose promises of infallible enlightenment and [has] emphasized that each must be his or her own redeemer. . . . 'Satan' is a representational concept, accepted by each according to his or her needs."[53] LaVey sometimes compared his church to an amusing circus, a spectacle that entertained the public and helped church members simply have fun. The Church of Satan was, for LaVey, a "Cosmic Joy Buzzer."[54]

The Ontology of the Image as Such

Thus far I have suggested that the logics of commodification explain how LaVey's creation of an ironic Satanic spectacle could be rendered so easily into a collection of visual representations and subsequently re-signified as something deadly serious. Yet the ease with which this occurs, as Baudrillard has suggested of the postmodern commodity, has much to do with the ontological status of the image as a particular kind of transactable thing. In other words, the exchange of the cover of *The Satanic Bible* as a totem is enabled by its being an iconic sign, a form that is capable of communicating a message visually. Unlike speech, music, and other modes of communicating, there is something particular to the image as such that makes it ideally suited for the logics of commodity form. By contending with the uniqueness of the image as such, then, one can better understand the rhetoric of rumor panics as the transaction of iconic or visual abbreviations in general, and the rhetoric of Satanism as a complex interplay and transaction of a limited set of visual abbreviations in particular.

The most successfully deceptive of social forms is the picture or visual image, and for the analysis that follows it is important to understand why this is the case (hereafter by "image" I mean "visual image").[55] The classic and widely referenced account of the ontology of image is found in the work of Roland Barthes, a philosopher and semiotician who provided what is perhaps the most comprehensive vocabulary for discussing the image as a kind of "sign" or visual mark. In a number of essays on film and photography, Barthes suggests that one can pragmatically contend with images as "messages" in order to unveil those elements particular to them, otherwise termed their "specificity." By treating images as messages, Barthes does not mean "message" in the ethereal sense in which one imagines two disembodied heads exchanging codes through some airy span, but rather as a material delivery device, much like the encased envelope of a New York City bike courier. Treating images as messages does not collapse their specificity onto speech or writing but rather attempts to forge an analogy that underscores the notion that the meaning of an image is not its assumed signified or that which it seems to depict but rather the dynamic relations among signifiers, both inside and outside the frame or boundaries of the image. Identifying something meaningful within an image is thus akin to catching a busy courier cycling from one office to another. The message that he or she is carrying changes depending on which street and at what time one stops him or her. Further, this meaning, Barthes says, is always a distillation in "proportion, in perspective, in color" of that which is represented in an image, its presumed "reality." The image is "at no point a *transformation*" of this reality (hence the protective envelope of the delivered message). Rather, the message of the image is a re-presentation or "transfer" of a reality onto a two-dimensional surface. With the example of the photograph, Barthes continues by suggesting that "the image is not the reality, but at least it is the perfect *analagon,* and it is just this analogical perfection which, to common sense, defines the photograph. Here appears the particular status of the photographic image: *it is a message without a code.*"[56] Barthes underscores two features particular to the image. First, the image appears to us as pure denotation, as if what it re-presents is, in fact, a reality. That it is actually a "transfer" of some prior reality, however, means that images qua images are kinds of dissimulations. The conceit of the image is that what it depicts is a reality, when in fact it is a selection of reality, a re-presentation that necessarily omits elements of the original. Our projection of a larger reality "behind" what the image presents (e.g., treating something patently two-dimensional as if it were three-dimensional) is commonly termed the "illusionism" of the image.[57] When the illusionism of the image is used to generate a sense of concrete reality—as in, for example, a fictional film—one can aptly describe it as a "reality effect." The reality effect of an image is recognized in the oft-heard phrase "Seeing is believing."

The second feature particular to the image that Barthes details is that an image does not contain a code or set of rules for interpreting it. Rather, an image is always interpreted in a context of presentation that adds connotations and evaluative clues. For example, although a photograph appears as if it is pure denotation, the context of its presentation—on the walls of an art exhibit, beside a didactic describing its history, with particular frame and matting, and so on—provides the interpretive codes. Juxtaposition among other images can provide comparative or "syntagmatic" codes in the moment of viewing (e.g., as in a slide show), and relationships to images of the past and present provide historical or "diachronic" codes of interpretation across time (e.g., the movement among rapid frames that gives film a sense of duration). Moreover, the interpretive codes used to make sense of a given image are not limited to the immediate context of its presentation, because they may also be found in a "learned vocabulary" based on one's life experiences as well as the general cultural knowledge one accrues through socialization in a given culture.[58] One aptly may locate the rhetorical or suasive movement of imagery, or the rhetoric of the image, in the use or imposition of these many kinds of codes of interpretation.[59]

The symbolism and imagery of Satanism created by LaVey depends on a general cultural knowledge of the signifiers of evil, which he used to create a rhetoric of mystery, as well as a rhetoric of irony premised on the need of imagery for code. As I mentioned in the previous chapter, the ability to separate a signifier from its signified, which is best exemplified by the image as a form in need of interpretive codes, is the logic behind the secrecy of occultism: what one sees is not necessarily what one gets, as dissimulation is a basic element of all occult organizations. Hence the notoriety and power of *The Satanic Bible* as a totem is derived from the purposively misleading connotations of the signifiers that compose it: the dark, minimalist composition of its front cover, LaVey's characteristically devilish appearance on the back cover, the humorously bombastic style of its text, the word "Satanic" in the title, and other elements that collectively connote "evil." This deliberate assembly of "dark" signifiers foregrounds irony as a central feature of LaVey's rhetoric, and as my remarks in chapter 6 suggest, his authority as the guarantee of meaning was destined to be undermined.[60] In light of the rumor panic of the late 1980s and early 1990s, LaVey's playful attempts to re-signify highly connotative signifiers of darkness and evil as "kitsch" backfired, as his church was later plagued by accusations of ritual murder, child abuse, and other occult crimes. In other words, although he was the architect of a successful

Satanic spectacle, LaVey was incapable of controlling that spectacle once it was released into the popular media and, by extension, the popular imaginary.

LaVey's inability to control the meaning of the imagery he created can be explained in reference to the ontology of the image: because images need contextualization for their meaning, they are more easily detached from primary or original contexts and moved to others that supply alternative codes. I term this ease of movement the "mobility of image." The mobility of image refers to the simple transaction of visual abbreviations among different, multiple texts (films, television programs, books, and so on), enabled by formalization and furthered by repeated transaction or use. In relation to what I have been describing as a visual abbreviation or trope, mobility refers to the ease with which an image, such as one that contains the Sigil of Baphomet, is wielded to mean different things in different contexts. The less ambiguous or discrete the image, the less mobile it will be (e.g., an image of an elephant is much less mobile than a strange symbol such as the Sigil of Baphomet). Hence the mobility of the image refers not only to the fact that images are discrete and can be moved and recontextualized but also to the fact that they can be assigned radically different meanings in the service of a given representation. From a rhetorical perspective, the mobility of the image is analogous to what rhetoricians refer to as a topos (or topoi in plural). Although scholars disagree about what topoi meant for ancient rhetoricians, today the term generally refers both to "the stuff of which arguments are made and the *form* of those arguments" (my emphasis).[61] If one substitutes "representation" for "argument" in this definition, then the mobility of image is synonymous with the idea of a visual or iconic topos. The perfect example of visual topoi in television production is "stock footage," fragments of films or other media texts that are made to signify different things depending on their contextualization.

In addition to the cover of *The Satanic Bible*, an excellent example of the mobility of Satanic imagery is the use of a 1969 documentary on the Church of Satan as stock footage. Examining this film as it moves through a number of televised representations helps one to observe better how Satanism was deployed as a collection of visual abbreviations that were recycled, time and time again, into new representations. Through the mapping of this stock footage, the rhetoric or suasive movement of rumor panics is shown to depend on the "reality effect" of the image, and at a more basic level, on the movement toward the sign-value typical of commodity fetishism within a circulatory network.

Double Deception: Satanic Imagery and the Invention of Rumor Panic

Directed and produced by Ray Laurent, *Satanis: The Devil's Mass* was yet another attempt by LaVey to spread the philosophy of the Church of Satan (and to sell copies of *The Satanic Bible*) within an ongoing publicity campaign headed by fellow Satanist and professional publicity agent Edward M. Webber.[62] The campaign began with a public "Satanic wedding" between journalist John Raymond and a New York socialite, Judith Case, in February 1967. The wedding was good copy for the national press and soon became a newsreel segment that ran in theaters through the late 1960s. The wedding was followed by a "Satanic baptism" of LaVey's daughter, and later a "Satanic funeral," both of which were also covered by the press. The movie *Satanis* was caught in the momentum of this publicity. Unfortunately for LaVey and Laurent, the film did poorly at local showings and failed to reach national distribution, seemingly passing into cult-movie obscurity by the mid-1970s. Presumably, Laurent failed to register the film and subsequently lost control of copyright, because today it is considered to be in the public domain.

According to Blanche Barton, LaVey's widow and current head of the Church of Satan, the film originally hit theaters in early "1970, often playing on a double bill with another movie Anton appeared in—Kenneth Anger's *Invocation of My Demon Brother*. The ads for the film, showcasing LaVey's scowling countenance, promised bloody, sexually explicit rituals. . . . [S]erious cautions were included in the large display ads: '*Satanis* is the most pertinent, and perhaps the most shocking film of our time. But it's definitely not a movie for everyone. If you choose not to see it, we will understand.' "[63] Although the film does feature nude women who serve as "altars" in a number of rituals, the "shockumentary" is relatively tame in comparison to contemporary mainstream Hollywood film.

In general, the film alternates between interviews of LaVey, interviews of his neighbors, and scenes from a kitschy, garishly lit Satanic ritual. The most memorable and frequently used part of the film is the opening, which depicts a "Satanic" ceremony that is both dramatic and humorous. The opening begins with a procession of hooded figures down a hallway dimly lit with green and red light. The sound track is of a pipe organ playing a gloomy set of notes that do not seem to constitute a formal work. The procession enters a ritual chamber fully furnished with ghoulish artifacts. A nude woman lies on her side, in the company of a skull and a bell, on an altar in the front of the room. An organist wearing a mask of a skull plays an organ in dramatic movements in the corner. Behind the altar is a large Sigil of Baphomet. The participants circle around the altar, and masks are presented to two of the participants: one is of a horse head, the other a devil's head. The participants put on the masks. Then, a bearded young man with priestly attire takes a bell from the altar and rings it in the directions of north, south, east, and west. He then returns to facing the altar and in deep, commanding voice intones, "*In dominis Satanis, Lucifer excelcis dei.* In the name of our most exalted god, Satan Lucifer, I command thee to come forth!" From a low angle, the camera cuts to a close-up of the bearded man's face as he picks up a ceremonial sword: "Come forth, and bestow these blessings of hell upon us. Come forth by these names: Satan, Lucifer, Belial, Leviathan, Shemhamferash!" The participants reply, "Shemhamferash." The man returns, "Hail Satan!," and they reply, "Hail Satan." A chalice is taken from an unseen location and ceremoniously given to Anton LaVey, who emerges from the circle wearing a hooded, horned devil costume. LaVey drinks and then comes to the center of the circle and continues the ritual. The film then cuts to interviews with neighbors, LaVey, and his followers, periodically returning to the ritual until the end of the film.

That the film is considered public domain has all but guaranteed its dominion over public conceptions of Satanism. Despite its obscurity as a whole, in pieces the film has had quite a showing as stock footage in a number of documentaries and local and national news stories. The most prominent of these programs, an ABC *20/20* segment titled "The Devil Worshippers" and a Geraldo Rivera special titled "Exposing Satan's Underground" on NBC, are responsible for broadcasting segments of *Satanis* to millions of viewers.

The first of these prime-time programs was the *20/20* segment, which aired on May 16, 1985. The television anchor, Hugh Downs, introduced the segment by claiming that the program would describe "perverse, hideous acts that defy belief. Suicides, murders, and ritualistic slaughter of children and animals." Witnesses in the program testified that "hearts were cut out, and . . . children were made to chew pieces of these children's hearts, pieces of their flesh."[64] Prominent in this program are clips from *Satanis,* which are used visually to stabilize the stories of Satanic ritual abuse survivors with memorable, concrete images. In one segment the film is used as an example of the "religious Satanist" as opposed to the "dabbler" or "generational" Satanist. The editing of the stock carefully weaves the sound track of one part of the film as a voice-over for another. In the chart below, the reporter's voice is signaled by his last name, "Wooden," and that of LaVey used from *Satanis* as a voice-over is denoted with "LaVey":

SHOT	AUDIO
1. From *Satanis:* LaVey takes a ceremonial sword in one hand and a book in another. He is in a devil outfit and lit by a green light.	Wooden: The Church of Satan and other organized devil-worship groups represent our second category . . .
Zoom out to a framing of the stock footage by a blue background. The words "Religious Satanist" appear above the framed footage.	. . . religious Satanists.
2. Cut to different part of *Satanis* ritual. A devil mask is handed to a participant by a hooded figure. The participant puts on the devil mask.	Although LaVey would not talk to us, we can get a glimpse of his theories and rituals in this 1970 documentary on his church.
3. Cut to organist wearing a skull mask. He or she is bathed in red light.	LaVey: "We feel a person should be free to indulge all the so-called fetishes that they would . . .
4. Overhead shot of ritual group in a circle, LaVey in the middle holding out a ceremonial sword.	. . . desire, as long as they don't hurt anyone that doesn't deserve or wish to be hurt."
5. Head shot of an older, male participant in dark, formal clothing.	
6. Head shot of LaVey.	Primary *Satanis* sound track: "Hail Satan!
7. Head shot of another participant wearing a hood. He repeats the words of LaVey in chorus.	"Hail Satan!"

8. Medium shot of LaVey with Sword LaVey turns toward camera with sword. The sword is put down. LaVey takes his cape and slowly, arms grasping it on each side, pulls it over his head.	LaVey: "We perform human sacrifices by proxy, you might say. The destruction of human beings who would, let's say, create an antagonistic situation towards us in the form of curses and hexes. Not in actual blood ritual, because, certainly, the destruction of a human being physically is illegal.
9. Cut to a different part of the ritual. A Coffin is opened, and a nude woman is revealed to be inside. "666" is written in black paint across her chest. A black bar obscures her breasts for television censors.	Wooden: Police we spoke to say they have never made a link between this Satanic church and the Satanic crimes being committed. However, some incidents described to us by witnesses . . .
10. Head shot of LaVey in green light.	. . . around the country are . . .
11. Medium shot of coffin. A man in a light colored robe climbs into the coffin with the nude woman, and other participants lower the lid.	. . . strikingly similar to these ritualistic scenes.

The segment continues by describing the coffin ritual as an "embrace of death" and then moves to a discussion of voodoo dolls. Although footage of *Satanis* is used in other parts of the program, the eleven shots described above are sufficient to illustrate how easily the film is used as a visual abbreviation of practices that they do not depict. The sound track of an interview of LaVey which appears much later in the film is used as a voice-over to contextualize the opening ritual as fetishistic (in the sexual sense) and as human sacrifice "by proxy." Although careful to avoid libel by noting that there is no evidence that the Church of Satan has committed crime, Wooden clearly implies there is a link by suggesting that "some incidents described to us by witnesses [of Satanic crime] around the country are strikingly similar to these ritualistic scenes." The necessary ambiguity of these images divorced from their original context is used to create the impression of an empirically verifiable Satanic ritual in which people are killed. The mobility of these Satanic images is reflected in the ease with which they are moved around in order to provide codes of interpretation that are different from their original codes. Their recontextualization in a program concerned with human atrocity and Satanic crime supplies new codes of interpretation that use the basic reality effect of the image to suggest the reality of Satanic murder. In other words, that these images depict a Satanic ritual at all helps to create kind of illusionism whereby an empirical crime that occurs outside the frame is implicated within the frame.

The alarmist tone of the *20/20* program continued with two high-profile programs by Geraldo Rivera, the first airing on November 19, 1987, as an episode of his *Geraldo* talk show, the second on October 25, 1988, as an NBC prime-time special titled "Devil Worship: Exposing Satan's Underground." In the latter, Rivera and his producers re-signify and contextualize *Satanis* footage in a more exaggerated manner than the *20/20* episode as undeniable evidence of crime. The difference is that Rivera's program implies that the ritual abuse and murder of adults and children is inspired by the supernatural forces of evil. The following example segment begins after a discussion of demonic possession:

SHOT	AUDIO
1. Medium shot of a woman, crying, clutching a wooden cross to her chest. Her voice is strained and she moves her head from side to side as she speaks.	"I won't let her go! No!" Organ music from the sound track of *Satanis* fades in.
2. Cut to ritual footage from *Satanis*. A participant in the ritual circle takes and puts on a devil mask.	Rivera: Devil worship is as old as religion itself. It's the grim alternative . . .
3. Cut to a medium shot of LaVey taking the ceremonial chalice. He drinks from the chalice.	. . . the flip side of life . . .

4. Cut to skull-masked organist bathed in red light.	. . . evil over good . . .
5. Caped participant sprinkling mock "holy water."	. . . dark over light, Satan over God himself!
6. Medium shot of LaVey picking up the ceremonial sword in his "devil" costume.	Primary sound track of *Satanis:* "Come forth, and bestow these blessings of hell upon us."
7. Cut to low angle shot of bearded man holding sword.	Rivera: Forced underground by the religious hysteria of the middle ages. . . .
8. Jump-cut to image of Eliphas Lévi's famous Sabbatic Goat (the "Baphomet")	

In Rivera's program, the ritual footage of *Satanis* is rearranged into a new chronological order, such that the first element the viewer sees after the image of a seemingly "possessed" woman is a devil mask, followed by the ominous figure of LaVey. The ending of the segment cuts to a scene previous to those depicting LaVey in the original chronology of *Satanis,* so that it features the dramatic, deep voice of the bearded man imploring Satan to "bestow these blessings of hell upon us." This new arrangement helps to highlight to the role of mobility of image in the creation of supernatural truths, as Rivera's program hijacks the reality effect of the image by using *Satanis* as evidence of the existence of demons: rituals like these are responsible for opening the portals to Hell.

Rivera's rhetorical excesses, however, deconstruct the program's underlying logic as one of deliberate and sensational deception. Rivera opened the widely watched news special with a galvanic warning: "The very young and impressionable should definitely not be watching this program tonight," which was later followed by, "I am begging you. . . . Please get them out of the room or change the station!" Ironically, during the daytime when many children are at home and awake, a number of popular talk shows—*Geraldo, Donahue, Sally Jesse Raphael,* and the *Oprah Winfrey Show*—devoted programming to survivors of the Satanic underground.[65] Notwithstanding their hypocrisy, the irony of Rivera's warnings about the impressionability of children undermines the fundamental assumption of those who insist on the validity of Satanic ritual abuse survivor stories, that the similarity of the stories is a measure of their authenticity and not of collective fantasy. What is implied in the warning is that a child cannot distinguish illusion from reality as well as an adult, and this much is true. But this assumption also implicitly challenges the notion that the similarity of survivor stories is not the product of media images. Rivera's warning about his program indicates he is at least partially aware of his furnishing the popular imaginary with powerful imagery—to wit, clips of *Satanis* juxtaposed with a hodgepodge of visual abbreviations of the occult. Indeed, that Rivera would urge children away implicates the media in blurring the distinction between illusion and reality—fundamentally for the sake of entertainment and, in turn, advertising dollars. The power of the genres of documentary and news resides precisely in their claim to truth, premised entirely on an amplification of the reality effect of the image. Such is the logic of the carefully edited tabloid news programs, and such is the logic of the reality of Satanic ritual abuse.

Concluding Remarks: The Death of Occultism?

Although I have discussed only a few of the ways in which the imagistic topoi of Satanism were created, disseminated, and taken up, these examples are sufficient to illustrate the highly associative logics of a kind of rhetoric not easily analyzed: the occultic. As a discourse, Satanism is diffuse and reducible neither to LaVey nor to the frenzied media portrayal of Satanic ritual abuse; rather, it consists in a seemingly infinite number of visual signs that circulate in the popular imaginary, some coming into focus while others are fading away. I have argued that the cover of *The Satanic Bible* and clips from *Satanis* were, and are, two of the most prominent signs in focus during the late 1980s and early 1990s.

Understood sympathetically, LaVey's Satanism represents an intellectualized form of play grafted onto an Objectivist philosophy of radical individualism, a praxis (theoretically informed practice) of ritual gaming that tapped into a human need for psychodrama. What LaVey failed to realize, just as much as those who believe strongly in the validity of Satanic ritual abuse stories, is the powerful and unruly logics of the popular imaginary, a reservoir of myth and trope that has been created by the mass media, that is maintained by mass media, and that is molded by the sensationalist and capitalist rhetorics of tabloid journalism. As Baudrillard has persuasively argued, in late capitalism power is located in the control of the codes of representation and signification, not in the control of the conditions and means of production.[66]

My mapping of two visual abbreviations, the cover of *The Satanic Bible* and portions of the film *Satanis,* reveals their distribution and their subsequent re-signification within the circuit of capital, a circuit that, I believe, with Baudrillard, Jameson, and other post-Marxian scholars, is almost synonymous with the circuit of mass media.[67] This cartography of the transaction of imagery describes one way in which discourses are created by the mass media and inserted into the popular imagination through the process of fetishization. An original object, such as an occult film, is released into the circuit of media/capital. In its transaction as stock footage, for instance, its original use-value and its content are hollowed out. It is reduced to a form or a series of fragments and transacted as imagistic topoi that can then be taken up and re-signified or re-situated into a different referent system, such as the discourse of demonic criminality. In regard to the Satanic panic, then, I have argued that LaVey's Satanic imagery provided a concrete and memorable set of condensation symbols, imagistic topoi, that were used to vivify and seemingly authenticate, on the basis of the reality effect of the image, the reality of cannibalism, human sacrifice, and blood ritual.

I also have argued that the formal repetition of commodity exchange is a larger, structuring logic that is reflected in the thinness or formalization of Satanic texts, to a lesser degree in the reduction of *The Satanic Bible* to its cover, and to a greater degree in the fragmentation of *Satanis* as stock footage. This analysis implies that contemporary rumor panics like that concerning Satanism can be understood as a phenomenon of late capitalism premised on the overall drive toward the commodification of culture and the consequent thinning of cultural objects into transactable, highly consumable forms. Unlike rumor panics of the past that were largely localized and contained (e.g., the Salem witch trials), contemporary rumor panics are widespread and perpetuate themselves on the basis of a limited set of iconic stimuli that is first disseminated or released into the popular imaginary and then re-signified as evidence for a given cultural narrative or myth. As I noted in the introduction, "blood ritual" is a very old narrative that has been a part of Western myth for centuries. The wide dissemination of visual topoi, such as that enabled by LaVey's publicity campaigns of the late 1960s and early 1970s, provided visual abbreviations that were taken up, stripped of their original content or use-value, re-signified, and used for their reality effects.

In terms of the story of occult discourse that this chapter continues, however, the Satanic panic of the late 1980s and early 1990s implicates an end: the eclipse of occulted content by the form of its presentation heralds the death of modern occultism as such and the arrival of something much messier, the occultic. Indeed, it is the position of Satanists that there are no more secrets, that there is no content to occultism. For them, Satanism comprises variations on ritual, pageantry, and form. LaVey himself prefaces *The Satanic Bible* by saying that "all great works on the subject of magic are nothing more than sanctimonious fraud—guilt-ridden ramblings and esoteric gibberish by chroniclers of magical lore unable or unwilling to present an objective view of the subject."[68] For LaVey, the "objective view" is that occultism appeals to our inherent need for ritual and that there is nothing supernatural or otherworldly about the occult tradition. Given the successes and failures of LaVey's publicity campaigns and the commodification such spectacles represented, Satanism sounded the death knell for occultism as the study of secret knowledge.

What remains, then, is a contemporary occultic that lends itself more easily to appropriation by mass-media producers, politicians, and cultural leaders, usually to either entertain and titillate or to quell widespread anxiety about this or that crisis stimulus. As I was writing the conclusion to the first draft of this book, a number of Islamic radicals slammed commercial airplanes into the World Trade Center and the Pentagon, killing thousands. The widespread experience of trauma by U.S. citizens quickly led to a mining of the occultic by the Bush II administration and its speechwriters, and later the mass media. As I am writing this, our current Satanism is called "terrorism," and its many "evil" followers are an endless font of secrets, including nefarious plots to murder women and children and to acquire "weapons of mass destruction." Stock footage of Muslims firing weapons or cheering and jeering in the streets has been re-signified as iconic tokens of a supernatural rage unleashed. Like the McMartin preschool case and the Salem witch trails centuries ago, uncovering these secrets has become an excuse for state-sponsored violence. Today, the crusade to uncover the secrets of the contemporary Yezedi has justified the invasion of Afghanistan and Iraq, and who knows how many countries since the publication this book? Whether his name is Osama bin-Laden or Anton LaVey, the Devil is here to stay.

8
The Allegory of *The Ninth Gate*

> BARONESS KESSLER: My knowledge of [*The Nine Gates of the Kingdom of Shadows*] is profound. I wrote a biography of its author.
> CORSO: Yes, I've read it. *Aristide Torchia: The Devil's Apprentice.* Excellent work.
> BARONESS KESSLER: A courageous man. He died for the sake of this very book in 1667. While studying the black arts in Prague, he acquired a copy of the dread *Delomelanicon.* This is Torchia's adaptation of that work, which was written by Lucifer himself. After they burned him at the stake, a secret society was founded to perpetuate its memory and preserve its secrets: the Order of the Silver Serpent.
> CORSO: A sect?
> BARONESS KESSLER: Yes, a kind of witches' coven. For centuries they have met to read from this book and worship the Prince of Darkness. Today they've degenerated into a social club for bored millionaires and celebrities who use its meetings as an excuse to indulge in their jaded sexual appetites. I myself belonged to the order years ago, but time is too precious at my age. Besides, my orgy days are over. I told them to go to the Devil.
>
> —Dialogue from *The Ninth Gate*[1]

In a key scene from Roman Polanski's 1999 occult thriller, *The Ninth Gate,* the "unscrupulous" book detective Dean Corso (played by Johnny Depp) learns that the occult book he is investigating has been protected by a secret society for centuries. Corso has been hired by the wealthy U.S. book publisher Boris Balkan to authenticate his recently acquired book titled *The Nine Gates of the Kingdom of Shadows* (alternately, *The Nine Gates*). Baroness Kessler (played by Barbara Jefford) is also a wealthy book collector and occult scholar who owns a copy of *The Nine Gates.* Another copy belongs to Victor Fargas, a book collector who makes his living by selling two or three of his family's valuable books each year. Balkan tells Corso that he is convinced that only one of the three known copies is the real deal, and thus Corso's task is to figure out which copy is authentic. During his visit to the baroness to examine her copy, she explains to Corso that the ritual hidden in the much-treasured *The Nine Gates*—presumably coauthored by Aristide Torchia and the "Devil himself" in 1666—has been performed time and time again without the desired results. Properly decoded, the ritual specified in the book is supposed to open a door to absolute knowledge—that is, the very gates of Hell.

During his investigation, Corso learns that the key to unlocking the secret of the book is comparative exegesis: the genuine book is dispersed among all three of the copies. While investigating Fargas's copy, Corso learned that Balkan's text was identical except for key alterations in a number of the book's nine illustrations; when a given illustration differed among the copies, it was signed "LCF" (viz., Lucifer). Impressed with Corso's explanation of the secret code, the baroness permits him to examine the third copy. Presumably, once all the "LCF" illustrations are identified, the authentic ritual will become clear.

Corso's examination of Kessler's copy comes to an abrupt end, however, when he is hit on the head and passes out. He awakens to a library in flames and discovers that the baroness's copy of *The Nine Gates,* like the baroness herself, is quickly turning to char. This traumatic turn of events comes as no surprise to the spectator, for as the film progresses we are made to witness the dead bodies of each onetime owner of *The Nine Gates*. After Corso visits Fargas, the collector is drowned in a fountain, and Corso later discovers Fargas's copy of the book in the fireplace with each illustration removed. Coming to in Kessler's library, Corso discovers that the baroness has been murdered (her tongue dangling from her mouth in a typical Polanskian flourish).[2] Illustrations have been removed from her copy of the occult tome as well. Clearly, someone wants these illustrations and believes they have tremendous power.

The spectator soon learns—without surprise—that the greedy capitalist who hired Corso to authenticate his copy of *The Nine Gates* is responsible for the murders. Trailing Corso during his international sleuthing, Balkan has been killing the unsuspecting and taking the relevant illustrations from each copy of *The Nine Gates* as soon as Corso departs the scene. Balkan's ultimate goal is to stroll through Hell and thereby (somehow) become a god, which he reveals in the first of the film's three climaxes. Storming into an Order of the Silver Serpent ceremony—replete with fifty or sixty extras in black hoods chanting Latin phrases—Balkan trumpets his supreme authority concerning the book:

> Mumbo-jumbo-mumbo-jumbo-mumbo-jumbo. . . . Look around you—yes, all of you. What do you see? I'll tell you: a

> bunch of buffoons in fancy dress. What are you expecting, an apparition? I'm the only apparition you'll see tonight. You really think the Prince of Darkness would deign to manifest himself to the likes of you? He never has and he never will—never! [He closes *The Nine Gates* with a snap and holds it up.] You read from his book, yes, but you have no conception of its true power. I alone have grasped its secret. I alone have fathomed the Master's grand design. I alone am worthy to enjoy the fruits of that discovery: absolute power to determine my own destiny.

Given the importance of the sovereign individual in occult discourse, it is not surprising that Balkan characterizes supreme occult power in terms of the achievement of absolute autonomy. For Balkan, mastery of secret knowledge is the apotheosis of the individual and the ultimate realization of agency freed from social and material constraints. In a manner similar to Milton's characterization of Lucifer's declaration of independence in *Paradise Lost* ("aspiring to set himself in Glory above his Peers, he trusted to have equall'd the most High"),[3] Balkan severs all ties with his former collective with a prideful screed and Satanic swagger.

After Balkan's spectacular interruption of the Satanic ceremony (during which he strangles the high priestess), the film unravels as the narrative meanders through two anticlimactic climaxes. First, having assembled all the Satanic illustrations, Balkan mistakenly burns himself alive in an ill-planned ritual sacrifice. Second, after this decidedly secular turn of events—and after a patently gratuitous lovemaking scene—Corso is told by a mysterious character known only as "the girl" that Balkan failed because one of his illustrations was a fake. "The girl" then provides Corso with clues about the location of the missing, authentic illustration. After he discovers it on the top of an old, dusty bookshelf in a Spanish bookshop, the ending shots seem to suggest that Corso does indeed unlock the ninth gate and learn the true secret of the book. To the annoyance of many moviegoers, however, the film's ending does not let the audience in on the secret, nor does it provide a clear suggestion as to whether the ending should be read as a secular or supernatural event.

This unsatisfying end to a tortuous plot was the most common reason given for panning *The Ninth Gate* as a failed effort. Across the board, critics were obsessed with the ambiguous ending. With both his thumbs plunging downward toward the fiery abyss, Roger Ebert condemned the ending as a mere whimper: "While at the end I didn't yearn for spectacular special effects," he writes, "I did wish for spectacular information—something awesome, not just a fade to white."[4] The *Sarasota Herald Tribune* criticized the film for starting with "a promising premise" but falling short with "an ending that doesn't work."[5] A critic from the Gannett News Service lamented that the film culminates "in an ending that is both confusing and anticlimactic."[6] A reviewer in the *Seattle Post-Intelligencer* noted that while the film was "sporadically enjoyable" it was still "rather pathetic," "suspenseless and fairly ludicrous," and that Polanski "seems almost to be making a parody of a demon movie" that fails to show us demons.[7] "Like pages falling out of an old tome," suggests *Entertainment Weekly,* "the film comes unglued slowly."[8] Jay Carr of the *Boston Globe* complained that *The Ninth Gate* is "a supernatural thriller that is neither super, natural, nor thrilling."[9] Nick Carter of the *Milwaukee Journal Sentinel* carped that while watching the film, it is "never clear what precisely those privy to the secrets of [*The Nine Gates*] know, fear and desire—and that's a hellish fate for the viewer who's been left in purgatory for the preceding 2 1/2 hours."[10] Polanski "has come up with 75 percent of a very good movie," reads a review in the *San Francisco Chronicle,* "but has a dickens of a time with the supernatural ending."[11]

The dominant reading of the film among critics is that *The Ninth Gate* is a movie about the dangers of obsession which, unfortunately, fails to supply convincing rationales for each character's obsession (why, pray tell, would anyone *want* to go to Hell?). Corso has no reason to be obsessed with the occult tome (unless, as some argue, he is himself a demon with amnesia),[12] yet he spends the last moments of the film hunting down the missing illustration. I would agree that, as a yarn about obsession and its consequences, the film does not hold together very well. Yet there is a reading, one which is sometimes termed an "oppositional" reading or a "productive misreading," that redeems the film: as a rhetorical object, *The Ninth Gate* reflects the transformation of occultism from the elite study of secrets to an aesthetic, commodified collection of iconic topoi.[13] In other words, the failure of the film mirrors, in content and form, the increasingly incoherent character of occultism as a contemporary discourse. Indeed, Polanski's wedding of capitalism and romantic individualism into a composite personification of the will to power is analogous to the story of occultism I have been telling. Furthermore, as the allegorical representative of the cultural or textual critic, the shamus sends us a warning: critics obsessed with fetishizing the discrete text or artistic object may, in the end, get burned.

For these reasons, as well as others I detail below, I think that Polanski's screen adaptation of Arturo Pérez-Reverte's novel *The Club Dumas* serves as an excellent allegorical frame for revisiting the arguments of this study.[14] The film also helps one to describe occult discourse simultaneously as text, intertext, and social form. The grammar of the occultic that I have developed and illustrated in this study can help one to recast the film as an epitaph for modern occultism, as if the film were an agent in itself, urging us to listen to the last, faint whispering of the occult, urging us to witness the death that it mourns.

In what follows, then, I first recharacterize this study as the provision of a grammar and a rhetoric of the occultic. I suggest that the former is a system of regularly appearing discursive elements that, properly articulated, helps one to make sense of an "occult" text, as well as an intertextual collection of occult texts, however disappointing, difficult, or diffuse. A rhetoric of the occultic (as opposed to *the* rhetoric), on the other hand, attempts to locate grammatical elements by moving among multiple levels of abstraction, by mediating texts, discourses, and social reality. After I detail a grammar and rhetoric of the occultic, I then illustrate their utility via a redemptive reading of *The Ninth Gate,* which I use as a platform for summary and discussion.

Recasting the Goals of Description and Diagnosis

> As we have said, our primary purpose has been to express towards language an *attitude* embodied in a *method.* This attitude is one of linguistic skepticism, which we synonymize with linguistic appreciation, on the grounds that an attitude of methodological quizzicality towards language may best equip us to perceive the full scope of its resourcefulness.
>
> —Kenneth Burke[15]

In his *Grammar of Motives,* Kenneth Burke set out to articulate a critical perspective (variously, attitude or disposition) for the criticism of literary objects by fashioning a metavocabulary that better enabled the rhetorician to perceive the critical object dialectically (e.g., a concern with multiple levels of abstraction, with mediation, with self-reflection, with a suspicion of language, and so on).[16] Burke's critical grammar, dubbed "dramatism," is an eclectic blend of rhetorical, psychological, sociological, and literary concepts that has been used fruitfully by critics in a number of ways.[17] Key among the grammar Burke specifies is the "pentad," a heuristic of five interrelated concepts that one could use to describe the motive, or world-orientation, of a given text: scene, act, agency, agent, and purpose (e.g., a text that tended to emphasize the importance of scene over the agent could be described as materialist). At the end of the book, Burke claims that dramatism is to accompany both a "rhetoric of motives" and a "symbolic of motives," complementary perspectives of study that "would examine *in detail* the ways in which the Grammatical resources are employed for the purposes of persuasion and self expression."[18] The rhetoric of motives Burke developed (in the book of the same title) actually abandoned the precise grammar he originally advanced, focusing instead on the ways in which anxiety about social hierarchy and mystery (alternately read, about class)[19] is embedded in rhetorical encounters. Unfortunately, Burke passed away before he could publish the symbolic of motives (which actually exists and may be published in the future by this press).

I have mentioned Burke here because his larger project resembles the present one.[20] If we replace Burke's term "dramatism" with "the occultic," then we could characterize the primary, descriptive goal of this study as the conjuring of a grammar of secrecy and magic applicable to any relevant discourse (e.g., dense scholarly prose). If we replace Burke's concern with attitude or motive with a concern for rhetoric as the suasive movement of grammatical elements, then the second, diagnostic goal of this study can be described as a rhetoric of the occultic. I discuss each in turn below.

Occultic Grammar: Describing Text, Intertext, and Social Form

The provision of an esoteric grammar for the occultic is an attempt to provide a nonreductive description of contemporary or postmodern occultism as a discourse or intersubjectively grounded social formation. The exigency for the more complex description of occultism has to do with the many ways in which it is used to describe a variety of phenomena today. In this study I have argued that although the meaning of occultism was more discrete and contained in the late nineteenth century (as the elite study of secrets), today it is best characterized as a diffuse and dynamic intertextual system of multiple bits, or as I put it previously, a totality of intersubjectively shared relations, of everything that is said to belong to it, including spells and images, books and symbols—even moods. Hence, as the story of modern occultism has moved from modernity toward postmodernity in each successive chapter, it has become increasingly abstract and diffuse. In Blavatsky's time, occultism primarily concerned the study of secrets as they were contained in cherished books. This understanding of occultism began to change during Crowley's time (late nineteenth century to the middle of the twentieth), however. For example, through sensational portrayals and exposés, the popular press began to democratize the secret knowledge of elite occult groups, effectively reversing occultism's association with the cultural elite. Jumping to the Satanic rumor panic at the end of the twentieth century, it is clear that within the span of forty years, not only have the elite and aristocratic been replaced by a disempowered Other's quest for social ascendancy (newspaper stories on youth gone wild, killing cats and torturing frogs in the name of Satan!), but the occult as such has exploded into an almost incoherent panoply of transactable forms. As with any object of history past, the horizons of occultism are easy to discern in yesterday but difficult to identify in the present.

To contend with the messiness of contemporary occult discourse, I first bracketed occultism to what I have termed its "modern" period, which I delimited in terms of common rhetorical features and the emergence of an economic motive for the creation of occult texts. Second, the description of modern occultism I forwarded operates at multiple levels of abstraction, or in terms of discourse: at the level of text, at the level of intertext, and at the level of social form. Each level corresponds to a different description of occultism as a textual practice, as an interpretive practice, and as an entertainment commodity, respectively. Only by moving among multiple iterations of the occult is one able to escape the deceptive unity of discrete critical objects and to place them within a social and historical context.

In regard to more traditional occult texts, I have suggested that occultism typically orbits a number of content themes and compositional forms. Most occult texts are saturated with the themes of secrecy, imagination, and authority, and their contents are often deployed in figurative or allegorical representations, frequently in a manner that is deliberately misleading. In addition to these thematic and generic features, I have also focused in detail on the rhetorical function of esoteric language as an occult poetics, which I characterized internally as an attempt to transcend the limits of language *through* language, and externally as a paradoxical mode of rhetorical invention. Blavatsky's texts, for example, forward a paradoxical rhetoric of revelation that promises secret knowledge in confusing and misleading terminology. Although such terminology represents Blavatsky's anxieties about the limits of language, her prolixity is demonstrative of her relative inability to control language as well. Indeed, Blavatsky's texts are representative of the role paradox plays in all religious discourse. The only way to end the chaining of occult modes of invention is to let go of the need for a transcendental presence; trapped in our own symbolicity, there is no access to the outside.

Second, as an intertextual discourse, the meaning of any given occult text is dependent on a psychical matrix of textual nodes that exist in the field of a shared, collective consciousness—the popular imaginary. Although anchored by texts, occult discourse necessarily concerns the relationships among texts, and especially the relationships among texts as they exist in the mental life of concrete individuals. In this respect, in the second part of the present study ("Exoterica") I describe occultism as an interpretive practice designed to empower the reader and, for some, an interpretive practice designed to establish the charismatic authority of occult leaders, a hermeneutic of authority. That the meaning of occultism is dynamic and intertextual is precisely the formal condition for assertions of charismatic authority as well as the condition for the erosion of charismatic authority. Through an analysis of texts by and about Crowley, I demonstrated how the magus's attempts at authorial control were undermined by the same rhetorical devices used by occultists for centuries, such as the rhetorical blind and other forms of dissimulation, largely as the result of evolving mass-media technologies. Innovations in mass media made occult texts cheaper to produce and made occult secrets widely available in the pages of magazines, tabloids, and newspapers. In the end, Crowley (and to a lesser extent LaVey) is the example figure of the failure of occult modes of authority in a media-saturated environment. Given the power of the "news" media and the speed with which information can move these days, the lesson here is that no charismatic leader is likely to succeed by means of deliberate misdirection or ironic spectacle. Of course there will always be exceptions, but in general the days of the Great Magus are over.

That occult themes became increasingly popular in newspapers and tabloids also highlights the impact of capitalism on occult practice: the content of occultism gave way to its form as highly evocative, imagistic topoi. Occult stories were and are popular because they are entertaining and because they tap into a human curiosity about the Other. They titillate middle-class audiences by promising the revelation of ancient, magical secrets or glimpses into the exotic world of "the other half." By the time LaVey was inventing his spectacular Church of Satan, occultism had been thoroughly commodified; it metamorphosed into books, films, and other media that emphasized transactability over use. The consequence of commodification was the reduction of occultism to a collection of visual abbreviations that are easily transacted in the field of the popular imaginary; put alternately by LaVey, when "the occult (hidden) becomes fashionable, it is no longer occult."[21]

Occultic Rhetoric: Dealing with Dynamism Dialectically

The diagnostic goal of this study concerned using the grammar of occultism—from its recurrent generic features as a text to its autonomous existence as a social form—to say something about the practice of criticism as well as to articulate the social character of a given time in relation to the concept of the individual. Both concern what Burke terms the "symbolic," which is caught up in the concept of rhetoric insofar as we can describe conscious rhetoric as persuasion and unconscious rhetoric as suasive movement.

In the course of writing this book I have also tried to demonstrate a multilayered, dialectical mode of criticism that can contend with the scattered and dynamic character of contemporary discourse. Like Corso's comparative exegesis of each seemingly identical copy of *The Nine Gates of the Kingdom of Shadows,* as a critic I have urged a comparative or dialectical hermeneutics of suspicion, a mode of critical interpretation that demands critical movement into different levels of abstraction, different contexts, in order to locate the traces of cultural logics like that of intertextual authority, commodity fetishism, class struggle, and so on. The fact that movement among multiple contexts is born out of political necessity refers to the dialectical intercourse between our necessary and pragmatic assumptions about agency and the unity of subjectivity, on the one hand, and the knowledge, vouchsafed by the discovery of the unconscious, that larger social forms, such as language and ideology, move us to do things in ways that are often beyond our conscious awareness, on the other. The unconscious movement of ideology does not mean we are precluded from locating its traces, for ideology moves precisely by means of contradiction, by covering over ruptures and eliding the very differences that critics are trained to notice (if there were no contradictions to elide, ideology as such would not exist). Nevertheless, given the manner in which ideology works through the concrete individual, the critic must be continuously self-doubting, reflexive, and suspicious of his or her critical moves; mediation among multiple, critical contexts is a political choice to manage the mystifications of demystification.

Insofar as my critical approach stresses the importance of the critic throughout, it should be said that I unavoidably reify the very concept of autonomous subjectivity that I begin to question when analyzing Crowley's work. This is a pragmatic and strategic (political) necessity. That we all are bundles of selves or "split" does not mean that we cannot intend things; nor does it mean that the critic cannot judge. Just as Corso persists in his exegeses despite his understanding that he does not know the whole story, although he recognizes someone is "playing a game with him," so too the critic should continue his or her projects guided by some political commitment. In other words, criticism is political because critics persist as critics even though our own symbolicity outwits us.

In each occultist's delusional striving to establish his or her prophetic authority over others, in each occultist's attempt to police meaning and interpretation, language outwits him or her by continually deferring the transcendental signified, by failing to produce God—or the Devil for that matter. Just as Blavatsky continued to generate book upon book and essay upon essay, Crowley was forced continuously to re-signify his texts in order to police interpretation. Further, in a media-saturated environment in which media producers exploit the appeal of occult themes for profit, LaVey was unable to control the powerful and far-reaching imagery that he deployed into the popular imaginary. In each case study that I examined, the fantasy of the intending subject in complete control of his or her rhetoric is made clear, as the logics of representation disperse fragments of their rhetorics among the millions upon millions of concrete mental spaces that compose the popular imaginary. In overtaking the traditional content of secrets, the form of occultism as a collection of intersubjective topoi eludes any one individual's attempt to channel it into something stable and impervious to re-signification. Take, for example, Roman Polanski's *The Ninth Gate.*

Through the Lens Darkly: The Occultic Object of *The Ninth Gate*

A productive oppositional reading of Polanski's failed film is possible if one reframes it as an occultic object itself, reading it as I have read occult discourse. Moving from the film as a text to the film as an intertextual site of cultural work, one can recast *The Ninth Gate* as an occult liturgy and, particularly, the administration of last rites. In both content and form, the film is an apt condensation of the present study.

The Ninth Gate *as Text*

Polanski's film evinces each of the themes and forms of traditional, modern occult texts in the figure of its titular book. *The Nine Gates* contains a secret ritual that has been studied and protected by a secret society, the Order of the Silver Serpent. In the film, authority is ultimately conferred by a "true" understanding of the secret of the book, and claims to this true understanding result in a number of struggles (between Balkan and the secret order, between Balkan and the other two owners of the book, and between Balkan and the individual who was the first to fathom "the Master's grand design," Dean Corso). Not surprisingly, the secret ritual is revealed by close textual analysis and comparative exegesis.

As Corso soon learns, the ability to understand the imagistic codes of Lucifer's nine illustrations resides in the power of association and imagination, not reason. The road to enlightenment/Hell is paved not with the good intentions of language (viz., the promise of linear meaning or a transparent relationship between the signifier and the signified) but with the deceptive, dreamlike qualities of imagery. *The Ninth Gate* is a threshold of intertextual links, a hieroglyph that is an illusion because it promises a deeper, *semantic* meaning. Ironically, the secret resides wholly within the imagistic surface.

Throughout the film, this liminal, imaginary crossroad is cued repeatedly in ways that resemble the intended, transportive function of occult texts, moving the reader from mundane reality to an imaginary one, presumably shot through with supernatural power: each "real" death witnessed by Corso (mundane) mirrors figures in the illustrations of the occult book (imaginary); key characters in the film's narrative are also represented in the illustrations (e.g., "the girl" as the Whore of Babylon in the ninth illustration). Although the film is all about books, the spectator is made to scrutinize the pictures in them, not the words they harbor; the castle that plays a large role at the ending of the film is first seen in a picture hanging in Balkan's office, which is seen again in a postcard found in the Kessler copy of *The Nine Gates,* which in turn is re-presented in the ninth illustration. Each key object, character, or place in the film is repeated in multiple imagistic iterations; their presumably real or mundane material basis is always under erasure. Characters are killed or simply disappear while their representations survive; the authentic book exists as an abstract trinity dispersed in three distinct places, not a single iteration; the castle, presumably the material site where the representation and the real are wed, goes up in flames. To wit: in the film the most "real" is the hyperreal—the floating signifier, the simulation, the lie, the husk or discarded skin of an absent spiritual existence. Insofar as traditional occult texts are Platonic in the sense that the world of appearances—mundane reality—is illusory and that ultimate reality is in the imaginary world of abstraction, Polanski's film follows through, true to form. In many ways, *The Ninth Gate* is an accurate, postmodern representation of modern occultism.

In the context of the film's story, that *The Nine Gates* has deceived its readers for centuries by hiding the authentic ritual in three seemingly identical books speaks directly to the suaveness of repetition. As repetitions, each copy of the book deceptively promises a unity, and if one describes rhetoric as the movement between repetitions (form), collectively the copies are a model of suasion: the secret of *The Nine Gates* has remained so for centuries because the images have been passed over as the totemic illustrations of *linguistic* meaning, not meaningful things in their own right. In this way the seductive mystery of the book is perpetuated. Given the necessarily deceptive nature of imagistic representation, the rhetorical blinds typical of occult texts are thus magnified by *The Nine Gates of the Kingdom of Shadows* in compositional form. The pictures obscure differences that, once noticed by means of intertextual comparison, promise to transport the reader beyond the material realm through the "gate" of the individual imagination and into ultimate reality.

Of course, that the secret secreted by the occult book concerns pictures is a necessary and expected innovation insofar as Polanski's text is a film. Yet the implicit cinematographic commentary, irrelevant of intention, should not be *over-looked:* in terms of the proverbial cliché, the secret here is that one cannot judge a book by its cover, a truth to which wealthy occultists and book collectors are blind because of their reification of the book as an fetishized object. "One of the sly jokes of 'The Ninth Gate,'" observes Stephanie Zacharek, "is that most book lovers, at least to an extent, succumb to the idea of books as totems, items that hold vast powers as physical objects."[22] Because the film repeatedly insists that we become suspicious of modes of totemic seduction, it can also be understood as advancing a characteristically rhetorical paradigm of interpretation and criticism: the hermeneutics of suspicion.

As the dialectical counterpart to seduction and obsession, the motif of suspicion is woven into the film in a number of ways. The most significant element of suspicion in respect to the spectator concerns the film's ambivalence toward the existence of the supernatural. This ambivalence renders *The Ninth Gate* an expression of, as well as a commentary upon, occultism. From a structural vantage, this ambivalence mirrors the riddle of the book at the level of the film's composition, linking content and form with the master trope of occultism: irony. For example, in one outside scene Corso wrestles with a bad guy at the landing of a stone staircase. The bad guy desperately wants

Balkan's copy of *The Nine Gates,* which Corso has in his satchel. "The girl" appears abruptly in a fleeting shot in which she seems to float down the staircase toward the scuffle. The scene is constructed to confuse the spectator about the role of the supernatural: Did "the girl" just fly? Does she have magical powers? Or is this simply Corso's mind playing tricks on him?[23]

The film's ironic conclusion also leaves the spectator confused. After finding the last, hidden illustration in a Spanish bookshop, Corso learns that he has happened upon the final, authentic piece that will solve the book's puzzle. In the succeeding shot, we watch Corso as he enters the gate of a castle into a blinding light, and the film, in an ironic reversal of cinematographic convention, fades to white. The audience is left wondering: Is this a filmic flourish? Is Corso entering the ninth gate? Didn't the castle burn up? Is this a supernatural event or simply a obtuse way to end the film? Indeed, the film leaves the spectator with more questions than answers. As Elvis Mitchell put it in his review in the *New York Times:* "Is ['the girl'] on Corso's side? Will Balkan get Satan's powers in his clutches through mastery of 'The Nine Gates'? And what about Satan? Since the rich in these Devil-quest spectaculars are always searching for the Devil but often come to a bad end, does this mean he's a socialist? Or perhaps, since money attracts money, that he's a supply-sider? These are questions to be answered sooner or later in an issue of *Cahiers du Cinéma.* Or *The Industry Standard.*"[24] Or in an academic book on occultism. In any event, the answers are not provided by the film itself (and yes, as I will shortly argue, the Devil *is* a socialist), and this fundamental ambiguity resembles in content the formal instability of the ironic devices that are so central to modern occult discourse. Just as the curious straight is horrified by Anton LaVey's Satanic gaming, or just as authorities expelled Crowley from Italy because his suggestion to sacrifice children was taken too literally, Polanski's ironic film disappoints (perhaps even angers) audiences by promising the Devil and failing to produce him.

Given this ending, the film's secret, for those inside the ironic circle, is that there are, in fact, no secrets—only deceptions. Just as Blavatsky would urge us to "see" behind the limitations of natural language, so too *The Ninth Gate* urges us to peer behind the misdirection and fetishized mystique of the visual image in ways that label the film an occultic text. The distinction to be made between Blavatsky's *Isis Unveiled* and Polanski's *The Ninth Gate,* however, is this: whereas there is an ultimate, metaphysical presence to which Blavatsky's text promises access, in *The Ninth Gate* the existence of this supernatural presence, that is, of a transcendental signified, is not guaranteed.

The Ninth Gate *as Intertext*

The filmic suggestion to distrust what one sees in any given shot is related to the intertextual understanding of occult discourse as well. Polanski's film is demonstrative of the dialectical interplay between interpretation and authority, and combined with its caution about imagery, it is an excellent commentary on the authorial function of textual exegesis. In the film, occult authority is conferred on the basis of authentic knowledge. Although all of the key players are wealthy aristocrats, no amount of money can "buy" the correct interpretation of *The Nine Gates*. In the scene in which Balkan dismisses a number of chanting Satanists as "buffoons in fancy dress," he insists that only he is competent to understand the secrets of *The Nine Gates*. His authority over the book's meaning is not conferred by means of reasoned argument, nor is it conferred in terms of his status as a wealthy capitalist. Rather, Balkan asserts his authority prophetically, offering self-evidence and self-assertion as the sole justification. "I alone have grasped its secret," he insists, "I alone have fathomed the Master's grand design." He cannot appeal to social contracts or established institutions, because none exist; he can only appeal to the mystical aura (or fetish character) of the occult book itself by aligning it with the mystique of his formidable ethos (the character is played by a campy, bespectacled Frank Langella, "wearing a hairpiece that is most assuredly from the Stygian depths of Hell").[25] It is not inconsequential that Balkan's dialogue closely resembles the charismatic rhetoric of Aleister Crowley: "I lay claim to be the sole authority competent to decide disputed points with regard to the Book of the Law, seeing that its Author, Aiwas, is none other than mine own Holy Guardian Angel, to Whose Knowledge and Conversation I have attained, so that I have exclusive access to him."[26]

The Ninth Gate *as Social Form*

The irony of the importance of pictures in the film is that Polanski intended *The Ninth Gate* as a nostalgic celebration of books. In the opening scene the camera seems to caress the bindings of books, leading the spectator to the next scene through a space in a bookshelf. Each succeeding scene that occurs in a library glorifies books in sepia-tinged shots, conveying a romantic, inviting feeling. Yet just as an child is drawn to picture books because little intellectual labor seems required, so too the traditional complexity of older occult texts is reduced to a series of pictures to appease the escapist motives of the typical moviegoing audience. In respect to the irony of its nostalgia, *The Ninth Gate* is not only an epitaph for occultism as the study of secrets but also a lamentation for the figure of the book.

As a commentary on the demise of the figure of the book, *The Ninth Gate* can be understood as an intertextual site that magnifies or hyperbolizes larger social logics. Insofar as every individual seeking authority, autonomy, and power is killed in a spectacularly grotesque way, *The Ninth Gate* enacts a commentary on democratizing forces of production (media technologies) and the resulting impact of these forces on social hierarchy: as new media technologies enabled the dissemination of occult knowledge in modernity, rare and old occult books became increasingly valuable as totems, irrelevant of their actual content; the secret societies sworn to protect infernal knowledge have devolved into social clubs and swinger societies; and from a metacritical vantage on the film itself, the reduction of *The Nine Gates of the Kingdom of Shadows* to a series of pictures implicates commodity fetishism, the tendency of cultural objects to become more valuable as transactable things—as forms—as opposed to being valuable for their uses. Each character's obsession with the figure of the book, as well as the film itself, is an object lesson in fetishism.

Again, in terms of the film's content we learn that the secret of the powerful occult tome is that there is, in fact, no secret (or rather, that the Devil alone chooses his disciples, and his choices have nothing to do with books). As I argued in the previous chapter, this kind of revelation is demonstrative of the demise of occultism as the study of secret knowledge and its transformation into a series of visual abbreviations for the sake of entertainment (as the baroness says to Corso, the cherished occult book and the society that protects it gives "bored millionaires" something to do—or a way to play—with themselves). In terms of its formal composition, however, Polanski's film also heralds the death of occultism as a textual practice; just as the iconic repertoire created by LaVey obscured the actual semantic content of *The Satanic Bible,* so too do the pictures in *The Nine Gates of the Kingdom of Shadows* obscure its printed text. The Satanic ritual performed by Balkan near the end of the movie is also significantly without esoteric language. Instead of chanting "mumbo-jumbo" or capering about with a bell, book, and candle, Balkan merely places the "LCF" illustrations side by side, briefly reads their captions, and sets himself on fire; the ritualistic depth typical of the demonic invocations in horror movies is conspicuously absent, as the substance and secrecy of the occult tradition gives way to style and the form of the image. The failure of this scene to terrify audiences can be explained in one of two ways. Polanski either misjudged the power of the image and occult icons to frighten audiences today (e.g., the inverted pentagram), or the "thinness" of the Satanic ritual was intentionally ironic: "There is nothing supernatural going on here!" In either case, the spoken and written word, like the book and occultism itself, is inconsequential.

The Ninth Gate's nostalgic celebration of occult books and their relationship to elites in the film speak directly to the demise of occultism as the sole province of a select group.[27] Today, occult texts are just as accessible to the lower and middle classes as they are to the elite. It makes sense, then, that empirical sociological research suggests that the majority of occult practitioners today are of the subclasses and disempowered groups such as youth. Polanski's film is thus also nostalgic in terms of the absence of us common folk; as in the days of Blavatsky and Crowley, the occult world of *The Ninth Gate* is one that belongs only to the ruling class. In its demystification of the occult the film is also demonstrative of the power of the mass media to demystify the lifestyles of the rich and famous. The pleasures of watching *The Ninth Gate* have something to do with its ability to invite a middle-class audience to mingle with millionaires. By learning more about the other half, the spectator can join (or destroy) them.[28]

Given the affinities between academic and traditional occult poetics, it is important to discuss how the voyeuristic pleasures of the film participate in a critique of elite academic culture: just as ivy-league schools are perceived to be sites of secret knowledge exclusively available to the cultural elite, the film characterizes the libraries of stately homes as the sites of occult knowledge exclusively available to the well educated and well-to-do. Although the theoretical implications of a symptomatic reading of occultism differ between academic and popular contexts, the critique of elitism converges in the concept of authority. The parallels between the occult authority and the academic scholar are obvious: just as the occultist promotes his or her novel vocabulary and urges a particular mode of interpretation that bolsters his or her authority as an expert, so, too, the scholar prescribes modes of analysis that reify the power of the critic and reinforce his or her claims (however implicit) to intelligence or brilliant insight. Just as the occultist seems to replicate the external hierarchy of class within a secret order, so, too, the academic carves out spaces of belonging in terms of a disciplinary argot and other rhetorics of inclusion and exclusion (e.g., admission standards). Indeed, as some first-generation scholars are likely to admit, academic success is motivated by a desire for class ascendancy, a motive that is frequently derided as a source of professorial arrogance. In this respect, it is not surprising that the unfavorable public reactions to occultists like Blavatsky and Crowley are similar to the unfavorable representations of academics in the popular media in general. Such representations even occur within the academy: Martha Nussbaum's comments in the *New Republic* about the feminist theorist Judith Butler are akin to calling her a witch: "Mystification and hierarchy are the tools of her practice," argues Nussbaum, and her "ponderous and obscure" writing is really only designed to create a cultish following.[29]

In *The Ninth Gate,* the scholar and occultist are wed in a number of composite characters, the most obvious being that of Boris Balkan (in the novel the Balkan character is two distinct individuals, one a wealthy scholar, the other a wealthy capitalist). The viewer is first introduced to Balkan while he is giving a lecture; his description in the screenplay is particularly telling:

> BORIS BALKAN, standing at a state-of-the-art lecturer's desk, is a bulky, imposing figure of a man around 50 years old. His thick gray hair is slicked back to reveal a domed forehead. The eyes beneath it radiate keen intelligence through a pair of heavy horn-rims. He speaks in a deep, slow, almost monotonous voice, but with great authority. BALKAN: "Relevant information may be found in Antoine Marin del Rio's *Disquisitionum Magicarum,* Louvain 1599, and earlier, in 1580, in *De la Demonomanle des Sorciers* by the Frenchman, Jean Bodin. . . . "

Balkan is described as the stereotypically arrogant professor whose authority in this scene is established by charismatic appeal; in other words, Balkan sounds and looks the part.

What is instructive about the narrative, however, is that Balkan's claims to authority and absolute independence are, in the end, denied; just as Nussbaum would symbolically burn Butler at the scholastic stake, so Polanski sets Balkan ablaze in a spectacular display of special-effects wizardry. In the ritualistic scene in which Balkan assembles the nine illustrations, it is clear to the audience that he believes he has finally solved the riddle of *The Nine Gates* (again, unbeknownst to Balkan, one of his illustrations is a fake). Dousing himself with gasoline, Balkan believes that he is finally a death-defying god, the right-hand man of the Prince of Darkness. He lights himself, giggling maniacally as Corso watches in horror. "I feel the power flowing through me like an electric current, rendering me capable of any achievement, mental or physical!" proclaims Balkan. "I could float on air, walk on water." Soon, however, the spectator is made aware that Balkan has realized his terrible mistake. His triumphant laughter becomes "a high-pitched scream of agony. He starts to caper around, slapping at his clothes, his face, his hair."[30] Corso shoots him to put him out of his misery, quickly putting an end to Balkan's delusions of grandeur.

Balkan's scripted delusion is important because it functions as a critique of the ruling class, a critique that plays on our own anxieties about hierarchy, perhaps on our inner wishes for wealth and prosperity: Balkan does not know everything after all, and despite his wealth and education, he is not immune to abject stupidity. His privilege, in other words, is punished. In *The Ninth Gate* all of the occultists are the wealthy elite, "bored millionaires" and the like, dissatisfied with their easy, privileged lives (a description, incidentally, commonly associated with the college professor).[31] Of course, the demonization of the wealthy and the valorization of the subclass is a common plot device in commercial film; that commercial film profits depend largely on the number of tickets it can sell to the middle and lower-middle classes explains precisely why this plot is so ubiquitous. Just as James Cameron's *Titanic* (1997) punishes the wealthy by drowning them and as Luis Buñel disciplines the upper class by denying them food in *The Discreet Charm of the Bourgeoisie* (1972), so Polanski's *The Ninth Gate* punishes aristocrats and bourgeoisie in particularly gruesome ways: Fargas is drowned; the baroness is strangled and incinerated; the leader of a secret order is choked to death; and Balkan commits suicide in an unglorified blaze of idiocy.

More than any other genre popular in commercial film today (typically variations of *Cinderella* or Random-Stuff-Exploding), the class-struggle formula saturates occult thrillers. The frequent association of the ruling class with supernatural forces on the screen suggests that occult discourse is particularly successful in arousing and quelling our anxieties about social hierarchy. For these reasons, in this study I have emphasized the discriminating function of occult discourse and, in particular, the social politics of irony. Occult films hyperbolize class anxiety in ways that mirror the negative coverage of occultists like Blavatsky, Crowley, and LaVey. Just as Crowley was demonized in the press as the "wickedest man in the world," for example, so the typical occult thriller disciplines, in one way or the other, social privilege. In *The Exorcist* (1973), the comfortable life of a rich and successful actress is wrecked when her daughter is possessed by a demon. In *The*

Omen (1976), the well-off, politically ensconced Thorn family is destroyed after unfortunately rearing the Antichrist. In Polanski's more commercially successful occult thriller, *Rosemary's Baby* (1969), a struggling actor named Guy makes a Faustian bargain with a number of wealthy Satanists who reside in his new, posh New York apartment building. The actor's wife, Rosemary, is given to Satan in a night of drugged debauchery in exchange for a successful career and social mobility. *The Ninth Gate* is simply one variation of the Faustian thriller in which the ruling class is either associated with the demonic, the secret source of their wealth and power, or punished by it. Read in light of the mysteries of social order and the anxieties any hierarchy produces, the occult thriller is a visual rendition of the talking cure.

In addition to its symbolic punishment of those who would keep secrets from us, *The Ninth Gate* can also be read as a critique of autonomy, of the notion that the individual is sovereign and free to govern the self as he or she wishes. In the film's depiction of the characteristic infighting of the occult tradition (viz., Balkan's bloodthirsty quest for Lucifer's pretty pictures), various occultists are pitted against each other in their common pursuit of supreme authority and autonomy. Balkan's spectacular death, for example, can be understood as the price one pays for narcissism, for failing to realize the importance of the Other. Balkan is so convinced of his "absolute power to determine [his] own destiny" that he fails to notice his own mistake, which, had he consulted Corso or others, might have been avoided. The antihero of the film, Dean Corso, is actually given the prized secret (or so the end of the film seems to suggest; whether this is the case is, again, not clear). Not only is Corso "like us" in terms of his lower- to middle-class affiliation, but he is also the only character who engages the community for companionship and for information, although he is painted as a selfish and greedy pirate. His eventual "obsession" with *The Nine Gates* is a negative quality, but the character of Corso is compelling precisely because he is not what he initially seems. Although he is described by other characters in the film as "unscrupulous," he is honest with the baroness and treats "the girl" with respect; although Corso claims to be interested only in his retainer and fees, he persists in investigating the book, succumbing to obsession, despite an increasing body count. Whereas Balkan is content unto himself, Corso depends on others to break the code of the occult book.

Corso is rewarded not only because of his scholarly humility (framed, significantly, as a businesslike disinterest in the contents of the book) but also because he seems to understand the fictive nature of his autonomy as an individual. That Corso understands he is not in control is revealed in a scene that follows his second visit to Fargas's mansion, where he discovers the aristocrat drowned in a fountain. He is seated on an airplane next to "the girl" as the next scene begins:

> CORSO looks down at THE GIRL.
> CORSO: What exactly happened back there?
> THE GIRL: Fargas caught someone stealing, I guess.
> CORSO: And what do you *guess* happened to him?
> THE GIRL: (simply) He drowned.
> CORSO: With a little help from who?
> THE GIRL: (Shrugs) He's dead. Who cares?
> CORSO: I care. I could wind up the same way.
> THE GIRL: Not with me to take care of you.
> CORSO: I see. You're my guardian angel.
> THE GIRL: Something like that. (She removes her head from his shoulder, turns away, and snuggles up against the window instead.)
> CORSO: Somebody's playing a game with me.
> THE GIRL: (drowsily): Of course. You're part of it. And you're getting to like it.

The dominant reading of this scene is not one that specifies a commentary on the fragmentation of subjectivity, yet from a rhetorical vantage the critique of humanism, particularly as it is expressed in terms of the illusion of the unity of subjectivity, helps to explain why Corso escapes the fate of every other character who touches the cursed book. The significant difference between Corso and the other characters is his sense of his own fallibility, his somewhat naive trust in the characters he meets, and his distrust of the image and other forms of representation. Those who do not "get it" are the Fools who have the strongest faith in their individual autonomy. Thus we can add a fourth to the many deaths of *The Ninth Gate:* not only does the film comment on the demise of the written text, the demise of the figure of the book, and the demise of occultism, but it is also a commentary on the demise of the autonomous individual. In the film, the Devil is a socialist in the sense that only those who do not assert their supreme independence from the collective are allowed to survive. Given his unfortunate expulsion from the idyllic collective know as "Heaven," perhaps the Devil has learned his lesson.

The Occultic as Postmodern Occultism

Having summarized this study as both an analysis of occultism in popular culture and a theoretical exploration of critical practice, questions about the larger significance of the occultic as a social form still remain: What does the death of modern occultism mean? If modern occultism is dead, then what can we describe as "occultic"? If the occult as such ended with the historical transition from modernity to postmodernity (or late capitalism), then is there such a thing as postmodern occultism? And what about the intending, concrete individual? The answers to these and similar questions can be broken down into the familiar categories of description and diagnosis. In concluding this book, I would like to speculate on a number of answers.

Occultic Identity Politics?

If the term "occult" is to retain its etymological roots in hiddenness and secrecy, then the concept of a "postmodern occultism" is oxymoronic. That the occult no longer coheres in the contemporary world as the elite study of secrets suggests that occultism as such no longer exists as a discrete practice. Yet popular culture continues to generate texts that appeal, nostalgically, to the occultism of modernity, and in this sense modern occultism continues to live in movies like *The Ninth Gate*. The occult also survives as a category that people continue to use in making generic sense of the world. "Postmodern occultism" or the occultic (or perhaps in fashionable, scholarly terms, "post-occultism") is a label for the death of modern occultism as the elite study of secrets and the birth of occultism as a kind of floating signifier. In light of the most popular occultic texts today, I suggest that this signifier is predominantly one of difference.

Although more traditional occult texts are widely available and continue to find audiences, the most ubiquitous form of the occultic is the entertaining commodity. At the time of my writing, the filmic version of *Harry Potter and the Sorcerer's Stone* is the current draw at the box office, and its debut has far surpassed *Jurassic Park* as having the most profitable opening weekend of all time. The film, based on a children's book by J. K. Rowling, is a male version of the Cinderella story: a young orphan living with an abusive aunt and uncle discovers he is fated to become a famous magus, and so he enrolls in the legendary Hogwarts School of Witchcraft and Wizardry. In a manner that resembles the appeal of the successful television program, *Bewitched*, the Harry Potter story appeals to middle-class sensibilities, offering the fantasy of effortlessly produced wealth and power by means of magic. The "magical formula" of laborlessly achieved status and power is common to all of the most popular "occult" phenomena today: in addition to the spate of films released in the last ten years (e.g., *The Craft, Practical Magic,* and so on), television shows like *Buffy the Vampire Slayer, Charmed,* and *Sabrina the Teenage Witch* feature middle-class youth wielding magic wands and casting spells, undoubtedly a reflection of the producers' effort to appeal to the highly desirable teenage target audience that, although disempowered socially, has a freedom from responsibility that translates into disposable income. Like the Harry Potter books, these television shows appeal to young people because they offer the fantasy of magically or effortlessly achieved empowerment.

Yet there is something else common to contemporary occult phenomena that is not so obvious. First, with few exceptions, contemporary occult texts predominantly appeal to women. All of the television shows I mentioned, and most of the more recent films highlighting occult themes, feature witches. Of course, witchery is and has been a means for contending with the oppressions of patriarchy; consequently, forms of entertainment that celebrate the witch are frequently about "getting a man" or punishing one. The relationship between the figure of the witch and issues of gender have been written about extensively,[32] yet in light of the demise of modern occultism and the posthumanist critique it suggests, the gendered aspects of contemporary occult phenomena could also be read as the emergence of an alternative, feminist ethic, a reclamation of the figure of the witch and, in turn, social power. Historically, as Blavatsky testifies, the occult has been a means by which women could achieve the power of leadership, enabling them to move more freely through "masculine," public spaces.[33] Contemporary occult texts are suggestive of similar means to empowerment, not because they suggest that women should become witches but because they function as a subtle reminder that women have a distinctive, albeit culturally determined, mode of agency different from that of men, an agency that can be exploited for change, magical or not.[34]

Second, and more disturbing, contemporary occult texts are employing the occult as a code for racial difference as well. For example, in a 1999 episode of the CBS drama *Judging Amy* titled "Witch Hunt,"[35] a man sues his ex-wife for custody of his son because she joined a witches' coven. In the narrative, witchcraft is used and discussed by the characters primarily as a marker of difference and marginality, as a sign of moral and intellectual deviance, which is used, in turn, to justify social and legal discrimination. What is significant about using the occult as a marker of difference in this manner is that the characters in each of these programs, films, and books are white.

In general, occultism has largely been the province of men and women who were racially coded "white," and in North America the practice, from Freemasonry to channeling and divination, has tended to exclude the racial Other.[36] The unfortunate exception, of course, is what has been coded in the mass media as "black magic," such as Santeria and voodoo, the magical practice of people of African American descent.[37] The use of occultism as a marker of difference may be a reinscription of the hegemony of racism insofar as it saps the political force of marginality from those who have been marginalized. In other words, popular uses of the occult as a marker of difference seek to claim a social and legal suspect status (the legal term for protected groups), drawing attention away from those who endure more violent and oppressive forms of discrimination. In light of the use of the occultic as a marker of difference, contemporary occultic entertainment texts seem to be a part of the emergence of "whiteness" as racial category in the 1990s[38] and therefore may be implicated in downplaying the effects of racism on African Americans.[39] Indeed, if there is a U.S. discourse that parallels the discriminating function of modern occultic discourse, it is the rhetoric of race.

The Occultic and Religion

That postmodern occultism is related to identity consciousness is, of course, a diagnostic claim, and in a larger sense it represents the collapse of description onto diagnosis, a collapse that also closes the conceptual distance between grammatical repetitions and rhetorical logics. This kind of collapse is simply a variation of the eclipse of content by form, an event that many thinkers hasten to add is not merely conceptual but symptomatic of representation in postmodernity or late capitalism, a superstructural, conceptual ripple caused by transformations of the base. Arguably, an identity politics that utilizes occult topoi is symptomatic of the complete erasure of occultism as a religious discourse concerned with the transhuman or supernatural, an erasure enabled by a consumerist logic that suggests one can simply purchase social change. In this respect, the death of modern occultism participates in an overall decline of religion, a fated decline that is considered "conventional wisdom" among a number of sociologists.[40]

Apparently, the cultural logic of late capitalism has led to the complete evaporation of Spirit. As Fredric Jameson puts it, "Capitalism, and the modern age, is a period in which, with the extinction of the sacred and the 'spiritual,' the deep underlying materiality of all things has finally risen dripping and convulsive into the light of day; and it is clear that culture itself is one of those things whose fundamental materiality is now for us not merely evident but quite inescapable."[41] I have already detailed, for example, how fetishism models the symbolic economy of Satanism in the terms of a consumerist system of exchange and in ways that erase the semantic dimensions of text. But how does this cultural logic—how does the particular capitalistic interaction of relations and forces—achieve the death of Spirit? Among sociologists (including Marx), the most common answer can be traced back to the Enlightenment: the death of religion is the triumph of almighty Reason. From the vantage of political economy, religion is in decline because of a secularization catalyzed by capitalism, a secularization inclusive of instrumental rationality. Positive accounts of this secularizing power of reason heralded "the overcoming of all the dualities that had divided consciousness . . . and made it so unhappy."[42] Negative accounts, like that of Horkheimer and Adorno in *Dialectic of Enlightenment,* see Spirit and its corresponding grammar of myth being replaced with mass deception and alienation, a discourse of domination that elides the contradictions of social existence. Max Weber argued that, because human character is shaped by the institutions in which we live, the progressivism of capitalistic economies has turned the workplace into an "iron cage." Capitalism has sapped the Puritan work ethic, combined it with a scientific rationality, and applied it to the workplace, thus turning the spaces in which we spend the most time into places of "mechanized petrifaction," effectively robbing people of a sense of duty to the spiritual or supernatural. Religion, in other words, has been replaced by overbureaucratized work:

> Victorious capitalism needs . . . [the support of religious asceticism] no longer. The rosy blush of its laughing heir, the Enlightenment, seems also to be irretrievably fading, and the idea of duty in one's calling prowls about in our lives like the ghost of dead religious beliefs. Where the fulfillment of the calling cannot directly be related to the highest spiritual and cultural values, or when, on the other hand, it need not be felt simply as economic compulsion, the individual generally abandons the attempt to justify it at all. In the field of its highest development, in the United States, the pursuit of wealth, stripped of its religious and

> ethical meaning, tends to become associated with purely mundane passions, which often actually give it the character of a sport.[43]

Those who counter the Marxist proclamation of the death or dying of religion often offer up the emergence of evangelical and prophetic sects or cults as evidence of the persistence of Spirit and the continued vitality of religious practice. Yet scholars such as Bryan Wilson counter by suggesting that cults are in fact "a confirmation of the process of secularization. They indicate the extent to which religion has become inconsequential for modern society." New Age religions, cults, and the like represent "the highly privatized preference that reduces religion to the significance of pushpin, poetry, and popcorns [*sic*]."[44] Emerging charismatic religions and New Age groups are mere buyers' clubs, the Sam's Warehouses of eternal salvation.

The decline of religion as a socially significant tradition, institution, and discourse has also been discussed by rhetoricians. James Darsey's book-length rumination on the Hebraic rhetorical tradition makes frequent mention of the decline of religious discourse and avers in the conclusion that "we have erred on the side of Hellenism. We are plainly uncomfortable with the unverifiable and the extraordinary. We prefer the blandness of the bureaucrat to the supernal vision of the seer. Our cynicism prevents us from crediting claims on the divine. . . . Our distrust of prophets is a reflection of a profound distrust of ourselves and our ability to tell true from false."[45] Darsey continues that the decline of prophetic rhetoric, and thus the disappearance of the prophet, is responsible for "the national malaise." The common, communal bonds that religion provides (e.g., God) are crumbling, and people in the West are losing a sense of community. The chronicle of modern occultism that I have told parallels the decline of the significance of prophecy. Not only are great magi a thing of the past, but modern occultism's Hellenic appeal to evidentiary support did not demand of the true believer an absolutist conviction in a leader's righteousness. Given its hybridism, from a sociological vantage, what began as the forbidden science of alchemy has returned to its roots: modern occultism is a snapshot of religion on its way to secularism.

Because modern occultism is a hybrid of Hellenic and Hebraic rhetorical traditions, its demise also parallels, in general, the simultaneous erosion of rational argument and textuality on the one hand and the decreasing social import of prophetic religiosity on the other. The simple prose of those who could be said to weakly continue the occult tradition—New Age gurus like Gary Zukav and psychics like

Sylvia Browne, for example—is representative of a transformation in literacy, a transformation that has been widely discussed as a movement toward the visual. In his widely read *Amusing Ourselves to Death,* Neil Postman assays the transformation as a retreat from linear thinking and logical argument toward a formulaic brave new world of intellectual pabulum devoid of complexity. Similarly, the ability of young people to tolerate logical contradiction (as well as their ability to tolerate cultural diversity, incidentally) is derided by Alan Bloom in his popular and widely praised *The Closing of the American Mind* as a failure of literacy and as a product of academic liberalism in general. The simplicity, and one might add the simple-mindedness, of contemporary occult texts is in keeping with the overall, general decline of textual complexity in the public arena.

Nevertheless, the long line of scholars who proclaim (lamentably or not) the death of God and the demise of religion are simply wrong. Insofar as one understands religion as the quest for the outside, as a hankering for something external to our symbolicity, religion will never go away; it will simply take new forms. For example, my discussion about the function of obtuse theory in academic discourse suggests that the motor beyond novel vocabularies is characteristically poetic, a struggle with the limitations of language as well as a symptom of our relative inability to communicate our subjective mental states to one another. That willingness, desire itself, is religious. If the demise of modern occultism is read as an exaggeration of the decline of religion in general, it only follows that traditional religion is losing its *public* significance.[46] It may be true that no invisible hand or Spirit animates the past, but it is certainly not the case that Spirit has been liquidated into something completely material; Spirit is simply moving into our private lives as the inevitable, human desire for something better. Indeed, the existence of the occultic and, therefore, the persistence of theological form can be located in a multitude of discourses and practices. From the conspiracy theories and alien abduction fantasies of popular culture, to the initiation rituals so familiar to members of Greek fraternities and sororities on campuses across the United States, to the litany of gatekeeping rituals academics seem to enjoy so much, the religious discourse of secrecy is everywhere.

Epilogue: The Fool's Yapping Cur

> The evidence of reality is quite useful for action, but can in no way help us to understand the meaning of our lives. As soon as we allow ourselves to be invaded by this obsession with evidence, the discretion of the word vanishes. We become insensitive to language, which, even if it is the Word of God, loses its meaning. Thus we no longer pay any attention to it.
>
> —Jacques Ellul[1]

> To be good for people. These words have a vaguely antediluvian ring in the sphere where the production of knowledge replaces the search for the good life. . . . If it is our compulsion towards speed and height that renders us immobile and hinders our vision, then it is only by propitiating the shunned dark god and not by stepping up that we will see where we want to go.
>
> —Janice Hocker Rushing and Thomas S. Frentz[2]

Anyone who has studied the occult tradition will recognize what I mean when I say that everything is related, in some sense, degree, or number, to everything else. Students of the occult may also identify with the frustration I experienced trying to make sense of the veritable word-salad of modern occult texts. The texts from the late nineteenth and early twentieth centuries, in particular, can test one's patience, not only because of their difficult language but also because their authors, indulgently, go on and on and on and on and on and on and on. The current edition of Lévi's *Transcendental Magic* is over 400 pages; the facsimile edition of Blavatsky's *Isis Unveiled* is 1,350 pages; and the latest edition Crowley's *Magick: Book IV* weighs in at almost three pounds. (Of course, if the patient reader has scanned these many pages cover to cover, he or she knows about whom I surely jest.)

To call attention to another not-so-secret secret, I hinted in the introduction that I might whisper the name of the figure who arose in the wake of the Great Orator and the Great Magus. Just like the "secrets" of a typical modern occult text, this figure should have been obvious from the start: she is the Learned Fool, Parsifal, the Great Professor, number zero in the Rider-Waite tarot. The composite character of Boris Balkan in Polanski's *The Ninth Gate* is, of course, this figure. Many readers will be quick to recognize, however, that unlike Balkan, there are no millionaire professors in the humanities, even among those of us who pen successful textbooks on public speaking, textual criticism, or English composition. Any pretense to wealth is simply a rhetorical blind. I want to close *Modern Occult Rhetoric* by suggesting that any pretense to intellectual mastery is also a ruse, and today, an increasingly troublesome one.

In the Rider-Waite tarot deck, the Fool is depicted as a young white man in garish clothes, his worldly belongings tied in a bundle at the end of a stick. The Fool feels free, engaged in a new beginning, and because his head is in the clouds he does not see the cliff he is swiftly approaching. A tiny dog barks at his heels trying to warn him. The scene depicted on the card is an allegory for the contemporary occultic enterprise of academics in the humanities, if not an apt condensation of how non-academics, especially cultural conservatives, view the professoriate. As Ellen Willis puts it, "protected by tenure, too many academics remain stubbornly liberal and attached to the ideal (if not always the reality) of intellectual independence. Their sense of entitlement to relatively autonomous and human working conditions is an offense to the prevailing corporate regime. . . . And so, even as the right's rhetoric invokes the noble heritage of the liberal arts and sciences against 'politicized nonsense,' its professor-bashing agenda incites and exploits the anti-intellectual currents endemic to American culture."[3] Like the justices presiding in the courtroom battle between Crowley and Mathers over magical secrets, academics are often regarded by outsiders as fools—intelligent, perhaps, but fools nonetheless. Understanding the ambivalent symbolism of the Fool, however, I think that there are good reasons to embrace the figure. Let me yap just a little bit more to make the case.

If the contemporary academic paradigm is occultic (and I think it is), then the story of modern occultism I have told suggests a litany of homologies. For example, there is the tenure and promotion system and the achievement of degrees or grades in modern secret societies; there is the mysterious process of publication and "blind review" and the "investigation" period of fraternal initiation;[4] there is "close textual reading" and the romantic hermeneutics of the Kabbalah; there is the esoteric language of modern occultism and the rhetoric of the project of the posts. But there are more serious parallels as well, particularly those concerning the corporatization or "McDonaldization" of education, which have led to a kind of neurotic obsession among scholars in the last decade. Book after book has been devoted to exploring the implications of commodified education, which is an irreversible trend that holds great possibilities for democracy as well as numerous challenges to intellectual freedom.[5]

Although I prefer to leave the discussion of academic capitalism to those better trained to discuss political economy, we academics should, in light of what happened to the great modern magi of the twentieth century, be expecting increasingly spectacular dramas of secrecy and publicity. Further, insofar as infighting and the emergence of a mediated star system abided the commodification of modern occultism, we should be able to locate competing vocabularies concerning secret truths, and a professoriate at odds with itself, mobilized into elite, discrete, and competing cabals that are, in turn, organized around the challenging work of this or that scholarly magus. Worse, in light of the death of modern occultism as a coherent tradition, we should discover that the "ivory tower," the central metaphor of a clandestine academic enterprise, has been leveled. Amid the smoldering rubble of this centuries-old artifice, we should find the Great Professor unprotected, naked, divided against him- or herself, unable to control or signify his or her texts, and, perhaps, under attack. If the rhetoric emerging from the academy these days is any measure, then these things are coming to pass—if they are not already a done deal. Willis argues that "there really is no ivory tower anymore," and that the most obvious symptom of its demise is the "Sokal hoax."

The Sokal hoax refers to the public prank played on the editors of the cultural studies journal *Social Text* and orchestrated by the previously little-known physicist Alan Sokal. Troubled by the "apparent decline in the standards of rigor in certain precincts of the academic humanities,"[6] and angered by the "mystification, deliberately obscure language, confused thinking, and the misuse of scientific concepts" often associated with "postmodern" thinkers,[7] Sokal composed a parodic essay in which he argued that the concept of quantum gravity had "profound political implications" that cultural studies scholars would find of interest. To this end he cobbled together a number of scientific and mathematical notions, the "bizarre New Age idea" of a "morphogenetic field," concepts from Lacanian psychoanalysis, and other scraps of theory into an increasingly ludicrous exercise in the fetishism of citation. For example, in one part of the essay Sokal asserts that "more recently, Lacan's *topologie du sujet* has been applied fruitfully to cinema criticism and to the psychoanalysis of AIDS. In mathematical terms, Lacan is here pointing out that the first homology group of the sphere is trivial. . . . Furthermore, as Lacan suspected, there is an intimate connection between the external structure of the psychical world and its inner psychological representation *qua* knot theory: this hypothesis has recently been confirmed by Witten's derivation of known invariants . . . from three-dimensional Chern-Simons quantum field theory."[8] After Sokal revealed his prank, the story made the front page of the *New York Times* on May 18, 1996, thereby sparking a years-long conversation on academic jargon and the (ir)relevance of critical and cultural studies to the academy. The responses to both academic and non-academic audiences have been numerous, but those that seem to have garnered the most sympathy are characteristically anti-theoretical and pragmatically realist (e.g., arguing for a return to the Enlightenment project of knowledge production and the pursuit of Truth).[9]

As a rhetorician, however, I am most interested in the defenses that were offered for the invention of difficult prose. The most common arguments had already been rehearsed among academics years before Sokal forced them into wider circulation. The first and most prominent argument was that jargon serves as a kind of shorthand for complex ideas. Lawrence Grossberg presents the case well: "I must acknowledge the difficulty of much of the language of this book. It is often too academic and occasionally hermetic, but I hope the analysis will have something to say to a broader audience. I would have liked to arrive at a more accessible vocabulary, but I do not want to fall into a common pseudo-populism which rejects such work as elitist. . . . Intellectuals are often criticized for introducing neologisms and dropping names, but these are often useful and efficient ways of bringing an entire argument or position quickly into the conversation."[10]

A second argument that has circulated, in one way or another, undermines the charge of inaccessibility by questioning the empirical existence of an "audience," meaning that what we typically refer to as audiences are brought into being by either those who study them or the texts that they share.[11] For example, Michael Warner has suggested that a given difficult writing "style" is a utopic gesture that attempts to speak to a future public, a style that escapes contemporary pressures to succumb to an academic populism that merely reinforces the harmful norms that difficult language is designed to combat (principally in terms of "defamiliarization," a corollary argument that Warner, like Butler, lays at the feet of Theodor Adorno).[12]

Third, there is the argument often made by public intellectuals like Richard Rorty, and which I have forwarded in this book with a little help from my friendly superstars, Uncle Burke and Jackie-D: namely, that difficult prose is the consequence of an occult poetics, which, in turn, is a consequence of the ineffability of human experience. Better than the first two arguments in defense of difficult language, I think this line of thinking roots difficult language in an ontology. I do not think for a moment, however, that this argument works for a wider audience, nor do I think it would ever sway an American public that already seems hostile to "high theory." To the outsider, I'm sure the ontological argument sounds like "we fools can't help it." This is, of course, the case I'm making, but to those who are trained to regard the image as certitude—at the expense of the humiliation of the word—it is likely understood as "the devil made us do it," a failure of accountability.

Perhaps to the chagrin of those readers who summarily dismiss difficult language as so much hocus-pocus, I find all three defenses of difficult language persuasive. But, the *rhetorical* lesson to be learned from the Great Magi of modernity is an ethical one, a lesson that has less to do with the inevitable alterity of language use (our ontological plight) and more to do with the ways in which we ignore or forget those whom we exclude or discipline with our words *in here, in the academy.* The numerous defenses of "pomo" in the academy that were published in response to Sokal's hoax almost universally acknowledge the anxiety and anger provoked by occultic prose but then proceed to discuss style only in respect to content, never fully exploring the relational information and the consequences that follow from form. While tacitly acknowledged, few discuss the humiliation, the discipline, of the fetishized word.

Consider, for example, the word "desire." I will never forget my first humiliating experience as an academic in training, my first rite of passage during Graduate Education Initiation. It seems minor today compared to being called "stupid fuck" by a journal editor,[13] but at the age of twenty-four my first taste of magickal warfare was in my maiden graduate seminar, a course on semiotic theory conducted by a highly regarded professor at the University of Minnesota. Much of the material we were reading (Peirce on "thirdness," e.g.) was very difficult to understand. I recall delivering a presentation for class on the readings, and then voicing some difficulty with a concept. An advanced graduate student from the Department of Cultural Studies and Comparative Literature laughed aloud, and then smugly posed a rhetorical question to me: "Haven't you read Lacan on *desire*?" I was embarrassed and felt stupid, having been taken to task by someone who knew a secret that I didn't know, someone smarter, more in control of his language, someone who knew how to read better. In a few months I learned that such sadistic agonism was not typical of all departments—and certainly not my own (Communication Studies). But, I do think that the professoriate too easily forget how contentious and competitive our degree system can be on the inside—especially among graduate students—and how the word humiliates at each successive rung of progress toward certification. Yes, difficult prose is shorthand for complex ideas and arguments. Yes, challenging styles defamiliarize and help us to envision better worlds. But the formal work and ideological function of occultic rhetoric can be sadistic. And where do graduate students learn how to spar and demean with secret vocabularies? By watching black-caped magi posture, argue, and stab backs at conferences and conventions, of course. I suppose the battle of magi is amusing on a number of levels, especially to those on the outside, but when I first experienced it on the inside, when I was laughed at because I had not read a single seminar of Lacan's, I was nauseous and wanted to throw up.

I do not mention my experience as a neophyte academic to exempt or excuse us "worker bees and ants" (to borrow a phrase from Rorty) from the standards of "rigor" or doing careful work. Nor do I share my experiences as a young initiate to call for the end of jargon. As this study attests, I think the production of new and challenging discourse is both helpful and inevitable. Indeed, I take great pleasure in reading, producing, and teaching challenging prose. Yet, if the demise of the Great Modern Magus provides a lesson for us academics, it must be that of recognizing our ignorance and celebrating the virtue of humility. I realize I must seem the naive fool—risking hypocrisy as I do—by extolling the virtue of humility, but in our era of publicity and corporatization there is immense pressure on us academics to popularize our work and to justify our existence, and consequently an intense desire to thicken our prose and to create the conditions that require our interpretive expertise and thereby guarantee our survival. In short, we are encouraged to be snotty. Our contemporary academic occultic is the ironic response to that globalizing corporate machine that accuses us of producing mere gibberish, "empty rhetoric." As our jobs become less plentiful and tenure goes the way of the dodo, as resources become more scarce and we are made to compete for a sense of security, the pressure to produce the contentious, argumentative Blue-Meanie Magus, or in the argot of graduate students, the "theory Nazi," is increasing.

The problem with the theory Nazi is that he or she ignores, deliberately or not, the relational structure of revelation and secrecy. Derrida, whom many regard as a wickedly brilliant yet kind, humorous, and self-deprecating superstar, touches on the problem in his latest work, which focuses on gifts, responsibility, and the limits of philosophical ethics. It is no surprise that secrecy is a significant part of his genealogy of responsibility. In a discussion that brings to mind Lacan's reading of Poe's "The Purloined Letter," a letter that always returns to the unconscious and which, consequently, belongs to no one, Derrida questions:

> How can another see into me, into my most secret self, without my being able to see in there myself and without my being able to see him in me? And if my secret self, that which can be revealed only to the other, to the wholly other, to God if you wish, is a secret that I will never reflect on, that I will never know or experience or possess as my own, then what sense is there in saying that it is "my" secret, or in saying more generally that a secret *belongs,* that it is proper to or belongs to some "one," or to some *other* who remains some*one*? It is perhaps there that we find the secret of secrecy, namely, that it is not a matter of knowing and that it is there for no-one.[14]

There is no home, no place of belonging, for the secret, continues Derrida. The relation is the only thing; this is the secret of the shibboleth.

The secret is a ruse, then, the content running cover for form. If we recognize that the undoing of the modern magus was caused, in part, by the arrogance of autonomy and the blackmail of secrecy, then we should embrace the Fool as our patron saint. The secret is not a secret without the shunned Other, and the Fool is not a fool without the loving Other who warns.

Appendix 1: Scholarship on Occultism

One way to describe occultism is as an object of scholarship composed of primary and secondary texts. The primary texts of occultism number in the thousands, and in a descriptive study such as the present one an exhaustive account would be not only impossible but probably not very helpful. Instead, I have selected a number of primary texts that were well known among the reading and viewing public during their respective moments: the work of H. P. Blavatsky and the Theosophists in the late nineteenth century; the public shenanigans of Aleister Crowley and the dictation of his holy book, *The Book of the Law,* during the early twentieth century; the overtly televisual occult texts of the world's most famous Satanist, Anton LaVey, in the late 1960s and early 1970s; and a major theatrical film written and directed by Roman Polanski, *The Ninth Gate,* which debuted in the United States in 1999. Notably, I began my analysis of primary texts in the nineteenth century, and I have done so for three reasons. First, by limiting myself to "modern" or more recent primary texts, the task of analyzing occult discourse is simply more manageable. Second and more important, however, are the ways in which occult texts from the nineteenth century and later are substantially different from those that preceded them: the condemnations of Catholics and Protestant reformists, as well as rise of scientific discourse during the Enlightenment, affected occult discourse in ways that distinguish it from its previous subsistence (see chapter 1). Third, as I conceptualize it, the popular imaginary did not exist until the emergence of mass culture and mass-communication media—media that placed public knowledge and encoded public memories into seemingly disposable objects of leisure. Modern occultism is a phenomenon goaded by the emergence of a popular imaginary, enabled by forms of mass technology, and constrained by the discourses of science and religion.

Having isolated the task of reviewing primary literature to the study itself, the task here is to provide some account of the secondary literature. Most of this body of work has been written by occultists and practitioners, and in these works one finds little concern for scholarly proprieties such as reflexivity, accuracy, or fidelity to presumed historical facts. One of the better, popular examples of this kind of work is Colin Wilson's *The Occult: A History,* a large, well-written origin narrative of the Western occult tradition. Wilson's proclamations of faith and frequent commentary about the existence of supernatural forces are typical of this kind of work as well. For example, in his book Wilson claims that human beings' "latent sense" that the world is not enough, that there must be something else, is "man's evolutionary appetite, the desire to make contact with reality. . . . I labeled this 'latent sense' Faculty X. . . . Faculty X is simply that latent power that human beings possess to *reach beyond the present.* After all, we know perfectly well that the past is as real as the present and that New York and Singapore and Lhasa and Stepney Green are all as real as this place I happen to be in at the moment. *Yet my senses do not agree.*"[1] Wilson continues to elaborate the concept at some length, linking it to psi phenomena and what is generally known as "pseudoscientific" research (investigations into extrasensory perception, telekinesis, and so on). While much of Wilson's historical work does seem to police factual detail with some degree of rigor, "Faculty X" appears and reappears from time to time in many chapters as the underlying explanation for magical workings and otherwise unexplainable behavior.

Because many occult writers do not conform to the codes of scholarly propriety, a great number of texts written by occultists are unreliable for critical-historical claims. Georgess McHargue speculates that, to some degree, this unreliability is in part born of the "general disrespect that is felt for the occult." It has led, "perhaps, to the formation of another unfortunate attitude . . . among those who do write about it. We have all seen occult books so sloppily researched and sketchily written that they seem to carry the message, 'This stuff is all fake anyway, so why bother to get the facts straight?' "[2] Although Kenneth Grant, for example, would adamantly deny fakery, his book *The Magical Revival* has been attacked by occultists and historians alike for its creative history-making. Grant, "not unlike a number of occult historians . . . appears content to link together and fuse into one continuous stream a variety of individuals, organizations and traditions which, as far as the exoteric historian is concerned, seem to have no direct connection."[3] (It should also be noted that many occultists' attacks on the work of other occultists, such Waite's critique of Lévi, are more competitive than scholarly.)

On the other hand, most of the academic literature on occultism is characteristically historical, descriptive, and uncritical. Further, very few works attempt to conjecture about the symbolic and rhetorical dimensions of occultism. The reasons for the lack of critical engagement with occult topics are many, but the most obvious are two in number. First, in the humanities the privileged objects of criticism have tended to be works of "great art," and a distinction between "high" and "low" culture can be said to underlie this privileging. Until recently, occultism has been characterized as a marginalized and "irrational" discourse unworthy of scholarly attention. Theodor Adorno, a philosopher associated with the Frankfurt school of critical theory, was one of the first to provide a serious critical study of the occult; his findings could be seen as an exaggeration of the bias against occultism as an irrational object of study. "The tendency to occultism is a symptom of the regression of consciousness," argued Adorno. "Occultists . . . feel drawn towards childishly monstrous scientific fantasies" and mindless platitudes.[4] Adorno describes the occult as a particular manifestation of the logics of capitalism that discourage rational, critical thought. The second reason why there is little critical academic work on the occult is a problem of description: because so many things are described as "occult," before any research begins scholars have had to engage in the difficult task of deciding what does and does not count. In this respect, the bulk of the scholarly work on occultism has been in sociological circles, and this work explicitly announces its primary task as that of describing occultism as a social phenomenon.

In general, occult scholarship by trained academics can be classified into four basic disciplinary frames: English and literary studies; anthropological and ethnographic studies; historical and descriptive scholarship; and sociological and cultural studies. Although each frame imbricates the others, each kind of study focuses on different themes. English and literary studies in occultism, for instance, tend toward two kinds of analyses: historical contextualization and the analysis of occult tropes. An example of the former is Paul H. Kocher's essay "The Witchcraft Basis in Marlowe's *Faustus,*" in which Kocher claims that Marlowe's knowledge of medieval witchcraft led to an accurate portrayal of the "motives and values" thought to be common among witches during his time. John Coates's "*Zanoni* by Bulwer-Lytton: A Discussion of Its 'Philosophy' and Its Possible Influences" urges a political reading of *Zanoni* against Disraeli's *Coningsby* and links Bulwer-Lytton's study of occultism to an estrangement from his wife. Although both of these kinds of readings offer good close textual analysis, neither explores the suasive, audience-centered dimensions of occult meanings. The work of figures like T. S. Eliot and William Butler Yeats are favorite objects of analysis in these kinds of contextual studies.

The tropic studies by literary critics are less directly related to the historical occult. The "occult" has been used as a trope for reading and as a characterization of the ontological status of all written texts. Allan Lloyd Smith has claimed, for instance, that the "mimetic quality of fiction has affinities with sympathetic magic," and Clive Bloom has argued that the occult experience is a good characterization of the "daemonic (or hidden compulsion) that defines textuality" in relationship to the unconscious in textual practice (writing and reading).[5]

The most relevant and interesting of these studies, however, are those that attempt to theorize the occult in relation to the psyche and cultural forms in reading. Foremost of this kind of work is Tzvetan Todorov's *The Fantastic: A Structural Approach to a Literary Genre.* To some extent Todorov is more interested in textual cartography than effect, but he suggests that the fantastic in literature can be cast in terms of the marvelous (when new laws of nature emerge) and the uncanny (no new laws emerge, but something explainable by natural law remains unsettling). All kinds of the fantastic, however, can be typified by indecision and uncertainty about events, both hallmarks of occultism. In the edited collection *Literature of the Occult: A Collection of Critical Essays,* Peter Messent extends Todorov's musings on the fantastic and argues that gothic literature is the example of the fantastic par excellence. For Messent, "occult literature stems initially from a point of intersection between 'realistic' and rationally 'unexplainable.'" Messent also observes that "in literature of the occult the supernatural is more often associated with the powers of darkness than those of light," but he fails to provide an explanation.[6]

Although the reasons for the association of dark tropes and the occult are many and complex, a few bear mentioning here. The first is historical: after Christianity was established as the official religion of the Roman Empire, the practice of magic and mysticism became illegal. The rationale frequently offered by influential priests, such as Augustine, was that all occult practice, whether done for good or ill, derived its power from demons. Although the association of darkness with the occult has been stronger in some historical periods than others, it persists to this day in the popular imaginary. A second explanation for why occultism is often associated with darkness in literature is the ideational proximity of the trope of darkness to human fear about the unknown.[7] This kind of psychological explanation is typically related to the concept of the uncanny developed by Freud, or the concept of the sublime, which has been a topic in aesthetic circles at least since Longinus's manuscript on the topic was rediscovered in the sixteenth century. Edmund Burke's 1757 treatise on the sublime and the beautiful is generally regarded as one of the great modern popularizers of the concept of the sublime. Burke argued that "whatever is fitted in any sort to excite the ideas of pain, and danger, that is to say, whatever is in any sort terrible, or is conversant about terrible objects, or operates in a manner analogous to terror, is a source of the sublime."[8] Later, Kant revised and deepened the concept, suggesting that the sublime was best characterized as "reason's inability to contain the experience of some sublime object, and the imagination's inability to limit its presentation to the understanding."[9]

However the concept of sublimity is understood, in literary studies there is an assumed relationship between the sublime and the occult. The occult, as a trope signifying hidden knowledge and sublime experience, could be used to quicken readers' pulses in anticipation of the secrets they were about to learn, or could be employed to cause curiosity, as readers learned about a magician "transformed, as the process of the natural universe became more comprehensible, into . . . a scientist." Such an explanation makes plain the tendency to associate the gothic novel with strange science and the occult (e.g., Mary Shelley's *Frankenstein* and Stevenson's *Dr. Jekyll and Mr. Hyde*).[10]

The work that forms the closest relationship to the "occult experience" of reading, however, is anthropological. In this body of literature, the overriding goal is a sympathetic understanding of the occult experience of groups of practicing occultists, usually by means of participant observation. This work tends to focus on the religious practices—much of which we would not describe as occult—of groups from geographically foreign cultures; currently, spirit possession seems to be the most popular topic. Closer to home yet characteristic of the goals of these studies is Karen McCarthy Brown's *Mama Lola: A Vodou Priestess in Brooklyn,* which details the daily life and religious practices of woman named Alourdes in a way that naturalizes spirit possession as a mundane coping mechanism.

The most outstanding anthropological work on occultism is Tanya M. Luhrmann's *Persuasions of the Witch's Craft,* a lengthy work that combines ethnographic and critical scholarship into a comprehensive and thorough explanation of "why some people, rather than others, have become involved in [the] practice."[11] Those people, claims Luhrmann, are "searching for powerful emotional and imaginative religious experience, but not for religion *per se*."[12] Luhrmann claims hers is a study of "psychological anthropology," an approach that focuses on "the conceptual play in the interstices between individual and society" and that employs a multifaceted method or approach to its objects of analysis.[13] Likening the occult experience to the re-creation of a "childhood world," Luhrmann explains over the course of some 350 pages the general beliefs of modern-day witches and magicians, the intellectual habits and cognitive training magicians seem to undergo, the use of language and the imagination in ritual magic, the arguments used against skeptics by believers, and the function of symbols in magical practice. At times ethnographic narrative overwhelms important critical points, but the larger project is insightful and is deserving of some discussion.

Luhrmann's larger, theoretical thesis is that sociological and anthropological work about "irrational" belief systems has wrongly assumed a unidirectional logic between belief and action. In the relevant anthropological literature on magic and ritual, it is often assumed either that magicians use ritual to achieve ends previously conceived in theory or that a magician's beliefs emerge from rituals, which are understood as a natural, sociological outworking of a higher cultural order.[14] Luhrmann claims that both approaches wrongly assume "the existence of clear cut, coherent beliefs." Debates within anthropology, often over the notion of rationality, consequently have "prejudged the issues, and the basic problem of irrational action has been ill-formed."[15] In response Luhrmann calls for a more interdependent understanding of belief, experience, and action (or ritual):

> This work on magic has suggested that beliefs are not the sorts of things they are stereotypically assumed to be: propositional commitments held consciously and claimed consistently and in a logical relationship to other such commitments. At least in the case of modern magicians, the ideas associated with their practice become persuasive because people rationalize an imaginative, emotional involvement. Their beliefs are not fixed or consistent, for they are often presented to justify some action. Beliefs do a job; they are not always disinterestedly asserted because they are felt to be true in themselves. Ideas and beliefs drift, in a complex interdependency of concept and experience. . . . This book has been an attempt to describe the way in which the interpretive drift may take place.[16]

Luhrmann's supposition that belief in magic is "irrational" causes some tension with her own thesis, but in general her model enables her to explain what one could characterize as the rhetorical dimensions of magic ritual. For example, in a series of observations that are important to my discussion about the function of esoteric language (jargon to some) in chapter 2, Luhrmann develops a theory of magical knowledge that depends on an oscillation between literal and figurative language by individual magicians. Luhrmann distinguishes between "knowing that" and "knowing of," the former being knowledge of explicit linguistic propositions and the latter "a feeling of intuitively grasping the sense of, the ambience of, the nature of."[17] On the basis of her personal experience with a coven, Luhrmann argues that the functions of each kind of knowledge are inversed as "magicians learn to use literal language to describe events which have not occurred in reality but have been imagined" and as they "use metaphorical language to describe actual events, feelings, and impressions."[18] These "linguistic somersaults" are offered up as kind of performance in which beliefs and actions interact in magical practice; both conscious and unconscious interplays between believing and doing explain the "persuasions of the witch's craft."

Related to Luhrmann's notion of interpretive drift are the arguments offered in the introduction to Bradford Verter's dissertation on the religious history of modern occultism, "Dark Star Rising: The Emergence of Modern Occultism, 1800–1950." Like Luhrmann, Verter presumes that "access to ideas is anterior to belief" and that these ideas only come to the occultist in an active interplay with experience. Verter's project differs from Luhrmann's insofar as his is not a concern for the epistemological as much as it is for the history and description of "the structure of knowledge and practice."[19] For Verter this structure is the social "nexus of ideas" offered in both scholarly literature on religion and occultism as well as the popular press. He announces his as a genealogical project, much like the present study, that traces the "category" of the occult across various literatures in order to highlight who had access to what was presumably occult knowledge. Along the way three important claims are made. First, "responsibility for cultivating popular occultism . . . lies not with cult leaders such as Eliphas Lévi, H. P. Blavatsky, or Aleister Crowley, but with scholars in the field of anthropology and comparative religion."[20] This claim is taken up largely in the first chapter and is little more than an excuse for wading through five centuries of comparative religious scholarship. Nevertheless, Verter's argument that comparative religious scholarship relativized religious work in the academy and helped to open the Western mind to Eastern mystical concepts is persuasive.

Second, Verter argues that occultism was not popularized by famous occult works, such as Blavatsky's *Isis Unveiled,* but "in the pages of popular novels, weekly periodicals, and anonymous pamphlets,"[21] a position with which this study is in partial agreement. Verter supports this claim by arguing that only the leisure class could afford to buy occult books; hence the popular imagination was most directly fueled by the coverage of public performances and pranks of figures like Crowley in newspapers and penny magazines. The present study extends Verter's contention, with the caveat that both occult books and the popular press are responsible for the popularization of the occult—both are components of mass media, and both contributed to popular imaginary, however directly or indirectly.

Finally, Verter claims that popular occultism should not be understood as emerging in revivals or crazes but rather as the gradual, "slow-ripening fruit of decades of intellectual inquiry" (comparative religious studies in the academy) and as more representative of "shifts in public discourse and social relations." By placing occult discourse within "social and cultural contexts," Verter claims to offer a "new narrative which restructures our understanding of the role of alternative spirituality in transatlantic religious history."[22]

Verter's historical work is just one of a number of careful scholarly histories I could mention, but I believe it is one of the most exemplary. His dissertation is perhaps the most thorough and wide-ranging scholarly account of occult literature from the nineteenth and early twentieth centuries, and it is an indispensable resource for the occult researcher as it details in rich, well-documented descriptions what occult works were available and read by the literate public.[23]

Historical and descriptive scholarship about the occult is not difficult to come by, but most of it is focused on witchcraft and witch-hunting (e.g., the Salem witch trials) and to a lesser extent cults (e.g., Scientology). With few exceptions, the historical work on occultism lacks critical observation. In addition to Verter's work, a recent exception is Diane Purkiss's *The Witch in History: Early Modern and Twentieth-Century Representations,* which chronicles the figure of the witch as both a coping fantasy for women and an object of fear for men. Like Verter's work with occultism, Purkiss's historical scholarship is unique in its attempt to treat "the witch" as a social form or "category" that is negotiated over time.[24]

The scholars most interested in analyzing sociocultural forms are, of course, sociologists, and all of the empirically minded work on occultism for the past fifty years has appeared in the pages of their journals. Marcel Mauss's trailblazing study, *A General Theory of Magic*, continues to provide the most helpful, functional account of the occult as a sociological form. In ways that are similar to Verter's treatment of "the occult" and Purkiss's treatment of "the witch," Mauss describes "magic" as a cultural form that is divorced from the individual as a social representation: "If the whole community does not believe in the efficacy of a group of actions, they cannot be magical. The form of the ritual is eminently transmissible and this is sanctioned by public opinion. It follows from this that strictly individual actions, such as the private superstitions of gamblers, cannot be called magical."[25] In other words, all the elements of "magic are created and qualified by the collectivity."[26] Magicians get their power from the collective, and as Edward A. Tiryakian notes, their existence is "contingent upon the popular imagination . . . which bestows on the magician (or the sorcerer, the witch, etc.) the powers and virtues that the practitioners of magic posses."[27]

Yet the same collective representations that give a magician power also mark him or her as a subaltern, inferior in social status and power. Mauss's observation that a "disproportionate number of magical practitioners . . . come from the ranks of those occupying a marginal social status" led Tiryakian to emphasize the social marginality or "liminality" of magic in his work.[28] In one of the first sociological works to take the "occult revival" of the late 1960s and early 1970s seriously, Tiryakian forwards a programmatic call for a "sociology of esoteric culture." His own contribution to the study of the occult is an argument for the use of the term "esoteric culture" over that of "magic" or "the occult": "By 'esoteric' I refer to those religio-philosophic belief systems which underlie occult techniques and practices; that is, it refers to the more comprehensive cognitive mappings of nature and the cosmos, the epistemological and ontological reflections of ultimate reality, which mappings constitute a stock of knowledge that provides the ground for occult procedures."[29] "Esoteric" culture is defined against common, or "exoteric" culture, which Tiryakian suggests, following Mauss, empowers the occult practitioner. Tiryakian also makes a number of more speculative claims about the occult's subcultural dynamic: "As a spiritual reaction against the rationalistic-industrial-bureaucratic ethos of modern society, it is part of the counterculture."[30] Esoteric culture is also highly dependent on an ethos of secrecy and the rigid hierarchies built in its fog.[31] Yet the boldest claims made by Tiryakian go without evidentiary support. Tiryakian claims that at the "very heart of the ideology of modernization, or modernism, is an esoteric influence," but exactly what that influence is remains unclear (it seems to be a progressive, messianic conception of time).[32] He claims that esotericism has contributed to a "breakdown of modernization" and also represents "flights into the irrational" and "escapes from the strains imposed by the complexity of the technological and social order."[33]

How the occult and magical practices have contributed to the breakdown of modernity is unclear and remains at the level of conjecture. Nevertheless, Tiryakian's conjectures are often interesting and insightful. One insight in particular is consequential: the magician and the occultist understand the world in terms of action, not motion. This observation is similar to the distinction Kenneth Burke makes in his rhetorical theory, which in turn is based on a key philosophical distinction made at the beginning of the Enlightenment by Descartes, namely, that science should be concerned with matter in motion, not questions of human free will or creativity. In this divorce between matter and spirit, Burke observed corresponding attitudes developed toward human activity and creativity vis-à-vis the physical world. The latter concerns "motion," the former, "action."[34] Given the large role the imagination and superphysical forces play in occult discourse, it makes sense that Tiryakian describes the magician as embracing "action." Even more significant, however, is his suggestion that the magician's world-as-action requires an active assembly of magical tropes and figures and that "each of these figures perceives the relationships between the visible and the invisible in terms of what might be called a *grammar of symbols*." Tiryakian continues that "a discussion of the grammar of symbols from each standpoint [of different forms of consciousness] is beyond the scope of this essay."[35] Describing such a grammar, of course, is a goal of this study.

In addition to building on the work of Mauss, Tiryakian's scholarship extends many of the more pragmatic arguments offered first by Marcello Truzzi, who claimed that the largest obstacle to the sociological study of the occult was the lack of agreement about what it comprises. Because the occult is not rigorous, Truzzi argues, it cannot be considered a science; however, it does seem to orbit knowledge claims. "In many ways," he muses, "the occult is a residual category, a wastebasket, for knowledge claims that are deviant in some way, that do not fit the established claims of science or religion. And once such a knowledge claim gains acceptance within establishment science or religion, it loses its status as an occultism."[36] As Truzzi's remarks are an apt testament, most of the sociological work on occultism is an exercise in typology.[37]

The functional aspects of occultism discussed by sociologists have already been discussed implicitly, but they bear an explicit summary. First, some sociologists have suggested—like Tiryakian—that an "occult revival" has occurred in response to a sense of social alienation, mostly on the part of young people. For example, in her study of Scientologists, Harriet Whitehead claims that over-rationalization and instrumentalization in U.S. society has created an "experiential void" in established religion, fostering a "gap" between the "accepted modes of comprehending the universe and our place in it" that the occult is able to bridge.[38] Similarly, Nachman Ben-Yehuda has argued that "the particular, contemporary blend of science, fiction, and occult, is a direct result of people having been socialized into positivistic science and being unable to provide satisfactory answers to existential problems."[39] Second, the occult "explosion" in the United States is explained as the result of a general dissatisfaction with the Christian Church and its relative inability to attend to the individual and personal needs of alienated people. Mircea Eliade summarizes this perspective when he notes that "it is primarily the attraction of a *personal* initiation that explains the craze for the occult."[40] Because traditional religions cannot keep pace with a rapidly changing world, people sensing anomie or crisis can turn to occultism for "individualized revitalization experiences."[41] Finally, the occult is attractive because it is often experienced as a "community" that provides more individually actualizing norms and values in a nondogmatic way.[42] Sociologists cannot seem to agree, however, about the degree of social organization among occultists.[43]

Appendix 2: Aleister Crowley's *The Book of the Law* (1904)

The Book of the Law
Liber AL vel Legis
sub figura CCXX
as delivered by XCIII = 418 to DCLXVI

[Chapter I]

1. Had! The manifestation of Nuit.
2. The unveiling of the company of heaven.
3. Every man and every woman is a star.
4. Every number is infinite; there is no difference.
5. Help me, o warrior lord of Thebes, in my unveiling before the Children of men!
6. Be thou Hadit, my secret centre, my heart & my tongue!
7. Behold! it is revealed by Aiwass the minister of Hoor-paar-kraat.
8. The Khabs is in the Khu, not the Khu in the Khabs.
9. Worship then the Khabs, and behold my light shed over you!
10. Let my servants be few & secret: they shall rule the many & the known.
11. These are fools that men adore; both their Gods & their men are fools.
12. Come forth, o children, under the stars, & take your fill of love!
13. I am above you and in you. My ecstasy is in yours. My joy is to see your joy.
14. Above, the gemmèd azure is
    The naked splendour of Nuit;
She bends in ecstasy to kiss
    The secret ardours of Hadit.
The wingèd globe, the starry blue,
Are mine, O Ankh-af-na-khonsu!

15. Now ye shall know that the chosen priest & apostle of infinite space is the prince-priest the Beast; and in his woman called the Scarlet Woman is all power given. They shall gather my children into their fold: they shall bring the glory of the stars into the hearts of men.

16. For he is ever a sun, and she a moon. But to him is the winged secret flame, and to her the stooping starlight.

17. But ye are not so chosen.

18. Burn upon their brows, o splendrous serpent!

19. O azure-lidded woman, bend upon them!

20. The key of the rituals is in the secret word which I have given unto him.

21. With the God & the Adorer I am nothing: they do not see me. They are as upon the earth; I am Heaven, and there is no other God than me, and my lord Hadit.

22. Now, therefore, I am known to ye by my name Nuit, and to him by a secret name which I will give him when at last he knoweth me. Since I am Infinite Space, and the Infinite Stars thereof, do ye also thus. Bind nothing! Let there be no difference made among you between any one thing & any other thing; for thereby there cometh hurt.

23. But whoso availeth in this, let him be the chief of all!

24. I am Nuit, and my word is six and fifty.

25. Divide, add, multiply, and understand.

26. Then saith the prophet and slave of the beauteous one: Who am I, and what shall be the sign? So she answered him, bending down, a lambent flame of blue, all-touching, all penetrant, her lovely hands upon the black earth, & her lithe body arched for love, and her soft feet not hurting the little flowers: Thou knowest! And the sign shall be my ecstasy, the consciousness of the continuity of existence, the omnipresence of my body.

27. Then the priest answered & said unto the Queen of Space, kissing her lovely brows, and the dew of her light bathing his whole body in a sweet-smelling perfume of sweat: O Nuit, continuous one of Heaven, let it be ever thus; that men speak not of Thee as One but as None; and let them speak not of thee at all, since thou art continuous!

28. None, breathed the light, faint & faery, of the stars, and two.

29. For I am divided for love's sake, for the chance of union.

30. This is the creation of the world, that the pain of division is as nothing, and the joy of dissolution all.

31. For these fools of men and their woes care not thou at all! They feel little; what is, is balanced by weak joys; but ye are my chosen ones.

32. Obey my prophet! follow out the ordeals of my knowledge! seek me only! Then the joys of my love will redeem ye from all pain. This

is so: I swear it by the vault of my body; by my sacred heart and tongue; by all I can give, by all I desire of ye all.

33. Then the priest fell into a deep trance or swoon, & said unto the Queen of Heaven; Write unto us the ordeals; write unto us the rituals; write unto us the law!

34. But she said: the ordeals I write not: the rituals shall be half known and half concealed: the Law is for all.

35. This that thou writest is the threefold book of Law.

36. My scribe Ankh-af-na-khonsu, the priest of the princes, shall not in one letter change this book; but lest there be folly, he shall comment thereupon by the wisdom of Ra-Hoor-Khuit.

37. Also the mantras and spells; the obeah and the wanga; the work of the wand and the work of the sword; these he shall learn and teach.

38. He must teach; but he may make severe the ordeals.

39. The word of the Law is THELEMA.

40. Who calls us Thelemites will do no wrong, if he look but close into the word. For there are therein Three Grades, the Hermit, and the Lover, and the man of Earth. Do what thou wilt shall be the whole of the Law.

41. The word of Sin is Restriction. O man! refuse not thy wife, if she will! O lover, if thou wilt, depart! There is no bond that can unite the divided but love: all else is a curse. Accursed! Accursed be it to the aeons! Hell.

42. Let it be that state of manyhood bound and loathing. So with thy all; thou hast no right but to do thy will.

43. Do that, and no other shall say nay.

44. For pure will, unassuaged of purpose, delivered from the lust of result, is every way perfect.

45. The Perfect and the Perfect are one Perfect and not two; nay, are none!

46. Nothing is a secret key of this law. Sixty-one the Jews call it; I call it eight, eighty, four hundred & eighteen.

47. But they have the half: unite by thine art so that all disappear.

48. My prophet is a fool with his one, one, one; are not they the Ox, and none by the Book?

49. Abrogate are all rituals, all ordeals, all words and signs. Ra-Hoor-Khuit hath taken his seat in the East at the Equinox of the Gods; and let Asar be with Isa, who also are one. But they are not of me. Let Asar be the adorant, Isa the sufferer; Hoor in his secret name and splendour is the Lord initiating.

50. There is a word to say about the Hierophantic task. Behold! there are three ordeals in one, and it may be given in three ways. The

gross must pass through fire; let the fine be tried in intellect, and the lofty chosen ones in the highest. Thus ye have star & star, system & system; let not one know well the other!

51. There are four gates to one palace; the floor of that palace is of silver and gold; lapis lazuli & jasper are there; and all rare scents; jasmine & rose, and the emblems of death. Let him enter in turn or at once the four gates; let him stand on the floor of the palace. Will he not sink? Amn. Ho! warrior, if thy servant sink? But there are means and means. Be goodly therefore: dress ye all in fine apparel; eat rich foods and drink sweet wines and wines that foam! Also, take your fill and will of love as ye will, when, where and with whom ye will! But always unto me.

52. If this be not aright; if ye confound the space-marks, saying: They are one; or saying, They are many; if the ritual be not ever unto me: then expect the direful judgments of Ra Hoor Khuit!

53. This shall regenerate the world, the little world my sister, my heart & my tongue, unto whom I send this kiss. Also, o scribe and prophet, though thou be of the princes, it shall not assuage thee nor absolve thee. But ecstasy be thine and joy of earth: ever To me! To me!

54. Change not as much as the style of a letter; for behold! thou, o prophet, shalt not behold all these mysteries hidden therein.

55. The child of thy bowels, *he* shall behold them.

56. Expect him not from the East, nor from the West; for from no expected house cometh that child. Aum! All words are sacred and all prophets true; save only that they understand a little; solve the first half of the equation, leave the second unattacked. But thou hast all in the clear light, and some, though not all, in the dark.

57. Invoke me under my stars! Love is the law, love under will. Nor let the fools mistake love; for there are love and love. There is the dove, and there is the serpent. Choose ye well! He, my prophet, hath chosen, knowing the law of the fortress, and the great mystery of the House of God.

All these old letters of my Book are aright; but [Tzaddi] is not the Star. This also is secret: my prophet shall reveal it to the wise.

58. I give unimaginable joys on earth: certainty, not faith, while in life, upon death; peace unutterable, rest, ecstasy; nor do I demand aught in sacrifice.

59. My incense is of resinous woods & gums; and there is no blood therein: because of my hair the trees of Eternity.

60. My number is 11, as all their numbers who are of us. The Five Pointed Star, with a Circle in the Middle, & the circle is Red. My

colour is black to the blind, but the blue & gold are seen of the seeing. Also I have a secret glory for them that love me.

61. But to love me is better than all things: if under the night stars in the desert thou presently burnest mine incense before me, invoking me with a pure heart, and the Serpent flame therein, thou shalt come a little to lie in my bosom. For one kiss wilt thou then be willing to give all; but whoso gives one particle of dust shall lose all in that hour. Ye shall gather goods and store of women and spices; ye shall wear rich jewels; ye shall exceed the nations of the earth in splendour & pride; but always in the love of me, and so shall ye come to my joy. I charge you earnestly to come before me in a single robe, and covered with a rich headdress. I love you! I yearn to you! Pale or purple, veiled or voluptuous, I who am all pleasure and purple, and drunkenness of the innermost sense, desire you. Put on the wings, and arouse the coiled splendour within you: come unto me!

62. At all my meetings with you shall the priestess say—and her eyes shall burn with desire as she stands bare and rejoicing in my secret temple—To me! To me! calling forth the flame of the hearts of all in her love-chant.

63. Sing the rapturous love-song unto me! Burn to me perfumes! Wear to me jewels! Drink to me, for I love you! I love you!

64. I am the blue-lidded daughter of Sunset; I am the naked brilliance of the voluptuous night-sky.

65. To me! To me!

66. The Manifestation of Nuit is at an end.

[Chapter II]

1. Nu! the hiding of Hadit.

2. Come! all ye, and learn the secret that hath not yet been revealed. I, Hadit, am the complement of Nu, my bride. I am not extended, and Khabs is the name of my House.

3. In the sphere I am everywhere the centre, as she, the circumference, is nowhere found.

4. Yet she shall be known & I never.

5. Behold! the rituals of the old time are black. Let the evil ones be cast away; let the good ones be purged by the prophet! Then shall this Knowledge go aright.

6. I am the flame that burns in every heart of man, and in the core of every star. I am Life, and the giver of Life, yet therefore is the knowledge of me the knowledge of death.

7. I am the Magician and the Exorcist. I am the axle of the wheel,

and the cube in the circle. "Come unto me" is a foolish word: for it is I that go.

8. Who worshipped Heru-pa-kraath have worshipped me; ill, for I am the worshipper.

9. Remember all ye that existence is pure joy; that all the sorrows are but as shadows; they pass & are done; but there is that which remains.

10. O prophet! thou hast ill will to learn this writing.

11. I see thee hate the hand & the pen; but I am stronger.

12. Because of me in Thee which thou knewest not.

13. for why? Because thou wast the knower, and me.

14. Now let there be a veiling of this shrine: now let the light devour men and eat them up with blindness!

15. For I am perfect, being Not; and my number is nine by the fools; but with the just I am eight, and one in eight: Which is vital, for I am none indeed. The Empress and the King are not of me; for there is a further secret.

16. I am The Empress & the Hierophant. Thus eleven, as my bride is eleven.

17. Hear me, ye people of sighing!
The sorrows of pain and regret
Are left to the dead and the dying,
The folk that not know me as yet.

18. These are dead, these fellows; they feel not. We are not for the poor and sad: the lords of the earth are our kinsfolk.

19. Is a God to live in a dog? No! but the highest are of us. They shall rejoice, our chosen: who sorroweth is not of us.

20. Beauty and strength, leaping laughter and delicious languor, force and fire, are of us.

21. We have nothing with the outcast and the unfit: let them die in their misery. For they feel not. Compassion is the vice of kings: stamp down the wretched & the weak: this is the law of the strong: this is our law and the joy of the world. Think not, o king, upon that lie: That Thou Must Die: verily thou shalt not die, but live. Now let it be understood: If the body of the King dissolve, he shall remain in pure ecstasy for ever. Nuit! Hadit! Ra-Hoor-Khuit! The Sun, Strength & Sight, Light; these are for the servants of the Star & the Snake.

22. I am the Snake that giveth Knowledge & Delight and bright glory, and stir the hearts of men with drunkenness. To worship me take wine and strange drugs whereof I will tell my prophet, & be drunk thereof! They shall not harm ye at all. It is a lie, this folly against self. The exposure of innocence is a lie. Be strong, o man! lust,

enjoy all things of sense and rapture: fear not that any God shall deny thee for this.

23. I am alone: there is no God where I am.

24. Behold! these be grave mysteries; for there are also of my friends who be hermits. Now think not to find them in the forest or on the mountain; but in beds of purple, caressed by magnificent beasts of women with large limbs, and fire and light in their eyes, and masses of flaming hair about them; there shall ye find them. Ye shall see them at rule, at victorious armies, at all the joy; and there shall be in them a joy a million times greater than this. Beware lest any force another, King against King! Love one another with burning hearts; on the low men trample in the fierce lust of your pride, in the day of your wrath.

25. Ye are against the people, O my chosen!

26. I am the secret Serpent coiled about to spring: in my coiling there is joy. If I lift up my head, I and my Nuit are one. If I droop down mine head, and shoot forth venom, then is rapture of the earth, and I and the earth are one.

27. There is great danger in me; for who doth not understand these runes shall make a great miss. He shall fall down into the pit called Because, and there he shall perish with the dogs of Reason.

28. Now a curse upon Because and his kin!

29. May Because be accursed for ever!

30. If Will stops and cries Why, invoking Because, then Will stops & does nought.

31. If Power asks why, then is Power weakness.

32. Also reason is a lie; for there is a factor infinite & unknown; & all their words are skew-wise.

33. Enough of Because! Be he damned for a dog!

34. But ye, o my people, rise up & awake!

35. Let the rituals be rightly performed with joy & beauty!

36. There are rituals of the elements and feasts of the times.

37. A feast for the first night of the Prophet and his Bride!

38. A feast for the three days of the writing of the Book of the Law.

39. A feast for Tahuti and the child of the Prophet—secret, O Prophet!

40. A feast for the Supreme Ritual, and a feast for the Equinox of the Gods.

41. A feast for fire and a feast for water; a feast for life and a greater feast for death!

42. A feast every day in your hearts in the joy of my rapture!

43. A feast every night unto Nu, and the pleasure of uttermost delight!

44. Aye! feast! rejoice! there is no dread hereafter. There is the dissolution, and eternal ecstasy in the kisses of Nu.

45. There is death for the dogs.

46. Dost thou fail? Art thou sorry? Is fear in thine heart?

47. Where I am these are not.

48. Pity not the fallen! I never knew them. I am not for them. I console not: I hate the consoled & the consoler.

49. I am unique & conqueror. I am not of the slaves that perish. Be they damned & dead! Amen. (This is of the 4: there is a fifth who is invisible, & therein am I as a babe in an egg.)

50. Blue am I and gold in the light of my bride: but the red gleam is in my eyes; & my spangles are purple & green.

51. Purple beyond purple: it is the light higher than eyesight.

52. There is a veil: that veil is black. It is the veil of the modest woman; it is the veil of sorrow, & the pall of death: this is none of me. Tear down that lying spectre of the centuries: veil not your vices in virtuous words: these vices are my service; ye do well, & I will reward you here and hereafter.

53. Fear not, o prophet, when these words are said, thou shalt not be sorry. Thou art emphatically my chosen; and blessed are the eyes that thou shalt look upon with gladness. But I will hide thee in a mask of sorrow: they that see thee shall fear thou art fallen: but I lift thee up.

54. Nor shall they who cry aloud their folly that thou meanest nought avail; thou shall reveal it: thou availest: they are the slaves of because: They are not of me. The stops as thou wilt; the letters? change them not in style or value!

55. Thou shalt obtain the order & value of the English Alphabet; thou shalt find new symbols to attribute them unto.

56. Begone! ye mockers; even though ye laugh in my honour ye shall laugh not long: then when ye are sad know that I have forsaken you.

57. He that is righteous shall be righteous still; he that is filthy shall be filthy still.

58. Yea! deem not of change: ye shall be as ye are, & not other. Therefore the kings of the earth shall be Kings for ever: the slaves shall serve. There is none that shall be cast down or lifted up: all is ever as it was. Yet there are masked ones my servants: it may be that yonder beggar is a King. A King may choose his garment as he will: there is no certain test: but a beggar cannot hide his poverty.

59. Beware therefore! Love all, lest perchance is a King concealed! Say you so? Fool! If he be a King, thou canst not hurt him.

60. Therefore strike hard & low, and to hell with them, master!

61. There is a light before thine eyes, o prophet, a light undesired, most desirable.

62. I am uplifted in thine heart; and the kisses of the stars rain hard upon thy body.

63. Thou art exhaust in the voluptuous fullness of the inspiration; the expiration is sweeter than death, more rapid and laughterful than a caress of Hell's own worm.

64. Oh! thou art overcome: we are upon thee; our delight is all over thee: hail! hail: prophet of Nu! prophet of Had! prophet of Ra-Hoor-Khu! Now rejoice! now come in our splendour & rapture! Come in our passionate peace, & write sweet words for the Kings.

65. I am the Master: thou art the Holy Chosen One.

66. Write, & find ecstasy in writing! Work, & be our bed in working! Thrill with the joy of life & death! Ah! thy death shall be lovely: whoso seeth it shall be glad. Thy death shall be the seal of the promise of our agelong love. Come! lift up thine heart & rejoice! We are one; we are none.

67. Hold! Hold! Bear up in thy rapture; fall not in swoon of the excellent kisses!

68. Harder! Hold up thyself! Lift thine head! breathe not so deep—die!

69. Ah! Ah! What do I feel? Is the word exhausted?

70. There is help & hope in other spells. Wisdom says: be strong! Then canst thou bear more joy. Be not animal; refine thy rapture! If thou drink, drink by the eight and ninety rules of art: if thou love, exceed by delicacy; and if thou do aught joyous, let there be subtlety therein!

71. But exceed! exceed!

72. Strive ever to more! and if thou art truly mine—and doubt it not, and if thou art ever joyous!—death is the crown of all.

73. Ah! Ah! Death! Death! thou shalt long for death. Death is forbidden, o man, unto thee.

74. The length of thy longing shall be the strength of its glory. He that lives long & desires death much is ever the King among the Kings.

75. Aye! listen to the numbers & the words:

76. 4 6 3 8 A B K 2 4 A L G M O R 3 Y X 24 89 R P S T O V A L. What meaneth this, o prophet? Thou knowest not; nor shalt thou know ever. There cometh one to follow thee: he shall expound it. But remember, o chosen one, to be me; to follow the love of Nu in the star-lit heaven; to look forth upon men, to tell them this glad word.

77. O be thou proud and mighty among men!

78. Lift up thyself! for there is none like unto thee among men or among Gods! Lift up thyself, o my prophet, thy stature shall surpass the stars. They shall worship thy name, foursquare, mystic, wonderful, the number of the man; and the name of thy house 418.

79. The end of the hiding of Hadit; and blessing & worship to the prophet of the lovely Star!

[Chapter III]

1. Abrahadabra; the reward of Ra Hoor Khut.

2. There is division hither homeward; there is a word not known. Spelling is defunct; all is not aught. Beware! Hold! Raise the spell of Ra-Hoor-Khuit!

3. Now let it be first understood that I am a god of War and of Vengeance. I shall deal hardly with them.

4. Choose ye an island!

5. Fortify it!

6. Dung it about with enginery of war!

7. I will give you a war-engine.

8. With it ye shall smite the peoples; and none shall stand before you.

9. Lurk! Withdraw! Upon them! this is the Law of the Battle of Conquest: thus shall my worship be about my secret house.

10. Get the stele of revealing itself; set it in thy secret temple—and that temple is already aright disposed—& it shall be your Kiblah for ever. It shall not fade, but miraculous colour shall come back to it day after day. Close it in locked glass for a proof to the world.

11. This shall be your only proof. I forbid argument. Conquer! That is enough. I will make easy to you the abstruction from the ill-ordered house in the Victorious City. Thou shalt thyself convey it with worship, o prophet, though thou likest it not. Thou shalt have danger & trouble. Ra-Hoor-Khu is with thee. Worship me with fire & blood; worship me with swords & with spears. Let the woman be girt with a sword before me: let blood flow to my name. Trample down the Heathen; be upon them, o warrior, I will give you of their flesh to eat!

12. Sacrifice cattle, little and big: after a child.

13. But not now.

14. Ye shall see that hour, o blessed Beast, and thou the Scarlet Concubine of his desire!

15. Ye shall be sad thereof.

16. Deem not too eagerly to catch the promises; fear not to undergo the curses. Ye, even ye, know not this meaning all.

17. Fear not at all; fear neither men nor Fates, nor gods, nor any-

thing. Money fear not, nor laughter of the folk folly, nor any other power in heaven or upon the earth or under the earth. Nu is your refuge as Hadit your light; and I am the strength, force, vigour, of your arms.

18. Mercy let be off; damn them who pity! Kill and torture; spare not; be upon them!

19. That stele they shall call the Abomination of Desolation; count well its name, & it shall be to you as 718.

20. Why? Because of the fall of Because, that he is not there again.

21. Set up my image in the East: thou shalt buy thee an image which I will show thee, especial, not unlike the one thou knowest. And it shall be suddenly easy for thee to do this.

22. The other images group around me to support me: let all be worshipped, for they shall cluster to exalt me. I am the visible object of worship; the others are secret; for the Beast & his Bride are they: and for the winners of the Ordeal x. What is this? Thou shalt know.

23. For perfume mix meal & honey & thick leavings of red wine: then oil of Abramelin and olive oil, and afterward soften & smooth down with rich fresh blood.

24. The best blood is of the moon, monthly: then the fresh blood of a child, or dropping from the host of heaven: then of enemies; then of the priest or of the worshippers: last of some beast, no matter what.

25. This burn: of this make cakes & eat unto me. This hath also another use; let it be laid before me, and kept thick with perfumes of your orison: it shall become full of beetles as it were and creeping things sacred unto me.

26. These slay, naming your enemies; & they shall fall before you.

27. Also these shall breed lust & power of lust in you at the eating thereof.

28. Also ye shall be strong in war.

29. Moreover, be they long kept, it is better; for they swell with my force. All before me.

30. My altar is of open brass work: burn thereon in silver or gold!

31. There cometh a rich man from the West who shall pour his gold upon thee.

32. From gold forge steel!

33. Be ready to fly or to smite!

34. But your holy place shall be untouched throughout the centuries: though with fire and sword it be burnt down & shattered, yet an invisible house there standeth, and shall stand until the fall of the Great Equinox; when Hrumachis shall arise and the double-wanded one assume my throne and place. Another prophet shall arise, and

bring fresh fever from the skies; another woman shall awake the lust & worship of the Snake; another soul of God and beast shall mingle in the globed priest; another sacrifice shall stain the tomb; another king shall reign; and blessing no longer be poured To the Hawk-headed mystical Lord!

35. The half of the word of Heru-ra-ha, called Hoor-pa-kraat and Ra-Hoor-Khut.

36. Then said the prophet unto the God:

37. I adore thee in the song—

I am the Lord of Thebes, and I
  The inspired forth-speaker of Mentu;
For me unveils the veiled sky,
  The self-slain Ankh-af-na-khonsu
Whose words are truth. I invoke, I greet
  Thy presence, O Ra-Hoor-Khuit!

Unity uttermost showed!
  I adore the might of Thy breath,
Supreme and terrible God,
  Who makest the gods and death
To tremble before Thee:—
  I, I adore thee!

Appear on the throne of Ra!
  Open the ways of the Khu!
Lighten the ways of the Ka!
  The ways of the Khabs run through
To stir me or still me!
  Aum! let it fill me!

38. So that thy light is in me; & its red flame is as a sword in my hand to push thy order. There is a secret door that I shall make to establish thy way in all the quarters, (these are the adorations, as thou hast written), as it is said:

The light is mine; its rays consume
  Me: I have made a secret door
Into the House of Ra and Tum,
  Of Khephra and of Ahathoor.
I am thy Theban, O Mentu,
  The prophet Ankh-af-na-khonsu!

By Bes-na-Maut my breast I beat;
  By wise Ta-Nech I weave my spell.
Show thy star-splendour, O Nuit!
  Bid me within thine House to dwell,
O winged snake of light, Hadit!
  Abide with me, Ra-Hoor-Khuit!

39. All this and a book to say how thou didst come hither and a reproduction of this ink and paper for ever—for in it is the word secret & not only in the English—and thy comment upon this the Book of the Law shall be printed beautifully in red ink and black upon beautiful paper made by hand; and to each man and woman that thou meetest, were it but to dine or to drink at them, it is the Law to give. Then they shall chance to abide in this bliss or no; it is no odds. Do this quickly!

40. But the work of the comment? That is easy; and Hadit burning in thy heart shall make swift and secure thy pen.

41. Establish at thy Kaaba a clerk-house: all must be done well and with business way.

42. The ordeals thou shalt oversee thyself, save only the blind ones. Refuse none, but thou shalt know & destroy the traitors. I am Ra-Hoor-Khuit; and I am powerful to protect my servant. Success is thy proof: argue not; convert not; talk not over much! Them that seek to entrap thee, to overthrow thee, them attack without pity or quarter; & destroy them utterly. Swift as a trodden serpent turn and strike! Be thou yet deadlier than he! Drag down their souls to awful torment: laugh at their fear: spit upon them!

43. Let the Scarlet Woman beware! If pity and compassion and tenderness visit her heart; if she leave my work to toy with old sweetnesses; then shall my vengeance be known. I will slay me her child: I will alienate her heart: I will cast her out from men: as a shrinking and despised harlot shall she crawl through dusk wet streets, and die cold and an-hungered.

44. But let her raise herself in pride! Let her follow me in my way! Let her work the work of wickedness! Let her kill her heart! Let her be loud and adulterous! Let her be covered with jewels, and rich garments, and let her be shameless before all men!

45. Then will I lift her to pinnacles of power: then will I breed from her a child mightier than all the kings of the earth. I will fill her with joy: with my force shall she see & strike at the worship of Nu: she shall achieve Hadit.

46. I am the warrior Lord of the Forties: the Eighties cower before

me, & are abased. I will bring you to victory & joy: I will be at your arms in battle & ye shall delight to slay. Success is your proof; courage is your armour; go on, go on, in my strength; & ye shall turn not back for any!

47. This book shall be translated into all tongues: but always with the original in the writing of the Beast; for in the chance shape of the letters and their position to one another: in these are mysteries that no Beast shall divine. Let him not seek to try: but one cometh after him, whence I say not, who shall discover the Key of it all. Then this line drawn is a key: then this circle squared in its failure is a key also. And Abrahadabra. It shall be his child & that strangely. Let him not seek after this; for thereby alone can he fall from it.

48. Now this mystery of the letters is done, and I want to go on to the holier place.

49. I am in a secret fourfold word, the blasphemy against all gods of men.

50. Curse them! Curse them! Curse them!

51. With my Hawk's head I peck at the eyes of Jesus as he hangs upon the cross.

52. I flap my wings in the face of Mohammed & blind him.

53. With my claws I tear out the flesh of the Indian and the Buddhist, Mongol and Din.

54. Bahlasti! Ompehda! I spit on your crapulous creeds.

55. Let Mary inviolate be torn upon wheels: for her sake let all chaste women be utterly despised among you!

56. Also for beauty's sake and love's!

57. Despise also all cowards; professional soldiers who dare not fight, but play; all fools despise!

58. But the keen and the proud, the royal and the lofty; ye are brothers!

59. As brothers fight ye!

60. There is no law beyond Do what thou wilt.

61. There is an end of the word of the God enthroned in Ra's seat, lightening the girders of the soul.

62. To Me do ye reverence! to me come ye through tribulation of ordeal, which is bliss.

63. The fool readeth this Book of the Law, and its comment; & he understandeth it not.

64. Let him come through the first ordeal, & it will be to him as silver.

65. Through the second, gold.

66. Through the third, stones of precious water.

67. Through the fourth, ultimate sparks of the intimate fire.

68. Yet to all it shall seem beautiful. Its enemies who say not so, are mere liars.

69. There is success.

70. I am the Hawk-Headed Lord of Silence & of Strength; my nemyss shrouds the night-blue sky.

71. Hail! ye twin warriors about the pillars of the world! for your time is nigh at hand.

72. I am the Lord of the Double Wand of Power; the wand of the Force of Coph Nia—but my left hand is empty, for I have crushed a Universe; & nought remains.

73. Paste the sheets from right to left and from top to bottom: then behold!

74. There is a splendour in my name hidden and glorious, as the sun of midnight is ever the son.

75. The ending of the words is the Word Abrahadabra.

The Book of the Law is Written
and Concealed.
Aum. Ha.

Notes

Introduction

1. Deleuze and Guattari, *Anti-Oedipus,* 5–6.
2. See Popkin, "Spinoza, Neoplatonic Kabbalist?"
3. See Copenhaver, *Hermetica.*
4. Lévi, *Transcendental Magic,* 25–27.
5. See Bacon, *New Atlantis.*
6. Lévi, *Transcendental Magic,* 26.
7. See Nietzsche, *Beyond Good and Evil.*
8. See Crowley, *Magick,* 206–7.
9. See Austin, *How to Do Things with Words,* esp. 4–11.
10. For helpful overviews of the rhetorical tradition see Bizzell and Herzberg, *The Rhetorical Tradition;* and Conley, *Rhetoric in the European Tradition.*
11. Readers familiar with the work of Kenneth Burke will recognize that I am riffing on his essay "Definition of Man." In a sense, one could read this book as a case study of that essay.
12. *Oxford English Dictionary,* 2nd ed. (online), s.v. "ineffable."
13. K. Burke, *The Rhetoric of Religion,* 15.
14. Isocrates argues that with the art of discourse "we both contend against others on matters which are open to dispute and seek light for ourselves on things which are unknown"; he further suggests that the faculty of speech is responsible for human civilization: "generally speaking, there is no institution devised by man which the power of speech has not helped to establish." In Bizzell and Herzberg, *The Rhetorical Tradition,* 75. For a contemporary extollation of the almighty, knowledge-centered power of rhetoric see Cherwitz and Hikins, *Communication and Knowledge.*
15. See Gay, *Understanding the Occult.*
16. In *Understanding the Occult,* Gay describes occultism in a very similar way: "I believe that occult experience occurs when people feel suddenly

that a hidden, yet vital, connection between themselves and other people is broken. . . . A person vulnerable to occult experience is one who is searching for a way to find again a road back to relationship, back to a sense of union, and back to a feeling of connectedness with others" (18).

17. Halyna Barannik, review of the film *What Lies Beneath,* Christian Spotlight on the Movies, http://www.christiananswers.net/spotlight/movies/2000/whatliesbeneath.htm (accessed August 18, 2001). It is interesting to note that many of the reviews of horror films on this site describe them as spells in themselves. Presumably, watching a "extremely offensive" occult-themed film like *The Ninth Gate, Stigmata,* or *Lost Souls* (all of which are about Satan in one guise or another) can open spiritual portals.

18. I explored this axiom in "Refitting Fantasy" in terms of "communication," of which rhetoric is a form.

19. Freud, *New Introductory Lectures,* 86–87.

20. See Dean, *Aliens in America;* and Knight, *Conspiracy Nation.*

21. Appendix 1 reviews the work that has been done in this area.

Chapter 1

1. Lévi, *Transcendental Magic,* 1.

2. Lévi, *The History of Magic,* 35.

3. See, e.g., McIntosh, *Lévi and the French Occult Revival;* E. M. Butler, *Ritual Magic,* esp. 94–99; and C. Wilson, *The Occult,* esp. 326–29.

4. E. M. Butler, *Ritual Magic,* 99.

5. Barrett, *The Magus,* bk. 2, 33.

6. Lévi, *History of Magic,* 45.

7. Agrippa, *Three Books of Occult Philosophy,* 202.

8. Lévi, *Transcendental Magic,* 247.

9. Ibid., 64–5.

10. A. E. Waite, "Biographical Preface," in Lévi, *Transcendental Magic,* xxxvi.

11. The *Clavicula Salomonis,* or *The Key of Solomon the King,* is one of the most famous *grimoires* attributed to King Solomon by occultists (it is not likely, however, that Solomon penned it). See Mathers, *The Key of Solomon the King.*

12. Qtd. in E. M. Butler, *Ritual Magic,* 97–8.

13. C. Wilson, *The Occult,* 326–7.

14. According to the current publisher of the book, Red Wheel/Weiser (formerly Samuel Weiser, Inc.), *Transcendental Magic* has been through thirteen printings since their first English-language reprint in 1968. This means that there are approximately 23,000 copies in print. Compared to popular novels of Stephen King, for example, 23,000 copies is relatively modest.

15. See Fisher, "Narration as a Human Communication Paradigm."

16. There are a number of excellent histories, many of which are lavishly illustrated. As one would expect, just about every occultist has his or her own "history" of the occult, and these are traditionally found in the introductions to books. The classic text is Lévi's *History of Magic;* however, many later historians have noted a substantial number of inaccuracies and sheer fictions. Lévi's popularizer, Arthur Edward Waite, has also written a popular account in *The Book of Ceremonial Magic,* although Waite's work suffers from the same charge of inaccuracy that he levied at Lévi. Colin Wilson's *The Occult: A History* is also a popular reference, but Wilson's expressed agenda (to prove the existence of psychic and astral forces) is sometimes an annoyance and detracts from the value of his scholarship. One of the best overviews is a coffee-table book by Charles Walker titled *The Encyclopedia of the Occult,* currently out of print but a frequent find in used book stores. Walker's book is well documented, clearly written, and full of helpful illustrations.

17. Wittgenstein, *Culture and Value,* 3.

18. See H. White, *Tropics of Discourse,* 84–85.

19. Also see Lecky, *Rise and Influence of Rationalism,* 1–138.

20. Eamon, "Magic and the Occult," 533.

21. Augustine, *City of God,* 339–40.

22. The undisputed classic survey of Renaissance occultism is Yates, *Giordano Bruno and the Hermetic Tradition.* For an interesting psychoanalytic reading of Renaissance magic see Couliano, *Eros and Magic in the Renaissance.*

23. Yates, *Giordano Bruno,* 25–28; Eamon, "Magic and the Occult," 536.

24. Scholars currently believe that the works attributed to Hermes Trismegistus were written by multiple authors and that he is in actuality a fictional character based on the Egyptian god of language, Thoth, which scholars mistook for a concrete individual.

25. The present English standard translation is Copenhaver, *Hermetica.*

26. The Kabbalah is, of course, Jewish in origin. It was taken up into Hermeticism by way of Arabic texts, the source of many ancient Greek "rediscoveries" (including the works of Aristotle). I describe the Kabbalah and related practices in greater detail in chapters 4, 5, and 6.

27. For a helpful discussion of the phrase "language of the birds" see Walker, *Encyclopedia of the Occult,* 7–27.

28. Agrippa, *Three Books of Occult Philosophy,* 711.

29. For an overview of Dee's career and the Enochian language see the introduction to Laycock, *Complete Enochian Dictionary.*

30. For a fascinating description of this kind of magic see Crowley, *The Vision and the Voice.*

31. Donald C. Laycock, "Enochian: Angelic Language or Mortal Folly?" in his *Complete Enochian Dictionary,* 63.

32. Laycock, *Complete Enochian Dictionary,* 250.

33. Lindley, *Trials of Frances Howard,* 50.

34. Montague Summers, "Introduction to 1928 Edition," in Kramer and Sprenger, *The Malleus Maleficarum,* vii–viii.

35. For a more extensive discussion of occultism in the Elizabethan and Jacobian periods see Thomas, *Religion and the Decline of Magic.*

36. Fraser, *King James VI of Scotland,* 55–58; also see Ashton, *James I by His Contemporaries,* 39–41, 144–45, 154–63; and O. J. Scott, *James I,* 209–32, 330–31.

37. Akrigg, *Letters of King James VI and I,* 114–15. The letter marks the beginning of a long period of insecurity on James's part regarding his primary political enemy, the Earl of Bothwell. James was becoming increasingly powerful only by reducing the power of the nobility. When Bothwell rebelled, James had him imprisoned, but Bothwell escaped before his trial and tormented James for years afterward with repeated assassination attempts. Shortly after his escape, James learned that Bothwell has consulted warlocks and witches ("wise men" and "cunning women") to put curses on him. James subsequently became obsessed with and fearful of the occult. Why James did not challenge Dee is unknown to me and is not discussed in the scholarly literature available; one can only surmise that Dee downplayed his dabbling and used his wide respect and influence among the English nobility to secure his continued survival.

38. Eamon, "Magic and the Occult," 539. Bacon knew Dee and, it is sometimes suggested, downplayed the role of mathematics in his "new science" because math was too closely associated with Dee. Bacon, anxious to secure the trust of James, even withheld the publication of *New Atlantis* because of its challenge to the divine right of kings and because of the magical overtones found throughout. See Yates, *The Rosicrucian Enlightenment.* To my knowledge, there no mention of Dee in the extant writings of Bacon.

39. Lindley, *Trials of Francis Howard,* 50.

40. The exception is David Hume, whose critique of causality rests on the notion that we cannot observe the "secret powers" of objects in motion: "Should it be said, that, from a number of uniform experiments, we *infer* a connexion between the sensible qualities and the secret powers." *An Enquiry Concerning Human Understanding,* 23.

41. Eamon, "Magic and the Occult," 538.

42. Barrett, *The Magus,* v.

43. See Eisenstein, *The Printing Press.*

44. Copy on the back jacket, *The Magus.* The actual number of copies printed is not known. Given the number of nineteenth-century occultists who

cite the work, it must have been readily available and probably underwent a number of reprintings.

45. See Jameson, *The Political Unconscious,* 105. In rhetorical studies, a representative critique is Conley, "The Linnaean Blues." Also see Benoit, "Beyond Genre Theory."

46. For a more extensive discussion of my understanding of genre see Gunn, "Gothic Music" and "The Rhetoric of Exorcism."

47. My views are similar to those articulated by Rosmarin in *The Power of Genre.* We differ significantly, however, in terms of the *use* of genre. Rosmarin locates genre as a basis for normative claims, whereas I see it as a useful *descriptive* tool only.

48. See Campbell and Jamieson, "Form and Genre in Rhetorical Criticism: An Introduction," in *Form and Genre,* 9–32.

49. Campbell and Jamieson, "Introduction," 294.

50. In a personal communication, Campbell writes: "My only interest as a critic is what use I can make of theory, how it can be applied to open up some symbolic process so that I can see it [and] understand it better, so I can interpret it in a fresh and interesting way." E-mail to author, August 21, 2001.

51. M. M. Smith, *The Title-Page.* For good examples of the study of titles (dubbed "titology" by those doing research in the "history of the book" area of composition and rhetorical studies) see Corbett and Lightbown, *The Comely Frontispiece;* and Genette, *Paratext,* esp. 55–103. The classic text in this field is dated but a delight to read: Pollard, *Last Words on the History of the Title-Page.* "Books are always books," muses Pollard, "but if any are to be selected for mutilation it would be hard to make a better choice than works of Dutch and German Theology."

52. Barrett, *The Magus,* 4.

53. Lévi, *Transcendental Magic,* 2–3.

54. Waite, *The Book of Ceremonial Magic,* xxii.

55. Walker, *Encyclopedia of the Occult,* 25.

56. Ibid., 26.

57. Lévi, *History of Magic,* 35.

58. Ibid., 158–61.

59. Lévi, *Transcendental Magic,* 317–19.

60. Ibid., 317.

61. As cited in E. M. Butler, *Ritual Magic,* 97–98.

Chapter 2

1. Joyce, *Ulysses,* 157.
2. Twitchell, *The Eck-Vidya,* 105.

3. Blamires, *The New Bloomsday Book*, 71.

4. See ibid., 72.

5. Joyce, *Ulysses*, 157.

6. Although it has its peculiarities, ECKANKAR resembles many other Western occult and New Age groups. Most groups provide a narrative of origins that features a familiar romantic tale of a solitary sojourner traveling to receive ancient wisdom from a secret wise person or group. For ECKers this man was Paul Twitchell, and it is the ECK Masters who bestowed to him, and later to the Mahanta Klemp, the most secret kinds of spiritual knowledge. For members of the Ishayas' Ascension, Maharishi Sadashiva Isham, referred to as the mysterious MSI in their literature, is the leader from Seattle who traveled to the Himalayas to meet the powerful Ishayas. For the best-selling New Age author and psychic extraordinaire, Sylvia Browne, earth travel was not necessary because the abode of secret wisdom is another plane of reality—"the Other Side." Gaining access to the Other Side requires either psychic power or death. Her spiritual guides are Francine and Raheim, spiritual emissaries of the collective of "advanced entities on the Other Side" known only as "the Council." And for Blavatsky, the advanced beings were the Secret Masters or Chiefs, collectively known as the "Great White Brotherhood." These supernatural beings lived in India and the Himalayas and, as Blavatsky tells it, commanded her to reveal their ancient secrets, paradoxically clothed in difficult language, in the name of world brotherhood and peace. See Browne, *Soul's Perfection*, esp. 16; Blavatsky, *Isis Unveiled;* and Van Mater, "The Writing of the Secret Doctrine."

7. One must be careful to distinguish between Joyce's protagonist and Joyce himself. After all, Joyce is responsible for writing the most jargon-rife, difficult work of literature in the twentieth century: *Finnegans Wake*.

8. In his *Poetics Handbook*, Abondolo remarks that the term is "often used to refer to a kind of creative process" (3). Additionally, keeping in mind that Aristotle wrote his *Poetics* to counter Plato's moral condemnation of literature and art as "irrational," an occult poetics is also an account of the basic logic of occult texts as sane and sensible. In other words, the term "poetics" is useful because it suggests a sensible logic or pattern. I also mean to employ the term in a manner similar to Kenneth Burke's "poetics of appeal," a poetics that is inherently suasive or rhetorical, thus dispensing with the hard, traditional distinction between poetics and rhetoric. Also see Heath, "Kenneth Burke's Poetics."

9. Katz, "Mystical Speech and Mystical Meaning," 3–4.

10. Lao Tzu and Chuang Tzu, *The Texts of Taoism*, 47.

11. Plato, *Republic*, 235–50. My use of masculine pronouns here is deliberate.

12. Ibid., 250–55.

13. Plato, *Phaedrus,* sec. 278, p. 101.

14. Klemp, *The Golden Heart,* 8–9.

15. Ibid., 151.

16. *The Urantia Book,* 1.

17. Ibid., 146.

18. In order to make sense of this complex book, I spent two months with two online discussion groups composed of readers of *The Urantia Book*. Even after this period of time and interaction, I was still unable to make sense of the cosmology. *The Urantia Book* is, in my opinion, one of the most baffling occult systems ever written/revealed.

19. Gurdjieff, *Beelzebub's Tales to His Grandson,* 815.

20. The quote is from the jacket cover.

21. James, *Varieties of Religious Experience,* 319.

22. Derrida, "*Différence.*"

23. Kamuf, *A Derrida Reader,* 126–28.

24. R. L. Scott, "Rhetoric and Silence," 146–47. Also see Ehrenhaus, "Silence and Symbolic Expression"; Johannesen, "The Functions of Silence"; Sewell, "Speech, Silence, and Authenticity"; and R. L. Scott, "Dialectical Tensions of Speaking and Silence."

25. I should mention that I am aware of the relevance of speech-act theory's "principle of expressibility." For John Searle, this principle holds that "whatever can be meant can be said," regardless of one's ability to express one's own private meaning. That is, because of the very structure of language as a system of relations, there always remains the possibility of expressing meaning in some relational set or means of expression yet to be discovered by an individual. The principle of expressibility is suggestive of two important observations. First, anything that can be thought is a languaging of some sort. This observation does not imply the use of "explicit verbal constructions" or the notion that one cannot be conscious without a language; rather, it implies that one is not aware of meaningful objects or experiences in the absence of some system of representation. Second, the principle of expressibility assumes the notion, marked in different terms by Derrida in the concept of *différence,* that meaning is a relational product typified by the fundamental absence of the signified. If it were possible to speak purely in the presence of objects of value, then there would be no need for language, or, one would be continuous or "one" with what Walter Benjamin has called a divine, "pure language." Thus the point here is that representation always implies *différence* and thus multiple absences and an inevitable interiority that absolutely denies the possibility of pure language. See Benjamin, "The Task of the Translator," esp. 74; and Searle, *Speech Acts.*

26. Blavatsky, *The Voice of Silence.*

27. *Différence* is, in fact, the ineffable. See Scharfstein, *Ineffability,* esp. 132.

28. Plato, *Republic,* secs. 502–11.

29. In a similar manner, Descartes's famous ruminations on the perfection of God presences God as the guarantor of truth and falsity. See his *Meditations* in *Philosophical Essays,* esp. 109.

30. Derrida, *Of Grammatology,* 3–5, 18–26.

31. See Wittgenstein, *Blue and Brown Books,* 16–17, and *Philosophical Investigations,* 23–36.

32. Rorty, *Contingency, Irony, and Solidarity,* 13.

33. Ibid., 12.

34. Barnes, *Kuhn and Social Science,* 28.

35. See Adorno, *Minima Moralia,* 101–2, 219–21.

36. J. Butler, "Changing the Subject," 765.

37. K. Burke, *A Grammar of Motives,* 134–39; also see Covino, *Magic, Rhetoric, and Literacy,* 1–3.

38. Aristotle, *Poetics,* sec. 8.

39. For example, P. D. Ouspensky recalled that Gurdjieff described his unique vocabulary as a reconfiguration of "old terms" in relationship to new principles concerning reality: "For exact understanding exact language is necessary. And the study of systems of ancient knowledge begins with the study of a language which will make it possible to establish at once exactly what is being said, from what point of view, and in what connection. This new language contains hardly any new terms or new nomenclature, but *it bases the construction of speech upon a new principle, namely, the principle of relativity;* that is to say, it introduces relativity into all concepts and thus makes possible an accurate determination of the angle of thought—for what precisely ordinary language lacks are expressions of relativity." Ouspensky, *In Search of the Miraculous,* 70. The deep paradox here, of course, is that Gurdjieff calls for a fluid view of language while simultaneously assuming the ubiquity of spiritual presences.

40. Kant, *Critique of Pure Reason,* 484–89.

41. Quine, *The Ways of Paradox,* 1–18.

42. See Derrida, "Plato's Pharmacy."

43. R. L. Scott, "On Viewing Rhetoric as Epistemic."

44. Rorty, *Truth and Progress,* 328.

45. Nussbaum, "The Professor of Parody."

46. For the present moment, however, this is all I wish to discuss about the contemporary occultic until I have began to exhaust the description of the occult; as a colleague frequently puts it, one must understand the concerto before beginning to study the symphony.

47. See K. Burke, *The Rhetoric of Religion.*

48. Weaver, "Language Is Sermonic."

Interlude: Mysteries of the Unknown

1. See Ellis, "Speak to the Devil: Ouija Boards and Deliverance," in *Raising the Devil,* 62–86.

2. "Mysteries of the Unknown," television commercial, Thinkfilm, Inc., 1996. Many thanks to Joseph Becker at Thinkfilm, who generously sent a copy of the commercial he directed.

Chapter 3

1. "The Theosophical Society," *Hartford Daily Times,* December 2, 1878, 1.

2. See Plato, *Cratylus,* sec. 439, *Republic,* secs. 514–21, and *Phaedrus,* secs. 244–58.

3. Zukav, *The Seat of the Soul,* 40.

4. Browne, *Soul's Perfection,* 63.

5. In his wildly entertaining pamphlet *Bluff Your Way in the Occult,* Rae puts it this way: "After the normal sort of apprenticeship for a religious leader (medium and snake charmer) [Blavatsky] founded Theosophy. The main aim of the movement was to spread knowledge of Eastern mysticism to such an extent that she virtually single-handedly introduced and made known all those vague philosophies and religions that are so popular now. So next time you are pestered in the street by someone with a shaven head and saffron in long-johns you know who to blame" (41). Regardless, the consensus of occultists and occult historians is that Blavatsky was at least the most visible popularizer of Eastern mysticism and occult ideas. See, e.g., Cuiley, *Harper's Encyclopedia of Mystical and Paranormal Experience,* 64–66.

6. To my knowledge, there are only three exceptions: Clark, "Rhetoric, Reality, and Rationalization"; McCarthy, "Andrew Jackson Davis"; and McGuire and Patton, "Preaching in the Mystic Mode."

7. Symonds, *Madame Blavatsky,* 80.

8. "The Objectives of the Theosophical Society," http://www.user.aol.com/tstec/hmpage/tsobject.htm (accessed December 16, 2000).

9. This relatively straightforward explanation is from the *Oxford English Dictionary* (1989), s.v. "theosophy." A more detailed but less clear description can be found in many of Blavatsky's writings. See especially *The Key to Theosophy.*

10. For an interesting account of the founding of the Theosophical Society see Olcott, *Inside the Occult.*

11. The rumors are perpetuated in Washington, *Madame Blavatsky's Baboon,* 68. Theosophists point out that some of Washington's claims about Blavatsky go undocumented.

12. De Zirkoff, "Introductory: How 'Isis Unveiled' Was Written": "the one thousand copies of the first printing were sold out in ten days. Even some of the advance subscribers had to wait for the second printing" (1). I am indebted to John Algeo of the Theosophical Society in America for this citation. Also see Washington, *Madame Blavatsky's Baboon,* 52. Algeo notes that "Blavatsky did not 'channel' as that term is understood today," however (e-mail to the author, November 1, 2000). Blavatsky claimed to be in "telepathic" contact with the Secret Masters, who were real individuals with physical bodies (despite possessing supernatural powers), and through this contact she wrote her books. I have used the term "channeled" because it is the closest approximation of what she claimed to do as an author. See Algeo, "Channeling."

13. Washington, *Madame Blavatsky's Baboon,* 52.

14. As cited in Blavatsky, "My Books," 46–47.

15. See Dupree, "Christianity and the Scientific Community"; Gregory, "The Impact of Darwinian Evolution"; Moore, "Geologists and Interpreters"; and Szasz, "Modern American Mainline Protestantism."

16. Schoepflin, "America's Innovative Nineteenth-Century Religions," 311; also see Noll, "Evangelicalism and Fundamentalism."

17. Jones, *History of Western Philosophy,* 176–77.

18. Paley, *Natural Theology,* 1–18.

19. Flew, "The Philosophical Implications of Darwinism," 8.

20. Warnick, "A Rhetorical Analysis of Episteme Shift," 36.

21. Russett, *Darwin in America,* 25.

22. Elliott-Binns, *Religion in the Victorian Era,* 172.

23. "No other genre of US literature," says Jeffrey Alan Melton, "enjoyed a greater popularity or a more enduring prominence in the nineteenth century than travel writing." Melton, "Touring Decay," 206. See also Dulles, *Americans Abroad.*

24. *Oxford English Dictionary* (1989), s.v. "spiritualism."

25. Braude, *Radical Spirits,* 10–31; Owen, *The Darkened Room,* 18–19; and Shepard, *Encyclopedia of Occultism and Parapsychology,* 1:345–49.

26. See Gunn, "Refitting Fantasy."

27. Rickels, *The Vampire Lectures,* 53.

28. Peters, *Speaking into the Air,* 94–95. Also see Sconce, *Haunted Media.*

29. See, e.g., Hart, *The Popular Book,* 157–79. Although Hart discusses the matter in a later period, his discussion of the popularity of the philosophical primer is also apropos (238–40). David D. Hall's characterization of the reading public is also helpful; see his *Cultures of Print,* esp. 36–78.

30. McCarthy, "Andrew Jackson Davis," 312.

31. Blavatsky, *Isis Unveiled,* 2:640.

32. I will only touch the surface of this cosmology. It is, I stress, extremely complex, and a number of Theosophists have spent a lifetime trying to make sense of it.

33. Theosophical cosmology is rife with similar paradoxes: If the universe is a unity, then how can it simultaneously be divided? The answer Blavatsky offers is similar to those offered by Spinoza, Schopenhauer, and Hegel: the split begins with the interplay between matter and mind, or thought and extension. Like Hegel's "the real is the rational and the rational is the real," Blavatsky maintains that minds and bodies are concurrent and are only understood as distinct because of the inherent limitations of individual consciousness—minds that have fallen from unity and thus taken on duality.

34. De Prurucker, *Occult Glossary,* 46–47.

35. Blavatsky, *The Key to Theosophy,* 1–71, and *Isis Unveiled,* 1:v–viii.

36. Blavatsky, *The Secret Doctrine,* 2:711.

37. Ibid.

38. Ibid., 300. Scholars often make two mistakes regarding Blavatsky's views on race. First, by "race" Blavatsky is suggesting a subspecies, and she disavows any notion of racial superiority; indeed, her touted project was to get the world's many subraces to realize their common ancestry. Second, many scholars have erroneously suggested that she proposed five root races instead of seven (two of which are in the future). See, e.g., Oppenheim, *The Other World,* 195. The reason for this second common mistake might be explained by the more recent attempts of Blavatsky's successors to eliminate eschatological and millennial overtones from her doctrines. According to Blavatsky, each root race underwent a cataclysm whereby one-half of the root race remained "pure" and the other half began to evolve characteristics and qualities of the coming race. To add to the complexity, among each root race are seven subraces, which in turn are divided into seven smaller races. Initially, Blavatsky suggested that there would be a final cataclysmic event in which a new race would emerge. This cataclysmic event would occur in the last evolutionary cycle of the fifth root race. Perhaps many scholars mistake the birth of a new race with the end of the world, which Blavatsky maintained would not happen for millions of years. See de Prurucker, *Occult Glossary,* 142–43.

39. See, e.g., Blavatsky, "Hypnotism."

40. Gomes, *Theosophy in the Nineteenth Century,* 180–85: "The October 1877 *American Bookseller* reported that the sale of *Isis Unveiled* was 'unprecedented for a work of its kind.'" There were at least thirteen printings (or "editions") during the century: those in 1877, 1877, 1878, 1882, 1884,

1886, 1887, 1888, 1889, 1891, 1892, 1893, 1896 are documented. My thanks, again, to John Algeo of the Theosophical Society in America for this source.

41. "A Visit to Madame Blavatsky," *Cincinnati Commercial Gazette,* October 13, 1889, 3.

42. "The Theosophical Society," *Hartford Daily Times,* December 2, 1878, 1; "H. P. Blavatsky's Adieux," *New York Daily Graphic,* December 10, 1878, 266.

43. "Blavatsky's Life: A Brief Account of Her Career in This Country," *Philadelphia Inquirer,* May 16, 1891, 12.

44. "Helena Petrovna Blavatsky," *New-York Daily Tribune,* May 10, 1891. Reprinted in *Sunrise,* August 1985, http://www.theosophy-nw.org (accessed December 16, 2000).

45. "Silence in the Lamasery," *New York Sun,* December 19, 1878, 1.

46. As many scholars of historical audiences and the history of the book have argued, it is practically impossible to determine what the general reader of Blavatsky's essays and books was like or how these publications were read. The best evidence one can marshal for claims about the character of historical audiences is memoir—direct accounts of reading practices by common readers. See Rose, "Rereading the English Common Reader"; and D. D. Hall, *Cultures of Print,* 37–78. Otherwise, one must be resigned to the representation of readers in texts, a critical move popularized by the reader-response critics and literary historians Stanley Fish and Wolfgang Isen. Essentially, such an approach attempts to reconstruct who the *author* believes the reader is by ferreting out assumptions made about them in the author's writing. Although Edwin Black was concerned with judging the ethical character of such assumptions, his rhetorical concept of the "second persona" is basically the same. See Black, "The Second Persona."

47. "Theosophy in New York," *New York World,* September 12, 1886, 13.

48. In general, however, it should be mentioned that newspapers are by and large unreliable as an account of factual occurrences. At best this article merely recapitulates rumors that circulated Blavatsky's name. In this respect, the mention of these individuals is a good indication of who was *thought* to be reading Blavatsky's books.

49. "English common reader" and "common reader" are terms used by the history of composition and book scholars to describe the reading subject in the abstract. See Rose, "Rereading the English Common Reader."

50. Barry Brummett has termed this strategy "transfer," a move that attempts to establish one's authority in two ways: first, transfer enhances one's characterizations of reality by "showing them as continuous with the readings" of sacred or expert texts; second, transfer attempts to "enhance one's own prestige by appearing to possess great powers of discernment and pre-

science not vouchsafed to the ordinary . . . reader." Brummett, "Exploiting Audience Commitment," 59.

51. Blavatsky, "Madame Blavatsky on the Views of the Theosophists." In this passage Blavatsky references the Theosophical doctrine of the soul. She argues that humans are a combination of body, soul, and spirit. The "soul" (which she variously terms "astral body," "astral man," or "double") is composed of three parts: a material body, an immaterial "vital energy" or sort of lust for life ("concupiscible nature"), and an immaterial consciousness ("mind"). Collectively, these three elements are "objective" or visible on earth yet invisible in the spiritual realm, and thus can be destroyed. The "spirit" (or "Nous"), however, is indestructible. It consists of an undifferentiated sort of vital, enduring energy that pervades all existence. Similar to Hegel's "World Spirit" or Schopenhauer's "Will," the Theosophist version of spirit is individuated when it unites with a "soul." Successful unification of the body, spirit, and soul, however, is only one step in the process of eternal living. To achieve eternal life, once individuated, the spirit in "man" must be allowed to grow and receive intuitions of the truth, which is aided by the terrestrial mind. Eventually, each individual is able to reunify with the divine principle yet remain an individual. Also see *Isis Unveiled,* 2:281–86, and *Key to Theosophy,* 107–8.

52. Elizabeth L. Saxon, "Madame Blavatsky: Her Opinions and Her Book," *New Orleans Daily Picayune,* November 4, 1877, 12.

53. Qtd. in Blavatsky, "My Books," 46.

54. Ibid., 47.

55. A reporter from the *Philadelphia Inquirer* writes: "The moment . . . that any one appeared who was antagonistic to her was the moment when she closed her shell. It happened in 1878 that she was interviewed by a man who saw both sides of the question. If she was really the person she claimed to be the world was bound to listen. If she was not it was certain that a worthy successor of Cagliostro had appeared. Accordingly he wrote a series of articles which attracted the attention of the whole country. From that moment the Theosophical Society became an accomplished fact." "Blavatsky's Life," 12.

56. Foote, *The New Cagliostro,* par. 12.

57. In Oppenheim, *The Other World,* 163–64.

58. C. Wilson, *The Occult,* 337.

59. The inadequacy of the name is the central theme in Plato's *Cratylus.* Additionally, in *Republic,* Plato names this technique of using language to surpass language as dialectic: "Here at last, then, we come to the main theme, to be developed in philosophic discussion. It falls within the domain of the intelligible world [that of the eternal Forms]; but its progress is like that of the power of vision in the released prisoner of our parable [the allegory of the

cave]. . . . [T]he summit of the intelligible world is reached in philosophic discussion by one who aspires, through the discourse of reason unaided by the senses, to make his way in every case to the essential reality and perseveres until he has grasped by pure intelligence the very nature of Goodness itself. This journey is what we call Dialectic" (secs. 532–33). The parallel here is that the difficult phrase or strange term comes to stand-in for a philosophic discussion that does not cue or inspire misleading sensations.

60. Blavatsky, "Occultism versus the Occult Arts," 12.

61. Ibid., 13.

62. Blavatsky, "My Books," 49.

63. Covino, *Magic, Rhetoric, and Literacy,* 2–3.

64. Blavatsky, *Key to Theosophy,* sec. 9.

65. In her exhaustive ethnography of practicing witches, *Persuasions of the Witch's Craft,* Tanya M. Luhrmann draws very similar conclusions about the epistemic function of esoteric language. For instance, she argues that the "imagined ambiguity" of magickal terms "grant[s] an imaginative richness because they allow one to respond to words not for their factual content but for the imaginative possibilities they offer. They are remarkable transformations, because they create a vivid let's-pretend world which is neither purely fiction nor confused with the tables-and-chairs reality" (220).

66. Some of the best if not most complex discussions of "pure language" are found in the writings of Walter Benjamin. See especially "The Task of the Translator" and "On Language as Such and the Language of Man."

67. Blavatsky, *The Secret Doctrine,* 1:269.

68. Ibid., 311.

69. Zukav, *The Seat of the Soul,* 13.

70. Ibid., 106.

71. Browne and Harrison, *Life on the Other Side,* 41.

72. David Byrne, Chris Frantz, Jerry Harrison, Tina Weymouth, and Brian Eno, "Once in a Lifetime," performed by the Talking Heads, on *Stop Making Sense,* Sire Records, 1984. Compact Disk.

Chapter 4

1. Crowley, *777,* 125.

2. I will use Crowley's conspicuous spelling of "Qabalah" to denote his version of practice. "Kabbalah" will continue to refer to the Jewish mystical tradition.

3. Crowley, *777,* 125.

4. K. Burke, *The Rhetoric of Religion,* 307. Also see Adorno, *The Stars Down to Earth,* 34–127.

5. Sutin, *Do What Thou Wilt,* 192.

6. Foucault discusses the interplay of social power with the concept of "power/knowledge." For a good overview see his *Power/Knowledge.*

7. Godzich, "Introduction: Caution! Reader at Work!" xxiii.

8. Crowley, *777,* xvii.

9. Ibid., 125.

10. See, e.g., Leff and Sachs, "Words the Most Like Things."

11. Leff, "Textual Criticism," 381.

12. Ibid., 380.

13. Ibid., 381.

14. For a remarkable overview of the theory of romantic criticism, with a number of astonishing parallels to contemporary close textual reading, see Benjamin, "The Concept of Criticism in German Romanticism." Also see Schulte-Sasse's edited collection *Theory as Practice.*

15. See, e.g., Wellek and Warren, *Theory of Literature,* esp. 7–19.

16. Redding, "Extrinsic and Intrinsic Criticism," 96.

17. Gaonkar, "The Oratorical Text," 259.

18. Campbell and Burkholder, *Critiques of Contemporary Rhetoric,* 18–19.

19. Campbell, "Nature of Criticism," 7.

20. Perhaps the masculinist (and therefore heterosexist) tincture of the disciplinary discussions over method need little more evidence than what I have cited here. "Rigor" and "vigor" are two words—and seemingly desirable goals—that appear quite frequently in this literature. Crowley's obsession with phallic symbolism, as I will soon demonstrate, is certainly apropos.

21. Campbell, "Nature of Criticism," 7.

22. Leff, "Interpretation and the Art of the Rhetorical Critic," 345.

23. Eliot, *Selected Prose,* 13.

24. These seem to be the implicit aims of Stephen E. Lucas's close textual analysis of the Declaration of Independence, which is often held up as an paradigm exemplar. See "The Stylistic Artistry of the Declaration of Independence," 531.

25. Lucas, "The Renaissance of American Public Address," 249.

26. Ibid.

27. See Whitson and Poulakos, "Nietzsche and the Aesthetics of Rhetoric"; and Nietzsche, *Nietzsche on Rhetoric and Language.*

28. Leff and Sachs, "Words the Most Like Things," 253.

29. Leff and Sachs argue that "a rhetorical discourse [is] a verbal construction that blends form and content into a concrete whole—a whole that assigns meaning to a region of shared public experience and solicits an audience to embrace the meaning it constructs." Ibid., 255.

30. Lucas, "The Renaissance of American Public Address," 247.

31. Medhurst, "Public Address and Significant Scholarship," 35–36.

32. Gaonkar, "The Disappearance of the Critical Object."

33. Crowley, *Equinox of the Gods,* 97.

34. Hymenaeus Beta, "Editor's Introduction," in Crowley, *Magick,* xli.

35. Ibid.

36. Ibid., xl.

37. Crowley, *Confessions,* 693.

38. Crowley, *Equinox of the Gods,* 117–18.

39. If one accepts Crowley's discussion of the book's authorship, then he or she is reading Crowley's understanding of what Aiwass said, who in turn was relaying the speech of three other gods—Nuit, Hadit, and Ra-Hoor-Khuit—but doing so on Horus's behalf, as Aiwass is his messenger. Being three times removed from the first entity or entities that had the power to signify meaning (which is manifestly unclear: it could be Horus speaking as these three entities, or rather, Horus in two incarnations with another guest, Nuit), one is confused about the authenticity and accuracy of the book. Immediately, confusion over the authorship of the book beckons the reader outside the text for clarification (making it difficult for one to discern the text's internal functions by staying "within" the text).

40. Wellek and Warren, *Theory of Literature,* 158.

41. I am aware that the New Critics René Wellek and Austin Warren would caution that the analysis of sound effects must resist the collapse of the "performance and pattern of sound," although such a collapse seems to be the poetic goal of musical texts. Wellek and Warren, *Theory of Literature,* 158. Patterns exist in texts that are not reducible to their performativity, and often performance can elide patterns that exist in the text.

42. See Crowley, *Equinox of the Gods,* 100–101.

43. See Wellek and Warren, *Theory of Literature,* 158–73.

44. See Klein-Hass, *The Book of the Centre of Pestilence,* pars. 8–10.

45. K. Burke, *A Rhetoric of Motives,* 271.

46. For example, the only poem of Crowley's to receive some critical acclaim, the "Hymn to Pan," reads very similarly: "Thrill with lissome lust of the light, / O man! My man! / Come careering out of the night / Of Pan! Io Pan! / Io Pan! Io Pan! Come over the sea / From Sicily and from Arcady! / Roaming as Bacchus, with fauns and pards / And nymphs and satyrs for thy guards." Crowley, *Magick,* 121. Also ibid., 663.

47. Crowley, *Equinox of the Gods,* 108.

48. Ibid., 94.

49. Ibid., 106.

50. J. G. Melton, "Thelemic Magick in America," 85.

51. In what is known as the "new commentary," Crowley explains that *The Book of the Law*'s symbolic references to "wine" signify ecstatic transportations and that "true religion is intoxication, in a sense. . . . Intoxica-

tion, that is, ecstasy, is the key to Reality. It is explained in 'Energized Enthusiasm' that there are 'three Gods whose function is to bring the Soul to the realization of its own glory: Dionysus, Aphrodite, Apollo—Wine, Women, and Song. . . . It is critics who deny poetry, people without capacity for Ecstasy and Will who call Mysticism moonshine and Magick delusion.'" Crowley, *The Law Is for All,* 85. In the essay "Energized Enthusiasm," Crowley argues that "wine, women, and song" are in actuality an ancient Greek recommendation for the attainment of ecstasy through music, alcohol or similar intoxicants, and sex. (Indeed, women are reduced to their sexual function in this essay; throughout his writings Crowley is ambivalent about the equality of women. Their inability to master the highest grades of the A:.A:., however, is telling.) Although *The Book of the Law*'s multiple references to music, alcohol, and sex are only implied in this essay, it is clear that Crowley finds their use in ritual extremely important and that their mention in *The Book of the Law* is not coincidental. Crowley concludes "Energized Enthusiasm" with an account of a secret ritual of the "Rose Croix degree of Masonry" in which the use of wine, music (primarily that of an organ), and sexual intercourse on the part of the priest and priestess succeed in transporting him to a higher level of consciousness. "I was lost to everything," he says, and "to me it seemed as if eternity itself could not contain the variety and depth of my experiences. Tongue nor pen could record them; and yet I am fain to attempt the impossible" (17).

52. As Lon Milo DuQuette suggests, "magickal exegesis is anything but a quiet, ponderous meditation on meanings. Rather, the Qabalist bombards the mind, drawing parallels and correspondences between absolutely everything and absolutely everything else, until there is no *anything else* left. Eventually something snaps—the mind is transcended, profound *fullness* is achieved, and suddenly the distinction between the perceiver and the perceived disappears." DuQuette, *Angels, Demons, and Gods,* 20.

53. See E. Burke, *A Philosophical Enquiry;* Kant, *Critique of Judgment,* 82–181.

54. E. Burke, *A Philosophical Enquiry,* 51.

55. Kant, *Critique of Judgment,* 82–85.

56. See R. Wilson, *American Sublime,* esp. 3–40.

57. See Schlegel, *Philosophical Fragments,* 1–16.

58. Crowley, *Equinox of the Gods,* 107.

59. Crowley, *The Law Is for All,* 141.

60. For an explanation see Verter, "Dark Star Rising," 299–348; and Crowley, *Crowley's Illustrated Goetia.*

61. Indeed, Crowley provides us with yet another brand of "the rhetoric of silence": Don't talk with your mouth full.

62. Lucas, "The Stylistic Artistry of the Declaration of Independence," 531.

63. In this regard my selection of Crowley is quite deliberate. Crowley's "religion," known as Thelema, is said to consist of sex-magic at the highest levels of initiation. It is only fitting that intrinsic criticism mirror the extrinsic act of intercourse at the intersection of Crowley's ghost.

64. The distinction is de Man's.

65. Gadamer, *Truth and Method,* 273.

66. Godzich, "Introduction," xxvii.

67. Gadamer, *Truth and Method,* 273.

68. Ricoeur, *Freud and Philosophy,* 28–32.

69. This definition comes from Idhe, *Experimental Phenomenology,* 32; also see Ricoeur, *Hermeneutics and the Human Sciences,* 28–30.

70. Ricoeur, *Hermeneutics and the Human Sciences,* 29–30.

71. Mailloux, *Rhetorical Power,* 145.

72. de Man, *Blindness and Insight,* 18.

73. Godzich, "Introduction," xxvii.

74. Leff and Sachs offer up the phenomenon of "iconicity" as evidence that the distinction cannot hold; this evidence, however, fails to address the ontological status of the political speech and the literary text. See "Words the Most Like Things," 269.

75. See Gaonkar, "The Oratorical Text," 275.

76. The best examples of these kind of investigations are found in Leff's work.

77. Greene, "The Textual Apparatus," par. 3.

78. Leff, "Interpretation and the Art of the Rhetorical Critic," 347.

79. Michel Foucault, "My Body, This Paper, This Fire," *Oxford Literary Review* 4 (1979), qtd. in Greene, "The Textual Apparatus," par. 8.

80. Pun intended. Of course, we all have an idea of what this means. Typically, "rigor" is simply a pseudonym for "smart" or "work like I would." Inferior critical work is thus described as "sloppy" and "facile."

81. These problems have been collected under the category of "critical invention." For an excellent examination of the problem see Nothstine, Blair, and Copeland, *Critical Questions.*

82. Jameson, *Marxism and Form,* 328–29.

Interlude: Re-membering Crowley

1. Readers familiar with the Christian Evangelical minister Bob Larson will recognize this kind of "seminar" or meeting. For an excellent historical account of the rise of Evangelical organizations obsessed with Satanism and demons see Ellis, *Raising the Devil,* esp. 32–61.

2. Ozzy Osborne, "Mr. Crowley," *Blizzard of Oz,* remastered version, performed by Ozzy Osborne. Epic Records, 1981. Compact Disk.

3. Langone and Blood, *Satanism and Occult-Related Violence,* 29.

4. Passantino and Passantino, *When the Devil Dares Your Kids.* Also see Larson, *Satanism;* and Raschke, *Painted Black.* Raschke's error-filled tome is frequently cited by the seemingly secular academics who profess a belief in an epidemic of Satanic ritual abuse.

5. Don Shirley, "Unlikely Characters Collide in Fanciful World," *Los Angeles Times,* January 29, 1999, 28.

6. Howard Cohen, "Ozzy, the Dead, Still Knows How to Rock Center Stage," *Buffalo News,* July 28, 1988, 6C.

7. "Library Files Checked in Zodiac Investigation," *New York Times,* July 18, 1990, 4.

8. March Franchetti Dortmund, "German Young Find Solace in Satanism," *Sunday Times* (U.K.), May 5, 1996, par. 3; available from http://www.crowleyana.co.uk (accessed January 22, 2001).

9. "Mother Accused of Murder Was Fascinated by the Occult and Black Magic, Jury Hears," *The Herald* (U.K)., October 4, 1996, 3.

10. Barbie Dutter, "Murdered Boy Laid Out for Sacrifice," *The Telegraph* (U.K.), October 4, 1996, par. 1–2; available from http://www.crowleyana.co.uk (accessed January 22, 2001).

11. Sinason, *Treating Survivors of Satanist Abuse,* 3. Similar alarmist essays can be found in Sakheim and Devine, *Out of Darkness.* A disturbing account of the hysteria of "professionals" regarding Satanic ritual abuse is Nathan and Snedeker's *Satan's Silence.* Helpful readings of Satanic panic among academics and professionals can be found in Richardson, Best, and Bromley, *The Satanism Scare,* esp. Mulhern, "Satanism and Psychotherapy." Finally, also of interest is Showalter, *Hystories,* esp. 171–88.

12. See Ellis, *Raising the Devil,* 1–61.

13. Verter, "Dark Star Rising," 286.

Chapter 5

1. Crowley, *777,* 125.

2. See Sutin, *Do What Thou Wilt,* 73–79.

3. Many of the rituals are also currently available in Regardie, *The Golden Dawn.*

4. Hutchinson, *Aleister Crowley,* 119. For another account of this trial see Sutin, *Do What Thou Wilt,* 204–6.

5. From "Secrets of the Rosicrucians: Protest against the Publication of Mysteries. Two Cats in the Bag," *Weekly News* (London), March 22, 1910. Accounts of the trial are fascinating and amusing. See "Secrets of a Mystic Society," *London Daily Express,* March 23, 1910; and "Rosicrucian Mysteries," *The Standard,* March 22, 1910. Hutchinson's account in *Aleister*

Crowley (204–7) is comical. All of these accounts are available online at http:www.crowleyana.co.uk (accessed January 22, 2001).

6. See Brummett, "Exploiting Audience Commitment."

7. See Scholes, *The Rise and Fall of English*, esp. 37–58.

8. The term "dialectic of control" comes from Giddens, *The Constitution of Society*, 16.

9. Kierkegaard, *The Sickness unto Death*, 99.

10. Ibid., 14–21. I should note that I chose the term "surrender" over "leap" because the latter is misleading. Aside from the fact that Kierkegaard never described religion as "a leap of faith," the term "leap" implies some sort of willed determination. As Kierkegaard himself puts it: "Suppose a man who wishes to acquire faith; let the comedy begin. He wishes to have faith, but he wishes also to safeguard himself by means of an objective inquiry and its approximation-process. What happens? . . . [Faith] becomes extremely and empathically probable. . . . Now he is ready to believe . . . and lo, now it has become precisely impossible to believe it . . . [because] anything that is almost probable, or probable, or extremely and emphatically probable, is something he can almost know . . . but it is impossible to *believe*. For the absurd is the object of faith, and the only object that can be believed." One does not, in other words, take a "leap of faith," but leaps *into* faith, as if to simply "give up." Kierkegaard, *Concluding Unscientific Postscript*, 220–21. Also see Ferreira, "Faith and the Kierkegaardian Leap," 207–34.

11. Darsey, *The Prophetic Tradition*, 19.

12. Crenshaw, *Prophetic Conflict*, qtd. in Darsey, *The Prophetic Tradition*, 30–33.

13. Adorno, *The Stars Down to Earth*, 38.

14. K. Burke, *The Rhetoric of Religion*, 307.

15. Analyzing Augustine's rhetoric, Burke also notes the ubiquity of the self-sealing argument: "If one doubts the faith, his will is impaired, which means that he lacks grace, which means that God is turning from him (thus allowing him of his free will to go to hell). Thus, any deficiency in the will to persevere was per se an indication that one was moving toward damnation." Ibid., 271.

16. This definition is informed by R. S. Downie's discussion of "authority" in the *Oxford Companion to Philosophy*, 68–69. This understanding of authority has been hotly debated in recent years, most especially in analytical philosophy and argumentation theory. For example, some argumentation scholars, following Aristotle's lead in *The Rhetoric*, argue that authority is a process or quality of communicative phenomena bound by a given rhetorical encounter, situation, or argumentative field and not a trait of character. See Liu, "Authority, Presumption, and Invention." For good overviews of the conceptual terrain of authority, also see Pennock and Chapman, *Nomos*

XXXIX, for the philosophical perspectives, and J. B. White, *Acts of Hope,* for the rhetorical and literary perspectives.

17. M. Weber, *Theory of Social and Economic Organization,* 328.

18. Ibid., 341.

19. Ibid., 358.

20. For a thorough discussion of traditional authority see Friedrich, *Tradition and Authority.* For a more wide-ranging overview of a number of authority forms see Lukes, "Perspectives on Authority," 59–75.

21. M. Weber, "The Prophet," in *Max Weber on Charisma and Institution Building,* 254.

22. See Luther, "Address to the Christian Nobility," 2.

23. For classic accounts see Oberman, *Luther;* and Brecht, *Martin Luther;* also see Todd, *Martin Luther.*

24. For other treatments of prophecy, particularly those that concern ethos and/or charisma, see Betz, "Fromm and the Rhetoric of Prophecy"; Bobbit and Mixon, "Prophecy and Apocalypse"; Pauley, "Reshaping Public Persona and the Prophetic Ethos"; O'Leary and McFarland, "The Political Use of Mystic Discourse"; and Zulick, "The Agon of Jeremiah." Insightful discussions of prophecy outside a rhetorical perspective include Clements, *Old Testament Prophecy;* and Russell, *Prophecy and the Apocalyptic Dream.* For work outside the discipline of rhetorical studies that nevertheless focuses on rhetorical aspects see Heschel, *The Prophets;* R. B. Y. Scott, *The Relevance of the Prophets;* and Westermann, *Basic Forms of Prophetic Speech.* Unfortunately, as Karlyn Kohrs Campbell has noted (in "A Toad in the Garden"), scholars have tended to overlook female prophets and the profound role women have played in the evolution of Protestantism. For discussions about the role of women in the prophetic tradition see Taber, *The Prophetic Stream.*

25. Darsey, *The Prophetic Tradition,* 6–8.

26. As R. L. Scott has remarked to me many times in personal communication, "In the beginning there was the error."

27. Aristotle, *On Rhetoric,* 121.

28. Darsey, *The Prophetic Tradition,* 9–10.

29. Ibid., 21.

30. Ibid., 20.

31. Ibid., 28.

32. For a more thorough discussion of why self-evidence and related forms are fallacious see Perelman and Olbrechts-Tyteca, *The New Rhetoric,* esp. 1–4, 32–33, and 510–511.

33. See, e.g., Randi, *Truth about Uri Geller.*

34. See Augustine, *On Christian Doctrine,* 2:34–78.

35. For an excellent discussion of the recollective versus more "repetitive"

or more forward-looking modes of critical interpretation see Caputo, *Radical Hermeneutics,* esp. 16–18.

36. Kierkegaard, *Fear and Trembling/Repetition,* 136.

37. See Ricoeur, *Freud and Philosophy,* 3–36.

38. Crowley, *Magick without Tears,* 44–47.

39. This kind of self-referencing is typical of many of Crowley's writings. Examples abound, for instance, in his magnum opus, *Magick;* see 137, 139, 182.

40. Crowley, *Magick without Tears,* 48.

41. Crowley, *777,* xix.

42. Crowley rejects the rabbinical Jewish tradition, which regards Qabalistic mysticism as heretical and dangerous (e.g., Jewish mystics do not believe the God of the Old Testament is the Supreme Being. "That honor goes to an inscrutable preexistent negative totality called *Ain Soph*—a great Zero, out of which emanates the one and subsequently the many"). See DuQuette, *Angels, Demons, and Gods,* 19. Further, Crowley also rejects the Jewish mystical tradition of Kabbalistic interpretation, which yearns for, in a profound spiritual sense, a primordial understanding of past worship and the reattainment of cosmic consciousness without giving up or abjuring the secular world. See Matt, *The Essential Kabbalah,* 2.

43. Crowley, *Liber Aleph Vel CXI,* 2. Also see DuQuette, *Angels, Demons, and Gods,* 19–20.

44. DuQuette, *Angels, Demons, and Gods,* 20.

45. Ibid., 29.

46. Crowley, *Equinox of the Gods,* 98.

47. Ibid., 98–99.

48. Parzival's story is often associated with Arthurian legends and with a very difficult poem written by Wolfram von Eschenback sometime in the thirteenth century. Parzival is a "fool" who wanted to be a knight of the Round Table but was often laughed away by the king and his court. Eventually, after many trials and tribulations, he becomes the keeper of the Holy Grail after being helped toward spiritual awakening by a hermit. Crowley is probably most familiar with this tale through Wagner, whose *Parsifal* is based on this difficult poem.

49. Crowley, *The Book of Thoth,* 53.

50. Crowley, *Equinox of the Gods,* 126.

51. See Fisher, "Toward a Logic of Good Reasons."

52. See Gunn, "Refitting Fantasy," 12–16.

53. K. Burke, *A Rhetoric of Motives,* 279.

54. See Kojève, *Introduction to the Reading of Hegel.*

55. Plato, *Gorgias,* secs. 462d–465.

56. Darsey, *The Prophetic Tradition,* 22.

57. Cicero, *On Oratory and Orators,* 1: sec. 8.
58. Lacan, "The Mirror Stage."

Interlude: On Stolen Letters and Lettered Secrets

1. Lacan, "The Purloined Letter," 198.
2. Ibid., 196.
3. See also Derrida, *The Gift of Death;* and Soros, "Giving Death."
4. See Lacan, "The Subversion of the Subject," 304.
5. Glynos and Stavrakakis, "Postures and Impostures," 685–86.
6. Lacan, "The Purloined Letter," 194.
7. Sokal and Bricmont, *Fashionable Nonsense,* 27.
8. "For the phallus is a signifier, a signifier whose function, in the intrasubjective economy of analysis, may lift the veil from the function it served in the mysteries. For it is the signifier that is destined to designate meaning effects as a whole, insofar as the signifier conditions them by its presence as signifier." Lacan, "The Signification of the Phallus," 275.
9. For example: "What then is the formula of the initiation of Horus? . . . It will be the natural growth of the Child. . . . The hieroglyph is 'The Fool': The innocent and impotent Harpocrates Babe becomes the Horus Adult by obtaining the Wand. *Der reine Thor* seizes the Sacred Lance. Bacchus becomes Pan. The Holy Guardian Angel is the Unconscious Creature Self—the Spiritual Phallus." Crowley, "*Ars Congressus Cum Daemone,*" in *Magick,* 523.
10. Fink, *Lacan to the Letter,* 130–31.
11. Fink, *Clinical Introduction,* 220.
12. Borch-Jacobson, *Lacan;* Althusser, *Writings on Psychoanalysis,* 21.

Chapter 6

1. Sutin, *Do What Thou Wilt,* 205–6.
2. "Secrets of the Rosicrucians: Protest against the Publication of Mysteries. Two Cats in the Bag," *Weekly News* (London), March 22, 1910; reprinted in Hutchinson, *Aleister Crowley,* 119.
3. A trend that one could argue began with the publication of Mozart's opera *The Magic Flute.* See Mellers, "Little Time to Spare." For an interesting discussion of Mozart's interest in the occult see Grattan-Guinness, "Why Did Mozart Write Three Symphonies in the Summer of 1788?"
4. T. Smith, *The Books of the Beast,* 18. The reader may recall from the previous chapter that the number 418 is a magic one for Crowley. Smith explains: "Like the pricing of the 'Blue' Equinox (Detroit, 1919) at 666 cents and the quarto-divisible sums charged for *Book Four, Parts One* and *Two,* [Crowley's pricing of the U.S. and German editions] have deeply significant

meanings. To begin with, Crowley believed the Law's messenger was spelled Avias, its Hebrew numerical equivalent being 78. . . . Just before [the publication of the creation of a fourth version of *The Book of the Law* in the U.K.], it was revealed to him that the correct spelling was Aiwza, which in Hebrew yields 93. '418' is the numerical equivalent of yet another, Greek, spelling of Aiwaz, 'AIFASS.' "

5. Verter, "Dark Star Rising," 96–115.

6. Ibid., 252.

7. See chapter 1 for a discussion of the transformation of occult style. It should also be noted that the most secret of occult books are widely available and relatively inexpensive. A facsimile copy of *The Book of the Law* costs one $7.98 on the amazon.com website.

8. See Anderson, *Imagined Communities.*

9. Arnold, *Culture and Anarchy,* 50–52.

10. See Leavis, *Mass Civilization and Minority Culture.*

11. Ibid., 9–10.

12. See Lowery and DeFleur, *Milestones in Mass Communication Research,* 21–67.

13. See Horkheimer and Adorno, *Dialectic of Enlightenment: Philosophical Fragments,* esp. 94–136.

14. See S. Hall, "The Rediscovery of Ideology"; Hoggart, *The Uses of Literacy;* Williams, "Culture Is Ordinary" and "The Masses."

15. Williams, "The Masses," 46.

16. Lang, *Irony/Humor,* 60.

17. Foucault, *The Archaeology of Knowledge,* 55.

18. For example, see Baudrillard, *The Illusion of the End.*

19. Hutcheon, *Irony's Edge,* 117. Also see Wimsatt and Brooks, *Literary Criticism.*

20. Wellek and Warren, *Theory of Literature,* 42.

21. In the landmark *Rhetorical Criticism: A Study in Method,* Edwin Black remarks that the critic is "invited to disaster" by Freudian approaches: someone "who speaks or writes reads Freud and learns that he can disguise his true motives by writing and speaking of arrows, for he knows that his auditors, themselves having been influenced by Freud, will interpret arrow to mean phallus and not, as it means to him, something entirely different. In short, just as Freud discovered that a person who has mastered ordinary language can use it to conceal his motives, so a person who has mastered Freudian vocabulary can use it too to conceal his motives. The possibilities of deception, deliberate or unconscious, seem endless, and consequently the problems presented the psychological critic seem insoluble" (26–27). Interestingly, intentionality is at the heart of Black's concern. In my mind, the

exemplar case is Hill, "Conventional Wisdom—Traditional Form." In his analysis of Nixon's speech, Hill deliberately brackets issues of intention and motive, focusing on the text itself. The ensuing debate with Karlyn Kohrs Campbell about whether ethical judgments can be made is particularly enlightening in this respect. See Campbell, " 'Conventional Wisdom—Traditional Form.' "

22. For interesting discussion see Becker, "Determinism as a Rhetorical Problem."

23. McKerrow, "Critical Rhetoric," 101.

24. "The 'denial' of an agent as productive of contingently derived social practices does not rule out the present role of persons as active participants in 'revolt' against the present dangers. Otherwise, there is no point to positing the possibilities of freedom—and a Sartrean angst is preordained as the condition of passive acceptance of one's fate." Ibid., 99.

25. Cloud, "The Materiality of Discourse as Oxymoron," 159.

26. See Davidson, "Intending"; and Pradhan, "The Dream of a Common Language."

27. Wittgenstein, *Culture and Value,* 3e.

28. Benjamin, "Theses on the Philosophy of History." My reading of this essay is detailed at length in Gunn, "Benjamin's Magic."

29. Swearingen, *Rhetoric and Irony,* 55–94.

30. Cicero, *On Oratory and Orators,* 2: sec. 252.

31. Booth, *A Rhetoric of Irony,* 6.

32. Perelman and Olbrechts-Tyteca, *The New Rhetoric,* 208.

33. Walker, *Encyclopedia of the Occult,* 7–27.

34. Kierkegaard, *The Concept of Irony,* 248–49.

35. Ibid., 249.

36. Hutcheon, *Irony's Edge,* 2.

37. K. Burke, "Four Master Tropes," 516–17.

38. Ibid., 512.

39. Jameson, *Marxism and Form,* 330–31.

40. Ibid., 329.

41. Crowley, *The Book of the Law,* chapter 3, verses 11–12.

42. Crowley, *Magick,* 207.

43. Ibid., 206.

44. Ibid., 207.

45. Ibid.

46. Ibid., 210 n. 3.

47. A humorous account is found in Sutin, *Do What Thou Wilt,* 242–51. Also, Verter argues that Crowley was party to a "Bohemian" conceit known as a *blague:* "Aleister Crowley was not content with privatized ritual,

and instead joined other members of the avant-garde in staging outrageous *blagues* calculated to attract publicity, including giving flip answers to the press." Verter, "Dark Star Rising," 283.

48. Crowley, *Magick without Tears,* 284–85.

49. Kierkegaard, *The Concept of Irony,* 247–48.

50. Crowley, *The Vision and the Voice,* 20.

51. In Sutin, *Do What Thou Wilt,* 277.

52. Cross, "Neither Either Nor Or," 136.

53. Kierkegaard, *The Concept of Irony,* 177.

54. Cross, "Neither Either Nor Or," 129.

55. Ibid.

56. Ibid.

57. Crowley, *The Law Is for All,* 33.

58. Ibid., 102.

59. Ibid., 115.

60. Ibid., 116.

61. Ibid., 131.

62. Ibid., 116.

63. Ibid., 37. In the light of these remarks, one might retitle the second commentary *The Law Is for All, But Not Necessarily You.*

64. Crowley, *Magick without Tears,* 442.

65. Ibid., 443.

66. Ibid., 444.

67. E. J. Hobsbawm, as qtd. in Sutin, *Do What Thou Wilt,* 17.

68. Sutin, *Do What Thou Wilt,* 37.

69. DuQuette, *The Magic of Thelema,* xv.

70. Booth, *A Rhetoric of Irony,* 39.

71. Crowley says: "The Eucharist of *Two* Elements has its matter of the passives. The wafer (apentacle) is of corn, typical of Earth; the wine (Cup) represents Water. (There are certain other attributions. The wafer is the Sun, for instance; and the wine is appropriate to Bacchus.) The wafer may, however, be more complex, the 'Cake of Light' described in *Liber Legis.* This is used in the exoteric 'Mass of Phoenix' mixed with the blood of the Magus. This Mass should be performed daily at sunset by every Magician. Corn and wine are equivalent to flesh and blood; but it is easier to convert live substance into the body and blood of God, than to perform this miracle upon dead matter." *Magick,* 268.

72. Ibid., 740, n. 238.

73. Another example: regarding the "Cakes of Light" and the *kind* of blood required for their making, Crowley says nothing in his published commentaries. In the larger, voluminous commentary that has gone mostly unpublished (the following being an exception, of course), Crowley interprets

Ra-Hoor-Khuit's recipe: "A: menstrual blood. B: possibly 'dragon's blood.' These two kinds of 'blood' are not to be confused. The student should be able to discover the sense of this passage by recollecting the Qabalistic statement that 'The blood is the life,' consulting *Book 4* Part III [*Magick*], and applying the knowledge which reposes in the Sanctuary of the Gnosis of the Ninth Degree of O.T.O. The 'child' is 'BABALON and THE BEAST conjoined, the Secret Savior' . . . It is inadvisable to word this explanation in terms too intelligible to the profane, since uninitiated attempts to make use of the formidable arcana of Magick presented in this passage could lead only to the most fulminating and irremediable disaster." Apparently the "disaster" is the sacrifice of an actual child that ends in death. Nevertheless, Crowley's intentional obfuscation about the meaning of "blood" and "sacrifice" here is indicative of a textual instability under the trope of irony, the sort that marks some kind of textual finitude. Ibid., 739–40, n. 238.

74. One finds the same the generative power of intertextuality—the consequence of the instability of occult irony—in the work of many modern occultists, from the thousand-page tomes of G. I. Gurdjieff to the deliberately deceitful Satanic tracts of Anton LaVey. Further, that verbal irony invites the problem of intertextuality is not limited to traditionally ironic occult texts, for esoteric jargon seems to invite the same sort of problems. Blavatsky kept writing to continually reproduce and re-signify occult meanings; current "New Age" systems like ECKANKAR and Scientology continuously produce books to elaborate their respective transcendental signifieds. Given that the logic of metaphor is that of replacement or re-signification (the interplay of the tenor and vehicle), one could even argue that belief systems based on particularly strange or appealing metaphors can also operate similarly, a given authority chaining out text after text to repeatedly circumscribe intertextual regress. For example, John Gray's wildly successful "Mars and Venus" books are "occult" in this regard. See especially E. S. Weber, "The Rhetoric of Mars and Venus."

75. R. R. McGuire, "Speech Acts," 31.

76. Crowley, *Magick without Tears*, 284.

77. "An Amazing Sect," *The Looking Glass*, October 29, 1910; available from http://www.crowleyana.co.uk (accessed May 5, 2001).

78. "Aleister Crowley's Orgies in Sicily," *London Sunday Express*, November 26, 1922; available from http://www.crowleyana.co.uk (accessed May 5, 2001).

79. "Crowley's Plans," *London Sunday Express*, precise date unknown (estimated late 1922 or early 1923); available from http:www.crowleyana.co.uk (accessed February 16, 2001).

80. "A Wizard of Wickedness," *John Bull*, March 17, 1923; available from http://www.crowleyana.co.uk (accessed February 16, 2001).

81. "The Wickedest Man in the World," *John Bull*, March 24, 1923; available from http://www.crowleyana.co.uk (accessed February 16, 2001).

82. Crowley, *Confessions*, 762.

83. See Sutin, *Do What Thou Wilt*, 367–74, for an account of the trial. Crowley is made the fool by the lawyers, and his refusal to demonstrate his powers by making himself invisible in court was widely reported.

84. From a *John Bull* story sometime in April 1923, as reprinted in Stephensen, *The Legend of Aleister Crowley*, 154. A number of similar stories are collected in Stephensen's book and quoted at length.

85. Stephensen, *The Legend of Aleister Crowley*, 155–56.

86. " 'Do Anything You Want to Do'—Their Religion," *American Weekly*, November 1922, in Verter, "Dark Star Rising," frontis.

87. "At the Sacrifice of a Cat" [illustration and caption], *New York American*, April 8, 1923. The illustration is only available for viewing in a special collection. A legible copy is reproduced in Verter, "Dark Star Rising," 321 (Verter has humorously retitled the picture "The Tabby of Thelema").

88. Ibid.

89. From the *New York World*, as printed in Stephensen, *The Legend of Aleister Crowley*, 117.

90. "An Amazing Sect."

91. "Rites of Eleusis: Classicism and Mysticism at Caxton Hall," *Morning Leader*, October 15, 1910; available from http://www.crowleyana.co.uk (accessed May 5, 2001).

92. "An Amazing Sect."

93. "The Kind of Depravity," *John Bull*, March 10, 1923; available from http://www.crowleyana.co.uk (accessed May 5, 2001).

94. "The Wickedest Man in the World."

95. March Franchetti Dortmund, "German Young Find Solace in Satanism," *Sunday Times*, May 5, 1996: par. 3; available from http://www.crowleyana.co.uk (accessed May 5, 2001).

96. Gustav Niebuhr, "Witches Cast as the Neo-Pagans Next Door," *New York Times*, October 31, 1999, 30.

97. Lisa J. Adams, "Exorcisms Maintain a Spirited Following among Mexican Faithful," *Los Angeles Times*, January 7, 2001, B3.

98. Mauss, *A General Theory of Magic*, 88.

Chapter 7

1. Felix, *Octavius*, 336–37.

2. Smith and Pazder, *Michelle Remembers*.

3. Not too coincidentally, Pazder and Smith also divorced their spouses and married each other.

4. These kinds of books continued to appear until the mid 1990s. See, e.g., R. Brown, *He Came to Set the Captives Free.*

5. Stratford and Michaelson, *Satan's Underground.*

6. A Christian magazine titled *Cornerstone* was responsible for exposing as frauds Stratford and a number of other Satanic ritual abuse survivors, such as Mike Warnke. See Passantino, Passantino, and Trott, "Satan's Sideshow"; and Hertenstein and Trott, *Selling Satan.* A number of academics continue to believe in Satanic ritual abuse, however; see Sakheim and Devine, *Out of Darkness;* and Sinason, *Treating Survivors of Satanist Abuse.* Challenges to hypnotic regression techniques can be found in Richardson, Best, and Bromley's excellent edited volume, *The Satanism Scare;* and Showalter, *Hystories,* 144–58.

7. On a CNBC program titled "Wrongly Accused and Convicted of Child Molesting," Geraldo Rivera recanted his sensational 1980s programs on Satanic ritual abuse: "I want to announce publicly that I was a firm believer of the 'Believe the Children' movement of the 1980s, that started with the McMartin trials in California, but now I am convinced that I was terribly wrong. . . . and many innocent people were convicted and went to prison as a result. . . . and I am equally positive [that the] 'Repressed Memory Therapy Movement' is also a bunch of crap." "Geraldo Rivera's Influence."

8. The definitive explanation is Victor, *Satanic Panic.* Victor argues that the Satanic panic was a scapegoating phenomenon goaded by a mass perception of moral decline in the United States. Another excellent analysis of the Satanic panic is Ellis, *Raising the Devil.*

9. Sinason, *Treating Survivors of Satanist Abuse,* 5.

10. Denna Allen and Janet Midwinter, "The Debunking of a Myth," *The Mail on Sunday* (London), September 20, 1990, 41.

11. Although there is little evidence to support the contention that there exists a vast Satanic underground, there is some evidence to suggest that *some* pedophiles have deliberately used cultish garb and pseudo-ritual to *frighten* their victims into silence. See Lanning, *Investigator's Guide.*

12. Qtd. in Bass and Davis, *The Courage to Heal,* 421.

13. Sinason, *Treating Survivors of Satanist Abuse,* 7.

14. See Felix, *Octavius,* 336–37.

15. Of course, rituals that were deliberately intended as Satanic or described as such already appeared in popular literature and occult tomes since the emergence of occultism as the study of secret knowledge and ritual—in the mid- to late seventeenth century. Hammer horror films are largely responsible for their emergence on the silver screen in the 1960s (see, e.g., *The Devil Rides Out,* released in 1968; Hammer is the name of the production studio). Widespread popular interest in Satanic ritual, however, can be laid at the feet of Anton LaVey and, to a lesser extent, the rituals that appear in Roman

Polanski's 1972 theatrical success, *Rosemary's Baby.* Prior to the creation of the Church of Satan, for instance, the now ubiquitous symbol for a goat's head circumscribed by an inverted pentagram—the Sigil of Baphomet—was not widely recognized as a Satanic symbol. After the book's publication and LaVey's publicity campaigns, the symbol began to appear frequently in horror movies, and Dennis Wheatley's popular "black magic" novel series was repackaged with the sigil prominently displayed on the covers.

16. Marx, *Capital,* 1:125–77.

17. Ibid., 270–80.

18. The term "late capitalism" first appeared in the work of Horkheimer and Adorno, for whom it denoted the emergence of a complex web of "bureaucratic control" and the "interpenetration of government and big business." See Jameson, *Postmodernism,* xviii.

19. Baudrillard, *Simulacra and Simulation,* 5.

20. Jameson, *Postmodernism,* xx–xxi, 1–54.

21. See Douglas and Isherwood, *The World of Goods,* 65; Jhally, *The Codes of Advertising,* 9–12.

22. Jhally, *The Codes of Advertising,* 9.

23. Ibid., 12; also see Baudrillard, *The Mirror of Production.*

24. Marx, *Capital,* 1:138.

25. This argument is made by Comaroff and Comaroff, "Millennial Capitalism."

26. See Campbell and Jamieson, *Form and Genre;* Miller, "Genre as Social Action."

27. Adorno, "On Jazz." Rhetoricians will recognize that Adorno's position on popular form is very similar to the definition of form offered by Kenneth Burke, which is derived from music: "Form is the creation of an appetite in the mind of the auditor, and the adequate satisfying of that appetite." *Counter-Statement,* 31.

28. Barton, *The Church of Satan,* 82.

29. LaVey, *The Satanic Bible,* 44.

30. Ibid., 97.

31. Barton, *The Church of Satan,* 9.

32. Ibid., 15–31. Zeena LaVey, as well as her mother and Diane, have since broken with the Church of Satan. Zeena currently performs in her gothic band Radio Werewolf (along with her partner Barry "Nikolas Schreck" Dubin) and is a member of the Temple of Set, a rival Satanic church. Again, the story of occultism is the story of infighting.

33. Ibid., 24–25.

34. Both Reuters and the Alternative Press issued obituaries, and a brief mention of LaVey's death was made on ABC's nightly news program.

35. These past odd jobs are frequently repeated in exposés of LaVey, al-

though there is little evidence to substantiate their truth. Given LaVey's penchant for dissimulation, it is likely that large parts of his autobiography are simply fabrications. See Aquino, *The Church of Satan,* 15–25. The "authorized" biography is Blanche Barton's *The Secret Life of a Satanist.*

36. Aquino, *The Church of Satan,* 52.

37. Ibid.

38. Ibid., 54. See Redbeard, *Might Is Right.* The book is very popular among neo-Nazis. It should be mentioned that Aquino's Temple of Set and the Church of Satan are at "war" with one another and that Aquino's accounts are not (as with any historical narrative) objective. Nevertheless, his research seemed balanced, and it is well documented. Zeena LaVey has corroborated all of Aquino's claims about the Church of Satan. The Church of Satan's official position about these claims is that Zeena and her partner wished to take control of the church.

39. Peter Gilmore (High Priest of the Church of Satan), e-mail to the author, July 4, 2001.

40. See Crowley, *Magick,* 47–116.

41. *Los Angeles Times,* July 17, 1979, sec. 1, 24–5.

42. LaVey, *The Satanic Bible,* 25.

43. These nine statements are an apt condensation of John Galt's screed against altruism and mysticism in *Atlas Shrugged.* See Ayn Rand, *Atlas Shrugged,* 927–93.

44. Aquino, *The Church of Satan,* 53.

45. LaVey, *The Satanic Bible,* 21.

46. Ibid., 22.

47. The statistics about the Church of Satan's membership and the number of Satanic bibles sold were unverifiable and likely exaggerations.

48. Comment made by Kenneth Wooden in his *20/20* program "The Devil Worshippers," which originally aired on May 16, 1985.

49. LaVey, *The Satanic Rituals,* 17–18.

50. Peter Gilmore, telephone conversation with author, May 24, 2001. Aquino disputes this claim as an ironic misdirection in his account of the early days of the church. In the beginning, Aquino argues, rituals were all about evoking the forces of darkness. Aquino suggests that one of the reasons for his break from the church had to do with its membership's declining interest in ritual as real magic.

51. See Delbanco's *The Death of Satan* for an interesting account of the United States' lack of a good repertoire of representations of evil. Also see Gunn, "The Rhetoric of Exorcism."

52. Baddeley, *Lucifer Rising:* "*There are a number of Satanists who identify their ideas with Nazism and the Far Right. What's your opinion on that.* [LaVey:] The link is often an aesthetic one. For example, there was this girl I

saw not long ago wearing a long coat. The coat was unmistakably a Nazi artefact [*sic*], while she was Jewish. Psychologically the two are irreconcilable, but on an aesthetic level they were understandable. The aesthetic appeal lies in the dramatic fashion of the Nazi militaria. The Nazis understood the meaning of visuals and sounds, and how to use them—take their use of a lot of black leather in their uniforms and 'oompah' music in their marches for example. There were some pretty smart guys involved with the Nazi movement—they knew how basic material could reach the soul. Their aesthetics appealed to the religiosity in people. My own prejudices are not ethnic but ethical—somebody's race or background really has nothing to do with it. Under Hitler many prominent Jews were 'Aryanised.' This has been documented, but it's been quietly swept under the carpet. There was a Zionist-Nazi pact establishing Madagascar as the Jewish homeland. Goebbels even struck a medal to commemorate the deal" (76). The nonchalant character of LaVey's musings on Nazi aesthetics, I think, is particularly telling—and highly troublesome. Also see LaVey, "The Jewish Question?"

53. LaVey, "The Church of Satan," 30.

54. Ibid., 30–32; also see LaVey, "Entertain Me," "How to Be God," and "Let Me Entertain You."

55. There is a great deal of disagreement among scientists and philosophers as to whether all images are visual. Mental images, e.g., are not explicitly visual yet appear to function in very similar ways. Nevertheless, by "image" I mean to refer to the picture.

56. Barthes, *Image, Music, Text,* 17.

57. More specifically, "illusionism" is premised on a kind of "guided projection," a cognitive experience of the viewer of an image moving from the materiality of the object (globs of paint, dots of ink, pixels of light) to a semblance of the whole representation as a discrete thing. See Gombrich, *Art and Illusion.*

58. Lancioni, "The Rhetoric of the Frame," 403.

59. See Barthes, *Image, Music, Text,* 32–52; and Foss, "Ambiguity as Persuasion." Because of the illusory reality effect of images and their need for contextual codes, most work on the rhetoric of image has focused on the manipulation of audiences by imagery. In cinema studies, the reality effect of images has been explored in terms of how the spectator is "positioned" in an ideological system through an identification with the camera. In visual studies, the reality effect of images has been explored in relationship to cognition, particularly in terms of how the brain is "hard wired" to perceive images in a certain way. In journalism, cultural, and rhetorical studies, the reality effect of the image has been explored in terms of how images are used to mislead audiences through their alteration (e.g., airbrushing) or by providing codes of interpretation that are ideologically or politically suspect. In the present context, the reality effect of images helps to explain why the images created

by LaVey in the late 1960s have come to take on radically different meanings. For an excellent literature review see Messaris, "Visual Literacy and Manipulation."

60. See especially Aquino, *The Church of Satan.*

61. Lanham, *A Handlist of Rhetorical Terms,* 152.

62. Aquino, *The Church of Satan,* 26–35.

63. Ibid., 25.

64. "The Devil Worshippers," a *20/20* program (ABC News), May 16, 1985.

65. For a description of the content of these programs see de Young, "Breeders for Satan." De Young notes that, overwhelmingly, Satanic ritual abuse survivors tend to be women, and he convincingly argues that at least part of the panic over Satanism can be explained as an obvious recapitulation of patriarchal norms.

66. See Baudrillard, *The Mirror of Production.* He expands this argument later in *Critique of the Political Economy of the Sign.*

67. Baudrillard, *The Mirror of Production;* Jameson, *Postmodernism,* esp. ix–xxii and 353–56.

68. LaVey, *The Satanic Bible,* 21.

Chapter 8

1. This dialogue is actually taken from the film. The version consulted in this chapter is *The Ninth Gate,* prod. and dir. Roman Polanski, 133 min., Artisan Home Entertainment, 2000, DVD. The screenplay is somewhat different; see Polanski, Brownjohn, and Urbizu, *The Ninth Gate.*

2. Perhaps such tongue-dangling is the proverbial "devil's mark."

3. Milton, *Paradise Lost/Paradise Regained,* 48.

4. Roger Ebert, review of *The Ninth Gate* in the *Chicago Sun-Times Online,* March 2000; available from http://www.suntimes.com/ebert/ebert_reviews/2000/03/031003.html (accessed October 23, 2001).

5. George Meyer, "Will 'Ninth Gate' Close the Book on Polanski?" *Sarasota Herald Tribute,* March 10, 2000, 18.

6. Marshall Fine, " 'The Ninth Gate': Weak Script Undermines Horror in Latest Polanski Film," *Gannet News Service,* March 10, 2000; available from http://www.rochestergoesout.com/mov/n/ninthg.html (accessed October 23, 2001).

7. William Arnold, "Exotic 'Ninth Gate' Breaks Down in Clichés," *Seattle Post-Intelligencer,* March 10, 2000; available from http://seattlep-i.nwsource.com/movies/gateq.shtml (accessed October 23, 2001).

8. Owen Gleiberman and Lisa Schwarzbaum, "The Week [movie reviews]," *Entertainment Weekly,* April 7, 2000, 76.

9. Jay Carr, "Polanski's 'Ninth Gate' Gives Satan a Bad Name," *Boston*

Globe, March 10, 2000; available from http://www.bostonglobe.com (accessed October 23, 2001).

10. Nick Carter, "Convoluted Story Slams Shut Polanski's 'Ninth Gate,'" *Milwaukee Journal Sentinel,* March 9, 2000; available from http://www.jsonline.com/enter/movies/reviews/mar00 (accessed October 23, 2001).

11. Bob Graham, "Summoning Silliness: Roman Polanski Salutes and Spoofs Satanic Thrillers," *San Francisco Chronicle,* March 10, 2000; available from http://www.sfgate.com/cgi-bin/article.cgi?file=/chronicle/archive/2000/03/10/DD108488.DTL (accessed October 23, 2001).

12. See Mitchell, *The Devil on Screen,* 208–13.

13. Oppositional readings are designed to escape and resist the gravity of the text, which I have discussed as the appeal of perfection and unity characteristic of all texts. An oppositional reading does not mean one can read a text as one pleases, however. In the reading below, the argument is that one can contend with the text, not on its own terms, but within the context of the demise of occultism as a social form. In other words, I am reading the film as an object of popular culture.

14. Pérez-Reverte, *The Club Dumas.* Pérez-Reverte's novel is a complex meditation in the practice of reading which weds a narrative about *The Three Musketeers* with Corso's quest for *The Nine Doors* (variously, *The Nine Lies*). In his screen adaptation, Polanski and his coauthors, John Brownjohn and Enrique Urbizu, strip the narrative of its many Eco-esque subplots and focus exclusively on the occult threads. Significantly, the film adds an ending that does not appear in the book and amplifies the supernatural elements. In the novel, the reader is encouraged to discount the role of supernatural forces (the evil goings-on being simply the evil of humans). Perhaps to appease the expectations of audiences, a number of scenes in Polanski's film are suggestive of the supernatural. Part of the film's commercial failure, I think, has to do with Polanski's amplification of the supernatural elements which resulted in a kind of supernatural ambivalence.

15. K. Burke, *A Grammar of Motives,* 441–42.

16. See ibid., 323–444.

17. For exemplary examples see Brummett, "Burke's Representative Anecdote as a Method in Media Criticism"; and Tonn, Endress, and Diamond, "Hunting and Heritage on Trial in Maine."

18. K. Burke, *A Grammar of Motives,* 442.

19. In my reading of Burke, social order and hierarchy are merely the surrogates for Marx's conception of class, with which Burke was very familiar. A one-time communist, Burke gradually moved away from political socialism, especially during and after the Red Scare in the United States. In reprints and new editions of his books, it was not uncommon for him to replace socialist concepts with less socially and politically dangerous con-

cepts. See Schiappa and Keehner, "The 'Lost' Passages of *Permanence and Change.*"

20. Yet perhaps not as well as Burke's conception of "logology," which he defined as "words about words" and used to make sense of "words about God." See K. Burke, *The Rhetoric of Religion,* esp. 1–7. My reasons for persisting with the analogy to dramatism will become clearer momentarily.

21. LaVey, "The Church of Satan," 31. For a variation of this theme see Fritscher, "The Selling of the Age of Aquarius."

22. Stephanie Zacharek, "'The Ninth Gate' [DVD review]," August 4, 2000; available from http://www.salon.com (accessed October 23, 2001).

23. In Polanski's running commentary on *The Ninth Gate* DVD, he suggests that this conundrum was precisely his intent with this scene. He notes that an important part of the film, as with the novel, is a nagging uncertainly about whether the events depicted have to do with the supernatural. As the movie moves closer to an ending, however, it is clear that Polanski wanted to emphasize the supernatural elements to appease audience expectation.

24. Elvis Mitchell, "'The Ninth Gate': Off to Hell in a Handbasket, Trusty Book in Hand," *New York Times on the Web,* March 10, 2000; available from http://www.nytimes.com/library/film/03100gate-film-review-html (accessed October 23, 2001).

25. Ibid.

26. Crowley, *Equinox of the Gods,* 127.

27. I should also mention that Polanski intended the film as a celebration of "old horror films," as he notes in the DVD commentary. This intentional nostalgia permeated every aspect of the film, Polanski notes. For example, instead of rendering the film's special effects on a computer, Polanski says that they used the "old" blue-screen (chroma keyed) techniques. When "the girl" flies in the fight scene, the crew used wires, even though the shot would have been much easier and cheaper to produce with computer technology.

28. The basic psychological logic here is that of "the gaze," particularly as it is described by Laura Mulvey: the contradictions of desires for independence (destruction of the Other) and unity (becoming one with the Other) are negotiated over the body of the wealthy aristocrat. See Mulvey, *Visual and Other Pleasures.*

29. Nussbaum, "The Professor of Parody."

30. This quotation is from the screenplay.

31. The stereotype is common in popular representations of the college professor. In a manner similar to John Houseman's depiction of the crusty old professor whose intelligence is an excuse for his arrogance and meanness in *The Paper Chase* (1973), Richard Dreyfuss plays an unpleasant, cranky college instructor in the canceled CBS drama *The Education of Max Bickford.* The show portrays Bickford as a man thoroughly dissatisfied with his

life, and each plot orbits his negotiation of the proverbial "mid-life crisis." In other words, examples of the "bored" and dissatisfied professor are not difficult to come by in popular culture texts.

32. See, e.g., Purkiss, *The Witch in History.*

33. See Braude, *Radical Spirits.*

34. I'm thinking, in particular, of Hélène Cixous's *écriture féminine.* See Cixous, "The Laugh of the Medusa."

35. Many thanks to Mimi White for this example. The program originally aired on October 19, 1999, and was rebroadcast on March 7, 2000.

36. Brother Wilmshurst wrote that the "true candidate [of Freemasonry] must indeed needs be, as the word *candidus* implies, a 'white man,' white within as symbolically he is white-vestured without, so that no inward stain or soilure may obstruct the dawn within his soul of that Light which he professes to be the predominant wish of his heart on asking for admission." Wilmshurst, *The Meaning of Masonry,* 12.

37. There are a number of historical exceptions, such as Prince Hall's charter of an African American Freemasonry Lodge in the United States. Putnam, "The House That Prince Hall Built."

38. See Giroux, "Rewriting the Discourse of Racial Identity."

39. See Gresson, *The Recovery of Race in America.*

40. Hammond, *The Sacred in a Secular Age,* 1.

41. Jameson, *Postmodernism,* 67.

42. Bell, "The Return of the Sacred?"

43. M. Weber, *The Protestant Ethic and the Spirit of Capitalism,* 181–82.

44. B. Wilson, *Contemporary Transformations of Religion,* 96. Wilson's use of the plural "popcorns" is a form of British slang (I think it refers to what folks in the United States know as popcorn balls).

45. Darsey, *The Prophetic Tradition,* 209.

46. See B. Wilson, *Religion in Sociological Perspective,* esp. 149–51.

Epilogue

1. Ellul, *The Humiliation of the Word,* n.p.; available http://www.religion-online.org/cgi-bin/relsearchd.dll/showchapter?chapter_id=490 (accessed June 25, 2004).

2. Rushing and Frentz, "The Gods Must Be Crazy," 244.

3. Willis, "My Sokaled Life," 134.

4. For an excellent examination of the nasty ways in which blind review perpetuates oppression see Blair, Brown, and Baxter, "Disciplining the Feminine."

5. See Hayes and Wynyard, *The McDonaldization of Higher Education;* Jary and Parker, *The New Higher Education;* R. Rand, *Logomachia;* Read-

ings, *The University in Ruins;* Slaughter and Leslie, *Academic Capitalism;* and White and Hauck, *Campus, Inc.*

6. Sokal, "Revelation," 49.

7. Sokal and Bricmont, *Fashionable Nonsense,* xi.

8. Sokal, "Transgressing the Boundaries," 230.

9. Although he does not shun theory, Robert Scholes argues that "concepts like *truth* and *reality* are necessary for the health of a discipline called English," and I suspect the humanities in general. Scholes, *The Rise and Fall of English,* x.

10. Grossberg, *We Gotta Get Out of This Place,* 30.

11. See Hartley, "'Text' and 'Audience.'"

12. Warner, *Publics and Counterpublics,* 125–58.

13. See Gunn, "Publishing Peccadilloes."

14. Derrida, *The Gift of Death,* 92.

Appendix 1

1. C. Wilson, *The Occult,* 58–59.

2. McHargue, "A Ride across the Mystic Bridge," 1639.

3. Tillett, "Encounters with Unfamiliar States," 77–78. Also see Grant, *The Magical Revival.*

4. Adorno, "Theses against Occultism," in *The Stars Down to Earth,* 128–33.

5. A. L. Smith, "The Occultism of the Text," 6; C. Bloom, *The "Occult" Experience and the New Criticism,* x.

6. Messent, *Literature of the Occult,* 5.

7. The ultimate unknown being, of course, death. The classic analysis here is Freud's commentary on the uncanny. See Freud, "The 'Uncanny'" (also of relevance is "Dreams and Telepathy," trans. C. J. M. Hubback, in the same volume, 169–92). Although it is currently out of print, George Devereux's edited volume *Psychoanalysis and the Occult* contains numerous insightful essays by Freud and others that investigate occultism and paranormal phenomena (the two are erroneously conflated). Gay's psychological account of the relation between occultism and darkness is very different. A student of Kohutian analysis (a view that centers on love objects and the Jungian *imago*), Gay argues that occult "experience" refers to an infantile wish to restore past relationships. See Gay, *Understanding the Occult.*

8. E. Burke, *A Philosophical Enquiry,* 16.

9. Gunn and Beard, "On the Apocalyptic Sublime," 276. Also see Kant, *Critique of Judgment,* secs. 23–54.

10. Messent, *Literature of the Occult,* 11. Gay offers up a similar explanation for the occult as a kind of "mood." *Understanding the Occult* (esp.

16) describes the occult "experience" as an encounter with one's fragmented self and as rooted in the "very early experience of surrender to a mothering person." Kohut's theory of the self-object is central to Gay's argument.

11. Luhrmann, *Persuasions of the Witch's Craft,* 7.

12. Ibid., 337.

13. Ibid., 16.

14. Ibid., 345.

15. Ibid., 352.

16. Ibid., 353.

17. Ibid., 203.

18. Ibid., 204.

19. Verter, "Dark Star Rising," 21.

20. Ibid., 4.

21. Ibid., 5.

22. Ibid.

23. Verter suggests that after Crowley, many occultists were feared to be sexually deviant. He emphasizes a relationship between homoerotic themes and occultism that at times seems overclaimed. A better, more in-depth engagement is Evan's *Witchcraft and the Gay Counterculture.*

24. It bears mentioning that Purkiss's work is a delightful read—well written, reflexive, and sharp.

25. Mauss, *A General Theory of Magic,* 19.

26. Ibid., 88.

27. Tiryakian, *On the Margin of the Visible,* 6.

28. Ibid.; see Mauss, *A General Theory of Magic,* 22–40, for the relevant material.

29. Tiryakian, "Toward a Sociology of Esoteric Culture," 265.

30. Ibid., 263.

31. Ibid., 267. These observations were inspired by Georg Simmel's famous essay on secrets, "The Sociology of Secrecy and of Secret Societies," which can also be found in Tiryakian's edited collection.

32. Tiryakian, "Toward a Sociology of Esoteric Culture," 268.

33. Tiryakian, *On the Margin of the Visible,* 2.

34. K. Burke, *A Grammar of Motives,* 134–38.

35. Tiryakian, *On the Margin of the Visible,* 9.

36. Truzzi, "Definition and Dimensions of the Occult," 245. All of Truzzi's articles are primarily definitional in scope. See also his "The Occult Revival as Popular Culture" and "Towards a Sociology of the Occult."

37. In "The Occult Establishment," e.g., Marty argues for a conceptual distinction between the occult "underground" and the occult "establishment." The "underground" would largely consist of those elements of occultism that are not objects of mass consumption. The "establishment" seems to

refer to those elements of occultism that many people characterize today as "New Age": astrology, spiritualism, etc. There are few exceptions to my claim that sociologists have been more interested in taxonomy than in critical claims. Patricia Hartman's survey of subscribers to an occult magazine is an exception. In "Social Dimensions of Occult Participation: The *Gnostica* Study," Hartman argues for nationwide surveys to get a handle on the scope of interest and basic demographic information about those drawn to the occult. Findings from her own survey were limited (e.g., she found that most people surveyed believed in "occult forces"), but this did not prevent her correctly predicting an explosion of "neo-paganism" (Wicca, Goddess worship, etc.) at the end of the century. For an excellent overview of neopagan religious beliefs see Graham Harvey's *Contemporary Paganism.*

38. Whitehead, "Reasonably Fantastic," 586.

39. Ben-Yehuda, "The Revival of the Occult," 13. Ben-Yehuda's essay is problematic because it too easily conflates science fiction with occultism yet offers no explanation or justification for such a conflation.

40. Eliade, *Occultism, Witchcraft, and Cultural Fashions,* 64.

41. Ben-Yehuda, "The Revival of the Occult."

42. Greeley, "Implications for the Sociology of Religion."

43. For example, Tiryakian seems to believe that secret societies make up a large portion of the occult subculture, while sociologists like Danny and Lin Jorgenson argue that there is a wide array of types of social organization, public and private. See Jorgenson and Jorgenson, "Social Meanings of the Occult." The authors are highly critical of the lack of empirical work in the sociology of the occult, and they offer a study in which they became adept readers of tarot cards. They claim that previous studies are too speculative and lack empirical evidence, that previous studies focus too narrowly on one group, and that previous studies lack insider perspectives. Their findings are predictable, and their method is dubious at best.

Selected Bibliography

Most of the materials consulted for this study are listed below; however, full citations for newspaper articles and non-text media can be found in the endnotes of each chapter.

Abondolo, Daniel. *A Poetics Handbook: Verbal Art in the European Tradition.* Richmond, U.K.: Curzon Press, 2001.

Adorno, Theodor W. *Minima Moralia: Reflections on a Damaged Life.* Trans. E. F. N. Jephcott. New York: Verso, 1999.

———. "On Jazz." Trans. Jamie Owen Daniel. *Discourse* 12 (Fall–Winter 1989–90): 45–69.

———. *The Stars Down to Earth and Other Essays on the Irrational in Culture.* Ed. Stephen Crook. New York: Routledge, 1994.

Agrippa, Henry Cornelius. *Three Books of Occult Philosophy.* Ed. Donald Tyson. Trans. James Freake. 1651. Reprint, St. Paul, Minn.: Llewellyn, 1997.

Akrigg, G. P. V., ed. *Letters of James VI and I.* Berkeley: University of California Press, 1984.

Algeo, John. "Channeling." In *The Concise Encyclopedia of Language and Religion,* ed. John F. A. Sawyer and J. M. Y. Simpson, 242–43. Amsterdam: Elsevier, 2001.

"All the Babies You Can Eat." *Humanist* 53 (March 1993): 40–41.

Althusser, Louis. *Writings on Psychoanalysis: Freud and Lacan.* Ed. Olivier Corpet and François Matheron. Trans. Jeffrey Mehlman. New York: Columbia University Press, 1996.

Anderson, Benedict. *Imagined Communities: Reflections on the Origin and Spread of Nationalism.* London: Verso, 1991.

Aquino, Michael. *The Church of Satan.* 4th ed. San Francisco: Temple of Set, 1999.

Aristotle. *On Rhetoric: A Theory of Civic Discourse.* Trans. George A. Kennedy. New York: Oxford University Press, 1991.

——. *Poetics*. Trans. Kenneth A. Telford. South Bend, Ind.: Gateway Editions, 1961.

Arnold, Matthew. *Culture and Anarchy*. Ed. Samuel Lipman. New Haven: Yale University Press, 1994.

Ashton, Robert, ed. *James I by His Contemporaries*. London: Hutchinson, 1969.

Augustine. *The City of God against the Pagans*. Ed. and trans. R. W. Dyson. New York: Cambridge University Press, 1998.

——. *On Christian Doctrine*. Trans. D. W. Robertson Jr. Upper Saddle River, N.J.: Prentice Hall, 1958.

Austin, J. L. *How to Do Things with Words*. 2nd ed. Cambridge: Harvard University Press, 1978.

Bacon, Francis. *New Atlantis and the Great Instauration*. Wheeling, Ill.: Harlan Davidson, 1989.

Baddeley, Gavin. *Lucifer Rising: Sin, Devil Worship, and Rock 'n' Roll*. London: Plexus, 1999.

Barnes, Barry. *T. S. Kuhn and Social Science*. New York: Columbia University Press, 1982.

Barrett, Francis. *The Magus: A Complete System of Occult Philosophy*. 1801. Reprint, York Beach, Maine: Samuel Weiser, 2000.

Barthes, Roland. *Image, Music, Text*. Trans. Stephen Heath. New York: Hill and Wang, 1977.

Barton, Blanche. *The Church of Satan*. New York: Hell's Kitchen Productions, 1990.

——. *The Secret Life of a Satanist: The Authorized Biography of Anton LaVey*. Portland: Feral House, 1990.

Bass, Ellen, and Laura Davis. *The Courage to Heal*. New York: Harper Perennial, 1994.

Baudrillard, Jean. *Critique of the Political Economy of the Sign*. Trans. C. Levin. St. Louis: Telos Press, 1981.

——. *The Illusion of the End*. Trans. Chris Turner. Stanford: Stanford University Press, 1994.

——. *The Mirror of Production*. Trans. Mark Poster. St. Louis: Telos Press, 1975.

——. *Simulacra and Simulation*. Trans. Sheila Faria Glaser. Ann Arbor: University of Michigan Press, 2000.

Becker, Lawrence C. "Determinism as a Rhetorical Problem." *Philosophy and Rhetoric* 4 (1971): 20–28.

Bell, Daniel. "The Return of the Sacred? The Argument on the Future of Religion." *British Journal of Sociology* 28 (1977): 420–21.

Benjamin, Walter. "The Concept of Criticism in German Romanticism." Trans. David Lachterman, Howard Eiland, and Ian Balfour. In *Walter Benjamin: Selected Writings, Volume One (1913–1926)*, ed. Marcus Bullock and Michael W. Jennings, 116–200. Cambridge: Harvard University Press.

———. "On Language as Such and the Language of Man." Trans. Edmund Jephcott. In *Reflections: Essays, Aphorisms, and Autobiographical Writings,* ed. Peter Demetz, 314–32. New York: Harcourt Brace Jovanovich, 1978.

———. "The Task of the Translator." Trans. Harry Zohn. In *Illuminations: Essays and Reflections,* ed. Hannah Arendt, 69–82. New York: Schocken, 1968.

———. "Theses on the Philosophy of History." Trans. Harry Zohn. In *Illuminations: Essays and Reflections,* ed. Hannah Arendt, 253–64. New York: Schocken, 1968.

Benoit, William L. "Beyond Genre Theory: The Genesis of Rhetorical Action." *Communication Monographs* 67 (2000): 178–92.

Ben-Yehuda, Nachman. "The Revival of the Occult and of Science Fiction." *Journal of Popular Culture* 20 (1986): 1–16.

Beta, Hymenaeus. "Editor's Introduction." In Aleister Crowley, *Magick: Book IV, Parts I–V,* 2nd rev. ed., xxiii–lxxiv. York Beach, Maine: Samuel Weiser, 1997.

Betz, Brian R. "Eric Fromm and the Rhetoric of Prophecy." *Central States Speech Journal* 26 (1975): 310–15.

Bizzell, Patricia, and Bruce Herzberg, eds. *The Rhetorical Tradition: Readings from the Classical Times to the Present.* Boston: Bedford Books, 2001.

Black, Edwin. *Rhetorical Criticism: A Study in Method.* New York: Macmillan, 1965.

———. "The Second Persona." *Quarterly Journal of Speech* 56 (1970): 109–19.

Blair, Carole, Julie R. Brown, and Leslie A. Baxter. "Disciplining the Feminine." *Quarterly Journal of Speech* 80 (1994): 383–409.

Blamires, Harry. *The New Bloomsday Book.* New York: Routledge, 1991.

Blavatsky, Helena Petrovna. "Hypnotism." In *Studies in Occultism,* 30–40. Pasadena: Theosophical University Press, 1987.

———. *Isis Unveiled: A Master Key to the Mysteries of Ancient and Modern Science and Theology.* 2 vols. Facsimile ed. 1877. Pasadena: Theosophical University Press, 1988.

———. *The Key to Theosophy, Being a Clear Exposition, in the Form of Question and Answer, of the Ethics, Science, and Philosophy.* Point Loma, Calif.: Theosophical University Press, 1939.

———. "Madame Blavatsky on the Views of the Theosophists." In *H. P. Blavatsky: Collected Works,* ed. Boris de Zirkoff, 1:290–300. Wheaton, Ill.: Theosophical Publishing House, 1960.

———. "My Books." Appendix to *Isis Unveiled: A Master Key to the Mysteries of Ancient and Modern Science and Theology,* 2 vols., facsimile ed., 2:45–53. Pasadena: Theosophical University Press, 1988.

———. "Occultism versus the Occult Arts." In *Studies in Occultism.* 11–24. Pasadena: Theosophical University Press.

———. *The Secret Doctrine: The Synthesis of Science, Religion, and Philosophy.* 2 vols. Facsimile ed. Pasadena: Theosophical University Press, 1977.

———. *The Voice of Silence.* 2nd ed. Pasadena: Theosophical University Press, 1992.

Bloom, Clive. *The "Occult" Experience and the New Criticism: Daemonsim, Sexuality, and the Hidden in Literature.* Totowa, N.J.: Barnes & Noble, 1987.

Bloom, Alan. *The Closing of the American Mind.* New York: Simon and Schuster, 1987.

Bobbit, David, and Harold Mixon. "Prophecy and Apocalypse in the Rhetoric of Martin Luther King, Jr." *Journal of Communication and Religion* 17 (1994): 27–38.

Booth, Wayne C. *A Rhetoric of Irony.* Chicago: University of Chicago Press, 1974.

Borch-Jacobson, Mikkel. *Lacan: The Absolute Master.* Trans. Douglas Brick. Stanford: Stanford University Press, 1991.

Braude, Ann. *Radical Spirits: Spiritualism and Women's Rights in Nineteenth-Century America.* Boston: Beacon Press, 1989.

Brecht, Martin. *Martin Luther.* Trans. James L. Schaaf. Philadelphia: Fortress Press, 1993.

Brown, Karen McCarthy. *Mama Lola: A Vodou Priestess in Brooklyn.* Berkeley: University of California Press, 1991.

Brown, Rebecca. *He Came to Set the Captives Free.* New Kensington, Pa.: Wittaker House, 1993.

Browne, Sylvia. *Soul's Perfection.* Carlsbad, Calif.: Hay House, 2000.

Browne, Sylvia, and Lindsay Harrison. *Life on the Other Side: A Psychic's Tour of the Afterlife.* New York: Dutton/Penguin Putnam, 2000.

Brummett, Barry. "Burke's Representative Anecdote as a Method in Media Criticism." *Critical Studies in Mass Communication* 1 (1984): 161–76.

———. "Exploiting Audience Commitment through 'Transfer,' Illustrated in Recent Apocalyptic Discourse." *Southern Journal of Communication* 54 (Fall 1988): 58–73.

Burke, Edmund. *A Philosophical Enquiry into the Origin of Our Ideas of the Sublime and Beautiful.* Ed. James T. Boulton. Notre Dame: University of Notre Dame Press, 1968.

Burke, Kenneth. *Counter-Statement.* 1931. Reprint, Berkeley: University of California Press, 1968.

———. "Definition of Man." In *Language as Symbolic Action: Essays on Life, Literature, and Method,* 3–24. Berkeley: University of California Press, 1968.

——. "Four Master Tropes." Appendix to *A Grammar of Motives,* 511–17. Berkeley: University of California Press, 1969.

——. *A Grammar of Motives.* Berkeley: University of California Press, 1969.

——. *A Rhetoric of Motives.* Berkeley: University of California Press, 1969.

——. *The Rhetoric of Religion: Studies in Logology.* Berkeley: University of California Press, 1970.

Butler, Elizabeth M. *Ritual Magic.* Gloucestershire, U.K.: Sutton, 1998.

Butler, Judith. "Changing the Subject: Judith Butler's Politics of Radical Resignification." Interview with Gary A. Olson and Lynn Worsham. *JAC* 20 (2000): 727–65.

Campbell, Karlyn Kohrs. " 'Conventional Wisdom—Traditional Form': A Rejoinder." *Quarterly Journal of Speech* 34 (1972): 126–27.

——. "The Nature of Criticism in Rhetorical and Communicative Studies." *Central States Speech Journal* 30 (Spring 1979): 4–13.

——. "A Toad in the Garden: A Response to James Darsey's *The Prophetic Tradition and Radical Rhetoric in America.*" Paper presented at the annual meeting of the National Communication Association, Chicago, November 2000.

Campbell, Karlyn Kohrs, and Thomas R. Burkholder. *Critiques of Contemporary Rhetoric.* 2nd ed. Belmont, Calif.: Wadsworth, 1997.

Campbell, Karlyn Kohrs, and Kathleen Hall Jamieson. "Introduction" (to special issue on generic criticism). *Southern Speech Communication Journal* 51 (1986): 293–99.

——, eds. *Form and Genre: Shaping Rhetorical Action.* Falls Church, Va.: Speech Communication Association, 1978.

Caputo, John D. *Radical Hermeneutics: Repetition, Deconstruction, and the Hermeneutic Project.* Bloomington: Indiana University Press, 1987.

Cherwitz, Richard A., and James W. Hikins. *Communication and Knowledge: Investigation in Rhetorical Epistemology.* Columbia: University of South Carolina Press, 1986.

Cicero. *On Oratory and Orators.* Trans. J. S. Watson. Carbondale: Southern Illinois University Press, 1986.

Cixous, Hélène. "The Laugh of the Medusa." Trans. Keith Cohen and Paula Cohen. *Signs* 1 (1976): 875–93.

Clark, Thomas D. "Rhetoric, Reality, and Rationalization: A Study of the Masking Function of Rhetoric in the London Theosophy Movement." *Communication Quarterly* 26 (1978): 24–30.

Clements, Ronald E. *Old Testament Prophecy: From Oracles to Canon.* Louisville: Westminster John Knox Press, 1996.

Cloud, Dana. "The Materiality of Discourse as Oxymoron: A Challenge to Critical Rhetoric." *Western Journal of Communication* 58 (1994): 141–63.

Coates, John. "*Zanoni* by Bulwer-Lytton: A Discussion of Its 'Philosophy' and Its Possible Influences." *Durham University Journal* 76 (June 1984): 223–33.

Comaroff, Jean, and John L. Comaroff. "Millennial Capitalism: First Thoughts on a Second Coming." *Public Culture* 12 (2000): 291–343.

Conley, Thomas. "The Linnaean Blues: Thoughts on the Genre Approach." In *Form, Genre, and the Study of Political Discourse,* ed. Herbert W. Simons and Aram A. Aghazarian, 59–78. Columbia: University of South Carolina Press, 1986.

——. *Rhetoric in the European Tradition.* Chicago: University of Chicago Press, 1990.

Copenhaver, Brian P., ed. *Hermetica.* New York: Cambridge University Press, 1992.

Corbett, Margery, and Ronald Lightbown. *The Comely Frontispiece: The Emblematic Title-Page in England, 1550–1660.* London: Routledge and Kegan Paul, 1979.

Couliano, Ioan P. *Eros and Magic in the Renaissance.* Trans. Margaret Cook. Chicago: University of Chicago Press, 1987.

Covino, William A. *Magic, Rhetoric, and Literacy: An Eccentric History of the Composing Imagination.* New York: State University of New York Press, 1994.

Crenshaw, James. *Prophetic Conflict.* Berlin: Walter de Gruyter, 1971.

Cross, Andrew. "Neither Either Nor Or: The Perils of Reflexive Irony." In *The Cambridge Companion to Kierkegaard,* ed. Alastair Hannay and Gordon D. Marino, 125–53. Cambridge: Cambridge University Press, 1998.

Crowley, Aleister. *Aleister Crowley's Illustrated Goetia: Sexual Evocation.* Ed. Lon Milo DuQuette and Christopher S. Hyatt. Tempe: New Falcon, 1994.

——. *The Book of Thoth: A Short Essay on the Tarot of the Egyptians.* 1944. Reprint, York Beach, Maine: Samuel Weiser, 1999.

——. *The Confessions of Aleister Crowley.* Ed. John Symonds and Kenneth Grant. New York: Arkana/Penguin, 1989.

——. "Energized Enthusiasm." *Equinox* 1 (rpt. Samuel Weiser, Inc., March 1993): 15–20.

——. *The Equinox of the Gods.* Tempe: New Falcon, 1991.

——. *The Law Is for All.* Ed. Louis Wilkinson and Hymenaeus Beta. Tempe: New Falcon, 1996.

——. *Liber Aleph Vel CXI: The Book of Wisdom and Folly.* York Beach, Maine: Samuel Weiser, 1991.

——. *Magick: Book IV, Parts I–IV (Liber ABA).* Ed. Hymenaeus Beta. 2nd rev. ed. York Beach, Maine: Samuel Weiser, 1997.

——. *Magick without Tears.* Ed. Israel Regardie. Tempe: New Falcon, 1999.

———. *777 and Other Qabalistic Writings of Aleister Crowley.* Ed. Israel Regardie. York Beach, Maine: Samuel Weiser, 1999.

———. *The Vision and the Voice, with Commentary and Other Papers.* York Beach, Maine: Samuel Weiser, 1999.

Cuiley, Rosemary Ellen. *Harper's Encyclopedia of Mystical and Paranormal Experience.* Edison, N.J.: Castle, 1991.

Darsey, James. *The Prophetic Tradition and Radical Rhetoric in America.* New York: New York University Press, 1997.

Davidson, Donald. "Intending." In *Essays on Actions and Events,* 83–102. New York: Oxford University Press, 1980.

Dean, Jodi. *Aliens in America: Conspiracy Cultures from Outerspace to Cyberspace.* Ithaca: Cornell University Press, 1998.

Delbanco, Andrew. *The Death of Satan: How Americans Have Lost the Sense of Evil.* New York: Farrar, Straus and Giroux, 1995.

Deleuze, Gilles, and Félix Guattari. *Anti-Oedipus: Capitalism and Schizophrenia.* Trans. Robert Hurley, Mark Seem, and Helen R. Lane. Minneapolis: University of Minnesota Press, 1996.

Derrida, Jacques. "*Différence.*" In *Margins of Philosophy,* trans. Alan Bass, 3–27. Chicago: University of Chicago Press, 1986. Also in *A Derrida Reader: Between the Blinds,* ed. Peggy Kamuf, 114–39. New York: Columbia University Press, 1991.

———. *The Gift of Death.* Trans. David Wills. Chicago: University of Chicago Press, 1995.

———. *Of Grammatology.* Trans. Gayatri Chakravorty Spivak. Baltimore: Johns Hopkins University Press, 1976.

———. "Plato's Pharmacy." Trans. Barbara Johnson. In *A Derrida Reader: Between the Blinds,* ed. Peggy Kamuf, 114–39. New York: Columbia University Press, 1991.

Descartes, René. *Philosophical Essays.* Trans. and ed. Laurence J. Lafleur. New York: Macmillan, 1989.

Devereux, George, ed. *Psychoanalysis and the Occult.* New York: International University Press, 1973.

Douglas, Mary, and Baron Isherwood. *The World of Goods.* New York: Basic Books, 1978.

Downie, R. S. "Authority." In *Oxford Companion to Philosophy,* ed. Ted Honderich, 68–69. New York: Oxford University Press, 1995.

Dulles, Foster Rhea. *Americans Abroad: Two Centuries of European Travel.* Ann Arbor: University of Michigan Press, 1964.

Dupree, A. Hunter. "Christianity and the Scientific Community in the Ag of Darwin." In *God and Nature: Historical Essays on the Encounter between Christianity and Science,* ed. David C. Lindberg and Ronald L. Numbers, 351–68. Berkeley: University of California Press, 1986.

DuQuette, Lon Milo. *Angels, Demons, and Gods of the New Millennium.* York Beach, Maine: Samuel Weiser, 1997.

———. *The Magic of Thelema: A Handbook of the Rituals of Aleister Crowley.* York Beach, Maine: Samuel Weiser, 1993.

Eamon, William. "Magic and the Occult." In *The History of Science and Religion in the Western Tradition: An Encyclopedia,* ed. Gary B. Ferngren, 533–49. New York: Garland, 2000.

Ehrenhaus, Peter. "Silence and Symbolic Expression." *Communication Monographs* 55 (March 1998): 41–57.

Eisenstein, Elizabeth L. *The Printing Press as an Agent of Change: Communications and Cultural Transformations in Early-Modern Europe.* New York: Cambridge University Press, 1980.

Eliade, Mircea. *Occultism, Witchcraft, and Cultural Fashions: Essays in Comparative Religion.* Chicago: University of Chicago Press, 1976.

Eliot, T. S. *Selected Prose of T. S. Eliot.* Ed. Frank Kermode. New York: Harcourt Brace, 1975.

Eliott-Binns, L. E. *Religion in the Victorian Era.* London: Lutterworth Press, 1964.

Ellis, Bill. *Raising the Devil: Satanism, New Religions, and the Media.* Lexington: University Press of Kentucky, 2000.

Ellul, Jacques. *The Humiliation of the Word.* Grand Rapids, Mich.: Eerdmans, 1985.

Evan, Arthur. *Witchcraft and the Gay Counterculture.* Boston: Fag Rag Books, 1978.

Felix, Minucius, *Octavius.* Trans. Rudolf Arbesmann, Emily Joseph Daly, and Edwin A. Quian. In *The Fathers of the Church,* 10:330–41. New York: Fathers of the Church, 1950.

Ferreira, M. Jamie. "Faith and the Kierkegaardian Leap." In *The Cambridge Companion to Kierkegaard,* ed. Alastair Hannay and Gordon D. Marino, 207–34. New York: Cambridge University Press, 1999.

Fink, Bruce. *A Clinical Introduction to Lacanian Psychoanalysis: Theory and Technique.* Cambridge: Harvard University Press, 1997.

———. *Lacan to the Letter: Reading* Écrits *Closely.* Minneapolis: University of Minnesota Press, 2004.

Fisher, Walter R. "Narration as a Human Communication Paradigm: The Case of Public Moral Argument." In *Readings in Rhetorical Criticism,* ed. Carl Burgchardt, 272–94. State College, Pa.: Strata, 1995.

———. "Toward a Logic of Good Reasons." *Quarterly Journal of Speech* 64 (1978): 376–84.

Flew, Anthony G. "The Philosophical Implications of Darwinism." In *Darwin, Marx, and Freud: Their Influence on Moral Theory,* ed. Arthur L. Caplan and Bruce Jennings, 3–33. New York: Plenum Press, 1984.

Foote, G. W. *The New Cagliostro: An Open Letter to Madame Blavatsky.* London: Progressive, 1889.

Foss, Sonia K. "Ambiguity as Persuasion: The Vietnam Veterans Memorial." *Communication Quarterly* 34 (1985): 326–40.

Foucault, Michel. *The Archeology of Knowledge and the Discourse on Language.* Trans. A. M. Sheridan Smith. New York: Pantheon, 1972.

———. *Power/Knowledge: Selected Interviews and Other Writings, 1972–1977.* Ed. Colin Gordon. New York: Pantheon, 1980.

Fraser, Antonia. *King James VI of Scotland, I of England.* London: Weidenfeld and Nicholson, 1974.

Freud, Sigmund. *New Introductory Lectures on Psycho-Analysis.* Trans. James Strachey. New York: Norton, 1961.

———. "The 'Uncanny.'" Trans. Alix Strachy. In *Sigmund Freud: Psychological Writings and Letters,* ed. Sander L. Gilman, 120–53. New York: Continuum, 1995.

Friedrich, Carl J. *Tradition and Authority.* London: Pall Mall, 1972.

Fritscher, John. "The Selling of the Age of Aquarius." In *Popular Witchcraft,* 53–101. Secaucus, N.J.: The Citadel Press, 1973.

Gadamer, Hans-Georg. *Truth and Method.* New York: Crossroad, 1984.

Gaonkar, Dilip Parameshwar. "The Disappearance of the Critical Object." Lecture given at the Northwestern University Institute for Cultural Studies and Method, Evanston, Illinois, July 25, 2000.

———. "The Oratorical Text: The Enigma of Arrival." In *Texts in Context: Critical Dialogues on Significant Episodes in American Political Rhetoric,* ed. Michael C. Leff and Fred J. Kauffeld, 255–75. Davis, Calif.: Hermagoras Press, 1989.

Gay, Volney P. *Understanding the Occult: Fragmentation and Repair of the Self.* Minneapolis: Fortress Press, 1989.

Genette, Gerard. *Paratexts: Thresholds of Interpretation.* Trans. Jane E. Lewin. New York: Cambridge University Press, 1997.

"Geraldo Rivera's Influence on the Satanic Ritual Abuse and Memory Hoaxes." *ReligiousTolerance.org,* n.d., n.p.; available at http://www.religioustolerance.org/geraldo.htm accessed May 5, 2001.

Giddens, Anthony. *The Constitution of Society: Outline of the Theory of Structuration.* Berkeley: University of California Press, 1984.

Giroux, Henry A. "Rewriting the Discourse of Racial Identity: Towards a Pedagogy of Politics and Whiteness." *Harvard Educational Review* 67 (1997): 285–320.

Glynos, Jason, and Yannis Stavrakakis. "Postures and Impostures: On Lacan's Style and Use of Mathematical Science." *American Imago* 58 (2001): 685–706.

Gombrich, E. H. *Art and Illusion.* London: Phaidon, 1960.

Gomes, Michael. *Theosophy in the Nineteenth Century: An Annotated Bibliography.* New York: Garland, 1994.

Godzich, Wlad. "Introduction: Caution! Reader at Work!" In Paul de Man, *Blindness and Insight: Essays in the Rhetoric of Contemporary Criticism,* ed. Wlad Godzich, 2nd ed., xv–xxx. Minneapolis: University of Minnesota Press, 1983.

Grant, Kenneth. *The Magical Revival.* London: Frederick Muller, 1972.

Grattan-Guinness, I. "Why Did Mozart Write Three Symphonies in the Summer of 1788?" *Music Review* 53 (February 1992): 1–6.

Greeley, Andrew M. "Implications for the Sociology of Religion of Occult Behavior in Youth Culture." In *On the Margin of the Visible: Sociology, the Esoteric, and the Occult,* ed. Edward A. Tiryakian, 295–302. New York: Wiley, 1974.

Greene, Ronald Walter. "The Textual Apparatus." Paper presented at the National Communication Association Convention, Seattle, Washington, November 2000.

Gregory, Frederick. "The Impact of Darwinian Evolution on Protestant Theology." In *God and Nature: Historical Essays on the Encounter between Christianity and Science,* ed. David C. Lindberg and Ronald L. Numbers, 369–90. Berkeley: University of California Press, 1986.

Gresson, Aaron David, III. *The Recovery of Race in America.* Minneapolis: University of Minnesota Press, 1995.

Grossberg, Lawrence. We *Gotta Get Out of this Place: Popular Conservatism and Postmodern Culture.* New York: Routledge, 1992.

Gunn, Joshua. "Benjamin's Magic." *Telos* 119 (2001): 68–74.

———. "Gothic Music and the Inevitability of Genre." *Popular Music and Society* 23 (1999): 31–50.

———. "Publishing Peccadilloes and the Idioms of Disposition: Views from the Habitus of Scholarly Adolescence." *Communication Studies* 54 (2003): 370–77.

———. "Refiguring Fantasy: Imagination and Its Decline in U.S. Rhetorical Studies." *Quarterly Journal of Speech* 89 (2003): 41–59.

———. "Refitting Fantasy: Psychoanalysis, Subjectivity, and Talking to the Dead." *Quarterly Journal of Speech* 90 (2004): 1–23.

———. "The Rhetoric of Exorcism: George W. Bush and the Return to Political Demonology." *Western Journal of Communication* 68 (2004): 1–23.

Gunn, Joshua, and David E. Beard. "On the Apocalyptic Sublime." *Southern Communication Journal* 65 (2000): 269–86.

Gurdjieff, G. I. *Beelzebub's Tales to His Grandson: An Objectively Impartial Criticism of the Life of Man.* 1950. New York: Penguin/Arkana, 1999.

Hall, David D. *Cultures of Print: Essays in the History of the Book.* Amherst: University of Massachusetts Press, 1996.

Hall, Stuart. "The Rediscovery of Ideology: Return of the Repressed in Media Studies." In *Culture, Society, and the Media,* ed. Michael Gurevitch, 56–90. New York: Routledge, 1988.

Hammond, Phillip E., ed. *The Sacred in a Secular Age: Toward Revision in the Scientific Study of Religion.* Berkeley: University of California Press, 1985.

Hart, James. *The Popular Book: A History of America's Literary Taste.* Berkeley: University of California Press, 1970.

Hartley, John. *Popular Reality: Journalism, Modernity, Popular Culture.* New York: Arnold/St. Martin's Press, 1996.

———. "'Text' and 'Audience': One and the Same? Methodological Tensions in Media Research" *Textual Practice* 13 (1999): 487–508.

Hartman, Patricia A. "Social Dimensions of Occult Participation: The *Gnostica* Study." *British Journal of Sociology* 27 (1976): 169–83.

Harvey, Graham. *Contemporary Paganism: Listening People, Speaking Earth.* New York: New York University Press, 1997.

Hayes, Dennis, and Robin Wynyard, eds. *The McDonaldization of Higher Education.* New York: Bergin and Garvey, 2002.

Heath, Robert L. "Kenneth Burke's Poetics and the Influence of I. A. Richards: A Cornerstone of Dramatism." *Communication Studies* 40, no. 1 (1989): 54–65.

Hertenstein, Michael, and John Trott. *Selling Satan: The Tragic History of Mike Warnke.* Chicago: Cornerstone Press, 1993.

Heschel, Abraham J. *The Prophets.* New York: Harper and Row, 1962.

Hill, Forbes I. "Conventional Wisdom—Traditional Form: The President's Message of November 3, 1969." *Quarterly Journal of Speech* 58 (December 1972): 373–86.

Hoggart, Richard. *The Uses of Literacy.* New Brunswick, N.J.: Transaction, 1997.

Horkheimer, Max, and Theodor W. Adorno. *Dialectic of Enlightenment.* Trans. John Cumming. New York: Continuum, 1999.

———. *Dialectic of Enlightenment: Philosophical Fragments.* Trans. Edmund Jephcott. Stanford: Stanford University Press, 2002.

Hume, David. *An Enquiry Concerning Human Understanding.* Ed. Eric Steinberg. Indianapolis: Hackett, 1993.

Hutcheon, Linda. *Irony's Edge: The Theory and Politics of Irony.* New York: Routledge, 1994.

Hutchinson, Roger. *Aleister Crowley: The Beast Demystified.* Edinburgh, U.K.: Mainstream, 1999.

Idhe, Don. *Experimental Phenomenology: An Introduction.* New York: State University of New York Press, 1986.

James, William. *The Varieties of Religious Experience.* New York: Penguin, 1958.

Jameson, Fredric. *Marxism and Form: Twentieth-Century Dialectical Theories of Literature.* Princeton: Princeton University Press, 1971.

———. *The Political Unconscious: Narrative as a Socially Symbolic Act.* Ithaca: Cornell University Press, 1981.

———. *Postmodernism, or, the Cultural Logic of Late Capitalism.* Durham: Duke University Press, 1995.

Jary, David, and Martin Parker, eds. *The New Higher Education: Issues and Directions.* Staffordshire, U.K.: Staffordshire University Press, 1998.

Jhally, Sut. *The Codes of Advertising: Fetishism and the Political Economy of Meaning in Consumer Society.* New York: Routledge, 1990.

Johannesen, Richard L. "The Functions of Silence: A Plea for Communication Research." *Western Journal of Speech Communication* 38 (Winter 1974): 25–35.

Jones, W. T. *A History of Western Philosophy: Hobbes to Hume.* 2nd ed. Fort Worth: Harcourt Brace Jovanovich College Publishers, 1980.

Jorgenson, Danny L., and Lin Jorgenson. "Social Meanings of the Occult." *Sociological Quarterly* 23 (1982): 373–89.

Joyce, James. *Finnegans Wake.* New York: Penguin, 1976.

———. *Ulysses.* Gabler ed. New York: Vintage, 1986.

Kamuf, Peggy, ed. *A Derrida Reader: Between the Blinds.* New York: Columbia University Press, 1991.

Kant, Immanuel. *Critique of Judgment.* Trans. J. H. Bernard. New York: Hafner Press, 1951.

———. *Critique of Pure Reason.* Ed. and trans. Paul Guyer and Allen W. Wood. New York: Cambridge University Press, 1999.

Katz, Steven T. "Mystical Speech and Mystical Meaning." In *Mysticism and Language,* ed. Katz, 3–41. New York: Oxford University Press, 1992.

Kierkegaard, Søren. *The Concept of Irony, with Continual Reference to Socrates.* Ed. and trans. Howard V. Hong and Edna H. Hong. Princeton: Princeton University Press, 1989.

———. *Concluding Unscientific Postscript to the "Philosophical Fragments."* Trans. David F. Swenson, Lillian Marvin Swenson, and Walter Lowrie. In *A Kierkegaard Anthology,* ed. Robert Bretall, 190–269. Princeton: Princeton University Press, 1973.

———. *Fear and Trembling/Repetition.* Ed. and trans. Howard V. Hong and Edna H. Hong. Princeton: Princeton University Press, 1983.

———. *The Sickness unto Death: A Christian Psychological Exposition for Upbuilding and Awakening.* Ed. and trans. Howard V. Hong and Edna H. Hong. Princeton: Princeton University Press, 1980.

Klein-Hass, Michelle. *The Book of the Centre of Pestilence.* Available from http:www.msgeek.com/heretic93/pestilence.html accessed February 11, 2000.

Klemp, Harold. *The Golden Heart: Mahanta Transcripts, Book 4.* Minneapolis: ECKANKAR, 1990.

Knight, Peter, ed. *Conspiracy Nation: The Politics of Paranoia in Postwar America.* New York: New York University Press, 2002.

Kocher, Paul H. "The Witchcraft Basis in Marlowe's *Faustus.*" In *Witchcraft and Demonology in Art and Literature,* ed. Brian P. Pevack, 257–84. New York: Garland, 1992.

Kojève, Alexandre. *Introduction to the Reading of Hegel: Lectures on the Phenomenology of Spirit.* Trans. Raymond Queneau. Ithaca: Cornell University Press, 1980.

Kramer, Heinrich, and James Sprenger. *The Malleus Maleficarum.* Ed. Montague Summers. New York: Dover Press, 1971.

Lacan, Jacques. "The Mirror Stage as Formative of the *I* Function." In *Écrits,* trans. Bruce Fink, 1–9. New York: Norton, 2004.

———. "The Purloined Letter." In *The Seminar of Jacques Lacan, Book II: The Ego in Freud's Theory and in the Technique of Psychoanalysis, 1954–1955,* trans. Sylvana Tomaselli, 191–205. New York: Norton, 1988.

———. "The Signification of the Phallus." In *Écrits,* trans. Bruce Fink, 271–80. New York: Norton, 2004.

———. "The Subversion of the Subject and the Dialectic of Desire in the Freudian Unconscious." In *Écrits,* trans. Bruce Fink, 281–312. New York: Norton, 2004.

Lancioni, Judith. "The Rhetoric of the Frame: Revisioning Archival Photographs in *The Civil War.*" *Western Journal of Communication* 60 (Fall 1996): 397–414.

Lang, C. D. *Irony/Humor: Critical Paradigms.* Baltimore: Johns Hopkins University Press, 1988.

Langone, Michael D., and Linda O. Blood. *Satanism and Occult-Related Violence: What You Should Know.* Weston, Mass.: American Family Foundation, 1990.

Lanham, Richard A. *A Handlist of Rhetorical Terms.* 2nd ed. Berkeley: University of California Press, 1991.

Lanning, Kenneth V. *Investigator's Guide to Allegations of "Ritual" Child Abuse.* Quantico, Va.: National Center for the Analysis of Violent Crime, Federal Bureau of Investigation, 1992.

Larson, Bob. *Satanism: The Seduction of America's Youth.* Nashville: Nelson, 1989.

LaVey, Anton Szandor. "The Church of Satan, Cosmic Joy Buzzer." In *The Devil's Notebook,* 66–67. Portland: Feral House, 1992.

———. "Entertain Me." In *Satan Speaks,* 23–24. Portland: Feral House, 1998.

———. "How to Be God (or the Devil)." In *The Devil's Notebook,* 66–67. Portland: Feral House, 1992.

——. "The Jewish Question? or, Things My Mother Never Taught Me." In *Satan Speaks,* 69–72. Portland: Feral House, 1998.

——. "Let Me Entertain You." In *The Devil's Notebook,* 104–7. Portland: Feral House, 1992.

——. *The Satanic Bible.* New York: Avon, 1969.

——. *The Satanic Rituals: Companion to* The Satanic Bible. New York: Avon, 1972.

Laycock, Donald C. *The Complete Enochian Dictionary.* York Beach, Maine: Samuel Weiser, 1994.

Leavis, F. R. *Mass Civilization and Minority Culture.* Cambridge: The Minority Press, 1930.

Lecky, W. E. H. *The Rise and Influence of Rationalism in Europe.* London: Longmans, Green, 1910.

Leff, Michael C. "Interpretation and the Art of the Rhetorical Critic." *Western Journal of Speech Communication* 44 (Fall 1980): 337–49.

——. "Textual Criticism: The Legacy of G. P. Mohrmann." *Quarterly Journal of Speech* 72 (1986): 377–89.

——. "Topical Invention and Metaphoric Interaction." *Southern Speech Communication Journal* 48 (1983): 214–29.

Leff, Michael, and Andrew Sachs. "Words the Most Like Things: Iconicity and the Rhetorical Text." *Western Journal of Speech Communication* 54 (Summer 1990): 252–71.

Lévi, Eliphas. *The History of Magic.* Trans. A. E. Waite. York Beach, Maine: Samuel Weiser, 1999.

——. *The Secret Tradition of Freemasonry.* Vol. 1. London: Rebman Limited, 1911.

——. *Transcendental Magic: Its Doctrine and Ritual.* Trans. A. E. Waite. York Beach, Maine: Samuel Weiser, 1999.

Lindberg, David C. "The Occult Revolution." *Christian Scholar's Review* 3 (1974): 370–76.

Lindley, David. *The Trials of Francis Howard: Fact and Fiction at the Court of King James.* New York: Routledge, 1993.

Liu, Yameng. "Authority, Presumption, and Invention." *Philosophy and Rhetoric* 30 (1997): 413–27.

Lowery, Shearon A., and Melvin L. DeFleur. *Milestones in Mass Communication Research.* 3rd ed. White Plains, N.Y.: Longman, 1995.

Lucas, Stephen E. "The Renaissance of American Public Address: Text and Context in Rhetorical Criticism." *Quarterly Journal of Speech* 74 (1988): 241–60.

——. "The Stylistic Artistry of the Declaration of Independence." In *Readings in Rhetorical Criticism,* ed. Carl R. Burgchardt, 531–46. State College, Pa.: Strata, 1995.

Luhrmann, Tanya M. *Persuasions of the Witch's Craft: Ritual Magic in Contemporary England.* Cambridge: Harvard University Press, 1989.

Lukes, Steven. "Perspectives on Authority." In *Nomos XXXIX: Authority Revisited,* ed. J. Roland Pennock and John W. Chapman, 59–75. New York: New York University Press, 1987.

Luther, Martin. "Address to the Christian Nobility of the German Nation." In *Readings in European History.* Boston: Ginn, 1906; available from http://history.haover.edu/texts/luthad.html accessed October 1, 2001.

Mailloux, Steven. *Rhetorical Power.* Ithaca: Cornell University Press, 1989.

de Man, Paul. *Allegories of Reading.* New Haven: Yale University Press, 1979.

———. *Blindness and Insight: Essays in the Rhetoric of Contemporary Criticism.* 2nd ed. Minneapolis: University of Minnesota Press, 1983.

Marty, Martin E., "The Occult Establishment." *Social Research* 37 (1970): 212–30.

Marx, Karl. *Capital.* Vol. 1. Trans. Ben Fowkes. New York: Penguin, 1990.

———. "Introduction to A Contribution to the Critique of Hegel's Philosophy of Right." In *Marx's Critique of Hegel's Philosophy of Right,* trans. Joseph O'Malley. New York: Oxford University Press, 1970; available from http://www.marxists.org/archive/marx/works accessed October 1, 2001.

Mathers, S. L. MacGregor, trans. *The Book of the Sacred Magic of Abramelin the Mage.* New York: Dover, 1975.

———, trans. and ed. *The Key of Solomon the King.* 1889. Reprint, York Beach, Maine: Samuel Weiser, 2000.

Matt, Daniel C. *The Essential Kabbalah: The Heart of Jewish Mysticism.* Edison, N.J.: Castle, 1997.

Mauss, Marcel. *A General Theory of Magic.* Trans. Robert Brian. Boston: Routledge and Kegan Paul, 1972.

McCarthy, Jan. "Andrew Jackson Davis: The Don Quixote of Spiritualism." *Southern Speech Journal* 30 (Summer 1965): 308–16.

McGuire, Michael D., and John H. Patton. "Preaching in the Mystic Mode: The Rhetorical Art of Meister Eckhart." *Communication Monographs* 44 (1977): 263–72.

McGuire, R. R. "Speech Acts, Communication Competence, and the Paradox of Authority." *Philosophy and Rhetoric* 10 (1977): 30–45.

McHargue, Georgess. "A Ride across the Mystic Bridge, or Occult Books: What, Why, and Who Needs Them?" *School Library Journal* 98 (1973): 1635–40.

McIntosh, Christopher. *Eliphas Lévi and the French Occult Revival.* New York: Samuel Weiser, 1974.

McKerrow, Raymie E. "Critical Rhetoric: Theory and Praxis." *Communication Monographs* 56 (1989): 91–111.

Medhurst, Martin J. "Public Address and Significant Scholarship: Four Challenges to the Rhetorical Renaissance." In *Texts in Context: Critical Dialogues on Significant Episodes in American Political Rhetoric,* ed. Michael C. Leff and Fred J. Kauffeld, 29–51. Davis, Calif.: Hermagoras Press, 1989.

Mellers, Wilfird. "Little Time to Spare." *Atlantic,* January 1992, 100–105.

Melton, J. Gordon. "Thelemic Magick in America." In *Alternatives to American Mainline Churches,* ed. Joseph H. Fichter, 67–87. New York: Rose of Sharon Press/Unification Theological Seminary, 1983.

Melton, Jeffrey Alan. "Touring Decay: Nineteenth-Century U.S. Travel Writers in Europe." *Papers on Language and Literature* 35 (1999): 206–22.

Messaris, Paul. "Visual Literacy and Manipulation." *Critical Studies in Mass Communication* 11 (1994): 180–203.

Messent, Peter B., ed. *Literature of the Occult: A Collection of Critical Essays.* Englewood Cliffs, N.J.: Prentice-Hall, 1981.

Miller, Carolyn R. "Genre as Social Action." *Quarterly Journal of Speech* 70 (1984): 151–67.

Milton, John. *Paradise Lost/Paradise Regained.* Ed. Christopher Ricks. New York: Signet/Penguin, 1968.

Mitchell, Charles P. *The Devil on Screen: Feature Films Worldwide, 1913 through 2000.* Jefferson, N.C.: McFarland, 2002.

Moore, James R. "Geologists and Interpreters of Genesis in the Nineteenth Century." In *God and Nature: Historical Essays on the Encounter between Christianity and Science,* ed. David C. Lindberg and Ronald L. Numbers, 322–50. Berkeley: University of California Press, 1986.

Mulhern, Sherrill. "Satanism and Psychotherapy: A Rumor in Search of an Inquisition." In *The Satanism Scare,* ed. James T. Richardson, Joel Best, and David G. Bromley, 145–72. New York: Aldine De Gruyter, 1991.

Mulvey, Laura. *Visual and Other Pleasures.* Bloomington: Indiana University Press, 1989.

Nathan, Debbie, and Michael Snedeker. *Satan's Silence: Ritual Abuse and the Making of a Modern American Witch Hunt.* New York: Basic Books, 1995.

Nietzsche, Friedrich. *Beyond Good and Evil: Prelude to a Philosophy of the Future.* Trans. Walter Kaufmann. New York: Vintage, 1989.

———. *Friedrich Nietzsche on Rhetoric and Language.* Ed. and trans. Sander L. Gilman, Carole Blair, and David J. Parent. New York: Oxford University Press, 1989.

Noll, Mark A. "Evangelicalism and Fundamentalism." In *The History of Science and Religion in the Western Tradition,* ed. Gary B. Ferngren, 298–306. New York: Garland, 2000.

Nothstine, William L., Carole Blair, and Gary A. Copeland, eds. *Critical Questions: Invention, Creativity, and the Criticism of Discourse and Media.* New York: St. Martin's Press, 1994.

Nussbaum, Martha. "The Professor of Parody." *New Republic*, February 22, 1999; available from http://tnr.com/archive/0299/nussbaum022299.html accessed May 5, 2001.

Oberman, Heiko Augustinus. *Luther: Man between God and the Devil.* Trans. Eileen Walliser-Schwarzbart. New Haven: Yale University Press, 1989.

Olcott, Henry Steel. *Inside the Occult: The Story of H. P. Blavatsky.* Philadelphia: Running Press, 1975.

O'Leary, Stephen, and Michael McFarland. "The Political Use of Mystic Discourse: Prophetic Interpretation in Pat Robertson's Presidential Campaign." *Quarterly Journal of Speech* 75 (1989): 433–52.

Oppenheim, Janet. *The Other World: Spiritualism and Psychical Research in England, 1850–1914.* New York: Cambridge University Press, 1985.

Ouspensky, P. D. *In Search of the Miraculous: Fragments of an Unknown Teaching.* 1949. San Diego: Harvest Books/Harcourt Brace, 1977.

Owen, Alex. *The Darkened Room: Women, Power and Spiritualism in Late Victorian England.* Philadelphia: University of Pennsylvania Press, 1990.

Paley, William. *Natural Theology, or, Evidences of the Existence and Attributes of the Deity, Collected from the Appearances of Nature.* Facsimile ed. Westmed, U.K.: Gregg International Publishers, 1970.

Passantino, Bob, and Gretchen Passantino. *When The Devil Dares Your Kids: Protecting Your Children from Satanism, Witchcraft, and the Occult.* Ann Arbor, Mich.: Servant Publications, 1991.

Passantino, Bob, Gretchen Passantino, and Jon Trott. "Satan's Sideshow." *Cornerstone Magazine* 18 (1989): n.p.

Pauley, John L. "Reshaping Public Persona and the Prophetic Ethos: Louis Farrakhan at the Million Man March." *Western Journal of Communication* 62 (1998): 512–36.

Pennock, J. Roland, and John W. Chapman, eds. *Nomos XXXIX: Authority Revisited.* New York: New York University Press, 1987.

Perelman, Chaïm, and L. Olbrechts-Tyteca. *The New Rhetoric: A Treatise on Argumentation.* Trans. John Wilkinson and Purcell Weaver. Notre Dame: University of Notre Dame Press, 1969.

Pérez-Reverte, Arturo. *The Club Dumas.* Trans. Sonia Soto. New York: Vintage International/Random House, 1998.

Peters, John Durham. *Speaking into the Air: A History of the Idea of Communication.* Chicago: University of Chicago Press, 1999.

Plato. *Cratylus.* Trans. D. D. C. Reeve. In *Plato: Complete Works,* ed. John M. Cooper, 101–56. Indianapolis: Hackett, 1997.

———. *Gorgias.* Trans. Donald J. Zeyl. In *Plato: Complete Works,* ed. John M. Cooper, 791–869. Indianapolis: Hackett, 1997.

———. *Phaedrus and Letters VII and VIII.* Ed. and trans. Walter Hamilton. New York: Penguin, 1973.

——. *The Republic of Plato.* Trans. Francis MacDonald Cornford. New York: Oxford University Press, 1945.

Polanski, Roman, John Brownjohn, and Enrique Urbizu. *The Ninth Gate.* Screenplay (n.d.); available http:www.godamongdirectors.com/scripts/ninthgate.html accessed May 3, 2000.

Pollard, Alfred W. *Last Words on the History of the Title-Page, with Notes on Some Colophons and Twenty-Seven Fac-similies of Title-Pages.* London: J. C. Nimmo, 1891.

Popkin, Richard. "Spinoza, Neoplatonic Kabbalist?" In *Neoplatonism and Jewish Thought,* ed. Lenn Goodman, 387–410. Albany: State University of New York Press, 1992.

Postman, Neil. *Amusing Ourselves to Death: Public Discourse in the Age of Show Business.* New York: Penguin, 1985.

Pradhan, Shekhar. "The Dream of a Common Language." In *Literary Theory after Davidson,* ed. Reed Way Dasenbrock, 180–200. University Park: Pennsylvania State University Press, 1993.

de Prurucker, G. *Occult Glossary: A Compendium of Oriental and Theosophical Terms.* Pasadena: Theosophical University Press, 1996.

Purkiss, Diane. *The Witch in History: Early Modern and Twentieth-Century Representations.* New York: Routledge, 1996.

Putnam, Aric. "The House That Prince Hall Built." Paper presented at the annual meeting of the National Communication Association, Atlanta, Georgia, November 2001.

Quine, W. V. *The Ways of Paradox.* Cambridge: Harvard University Press, 1976.

Rae, Alexander C. *Bluff Your Way in the Occult.* London: Ravette, 1992.

Rand, Ayn. *Atlas Shrugged.* New York: Signet/Penguin, 1992.

Rand, Richard, ed. *Logomachia: The Conflict of the Faculties.* Lincoln: University of Nebraska Press, 1992.

Randi, James. *Truth about Uri Geller.* Amherst, N.Y.: Prometheus Books, 1982.

Raschke, Carl. *Painted Black.* San Francisco: Harper and Row, 1990.

Readings, Bill. *The University in Ruins.* Cambridge: Harvard University Press, 1997.

Redbeard, Ragnar. *Might Is Right: Survival of the Fittest.* St. Maries, Iowa: 14 World Press, 1999.

Redding, W. Charles. "Extrinsic and Intrinsic Criticism." *Western Journal of Speech* 21 (Spring 1957): 96–103.

Regardie, Israel. *The Golden Dawn: A Complete Course in Practical and Ceremonial Magic.* 6th ed. St. Paul, Minn.: Llewellyn, 1997.

Richardson, James T., Joel Best, and David G. Bromley, eds. *The Satanism Scare.* Hawthorn, N.Y.: Aldine De Gruyter, 1991.

Rickels, Laurence A. *The Vampire Lectures.* Minneapolis: University of Minnesota Press, 1999.

Ricoeur, Paul. *Freud and Philosophy: An Essay on Interpretation.* Trans. Denis Savage. New Haven: Yale University Press, 1970.

——. *Hermeneutics and the Human Sciences.* Trans. John B. Thompson. Cambridge: Cambridge University Press, 1994.

Rorty, Richard. *Contingency, Irony, and Solidarity.* New York: Cambridge University Press, 1989.

——. *Truth and Progress: Philosophical Papers, Volume 3.* New York: Cambridge University Press, 1998.

——, ed. *The Linguistic Turn: Essays in Philosophical Method.* Chicago: University of Chicago Press, 1992.

Rose, Jonathan. "Rereading the English Common Reader: A Preface to a History of Audiences." *Journal of the History of Ideas* 53 (January–March 1992): 47–70.

Rosmarin, Adena. *The Power of Genre.* Minneapolis: Minneapolis University Press, 1985.

Rowling, J. K. *Harry Potter and the Sorcerer's Stone.* New York: Arthur A. Levine/Scholastic Press, 1998.

Rushing, Janice Hocker, and Thomas S. Frentz. "The Gods Must Be Crazy: The Denial of Descent in Academic Scholarship." *Quarterly Journal of Speech* 85 (1999): 229–44.

——. *Projecting the Shadow: The Cyborg Hero in American Film.* Chicago: Chicago University Press, 1995.

Russell, D. S. *Prophecy and the Apocalyptic Dream.* Peabody, Mass.: Hendrickson, 1994.

Russett, Cynthia Eagle. *Darwin in America: The Intellectual Response, 1865–1912.* San Francisco: Freeman, 1976.

Sakheim, David K., and Susan E. Devine, eds. *Out of Darkness: Exploring Satanism and Ritual Abuse.* New York: Lexington Books, 1992.

Scharfstein, Ben-Ami. *Ineffability: The Failure of Words in Philosophy and Religion.* Albany: State University of New York Press, 1993.

Schiappa, Edward, and Mary F. Keehner. "The 'Lost' Passages of *Permanence and Change.*" *Communication Studies* 42, no. 3 (1991): 191–98.

Schlegel, Friedrich. *Philosophical Fragments.* Trans. Peter Firchow. Minneapolis: University of Minnesota Press, 1991.

Schoepflin, Rennie B. "America's Innovative Nineteenth-Century Religions." In *The History of Science and Religion in the Western Tradition,* ed. Gary B. Ferngren, 307–12. New York: Garland, 2000.

Scholes, Robert. *The Rise and Fall of English: Reconstructing English as a Discipline.* New Haven: Yale University Press, 1998.

Schulte-Sasse, Jochen, ed. *Theory as Practice: A Critical Anthology of Early*

German Romantic Writings. Minneapolis: University of Minnesota Press, 1997.

Sconce, Jeffrey. *Haunted Media: Electronic Telepresence from Telegraphy to Television*. Durham, N.C.: Duke University Press, 2000.

Scott, Otto J. *James I*. New York: Mason/Charter, 1976.

Scott, R. B. Y. *The Relevance of the Prophets*. New York: Macmillan, 1968.

Scott, Robert L. "Dialectical Tensions of Speaking and Silence." *Quarterly Journal of Speech* 79 (1993): 1–18.

——. "On Viewing Rhetoric as Epistemic." *Central States Speech Journal* 18 (1967): 9–17.

——. "Rhetoric and Silence." *Western Speech* 36 (Summer 1972): 146–58.

——. "Why I Am Not a Satanist: A Reply to Bertrand Russell." *Cloven Feet: International Newsletter of Satanists* 66 (1966): 6–66.

Searle, John R. *Speech Acts: An Essay in the Philosophy of Language*. London: Cambridge University Press, 1978.

Sewell, Edward H. "Speech, Silence, and Authenticity." *Southern Speech Communication Journal* 40 (Winter 1975): 169–79.

Shepard, Leslie, ed., *Encyclopedia of Occultism and Parapsychology*. 2 vols. Detroit: Gale, 1978.

Showalter, Elaine. *Hystories: Hysterical Epidemics and Modern Media*. New York: Columbia University Press, 1997.

Simmel, Georg. "The Sociology of Secrecy and of Secret Societies." *American Journal of Sociology* 11 (1906): 441–98.

Sinason, Valerie, ed. *Treating Survivors of Satanist Abuse*. New York: Routledge, 1994.

Slaughter, Sheila, and Larry L. Leslie. *Academic Capitalism: Politics, Policies, and the Entrepreneurial University*. Baltimore: Johns Hopkins University Press, 1997.

Smith, Allan Lloyd. "The Occultism of the Text." *Poetics Today* 3 (1982): 5–20.

Smith, Margaret M. *The Title-Page: Its Early Development, 1460–1510*. New Castle, Del.: Oak Knoll Press, 2000.

Smith, Michelle, and Lawrence Pazder. *Michelle Remembers*. New York: Simon and Schuster, 1980.

Smith, Timothy d'Arch. *The Books of the Beast*. Oxford, U.K.: Mandrake, 1991.

Sokal, Alan. "Revelation: A Physicist Experiments with Cultural Studies." In *The Sokal Hoax: The Sham That Shook the Academy*, edited by the editors of *Lingua Franca*, 49–53. Lincoln: University of Nebraska Press, 2000.

——. "Transgressing the Boundaries: Towards a Transformative Hermeneutics of Quantum Gravity." In Alan Sokal and Jean Bricmont, *Fashion-*

able Nonsense: Postmodern Intellectuals' Abuse of Science, 212–58. New York: Picador, 1998.

Sokal, Alan, and Jean Bricmont. *Fashionable Nonsense: Postmodern Intellectuals' Abuse of Science.* New York: Picador, 1998.

Soros, Erin. "Giving Death." *Differences: A Journal of Feminist Thought* 10 (1998): 1–29.

Stephensen, P. R. *The Legend of Aleister Crowley.* Ed. Israel Regardie. Las Vegas: New Falcon Publications, 1986.

Stratford, Lauren, and Johanna Michaelson. *Satan's Underground: The Extraordinary Story of One Woman's Escape.* Gretna, La.: Pelican, 1991.

Sutin, Lawrence. *Do What Thou Wilt: A Life of Aleister Crowley.* New York: St. Martin's Press, 2000.

Swearingen, C. Jan. *Rhetoric and Irony: Western Literacy and Western Lies.* New York: Oxford University Press, 1991.

Symonds, John. *Madame Blavatsky: Medium and Magician.* London: Odhams Press, 1959.

Szasz, Ferene M. "Modern American Mainline Protestantism." In *The History of Science and Religion in the Western Tradition: An Encyclopedia,* ed. Gary B. Ferngren, 291–306. New York: Garland, 2000.

Taber, William P. *The Prophetic Stream.* Wallingford, Pa.: Pendle Hill, 1984.

Thomas, Keith. *Religion and the Decline of Magic.* London: Weidenfeld and Nicholson, 1971.

Tillett, Gregory. "Encounters with Unfamiliar States: A Review of Five Books by Kenneth Grant." *Theosophical History* 4 (1992): 77–84.

Tiryakian, Edward A. "Toward a Sociology of Esoteric Culture." In *On the Margin of the Visible: Sociology, the Esoteric, and the Occult,* ed. Tiryakian, 257–80. New York: Wiley, 1974.

——, ed. *On the Margin of the Visible: Sociology, the Esoteric, and the Occult.* New York: Wiley, 1974.

Todd, John M. *Martin Luther: A Biographical Study.* London: Burns and Oates, 1964.

Todorov, Tzvetan. *The Fantastic: A Structural Approach to a Literary Genre.* Cleveland: Press of Case Western Reserve University, 1973.

Tonn, Mari Boor, Valerie A. Endress, and John N. Diamond. "Hunting and Heritage on Trial in Maine: A Dramatistic Debate Over Tragedy, Tradition, and Territory." *Quarterly Journal of Speech* 79 (1993): 165–81.

Truzzi, Marcello. "Definition and Dimensions of the Occult: Toward a Sociological Perspective." In *On the Margin of the Visible: Sociology, the Esoteric, and the Occult,* ed. Edward A. Tiryakian, 243–55. New York: Wiley, 1974.

——. "The Occult Revival as Popular Culture: Some Random Observations on the Old and the Nouveau Witch." *Sociological Quarterly* 13 (1972): 16–36.

——. "Towards a Sociology of the Occult: Notes on Modern Witchcraft." In *Religious Movements in Contemporary America,* ed. Irving I. Zaretsky and Mark P. Leone, 628–45. Princeton: Princeton University Press, 1974.

Twitchell, Paul. *The Eck-Vidya: Ancient Science of Prophecy.* Menlo Park, Calif.: IWP Publishing, 1982.

Tzu, Lao, and Chuang Tzu. *The Texts of Taoism.* Trans. James Legge. New York: Dover, 1962.

The Urantia Book. Chicago: Urantia Foundation, 1999.

Van Mater, Kirby. "The Writing of the Secret Doctrine." In *An Invitation to the Secret Doctrine,* appendix, n.p. Pasadena: Theosophical University Press, 1994.

Verter, Bradford J. M. "Dark Star Rising: The Emergence of Modern Occultism, 1800–1950." Ph.D. diss., Princeton University, 1998.

Victor, Jeffrey S. *Satanic Panic: The Creation of a Contemporary Legend.* Chicago: Open Court, 1993.

Waite, Arthur Edward. *The Book of Ceremonial Magic.* 1911. New York: Barnes and Noble, 1999.

Walker, Charles. *The Encyclopedia of the Occult.* New York: Crescent, 1995.

Warner, Michael. *Publics and Counterpublics.* New York: Zone Books, 2002.

Warnick, Barbara. "A Rhetorical Analysis of Episteme Shift: Darwin's *Origin of the Species.*" *Southern Speech Communication Journal* 49 (1983): 26–42.

Washington, Peter. *Madame Blavatsky's Baboon: Theosophy and the Emergence of the Western Guru.* London: Secker and Warburg, 1993.

Weaver, Richard. "Language Is Sermonic." In *Language Is Sermonic: Richard M. Weaver on the Nature of Rhetoric,* ed. Richard L. Johannesen, Rennard Strickland, and Ralph T. Eubanks, 201–5. Baton Rouge: Louisiana State University Press, 1970.

Weber, Elizabeth Sue. "The Rhetoric of Mars and Venus." Ph.D. diss., University of Minnesota, 2001.

Weber, Max. *Max Weber on Charisma and Institution Building: Selected Papers.* Ed. S. N. Eisenstadt. Chicago: University of Chicago Press, 1968.

——. *The Protestant Ethic and the Spirit of Capitalism.* 1905. Reprint, London: Unwin, 1985.

——. *Theory of Social and Economic Organization.* Trans. A. M. Henderson and Talcott Parsons. Ed. Talcott Parsons. New York: The Free Press, 1968.

Wellek, René, and Austin Warren. *Theory of Literature.* 3rd ed. San Diego: Harcourt Brace, 1984.

Westermann, Claus. *Basic Forms of Prophetic Speech*. Trans. Hugh Clayton White. Philadelphia: Westminster Press, 1967.

White, Geoffrey D., and Flannery C. Hauck, eds. *Campus, Inc.: Corporate Power in the Ivory Tower.* Amherst, N.Y.: Prometheus Books, 2000.

White, Hayden. *Tropics of Discourse: Essays in Cultural Criticism.* Baltimore: John Hopkins University Press, 1979.

White, James Boyd. *Acts of Hope: Celebrating Authority in Literature, Law, and Politics.* Chicago: University of Chicago Press, 1994.

Whitehead, Harriet, "Reasonably Fantastic: Some Perspectives on Scientology, Science Fiction, and Occultism." In *Religious Movements in Contemporary America,* ed. Irving I. Zaretsky and Mark P. Leone, 577–89. Princeton: Princeton University Press, 1974.

Whitson, Steve, and John Poulakos. "Nietzsche and the Aesthetics of Rhetoric." *Quarterly Journal of Speech* 79 (May 1993): 131–45.

Williams, Raymond. "Culture Is Ordinary." In *The Raymond Williams Reader,* ed. John Higgins, 10–24. Malden, Mass.: Blackwell, 2001.

———. "The Masses." In *The Raymond Williams Reader,* ed. John Higgins, 42–64. Malden, Mass.: Blackwell, 2001.

Willis, Ellen. "My Sokaled Life; Or, Revenge of the Nerds." In *The Sokal Hoax: The Sham That Shook the Academy,* ed. by the editors of *Lingua Franca,* 133–38. Lincoln: University of Nebraska Press, 2000.

Wilmshurst, W. L. *The Meaning of Masonry.* New York: Grammercy, 1980.

Wilson, Bryan. *Contemporary Transformations of Religion.* Oxford: Clarendon Press, 1979.

———. *Religion in Sociological Perspective.* New York: Oxford University Press.

Wilson, Colin. *The Occult: A History.* New York: Barnes and Noble, 1995.

Wilson, Rob. *American Sublime: The Genealogy of a Poetic Genre.* Madison: University of Wisconsin Press, 1991.

Wimsatt, W. K., Jr. and Cleanth Brooks. *Literary Criticism: A Short History.* New York: Knopf, 1964.

Wittgenstein, Ludwig. *The Blue and Brown Books.* New York: HarperCollins, 1976.

———. *Culture and Value.* Ed. G. H. Von Wright and trans. Peter Winch. Chicago: University of Chicago Press, 1984.

———. *Philosophical Investigations.* Trans. G. E. M. Anscombe. 2nd ed. Malden, Mass.: Blackwell, 1997.

Yates, Frances A. *Giordano Bruno and the Hermetic Tradition.* Chicago: University of Chicago Press, 1991.

———. *The Rosicrucian Enlightenment.* New York: Routledge, 1999.

de Young, Mary. "Breeders for Satan: Toward a Sociology of Sexual Trauma Tales." *Journal of American Culture* 19 (Summer 1996): 111–18.

de Zirkoff, Boris. "Introductory: How 'Isis Unveiled' Was Written." In H. P. Blavatsky, *Isis Unveiled,* 2 vols., ed. Boris de Zirkoff, 1:1–7. Wheaton, Ill.: Theosophical Publishing House, 1972.

Zukav, Gary. *The Seat of the Soul.* New York: Fireside, 1990.

Zulick, Margaret D. "The Agon of Jeremiah: On the Dialogic Invention of Prophetic Ethos." *Quarterly Journal of Speech* 78 (1992): 125–48.

Index

Abramelin oil: use in occult rituals, 163–164
academics: as occult practice, xxix, 219–220
academic terminology: as jargon, 48; as occult, 51–52
Adorno, Theodor: on astrology and irrationality, 119, 239; critique of popular music forms, 181–182. *See also* Horkheimer, Max
agency: of the signifier, 139; relationship to intentionality and determinism, 149
Agrippa, Henry Cornelius, 4, 12
alchemy, 10
alcohol: role in Crowley's magical system, 280n51
allegory: use in occult rhetoric, 22
ambiguity: deliberate use of in occult rhetoric, 72; and language, 81
Anger, Kenneth, 195
antinomy: defined, 37; rhetorical, 47–50. *See also* rhetorical antimony
Aquinas, St. Thomas: and scholasticism, 125
Aquino, Michael, 184
Aquarius, Age of. *See* New Age
argument from design. *See* Paley, William
Aristotle: on science, 48
astral projection: defined, 36; in ECKANKAR, 36
astrology, 6
Attali, Jacques: on the commodification of music, 178–179
audience: concept of 233–234. *See also* mass audience
Augustine of Hippo: and occultism, 13; and scholastic interpretation (hermeneutics), 125–126
authority: in ancient rhetorical tradition, 136–138; controversy over defining 284n16; defined, 120–121; and H. P. Blavatsky, 68–69; in *The Ninth Gate* 214, 217, 220; and the occult tradition, 20–21; and rhetoric, xx. *See also* authority, occult; authority, religious
authority, occult: achievement via struggle, 117; in the occult tradition, 20–21; in *The Ninth Gate,* 217, 220. *See also* authority, religious
authority, paradox of. *See* paradox of authority
authority, religious: and hierarchy, 120; and self-evidence, 119; and self-sealing argument. *See also* authority, occult; self-sealing argument
autonomy: fantasy of, 222–223; as undermined by language, 135

backward masking: and heavy metal music, 109; and Led Zeppelin's "Stairway to Heaven," 109

Bacon, Francis: and the doctrine of twofold truth, xviii; relationship to John Dee, 268n38
Baphomet, Sigil of: commodity fetishism and, 189; description of 187; influence of in popular culture, 293–294n15
Barnes, Barry: on the limits of language, 46
Barrett, Francis, 4, 15
Barthes, Roland: on image and photography, 191–192
Barton, Blanche: and the history of the Church of Satan, 195. *See also* LaVey, Anton S.
Baudrillard, Jean: on signs and commodities, 176–178
Beatles, the: and representation of Crowley on music album, 110
Benjamin, Walter: on the relationship of historical materialism to determinism, 151; and pure language, 271n25, 278n66
Ben-Yehuda, Nachman: on religion and occultism, 297
Besant, Annie: and Theosophy, 70
bible, the: and Freemasonry, xix, 91; and speech 45
Black, Edwin: on Freudian criticism, 288–289n21; and the second persona, 276n46
black magic: Francis Barrett on, 15; in popular literature, 143; and race, 226; Arthur Edward Waite on, 24. *See also* voodoo
Blavatsky, Helena Petrovna: and the development of the Theosophical Society, 58–61; her importance in the occult tradition, 55, 273n5; and the process of invention, xxvii; in Joyce's *Ulysses*; on metalanguage, 73; newspaper stories about, 66–68; on race, 275n38; on silence, 44
Bloom, Alan: on literacy and youth, 229
Bloom, Clive: on textuality and occultism, 240
Book of the Law, The: description of 86–87; personae in, 88–89
Booth, Wayne: on stable irony, 152, 163
Brooks, Cleanth: and New Criticism, 83. *See also* New Criticism
Browne, Sylvia: as contemporary occultist, 229; on karma, 57
Brummett, Barry: on authority and the concept of "transfer," 276n50
Bruno, Giordano: and the occult tradition, 12
Burke, Edmund: on the sublime, 94, 241
Burke, Kenneth: on action versus motion, 246; on ambiguity, 47; and the concept of the symbolic, 212; on dramatism, 208; on the grammar of motives, 208; on form, 294n27; on the human barnyard, 52; on interpretation and hierarchy, 135; on irony, 154; on mystery and hierarchy, 79; and the pentad, 208–209; and pure persuasion, 91; and *The Rhetoric of Religion,* xxi–xxii; on religious authority, 119–120; on the self-sealing argument, 289n15
Burkenholder, Thomas R.: on organic criticism, 83
Butler, Elizabeth: on Eliphas Lévi's writing, 3–4
Butler, Judith: on difficult prose, 46–47, 52; response to Martha Nussbaum, 52
Byrne, David: as a Talking Head, 78

cakes of light: recipe for in Crowley's work, 290–291n73
Campbell, Karlyn Kohrs: and description of organic criticism, 83; on ethics and criticism, 289n21; on genre, 17, 269n50
capitalism: as a mode of production,

176; impact on occult practice, 211–212; relation to occultism, 15. *See also* capitalism, late
capitalism, late: and economies of prestige and sustenance, 177–178; explained, 176
chain of signifiers: and the hermeneutic of authority, 134
channeling: practice of, 274n12
charisma: defined, 121; relationship to authority, 121; and the rhetorical tradition, 136–137
Christianity: and the challenge of science, 61–62; and occult rhetoric, 21
Christian Science: and religion in the United States, 61, 64. *See also* Eddy, Mary Baker
Church of Satan. *See* LaVey, Anton S.
Cicero: on authority, 136–137; on irony and dissimulation, 152
Civil War: and the emergency of Theosophy, 58, 61
class: function in horror films, 221–222; and hierarchy in the work of Kenneth Burke, 298–299n19; and occultism in the popular press, 168–171; and social discrimination in Crowley's work, 160–161
close textual criticism. *See* intrinsic criticism
cogito. *See* Descartes, René
cold reading: and the practice of tarot and astrology, 134
commodity: as an image, 191–192; and sign value, 178; and transaction value, 178
commodity fetishism: in late capitalism, 179; and *The Ninth Gate,* 218
commodity occultism: explained, 175–182; and *The Satanic Bible,* 187
common reader: defined, 68
communication, fantasy of: and spiritualism, 63
Covino, William: on literacy, 73
Crenshaw, James: on prophecy, 119
critical rhetoric: Raymie McKerrow and, 149
Cross, Andrew: on irony, 159
Crowley, Aleister: on aesthetics and *The Book of the Law,* 91–93; and authority, 79–80; and *The Book of the Law,* xxvii, 81, 86–97, 101; and the Cairo Working, 87–88; and class anxiety, 115; court battle with Mathers, 116, 143; on function of alcohol and magick, 280n51; as a gigolo, 161; and popular representation, 111–115, 166–168; and the *Ordo Templi Orientis,* 87; on the study of the Qabalah, 79; on the tarot, 131–132; on women, 281n51

Darsey, James: on the decline of religious righteousness, 228; on prophecy, 119, 122
Darwin, Charles: and the theory of evolution, 61–62
Davis, Andrew Jackson: and spiritualism, 63
degree system (in secret orders): occult origins of, 93
Deleuze, Gilles, and Félix Guattari: and difficult language, xxiv; and the occult tradition, xvii–xviii
Deliverance movement: and exorcism, 114
demonology, 6
Derrida, Jacques: on *différence,* 43–44; on Plato's *Phaedrus,* 43–44; on secrecy and secrets, 235–236
Descartes, René: and dualism, xvii–xviii; and the compromise between science and religion, 61, 246. *See also* Bacon, Francis
Desmond, Arthur: relationship to *The Satanic Bible,* 184
determinism: and agency, 149; and mass media technology, 151
development hypothesis. *See* Darwin; evolution

Devil, the. *See* Satan
devil worship. *See* Satanism
dialectic: and the trope of irony, 154; language and, 52; Platonic, 38–39, 56, 277n59
dialectical criticism: Fredric Jameson on, 104, 155
dialectic of control: and occult authority, 132
différence: and absence, 43–44, 271n25; explained, 43–44; and the hermeneutic of authority, 134; and ineffability, 51; and language, 44–45
dissimulation: and irony, 152
doctrine of twofold truth. *See* Bacon, Francis
Downs, Hugh: and *20/20*'s role in the Satanic panic of the 1980s and 1990s, 196
dramatism: as a theory of rhetoric, 208. *See also* Burke, Kenneth
dualism: ontological, xix, 275n33; *See also* Descartes, René
DuQuette, Lon Milo: on Crowley's rhetorical blinds, 162

Eamon, William: on the occult tradition, 15
Ebert, Roger: review of *The Ninth Gate,* 206–207
ECKANKAR: language of, 37; as occult organization, 36–38, 40, 42
Eddy, Mary Baker: and Christian Science as prophecy, 122. *See also* Christian Science
Eliade, Mircea: on the appeal of occultism, 247
Eliot, T. S.: on textual erotics, 84
Ellul, Jacques: on the humiliation of the word, 230
Emerald Table, The, 11
Emerson, Ralph Waldo: and transcendentalism, 64
Enochian magic, 12
enthymeme: function in occult rhetoric, 75
epochê: and intrinsic criticism, 99. *See also* phenomenology
erotics, textual: and intrinsic criticism, 83–85
esoteric grammar: occult rhetoric as, 209
esoteric language: function of, 37, 210; in the work of H. P. Blavatsky, 68–76
ethos: and authority in the rhetorical tradition, 136
evil: occult represented as, 113–114
evolution, theory of, 61–62. *See also* Darwin, Charles; Paley, William
exoterica: defined, xxvii
existential irony: and occultism, 157–159
Exorcist, The: and class representation in film version, 221–222

faith: "leap of," 284n10
fantastic, the: Todorov's concept of, 240
fetishism: of *The Book of the Law* 97; in late capitalism, 179
feudalism: versus capitalism, 176
figurative language: and occult rhetoric, 22
Fink, Bruce: on Lacan's theory of the phallus, 140
Fool, the figure of: defined, 130; in Crowley's occult system, 129–139; relation to irony, 154–155; and the tarot, 131–132, 230–231. *See also* Gunn, Joshua; Parzifal
Foote, George W.: attack on H. P. Blavatsky, 70
form: and figurative language, xix; and irony, 155; Fredric Jameson on, 155; Platonic, 39
fortune telling: as an occult practice, 6
Foucault, Michel: and posthumanism,

148; on power, 80; and the humanist subject, 150
Fox, Kate, and Margaret: and the birth of spiritualism, 62
Frankfurt School, the: and the mass culture debate, 146–147. *See also* Horkheimer, Max, and Theodor Adorno; mass audience
Freemasonry: and the holy bible, 91; and the New Age, 56; occult tradition, xviii
French occult revival, the, 16
Fuld, William: and invention of the Ouija board, 63

Gadamer, Hans-Georg: on hermeneutics, 98
Galileo: on mathematics as the language of the universe, 128
Gaonkar, Dilip: on the disappearance of the critical object, 85; on the origin of textualism, 83
Geller, Uri: and spoon-bending, 125
genre: defined, 16–18; and the occult, 18
Gilmore, Peter: and the Church of Satan, 190
God, death of, 229
Godzich, Wlad: on textual fetishization, 98; on textual interpretation, 81
goety (evocation of evil spirits), 12, 23–25
Golden Dawn, Order of the: Crowley's expulsion from, 116; Israel Regardie on, 20; Mather's leadership of, 116; and the Qabalah, 4, 128
good reasons: rejection of in occult arguments, 134
goth: and youth, xxviii
gothic literature: relation to occultism, 240
grade system (in a secret order). *See* degree system
grammar of occultism, 246
Grant, Kenneth, 238
Great White Brotherhood. *See* Secret Masters
grimoire, 5
Grossberg, Lawrence, 233
Gurdjieff, G. I.: on allegory, 41; on difficult language, 272n39
Gunn, Joshua. *See* Fool, the figure of

heavy metal music: and devil worship, 7
Heidegger, Martin: and the difficult prose of *Being and Time,* 46
Hermetica, the. *See* hermeticism; Trismigestis, Hermes
hermeticism, xvii. *See also* Trismigestis, Hermes
hermeneutics: of authority, 125–126; of faith, 99; relation to power, 80–81; of suspicion, 104, 211
Hindu language: and occult rhetoric, 66
history. *See* origin narrative
Horkheimer, Max, and Theodor Adorno: the difficult prose of, 46; and *Dialectic of Enlightenment* 227
horror film: function of class in, 221–222; and relation to the occult, xxiii; Hammer Studios and, 293n15
human sacrifice: in the work of Crowley, 156; rumors of in occult rituals, 174
Hume, David: on secret powers, 268n40
Hutcheon, Linda: on irony, 152
hyperreal, 214–215
hypnotic regression: role in Satanic rumor panic, 173

illusionism: of the image, 192. *See also* image

identity politics: and contemporary occult rhetoric, 224–226
ideology: relation to the unconscious, 212
image: illusionism and reality effect of, 296n59; mobility of, 194; rhetoric of, 193
imagination: in occult tradition, 5; rhetorical power of, 174; role in *The Ninth Gate,* 214
Indian mysticism: and the *neti neti* method, 74
ineffability: in Derrida's philosophy, 42–46; and religious discourse, 38–42; and Rorty's philosophy, 45–46
Inquisition, Spanish, 13–14
instrumental rationality: in religion, 227
intentionality: and agency, 148; and the unconscious, 150
intentional fallacy: and textual criticism, 148–149
interpretation, art of. *See* hermeneutics; intrinsic criticism
intertextuality: and irony, 155; and invention, 291n74; and occultism, 211, 291n74; problem of in interpretation, 132
intrinsic criticism: as close textual interpretation, 82as erotic process, 83–85; method of, 82–86, 96–103; in *The Ninth Gate,* 214
Ipissimus, magical grade of, 158
irony: described, 152–155; Wayne Booth on, 163–165; Kenneth Burke on, 154; and dialectic, 154; and form, 155; and intertextuality, 155; and occult rhetoric, 22; and social discrimination, 153; stable, 163; unstable 163–165
irrationalism: and occult beliefs, 242–243. *See also* Adorno, Theodor
Ishaya's Ascension, 27–34
Isis Unveiled: publication of, 60. *See also* Blavatsky, Helena Petrovna
Isocrates, 265n14

James VI, King: and persecution of witches, 14, 268n37
Jameson, Fredric: on dialectical criticism, 104, 155; on form, 155; on the spiritual in late capitalism, 227
Jamieson, Kathleen Hall: on genre, 17
jargon, academic, xix, 48. *See also* academic terminology
Jhally, Sut: on fetishism, 179; on political economy, 178
Joyce, James: and Theosophy, 35–36

Kabbalah: and dualism, xvii. *See also* Qabalah
Kant, Immanuel: on philosophical antinomies, 48; and occultism, 14; on the sublime, 94, 241
karma: contested meaning of, 56–57
Kelley, Edward, 12
Kierkegaard, Søren: on faith, 118–119, 284n10; on existential irony 157–159; on irony in general, 153; on role of remembrance in interpretation, 126
Klemp, Sri Harold: as head of ECKANKAR, 36; on the limits of language, 40

Lacan, Jacques: on the agency of the signifier, 138; function of his difficult prose, 141; and lack, 31; as occult authority, 141; reading of "The Purloined Letter," 138; on subjectivity, 137
lack: and literature, 100–101. *See also* de Man, Paul; Lacan, Jacques
language: difficult, xix–xx; fixed view of, 42, 44–45; fluid view of, 45–46
late capitalism. *See* capitalism, late
Laurent, Ray. See *Satanis: The Devil's Mass*

LaVey, Anton S.: and origin of the Church of Satan, 182–183; on Nazism, 296n52; on function of Satanic rituals, 189–190
Led Zeppelin: and backward masking, 109
Leff, Michael: description of intrinsic criticism, 82; on textual erotics, 84. *See also* intrinsic criticism
Lévi, Eliphas: on astral travel, 4; biography of, 3; and evil, xviii; on the imagination, 5; and *Transcendental Magic,* 3
liquor. *See* alcohol
Longinus (pseudo-): on the sublime, 94, 241
logocentrism: and religious discourse, 45. *See also* Derrida, Jacques
Long, Earl, xxv
Lucas, Stephen E.: on intrinsic criticism, 84, 96
Luhrmann, Tanya M.: on witchcraft and ceremonial magic, 241–243
Luther, Martin: and the challenge to religious authority, 121; and charismatic authority, 122. *See also* Reformation, the

magic, xxii
magical powers: demonstration of, 124–125. *See also* Geller, Uri
Mahatmas. *See* Secret Masters
Mailloux, Steven: on rhetorical hermeneutics, 100
Maleus Maleficarum, 14
de Man, Paul: on literature and lack, 100–101
Marx, Karl: on the commodity, 176
Masonry. *See* Freemasonry
mass audience: emergence of, 144–145; as rhetorical category, 145–147. *See also* Frankfurt School, the
Mathers, Samuel Liddell Macgregor: courtroom battle with Crowley, 116–118, 143; and the Golden Dawn, 116. *See also* Golden Dawn, order of the
Mauss, Marcel: on marginality of occult practitioners, 171; on this theory of magic, 245
McHargue, Georgess: on lack of rigor in occult scholarship, 238
McKerrow, Raymie: on critical rhetoric and Foucault, 144
Medhurst, Martin J.: advocacy of intrinsic criticism, 85
Melton, J. Gordon: and the degree system of the *Ordo Templi Orientis,* 93
Messent, Peter: on gothic literature and the occult, 240
metalanguage: Blavatsky on, 73
metaphor: tenor and vehicle of, 92. *See also* Richards, I. A.
meditation: as occult practice, 38
Michelle Remembers: and Satanic ritual abuse, 172. *See also* Smith, Michelle
Milton, John: and Satan in *Paradise Lost,* 206
miracles: as evidence of religious authority, 124–125. *See also* prophecy
modernity: and occultism, xxvi, 210
Mohrmann, G. P.: on historical biography and rhetorical criticism, 83
Morse code: and spiritualism, 63
Mozart, Wolfgang Amadeus: and Freemasonry, 287n3
Müller, Max: on Blavatsky's writings, 70
"Mysteries of the Unknown" (Time/Life book series), 53–55
mysticism: and the concept of occultism, xxii
mystification: in late capitalism, 180. *See also* commodity fetishism

Nazism: LaVey on, 295n52
necromancy: and summoning the devil, 23–25. *See also* Satanism

neologism: in occult discourse, 37. *See also* difficult language; jargon
New Age: original meaning of, 56
New Criticism: description of, 82–83; comparison to intrinsic criticism, 82–83. *See also* intrinsic criticism; Leff, Michael; Lucas, Stephen E.
Nietzsche, Friedrich: in the work of Crowley, 160; lectures on rhetoric, 85; and the figure of Zarathustra, xviii, 91
Ninth Gate, The: description of film, 204–207
nostalgia: and *The Ninth Gate,* 219
novelty: as central characteristic of occult rhetoric, 48. *See also* difficult language; neologism
Nussbaum, Martha: attack on Judith Butler, 52. *See also* Butler, Judith

Objectivism. *See* Rand, Ayn
Ockham, William: and scholasticism, 125
occult, the: and academics, xxix; and authority, 20–21; and class, 168–171; definition of, xxii, 10, 26; and financial gain, 16; and ineffability, xxiv; and in-fighting, 6; as "modern," 3; versus the occultic, 7; and sensationalism, 16; and urban legend, 110
occult economy: emergence in late capitalism, 180–181
occult poetics: function of, 210; and ineffability, 233–234; and resignification, 132; and the Sokal hoax, 140; and Theosophy, 70–71
occultic: emergence of, 175; versus the occult, 7
Olcott, Henry Steel: relation to H. P. Blavatsky, 59–60
Omen, The: and class representation, 222
oppositional reading: described, 298n13; of *The Ninth Gate,* 207, 213–223
Oprah Winfrey Show: talk show, 56; role in Satanic rumor panic, 173
Ordo Templi Orientis: and Crowley's leadership of, 87; and the degree system, 93
organic criticism. *See* intrinsic criticism
origin narrative: defined, xxvi, 7–8
Origin of Species: rhetoric of, 64. *See also* Darwin, Charles; evolution, theory of
Osborne, Ozzy: and Satanism, 109–110
Ouija board, xxv, 53, 63. *See also* Fuld, William

Paley, William: and the argument from design, 61. *See also* evolution, theory of
palmistry. *See* fortune telling
Paracelsus, 12
Paradise Lost: depiction of Satan in, 206
paradox of authority: described, 165–166. *See also* authority
parapsychology, 64
Parzifal (Parsifal), 131, 286n48. *See also* Fool, the figure of
Pazder, Lawrence: and the Satanic rumor panic, 172–173
pentad, the: as method of interpretation, 208. *See also* Burke, Kenneth
Perelman, Chaïm, and L. Olbrechts-Tyteca: on irony, 153
Peters, John Durham: on spiritualism, 63
phallus: in Crowley's occult system, 140; 287n9; as metaphor for intrinsic criticism, 279n20; Lacan's theory of, 140, 287n8
phenomenology, 83, 99
piety, false: role in occult rhetoric, 21–25
philosophical irony. *See* existential irony
Plato: on allegory (*mythoi*), 56; and

the Kabbalah, xviii; and paradox, 42–43
Platonic dialectic, 38, 39. *See also* dialectic
Poe, Edgar Allen: and "The Purloined Letter," 138
poetics: defined 37; and relation to invention, xxvi, 270n8
Polanski, Roman: and *The Ninth Gate,* xxvii, 204
popular imaginary, 237
posthumanism: and subjectivity, 148–151
Postman, Neil: on the effects of television, 229
postmodernism: versus modernity, 204–210; and *The Ninth Gate,* 215
power: Foucault's view, 80; in textual interpretation, 80–81
Price, Vincent, 53
professor: figure of, 231; relationship to fool 231; stereotype of, 299–300n31
prophecy: defined, 122; lack of discussion about women and, 285n24
pseudo-science, 64
psychoanalysis: Lacanian, 232–233; as occult discourse, 140; as the talking cure, 31; and psychobabble, 32; and rhetoric, xxv
publicity: and the difficulty of secrecy, 145; in postmodernity, 142; and technology, xxi
pure language: Sanskrit as, 50, 73–76
pure persuasion: and Crowley's *The Book of the Law,* 91
Purkiss, Diane: on the figure of the witch, 244. *See also* witch

Qabalah: Crowley's description, 79; Crowley on the significance of, 127; explained, 127–129; versus the Kabbalah, 286n42; *See also* Kabbalah, the
Quine, W. V.: on paradox, 48–49

race: misunderstanding of in Blavatsky's work, 275n38; and the occult tradition, 225–226
Rand, Ayn: and Objectivism, 185
rationalism: occultism as a response to, 47
reality effect. *See* illusionism
Redbeard, Ragbar. *See* Desmond, Arthur
Redding, W. Charles: on textualism, 83
reflection: romantic doctrine of, 12; in German romanticism, 164
Reformation, the: and occultism, 12
Regardie, Israel: and the Golden Dawn, 20
religion: death of, 227; decline of public significance, 226–229; and rhetoric, xxi–xxii; and theological form, xxi–xxiii. *See also* theological form
Renaissance, the: and occultism, 10–12
repetition: and rhetoric, 215
representation: as linguistic burden, 81
rhetoric: and charisma, 136–137; defined, xx; as empty speech, xx; and flattery, 136; role of repetition, 215; as representation, xx; and religion, xxi–xxii; and social discrimination, xx
rhetorical antimony: defined, 47–50; and invention, 57
rhetorical blind: and the ritual sacrifice of children, 156
rhetorical criticism: described, xx–xxi; object of, xxiii. *See also* intrinsic criticism
rhetorical hermeneutics: and intrinsic interpretation, 100. *See also* Mailloux, Steven
rhetorical power: in relation to intrinsic criticism, 84. *See also* Mailloux, Steven
rhetoric of motives: Burke's theory of, 209

Richards, I. A.: and New Criticism, 83; theory of metaphor, 92
Ricoeur, Paul: on hermeneutics of faith, 99
right-hand path. *See* white magic
Rivera, Geraldo: role in the Satanic rumor panic, 199–201; recanting of claims about Satanic ritual abuse, 293n7
role-playing games, 53
romanticism, German: concept of reflection and, 164; and intrinsic criticism, 82
romantic pedagogy: perils of, 103–104
root race: in Blavatsky's work, 66. *See also* race
Rorty, Richard: on the contingency of language, 45–46; on poetry, 51; on poetics, 233–234
Rosemary's Baby, 183, 222
rumor panic: defined, 173; role of television in creating, 190–191; and Satanism, xxviii
Rushing, Janice Hocker, and Thomas S. Frentz, 230

Sabbatic Goat: illustrated and explained, 5
Sanskrit: as pure language, 73–76. *See also* pure language
Satan: how to summon, 23; LaVey's resignification of as human nature, 185; and rumor panic, xxviii. *See also* Satanism
Satanic Bible, The: description of, 183–184; outline of contents, 184–186; packaging of, 186–187
Satanic Ritual Abuse: and rumor panic, 113–114; exposure as fraud, 293n6. *See also* rumor panic
Satanis: The Devil's Mass: description of, 195–196; use as stock footage, 196–201
Satanism: defined as discourse, 201; and Aleister Crowley, xxvii; as imagistic vocabulary, 173–175; and ritual abuse, 113–114; and secrecy, 203
science: versus occultism, xxiv; relation to occult in history, 14–15
Scientology, 78, 247
Scott, Robert L., 44
Scotus, John Duns: and scholasticism, 125
Searle, John, 271n25
Second Great Awakening, 62
second persona: *See* Black, Edwin
secrecy: and occultism, 3, 9
Secret Doctrine, The: Blavatsky on, 60; as concept, 65; and pure language, 75–76
Secret Masters (Chiefs): relation to Theosophy, 60; as common figures in occult discourse, 270n6
self-evidence: and occult authority in *The Ninth Gate,* 217
self-sealing argument, 119
shibboleth: defined, xix; and Freemasonry, xix; and genre, 17; and rhetoric, xix–xxi
signifying chain: and hermeneutic of authority, 134
sign value. *See* commodity
silence: as response to ineffability, 38, 50; rhetoric of, 44
Silver Star, Order of (A:.A:.): and Crowley's *The Book of the Law,* 87
Sinason, Valerie: and the Satanic Ritual Abuse movement, 113, 173
Smith, Allan Lloyd: on occultism and fiction, 240
Smith, Michelle: and the Satanic rumor panic of the 1980s and 1990s, 172–173. See also *Michelle Remembers*
Society for Ascension. *See* Ishaya's Ascension
Socrates: as existential ironist, 158–159
Sokal, Alan and Jean Bricmont: on postmodern theory, 139

Sokal hoax: explained, 232–233. *See also* Sokal, Alan and Jean Bricmont
soul: Theosophical doctrine of, 277n51
speech: Derrida on, 43–45; Plato on, 40
speech act theory: and form, xix–xx; and the principle of expressability, 271n25
Spinoza, Benedict De, xvii
spiritualism: defined, 62; history of 62–63; as occult practice, 6; rhetoric of 63–65
star system: in the academy, 117, 141; in occult tradition, 117
stock footage: as *topoi,* 19
Stratford, Lauren: and the Satanic rumor panic of the 1980s and 1990s, 172–173
style, 85
subjectivity: and fantasy of autonomy, 213; and posthumanism, 148–151
sublime: defined, 93–94; and *The Book of the Law,* 93–96; relation to occultism, 241. *See also* Burke, Edmund; Kant, Immanuel; Longinus
supernaturalism: and religion, xxi
suspicion: motif in *The Ninth Gate,* 215. *See also* hermeneutics
syzygy, xvii

Taoism, 38. *See also* Tzu, Lao
tarot, 131–132. *See also* Fool, the
telegraph: role in spiritualism, 63
telepathy: role in spiritualism, 63
text: versus discourse, 181
textualism. *See* intrinsic criticism
textual occultism: defined, 81, 97
Thelema. *See* Crowley, Aleister
theological form: definition of, xxi; in relation to transcendence and immanence, xxi
Theosophy: cosmology of, 65–66; definition, 58; and the doctrine of the soul, 277n51; goals of, 58–59; history of, 57–62; in Joyce's *Ulysses,* 35–36. *See also* Blavatsky, Helena Petrovna
Tiryakian, Edward A.: on occultism versus esoteric culture, 245–246
title page: of occult books, 18
Todorv, Tzvetan, 240. *See also* fantastic, the
topoi: described, 194
topos. See topoi
totem: in capitalism, 177–178; occult book as, 218
transcendence: and religion, xxi
transcendentalism, 64. *See also* Emerson, Ralph Waldo
transfer: as strategy of authority, 276n50. *See also* Brummett, Barry
tree of life. *See* Kabbalah; Qabalah
Trismigestus, Hermes, 10. *See also* hermeticism
Truzzi, Marcello: on the occult versus science, 246
Twitchell, Paul: on ECKANKAR, 35–36, 40. *See also* ECKANKAR
Tzu, Lao: and Taoism, 38

uncanny: and relation to occultism, 241
unconscious: and conscious intention, 150; discovery of, 212; relation to ideology, 212; relation to subjectivity, 212–213
Urantia Book, The, 40–41
urban legend: and the occult, 110

Verter, Bradford: on Crowley, 114; on history of occultism, 243–244; on the occult in popular literature, 143
voodoo: and racial identity, 226

Waite, Arthur Edward: on Eliphas Lévi, 5
Walpurgisnacht: explained, 183

Warner, Michael: on audience, 233
Warnick, Barbara: on Darwin, 62
Weaver, Richard: on language as sermonic, 52
Webber, Edward M.: and publicity for the Church of Satan, 195
Weber, Max: and the iron cage, 227; on types of authority, 120–121
Wellek, René, and Austin Warren: and the intentional fallacy, 148–149. *See also* intentional fallacy; Wimsatt, W. K., and Monroe Beardsley
Whitehead, Harriet: on Scientology, 247
white magic, 15
Wilson, Bryan: on cults and consumerism, 228
Wilson, Colin: and the history of the occult, 238; on Eliphas Lévi, 6
Wimsatt, W. K., and Monroe Beardsley: on the intentional fallacy, 148–149
witch, figure of, 225
witchcraft, 241–243
Wittgenstein, Ludwig, 45

Yezidi: and Satanism, 182

Zodiac gunman: murder case and occultism, 112
Zukav, Gary: as contemporary occultist, 228–229; on karma, 56; and occultism, 20; and *Seat of the Soul,* 77–78